PSYCHOLOGY
AND
MENTAL HEALTH

PSYCHOLOGY AND MENTAL HEALTH

VOLUME II

Group Therapy — Type A Behavior Pattern

Index

edited by

Jaclyn Rodriguez, Ph.D.

Occidental College

project editor

Tracy Irons-Georges

SALEM PRESS, INC.

PASADENA, CALIFORNIA   HACKENSACK, NEW JERSEY

Most of the essays in *Magill's Choice: Psychology and Mental Health* originally appeared in *Magill's Survey of Social Science: Psychology*, 1993, edited by Dr. Frank N. Magill and Jaclyn Rodriguez; some of them were updated for *Magill's Choice: Psychology Basics*, 1998. The remainder of the essays were taken from *Magill's Medical Guide: Revised Edition 1998*. All bibliographies have been updated, and some formats have been changed.

∞ The paper used in these volumes conforms to the American National Standard for Permanence of Paper for Printed Library Materials, Z39.48-1992 (R1997).

Library of Congress Cataloging-in-Publication Data
Psychology and mental health / edited by Jaclyn Rodriguez ; project editor Tracy Irons-Georges.
        p.   cm. — (Magill's choice)
Includes bibliographical references and index.
ISBN 0-89356-066-9 (set : alk. paper). — ISBN 0-89356-167-7 (vol. 1 : alk. paper). — ISBN 0-89356-068-5 (vol. 2 : alk. paper)
1. Psychology, Pathological—Encyclopedias. 2. Mental illness— Encyclopedias. 3. Mental health—Encyclopedias. I. Rodriguez, Jaclyn. II. Irons-Georges, Tracy. III. Series.

RC437 P795 2001
616.89'003—dc21

                                                                00-046312

First Printing

TABLE OF CONTENTS

PSYCHOLOGY
AND
MENTAL HEALTH

GROUP THERAPY

Type of psychology: Psychotherapy
Fields of study: Group and family therapies

Group therapy allows individuals to enter into the therapeutic process with others who have the same or similar problems. This gives an individual much more freedom of expression and the support of others from within the group.

Principal terms

DISCLOSURE: the point at which a member of a group will share private feelings and concerns

GROUP DYNAMIC: the commonality of purpose that unites a group of people and their desire to succeed

GROUP LEADER: a qualified and trained therapist whose work is to lead the group through the therapeutic process

SESSION: the time span allotted to and agreed on by the group as an acceptable time in which to complete the necessary therapy

THERAPEUTIC PROCESS: the various stages of understanding through which an individual will pass during a therapy session

Overview

Society to a greater or lesser degree always forms itself into some kinds of groupings, whether they are for economic stability, religious expression, educational endeavor, or simply a sense of belonging. Within the field of psychotherapy, many theories and practices have been developed that deal with specific problems facing individuals as they try to relate to their environment as a whole and to become valuable members of society. Available approaches range from psychoanalysis to the more recently formulated transpersonal therapy. Taking advantage of the natural tendency for people to form groups, therapists, since the years following World War II, have developed various forms of group therapy. Therapy groups, although they do not form "naturally," are most frequently composed of people with similar problems.

Among the different types of group counseling available are those that focus on preventive and developmental aspects of living. Preventive group counseling deals with enhancing the individual's understanding of a specific aspect of life. These aspects range from simple job-seeking skills to more complex studies of career changes in midlife. Developmental groups are composed of well-adjusted people who seek to enhance their social and emotional skills through personal growth and transformation. Conversely, group therapy is concerned with remedial help. The majority of people entering group therapy are aware that they have dysfunctional components in their life; they are seeking group work as a possible way of resolving those problems. The size of most groups ranges from four to twelve participants. Sometimes all the members in the group belong to one family, and the group becomes a specialized one with the emphasis being on family therapy. Treating the problems of one family member in the larger context of the whole family has proved successful.

There are as many approaches to therapy as there are therapists; thus, the direction that any given group takes will be dependent on the group leader. Group leadership is probably the one factor that is vital in enabling a group to succeed in reaching both individual and group goals. Often there will be two therapists involved with the one group, the second therapist sometimes being an intern or trainee.

There are definite advantages, both economic and therapeutic, to group therapy. The economic burden of paying for therapy does not fall solely on one person's shoulders; moreover, the therapist can use his or her time economically, helping a larger number of people. More important, group work may be much more beneficial than individual therapy for certain people. Often the group setting will produce conditions similar to those the member faces in real life and can thus offer an opportunity to face and correct the problem.

In group therapy, a "session" consists of a number of meetings; the number is specific and is usually determined at the beginning by the group leader. Flexibility is a key concept in counseling, however, and if a group requires more time and all the participants agree, then the number of sessions can usually be extended. Therapists have generally come to accept five stages as being necessary for a group to complete a therapy session. These five stages do not have definite boundaries; indeed, if a group experiences problems at any stage, it may return to earlier stages.

Orientation is a necessary first step in establishing a sense of well-being and trust among the group's members. A therapy group does not choose its own members; it is a random and arbitrary gathering of different people. Each member will critically assess the group as to whether this group will benefit them significantly. One way for participants to discover the sincerity of the membership of the group is to reveal something of the problem which brought them to the group in the first place, without going into a full disclosure. An individual can then assess from the responses of the other members of the group whether they are going to be empathetic or critical. After the orientation stage comes the transitional stage, in which more self-revelation is required on the part of the individual members. This is usually an anxious time for members of the therapy group. Yet despite this anxiety, each member must make a commitment to the group and must further define the problem that has brought him or her to the group in the first place.

When the transitional stage has proved successful, the group will be able to begin the third stage, which involves a greater sense of cohesiveness and openness. This sense of belonging is a necessary and important aspect of group therapy. Without this feeling, the subsequent work of resolving problems cannot be fully addressed. By this time, each member of the group will have disclosed some very personal and troubling part of their lives. Once a group cohesiveness has been achieved, the fourth stage—actually wanting to work on certain behavior-modifying skills—becomes dominant. At this point in the therapeutic continuum, the group leader will play a less significant role in what is said or the direction taken. This seeming withdrawal on the part of the leader allows the group participants to take the primary role in creating changes that will affect them on a permanent basis.

As with all therapeutic methods and procedures, regardless of school or persuasion, a completion or summation stage is vital. The personal commitment to the group must be seen in the larger context of life and one's need to become a part of the greater fabric of living. By consciously creating a finale to the therapy sessions, members avoid being limited in their personal growth through dependence on the group. This symbolic act of stepping away from the group reaffirms all that the group work achieved during the third and fourth stages of the therapeutic process.

Applications

Group work offers participants an opportunity to express their feelings and fears in the hope that behavioral change will take place. Group therapy only takes on significance and meaning when the individual members of the group want to change their old behavioral patterns and learn a new behavioral repertoire. Most individuals come from a background where they have experienced difficulties with other members of their immediate family. Whether the problem has been a spousal difficulty or a parental problem, those who enter into therapy are desperately looking for answers. The very fact that there is more than one person within the group who can understand and sympathize with another's problem begins the process of acceptance and change.

A group will very quickly become close, intimate, and in some ways self-guarding and self-preserving. Through continually meeting with one another in an intense emotional environment, members begin to look upon the group as a very important part of their life. When one member does not come to a meeting, it can create anxiety in others, for the group works as a whole; for one person not to be present undermines the confidence of those who already lack self-esteem. There are also those who come to group meetings and express very little in the way of what is actually bothering them. While even coming into the therapeutic process is one large step, to disclose anything about themselves is too painful. For those who remain aloof and detached, believing that they are the best judge of their own problems, the group experience will be a superficial one.

According to Irvin D. Yalom, therapy is "an emotional and a corrective experience." The corrective aspect of therapy takes on a new meaning when placed in a group setting. There is general agreement that a person who seeks help from a therapist will eventually reveal what is truly troubling him or her. This may take weeks or even months of talking—generally talking around the problem. This is equally true of group participants. Since many difficulties experienced by the participants will be of an interpersonal nature, the group acts as a perfect setting for creating the conditions in which those behavioral problems will manifest. One major advantage that the group therapist has over a therapist involved in individual therapy is that the conditions that trigger the response can also be observed.

For those people who believe that their particular problem inhibits them from caring or even thinking about others, particularly the narcissistic or schizoid personality, seeing the distress of others in the group often evokes strong sympathy and caring. The ability to be able to offer some kind of help to another person often acts as a catalyst for a person to see that there is an opportunity to become a whole and useful member of the greater community. For all of its limitations, the group reflects, to some degree, the actual real-life situations that each of its members experiences each day.

The acknowledgment of another member's life predicament creates a cohesiveness among the members of the group, as each participant grapples with his or her own problems and with those of the others in the group. As each member becomes supportive of all other members, a climate of trust and understanding comes into being. This is a prerequisite for all group discovery, and it eventually leads to the defining of problems and thus to seeking help for particular problems shared by members. When the individual members of a group begin to care and respond to the needs of the other members, a meaningful relationship exists that allows healing to take place. Compassion, tempered by understanding and acceptance, will eventually prove the ingredients of success for participating members.

Perspective and Prospects

Immediately after World War II, the demand for therapeutic help was so great that the only way to cope with the need was to create therapeutic groups. Group therapy did not boast any one particular founder at that time, although among the first counseling theorists to embrace group therapy actively were Joseph Pratt, Alfred Adler, Jacob Moreno, Trigant Burrow, and Cody Marsh. Psychoanalysis, so firmly placed within the schools for individual psychotherapy, nevertheless became one of the first therapeutic approaches to be applied to group therapy. Gestalt therapy and transactional analysis have proved extremely successful when applied to the group dynamic. Fritz Perls was quick to apply his theories to group therapy work, although he usually worked with one member of the group at a time. Gestalt group therapists aim as part of their treatment to try and break down the numerous denial systems which, once overcome, will bring the individual to a new and more unified understanding of life. Eric Berne, the founder of transactional analysis, has postulated that the group setting is the ideal therapeutic setting.

Group therapy has certainly not been fully accepted in all quarters of the therapeutic professions. Advocates of group therapy have attempted to show, through research and studies, that group therapy is equally effective as individual therapy, but this claim has not settled all arguments. In fact, what has been shown is that if the group leader shows the necessary warmth, understanding, and empathy with the members, then success is generally assured. If the group leader is more on the offensive, however—even taking on an attacking position—then the effects are anything but positive.

Group therapy continues to play an important role within the field of professional care. Perhaps what has been lacking and will need to be reassessed is not so much whether the theories work but whether the participants gain as much as they can from group work. There has been a general lack of systematized study and research into the effectiveness of group therapy, especially as far as feedback from the participants of the group therapy experience is concerned. This reluctance on the part of psychologists and counselors to assess more closely the type of therapy that is being offered will change as participants of group work expect a greater degree of accountability from the professionals who serve them.

Bibliography

Corey, Marianne Schneider, and Gerald Corey. *Groups: Process and Practice.* 5th ed. Pacific Grove, Calif.: Brooks/Cole, 1997. This book is primarily concerned with identifying the main therapeutic stages and assessing the important role that the group leader plays in the process.

Donigian, Jeremiah, and Richard Malnati, *Critical Incidents in Group Therapy.* Monterey, Calif.: Brooks/Cole, 1987. Six incidents are chosen by the authors and are presented to therapists from six different therapeutic approaches. Client-centered therapy, Gestalt therapy, individual psychology, reality therapy, rational-emotive therapy, and transactional analysis approaches are then applied to the same incidents.

Peterson, Vincent, and Bernard Nisenholz. "Group Work." In *Orientation to Counseling.* 2d ed. Needham Heights, Mass.: Allyn & Bacon, 1990. This chapter gives a very concise yet broad survey of group work as it relates to the general field of counseling and counseling theory. Acts as a good introduction to the field.

Rogers, Carl Ransom. *On Becoming a Person.* Boston: Houghton Mifflin, 1961. Carl Rogers's influence on group work is acknowledged by all in the field. Rogers was mostly involved with encounter groups, but the theories and approaches spoken about in his book form the basis of much of group therapy practice today.

Rose, Sheldon D. *Group Therapy with Troubled Youth: A Cognitive-Behavioral Interactive Approach.* Thousand Oaks, Calif.: Sage Publications, 1998. Intended for those leading cognitive-behavioral groups for troubled young people. Includes bibliographical references and indexes.

Yalom, Irvin D. *The Theory and Practice of Group Psychotherapy.* New York: Basic Books, 1985. Yalom's book is a comprehensive work on group therapy. The entire subject of group therapy, from method to application, is covered both from a theoretical viewpoint as well as from the experiential perspective. Actual cases are used as examples of what happens during a group therapy session, making this work indispensable.

Richard G. Cormack

See also:

Behavioral Family Therapy; Community Psychology; Gestalt Therapy; Person-Centered Therapy; Psychotherapy: Goals and Techniques; Strategic Family Therapy.

HYPOCHONDRIASIS, CONVERSION, SOMATIZATION, AND SOMATOFORM PAIN

Type of psychology: Psychopathology
Fields of study: Anxiety disorders; models of abnormality

Conversion, hypochondriasis, somatization, and somatoform pain are a group of mental disorders that are typically referred to as the somatoform disorders. The primary feature of these disorders, as their name suggests, is that psychological conflicts take on a somatic, or physical, form.

Principal terms

CATHARTIC METHOD: a therapeutic procedure in which the patient recalls an earlier emotional trauma in order to express the accompanying tension and unhappiness in a useful manner

CONVERSION DISORDER: the loss or impairment of some motor or sensory function when no organic illness is present

HYPOCHONDRIASIS: a mental disorder in which the person is unrealistically preoccupied with the fear of disease and worries excessively about his or her health

SOMATIZATION DISORDER: a mental syndrome in which the person chronically has a number of vague but dramatic medical complaints, which apparently have no physical cause

SOMATOFORM DISORDERS: a group of mental disorders in which the person has physical complaints or symptoms that appear to be caused by psychological rather than physical factors

SOMATOFORM PAIN: the experience of sensory pain which appears to be caused by psychological rather than physical factors

Causes and Symptoms

Conversion, hypochondriasis, somatization, and somatoform pain are thought by most mental health professionals, such as psychiatrists and clinical psychologists, to be the four major types of somatoform disorders. These disorders are typically studied together because they have an important similarity. With each of these disorders, a psychological conflict is expressed through a somatic, or physical, complaint.

The manifestation of a psychological conflict through a physical complaint is perhaps most apparent with conversion disorders. When an individual suffers from a conversion disorder, the psychological conflict results in some type of disability. While conversion disorders vary widely, some of the most common involve blindness, deafness, paralysis, and anesthesia (loss of sensation). In all these cases, medical examinations reveal that there is nothing wrong physiologically with the individual. The handicap stems from a psychological or emotional problem.

In many instances, the handicap is thought to develop because it gives the person an unconscious way of resolving his or her conflict. For example, an adult who is feeling powerful yet morally unacceptable feelings of anger and rage may wish to strike his or her young child. Rather than carry out this dreadful action, this person

*Josef Breuer, who reported the classic case study of conversion disorder sufferer "Anna O."
in 1895.*

will suddenly develop a paralyzed arm. The unacceptable emotion impulse is then "converted" (thus the term "conversion") into a physical symptom. When this happens, individuals will sometimes seem strangely unconcerned about their new physical disabilities. They will have what is known by the French term *la belle indifference* (or "beautiful indifference"). While most people would be quite upset if they suddenly became blind or paralyzed, conversion patients will often be rather calm or nonchalant about their disability, because their symptom unconsciously protects them from their desire to act on an unacceptable impulse.

The situation is somewhat different for individuals with hypochondriasis or somatization disorder, since individuals with these syndromes generally do not experience a dramatic physical disability. Individuals with hypochondriasis or somatization disorder are troubled instead either by fear of illness or by complaints about being sick.

With hypochondriasis, the afflicted individual, who is typically referred to as a hypochondriac, often misinterprets ordinary physical symptoms as a sign of some extremely serious illness. For example, the hypochondriac with mild indigestion may think that he or she is having a heart attack. In a similar fashion, a mild headache may be interpreted as a brain tumor. Hypochondriacs are usually quite interested in medical information and will keep a wide array of medical specialists at their disposal. After a visit to the physician, the typical hypochondriac is relieved to learn that he or she does not suffer from some dreaded disease. When this person again experiences an everyday ache or pain, such as muscle soreness or indigestion, however, he or she will again mistakenly believe that he or she has come down with some terrible illness.

While the hypochondriac is typically afraid of having one particular disease, the individual with a somatization disorder will often have numerous medical complaints with no apparent physical cause. Somatization disorder is also sometimes known as Briquet syndrome, because a physician by that name described it in detail in 1859. The individual who develops a somatization disorder, or Briquet syndrome, is known as a somatizer. This person is not bothered by the fear of disease, but rather by the actual symptoms that he or she reports. This individual will generally describe numerous aches and pains in a vague and exaggerated manner. Like the hypochondriac, the somatizer will often seek out frequent, unnecessary medical treatment. The somatizer, however, will be a particularly difficult patient for the physician to handle. The somatizer will often present his or her physician with a long, vague, and confusing list of complaints. At times, it may seem as if the somatizer is actually developing new symptoms as he or she talks to the physician. The dramatic and disorganized manner in which these patients describe their problems, and their tendency to switch from one doctor to the next with great frequency, make somatizers some of the most frustrating patients that medical professionals are likely to encounter.

It will also be difficult for even the most capable of medical professionals to work effectively with an individual who is suffering from somatoform pain. The concept of somatoform pain is a relatively new diagnostic category, in which the individual experiences physical pain that is thought to be caused by emotional factors. Somatoform pain is similar to conversion disorder, except that the individual experiences pain rather than some type of disability or anesthesia. Since pain is a subjective sensory experience rather than an observable symptom, it is often quite difficult for physicians to determine whether pain is caused by psychological or physical factors. It is therefore very hard to diagnose somatoform pain with any certainty.

The somatoform disorders, like all psychiatric diagnoses, are worth studying only when they can contribute to an understanding of the experience of a troubled individual. In particular, the somatoform disorders are useful when they help show that while an individual may genuinely feel sick, or believe he or she has some physical illness, this is not always the case. There are times when a psychological conflict can manifest itself in a somatic form.

A classic example of this situation is a famous case of conversion disorder that was reported by Josef Breuer and Sigmund Freud in 1895. This case involved "Anna O.," a well-educated and extremely intelligent young Viennese woman who had rapidly become bedridden with a number of mysterious physical symptoms. By the time that Anna O. sought the assistance of Breuer, a prominent Austrian physician, her medical condition was quite serious. Both Anna O.'s right arm and her right leg were paralyzed, her sight and hearing were impaired, and she often had difficulty speaking. She also sometimes went into a rather dreamlike state, which she referred to as an "absence." During these periods of absence, Anna O. would mumble to herself and appear quite preoccupied with disturbing thoughts.

Anna O.'s symptoms were quite troubling to Breuer, since she did not appear to suffer from any particular physical ailment. To understand this young woman's condition, Breuer encouraged her to discuss her symptoms at length, and used hypnosis to explore the history of her illness. Over time, Breuer began to get Anna O. to talk more freely, until she eventually discussed some troubling past events. Breuer noticed that as she started to recall and discuss more details from her emotionally disturbing history, her physical symptoms began to go away.

Eventually, under hypnosis, Anna O. described what Breuer thought was the original trauma that had precipitated her conversion reaction. She indicated that she had been spending a considerable amount of time caring for her seriously ill father. After many days of patiently waiting at her father's bedside, Anna naturally grew somewhat resentful of the great burden that his illness had placed upon her. These feelings of resentment were morally unacceptable to Anna O., who also experienced genuine feelings of love and concern for her father. One day, she was feeling particularly tired as she sat at her father's bedside. She dropped off into what Breuer describes as a waking dream, with her right arm over the back of a chair. After she fell into this trancelike state, Anna O. saw a large black snake emerge from the wall and slither toward her sick father to bite him. She tried to push the snake away, but her right arm had gone to sleep. When Anna O. looked at her right hand, she found that her fingers had turned into little snakes with death's heads.

The next day, when Anna O. was walking outside, she saw a bent branch. This branch reminded her of her hallucination of the snake, and at once her right arm became rigidly extended. Over time, the paralysis in Anna O.'s right arm extended to her entire right side; other symptoms began to develop as well. Recalling her hallucination of the snake and the emotions that accompanied it seemed to produce a great improvement in her condition. Breuer hypothesized that Anna O. had converted her original trauma into a physical symptom, and was unable to recover until this traumatic memory was properly expressed and discussed. The way in which Breuer treated Anna O. eventually became known as the cathartic method.

Anna O.'s case and the development of the cathartic method eventually led to widespread interest in conversion disorders, as well as in the other types of somatoform disorders. Many mental health professionals began to suspect that all the somatoform disorders involved patients who were unconsciously converting unpleasant or unacceptable emotions into somatic complaints. The manner in which somatoform patients could misinterpret or misperceive their bodily sensations, however, remained rather mysterious. For example, how can an individual who has normal vision truly believe that he or she is blind? Research conducted by the team of Harold Sackheim, Johanna Nordlie, and Ruben Gur has suggested a possible answer to this question.

Sackheim and his colleagues studied conversion patients who believed they were blind. This form of blindness, known as hysterical blindness, can be quite debilitating. Patients who develop hysterical blindness are generally unable to perform their usual functions, and often report total loss of vision. But when the vision of these patients was tested in an empirical fashion, an interesting pattern of results emerged. On each trial of a special visual test there were two time intervals, each of which was bounded by the sounding of a buzzer. During each trial, a bright visual target was illuminated during one of the intervals. Hysterically blind subjects were asked to report whether the visual target was illuminated during the first or the second interval. If truly blind subjects were to attempt this task, they should be correct by chance approximately 50 percent of the time. Most hysterically blind subjects were correct only 20 to 30 percent of the time, as if they were deliberately trying to demonstrate poor vision. A smaller number of hysterically blind subjects were correct on almost every trial, suggesting that they were actually able to see the visual stimuli before them.

Sackheim and his colleagues have suggested that a two-state defensive reaction can explain these conflicting findings. First, the perceptual representations of visual stimuli are blocked from conscious awareness, so that subjects report that they are blind. Then, in the second part of the process, subjects continue to gain information from the perceptual representations of what they have seen. The performance of subjects on a visual task will then depend on whether the subjects feel they must deny access to the information that was gained during the second part of the visual process. If subjects believe that they must deny access to visual information, they will perform more poorly on a visual task than would be expected by chance. If subjects believe that they do not need to deny access to visual information, then they will perform like a normal subject on a visual task. In other words, according to Sackheim and his colleagues, hysterically blind patients base their responses on the consequences of their behavior.

The way in which hysterically blind patients can manipulate their ability to see has led many scholars to question whether these patients are being truthful. Sackheim, Nordlie, and Gur, however, report that there are patients with lesions in the visual cortex (a part of the brain which processes visual information) who report that they are blind. These patients believe that they cannot see, even though they have normal eyes and can respond accurately to visual stimuli. They believe they are blind because they have trouble processing visual information. It is thus possible that an individual can have normal eyesight and still believe that he or she is blind. It may thus be the case that many somatoform patients truly and honestly believe that they have a physical symptom, even though they are actually quite healthy.

Treatment and Therapy

The study of somatoform disorders is an important area of concern for both medical professionals and social scientists. The somatoform disorders are relatively common, and their great prevalence poses a serious problem for the medical establishment. A tremendous amount of professional energy and financial resources is expended in the needless medical treatment of somatoform patients, who really suffer from emotional rather than physical difficulties. For example, when Robert Woodruff, Donald Goodwin, and Samuel Guze compared fifty somatization patients with fifty normal control subjects in 1974, they found that the somatization patients had undergone major surgical procedures three times more frequently than had the normal controls. Since an effort was made to match the somatizing and control patients on the basis of their actual medical condition, one can assume that much of the surgery performed on the somatization patients was unnecessary.

On the other hand, there is also a considerable amount of evidence to indicate that many people who are genuinely ill are misdiagnosed with somatoform disorders. Charles Watson and Cheryl Buranen published a follow-up study of somatization patients in 1979 which found that 25 percent of the patients actually suffered from real physical disorders. It seems physicians who are unable to explain a patient's puzzling medical problems may be tempted to label the patient prematurely with a somatoform disorder. The diagnosis of a somatoform disorder needs to be made with great caution, to ensure that a genuine medical condition will not be overlooked. There is also a need for further research into the causes and nature of the somatoform disorders, so that they can be diagnosed in a more definitive fashion.

Perspective and Prospects

One hopes that further research will also shed light on the ways in which somatoform disorders can be treated. Most somatoform patients are truly in need of assistance, for while their physical illness may be imaginary, their pain and suffering are real. Unfortunately, at this time, it is often difficult for mental health professionals to treat somatoform patients effectively since these individuals tend to focus on their physical complaints rather than on their emotional problems.

More research is needed on the treatment of somatoform patients so that they can overcome the psychological difficulties that plague them.

Bibliography

Alloy, Lauren B., Neil S. Jacobson, and Joan Acocella. *Abnormal Psychology: Current Perspectives*. 8th ed. New York: McGraw-Hill, 1998. This textbook contains an excellent chapter on the somatoform disorders which describes relevant case studies and explains how different psychological theorists view the somatoform diagnoses. Discussion of hypochondriasis and conversion disorder is particularly informative. Clear, easy to read, and comprehensible to the high school or college student.

Breuer, Josef, and Sigmund Freud. *Studies in Hysteria*. Translated and edited by James Strachey, with the collaboration of Anna Freud. New York: Basic Books, 1982. In many ways, this landmark book, first published in 1895, was the genesis of contemporary psychotherapy. Describes the famous case of Anna O., as well as the histories of a number of other conversion patients. A challenging book, useful to the college student who has a serious interest in either conversion disorders or the history of psychology.

Jacob, Rolf G., and Samuel M. Turner. "Somatoform Disorders." In *Adult Psychopathology and Diagnosis*, edited by Samuel M. Turner and Michel Hersen. New York: John Wiley & Sons, 1984. Provides the reader with a scholarly overview of somatoform disorders. Relevant diagnostic issues are discussed, in conjunction with a thorough review of the major research studies that have been conducted on somatization disorder, hypochondriasis, and conversion disorder.

Ono, Yukata, et al., eds. *Somatoform Disorders*. New York: Springer, 1999. Examines the social aspects of somatoform disorders from a worldwide, cross-cultural perspective. Includes bibliographical references and an index.

Pilowsky, Issy. *Abnormal Illness Behaviour*. New York: John Wiley & Sons, 1997. Provides a general introduction to the early recognition and management of abnormal illness behavior.

Sackheim, Harold A., Johanna W. Nordlie, and Ruben C. Gur. "A Model of Hysterical and Hypnotic Blindness: Cognition, Motivation, and Awareness." In *Journal of Abnormal Psychology* 88 (October, 1979): 474-489. Recommended for the college student or serious reader who is interested in learning about contemporary research on conversion disorders. In particular, research on hysterical blindness is described in a complete and detailed fashion. The authors attempt to explain why hysterically blind patients believe they have lost their vision, when in reality they are able to see.

Sarason, Irwin G., and Barbara R. Sarason. *Abnormal Psychology: The Problem of Maladaptive Behavior*. 8th ed. Upper Saddle River, N.J.: Prentice Hall, 1996. Includes a very readable chapter on the psychological factors which can produce physical symptoms. A well-organized overview of somatization disorders is enhanced with a number of lively examples. Recommended for the high school student, college student, or casual reader.

Steven C. Abell

See also:

Abnormality: Biomedical Models; Abnormality: Psychodynamic Models; Anxiety Disorders; Grief and Guilt; Phobias; Post-traumatic Stress; Psychosomatic Disorders; Stress: Behavioral and Psychological Responses; Stress: Physiological Responses.

IDENTITY CRISES

Type of psychology: Developmental psychology
Fields of study: Adolescence; adulthood

Identity crises are the internal and external conflicts faced by the adolescent/young adult when choosing an occupation and coming to terms with a basic ideology. Development of a personal identity is a central component of psychosocial maturity.

Principal terms

IDENTITY: a configuration of occupational, sexual, and ideological commitments; according to Erikson, the positive pole of the fifth stage of psychosocial development

IDENTITY CONFUSION/DIFFUSION: an incomplete or inadequate sense of self, which can range from a state of occasional uncertainty to a psychotic state

IDENTITY STATUS: a description of one's self-structure based on evidence of exploration of alternatives and commitments to a career and a basic set of values

NEGATIVE IDENTITY: a self-structure that reflects a deviant lifestyle such as that taken on by a delinquent

PSYCHOSOCIAL MATURITY: the completion of development in those areas that include both psychological and social aspects, such as identity and sexuality

PSYCHOSOCIAL MORATORIUM: a period during which the adolescent is free from responsibilities and obligations in order to explore the meaning of life

Overview

Identity crises are an integral phase in human development. According to Erik Erikson, successful resolution of the identity crisis is contingent on the earlier resolution of the crises associated with infancy and childhood, such as trust, autonomy, initiative, and industry. Further, the extent to which the conflict surrounding identity is resolved will influence how the individual will cope with the crises of adulthood.

According to Erikson's model of the human life cycle, an identity crisis is one of the psychosocial conflicts faced by the adolescent. In Erikson's model, which was published in the 1960's, each age period is defined by a certain type of psychosocial crisis. Adolescence is the life stage during which acquiring an identity presents a major conflict. Failure to resolve the conflict results in identity confusion/diffusion—that is, an inadequate sense of self.

Identity implies an existential position, according to James Marcia, who construes identity as a self-structure composed of one's personal history, belief system, and competencies. One's perception of uniqueness is directly related to the development of this self-structure. A somewhat similar position has been taken by Jane Kroger, who views the identity crisis as a problem of self-definition. The resulting identity is a balance between self and others. Erikson defines identity as the belief that one's past experiences and identity will be confirmed in the future—as exemplified in the choice of a career. Identity is a composite of one's sexuality, physical makeup, vocation, and belief system. Identity is the pulling together of who one is and who one can become, which involves compositing one's past, present, and future. It is a synthesis of earlier identifications. Successfully resolving the identity crisis is contingent on the interactions that the adolescent/young adult has with others. Erikson contends that interacting with others provides the needed feedback about who one is and who one ought to be. These interactions with others enable the adolescent/young adult to gain a perspective of self that includes an evaluation of his or her physical and social self. Identity acquisition is cognitive as well as social.

From Erikson's perspective, as discussed by James Cote and Charles Levine (1987), four conditions are necessary for an identity crisis: Puberty has been reached; the requisite cognitive development is present; physical growth is nearing adult stature; and societal influences are guiding the person toward an integration and resynthesis of identity. The dialectics of society and personality, implicit in the last condition, are given the most attention by Erikson, according to Cote and Levine, because the other three conditions are part of normative development. Developmental level of the individual and societal pressures combine to elicit an identity crisis; but Cote and Levine note that timing of this crisis is contingent on factors such as ethnicity, gender, socioeconomic status, and subculture, as well as personality factors (for example, authoritarianism or neuroticism) and socialization practices. The severity of the identity crisis is determined by the extent to which one's identity portrayal is interfered with by the uncertainty inherent in moving toward self-definition and unexpected events.

An integral part of the identity crisis is the psychological moratorium, a time during which society permits the individual to work on crisis resolution. During this moratorium, the adolescent/young adult has the opportunity to examine societal roles, career possibilities, and values, free from the expectation of commitments and long-term responsibilities. Although some individuals choose to remain in a moratorium indefinitely, Erikson contends that there is an absolute end to the recognizable moratorium. At its completion, the adolescent/young adult should have attained the necessary restructuring of self and identifications so that he or she can find a place in society which fits this identity.

Based on Erikson's writings, Cote and Levine identify two types of institutionalized moratoria: the technological moratorium, which is highly structured, and the humanistic moratorium, which is less highly structured. The technological moratorium is the product of the educational system, which is charged by society with socializing youth to fit in adult society. Individuals in this moratorium option experience less difficulty in resolving the identity crisis because they move into occupations and societal roles for which they have been prepared with significantly less intrapsychic trauma in accepting an ideology. The school takes an active role in easing this transition by providing vocational and academic counseling for students, facilitating scheduling so that students can gain work experience while enrolled in school, and encouraging early decision making as to a future career.

The identity crisis for individuals in the humanistic moratorium is more stressful, painful, and of longer duration than for those in the technological moratorium. The focal concern of the adolescent/young adult in the humanistic moratorium is humanistic values, which are largely missing from the technological moratorium. There is more variability in this concern for humanistic values, which is reflected in the moratorium that is chosen and the commitments that are made. These conditions elicit an alternation between progressive and regressive states, with the individual making commitments at one time and disengaging at another. The character Holden Caulfield in J. D. Salinger's classic novel *The Catcher in the Rye* (1951) is an example of this type of identity problem. More extreme identity confusion is found among individuals in this moratorium. According to Cote and Levine, social support is often lacking, which hinders formation of a stable identity. Family and community support is especially important for these individuals. Yet these are the adolescents/young adults who, because their lifestyle departs from the societal mold, are often ostracized and denied support. Individuals may promote a cause of some type. Those who choose a humanistic moratorium are more likely to be intellectual, artistic, antiestablishment, and ideologically nonconforming. After a time, some of these individuals accept technological values and roles.

Individuals whose identity seeking is not influenced by technological or humanistic moratoria face a rather different situation. Some remain in a constant state of flux in which choices are avoided and commitments are lacking. Others take on a negative identity by accepting a deviant lifestyle and value system (for example, delinquency or gang membership). In this instance, the negative elements of an identity outweigh the positive elements. This type of identity crisis resolution occurs in an environment which precludes normative identity development (for example, excessively demanding parents, absence of an adequate role model).

Applications

Erikson's writings on identity crises have been responsible for an extensive literature, consisting of conceptual as well as empirical articles. Perhaps the most widely used application is Marcia's identity status paradigm, in which he has conceptualized and operationalized Erikson's theory of identity development in terms of several statuses which result from exploration and commitment. More than one hundred empirical studies have been generated from this paradigm, according to a review by Cote and Levine (1988). The identity status paradigm provides a methodological procedure for determining identity statuses based on resolution of an identity crisis and the presence of commitments to an occupation and an ideology.

According to the Marcia paradigm, an ego identity can be one of several statuses consisting of achievement, foreclosure, moratorium, or diffusion. An achievement status indicates resolution of the identity crisis and firm commitments to an occupation and an ideology. In a foreclosure status, one has formed commitments but has not experienced a crisis. The moratorium status denotes that an identity crisis is currently being experienced, and no commitments have been made. The diffusion status implies the absence of a crisis and no commitments. Much of the research has focused on identifying the personality characteristics associated with each of these statuses. Other studies have examined the interactional patterns as well as information-processing and problem-solving strategies. Achievement and moratorium statuses seek out, process, and evaluate information in their decision making. Foreclosures have more rigid belief systems and conform to normative standards held by significant others, while those in the diffusion status delay decision making. Significant differences have been found among the statuses in terms of their capacity for intimacy, with diffusions scoring lowest, followed by foreclosures. Achievement and moratorium statuses have a greater capacity for intimacy.

Two areas of research that continue to attract attention are parental socialization patterns associated with crisis resolution, and identity crises in females. The findings to date reveal distinctive parental patterns associated with each status. Positive but somewhat ambivalent relationships between parents and the adolescent/young adult are reported for achievement status. Moratorium-status adolescents/young adults also seem to have ambivalent relationships with their parents, but they are less conforming. Males in this status tend to experience difficulty in separating from their mothers. Foreclosures view their parents as highly accepting and encouraging. Parental pressure for conformity to family values is very evident. Diffusion-status adolescents report much parental rejection and detachment from parents, especially from the father. In general, the data from family studies show that the same-sex parent is an important figure in identity resolution.

The interest in female identity has arisen because different criteria have been used to identify identity status based on the Marcia paradigm. Attitudes toward premarital sexual relations is a major content area in status determination. The research in general shows that achievement and foreclosure statuses are very similar in females, as are the moratorium and diffusion statuses. This pattern is not found for males. It has been argued by some that the focal concerns of females, in addition to concerns with occupation and ideology, involve interpersonal relationships more than do the concerns of males. Therefore, in forming a self-structure, females may examine the world outside for self-evaluation and acceptance in addition to the internal examination of self which typically occurs in males. The effect of an external focus on identity resolution in females is unknown, but this type of focus is likely to prolong the identity crisis. Further, it is still necessary to determine the areas in which choices and commitments are made for females.

The concept of negative identity has been used frequently in clinical settings to explain antisocial acts and delinquency in youth, as well as gang-related behavior. Randall Jones and Barbara Hartman (1988) found that the use of substances (for example, cigarettes, alcohol, and other drugs) was higher and more likely in youths of identity-diffusion status. Erikson and others have argued that troubled youths find that elements of a negative identity provide them with a sense of some mastery over a situation for which a positive approach has been continually denied them. In the examples cited, deviant behavior provided this sense of mastery and an identity.

Perspective and Prospects

The identity crisis is the major conflict faced by the adolescent. Erikson's theorizing about the identity crisis made a major contribution to the adolescent literature. Marcia's reconceptualization of ego identity facilitated identity research and clinical assessment by providing a methodological approach for determining identity development and the psychological concomitants of identity. As a result, the study of identity and the awareness of the psychological impact on the individual has become a major research area and has provided a basis for clinical intervention.

The concept of identity crises originated with Erikson, based on the clinical experiences which he used to develop a theory of ego identity development. Explication of this theory appeared in his writings during the 1950's and 1960's. Erikson's theory of the human life cycle places identity resolution as the major crisis faced by the adolescent. The success of this resolution is determined by the satisfactory resolution of crises in the stages preceding adolescence.

Identity formation is a major topic in most textbooks on adolescence, and it is a focal concern of practitioners who treat adolescents with psychological adjustment problems. Until the appearance of Erikson's writings, the field of adolescence was mostly a discussion of physical and sexual development. His focus on psychosocial development, especially the emergence of a self-structure, increased immeasurably the understanding of adolescent development and the problems faced by the adolescent growing up in Western society. As Cote and Levine have noted, identity is a multidimensional construct, consisting of sociological perspectives, specifically the social environment in which the individual interacts, as well as psychological processes. Thus, a supportive social environment is critical to crisis resolution. The absence of this supportive environment has frequently been cited as an explanation for identity problems and the acquisition of a negative identity.

It is important to realize that identity has a temporal element as well as a lifelong duration. That is, identity as a personality characteristic undergoes transformations throughout the life cycle. While crisis resolution may be achieved during adolescence/young adulthood, this self-structure is not permanent. Crises can reemerge during the life span. The midlife crises of middle adulthood, written about frequently in the popular press, are often viewed as a manifestation of the earlier identity crisis experienced during adolescence/young adulthood.

A future role for identity crises is difficult to forecast. The psychological moratorium will continue to be an important process. Given the constant change in American society, the moratorium options available for youth may be more restricted, or more ambiguous and less stable. This scenario is more probable for humanistic moratoria as society moves toward more institutional structure in the form of schools taking on increased responsibility for the socialization of children and youth. The provision of child care before and after school is one example of the school's increased role. The erosion which has occurred in family structure presents another problem for identity crisis resolution.

Bibliography

Cote, James E., and Charles Levine. "A Critical Examination of the Ego Identity Status Paradigm." *Developmental Review* 8 (June, 1988): 147-184. Critiques the Marcia identity-status paradigm and notes several areas of divergence from Erikson's conceptualization theory of identity. Advances the argument for an interdisciplinary approach to understanding identity, and identifies several questions about identity crises that need to be considered.

_____. "A Formulation of Erikson's Theory of Ego Identity Formation." *Developmental Review* 7 (December, 1987): 209-218. A comprehensive review of Erikson's theory of ego identity and the role of psychological moratoria in the resolution of identity crises. Discusses Erikson's concepts of value orientation stages and the ego-superego conflict over personality control. Offers criticisms of Erikson's work and suggests cautions for the researcher.

Erikson, Erik Homburger. *Childhood and Society*. 2d ed. New York: W. W. Norton, 1963. A presentation of case histories based on Erikson's clinical experiences, as well as a discussion of Erikson's lifecycle model of human development. One section of the book is devoted to an examination of youth and identity. Clinical studies are used to illustrate the problems youth face in identity resolution.

_____. *Identity: Youth and Crisis*. New York: W. W. Norton, 1968. A theoretical discussion of ego identity formation and identity confusion, with special attention given to issues such as womanhood, and race and identity. Erikson relies heavily on his vast clinical experiences to illustrate the concepts that he discusses. The life cycle as it applies to identity is examined from an epigenetic perspective.

Evans, Richard I. *Dialogue with Erik Erikson*. Reprint. Northvale, N.J.: Jason Aronson, 1995. This volume in the Master Work series was originally published in 1964. Includes reactions from Ernest Jones, bibliographical references, and an index.

Kroger, Jane. *Identity in Adolescence*. London: Routledge & Kegan Paul, 1989. A presentation of identity development as conceptualized by Erikson and others. Each approach is criticized, and the empirical findings generated by the approach are summarized. The first chapter of the book is devoted to an overview of identity from a developmental and sociocultural perspective. The final chapter presents an integration of what is known about identity.

Marcia, James E. "Identity in Adolescence." In *Handbook of Adolescent Psychology*, edited by Joseph Adelson. New York: John Wiley & Sons, 1980. A discussion of the identity statuses developed by Marcia, based on a paradigm derived from Erikson's conceptualization of ego identity. Reviews the research literature on personality characteristics, patterns of interaction, developmental studies, identity in women, and other directions in identity research. Ends with a discussion of a general ego-developmental approach to identity.

Moshman, David. *Adolescent Psychological Development: Rationality, Morality, and Identity*. Mahwah, N.J.: Lawrence Erlbaum Associates, 1999. Presents a constructivist approach to the development of rationality, morality, and identity in adolescence and early adulthood. Reviews post-Piagetian approaches to adolescent cognition, examining classic theories and current research. Accessible to students with no background in psychology.

Psychoanalysis and Contemporary Thought 19, no. 2 (1996). A special issue entitled "Ideas and Identities: The Life and Work of Erik Erikson," edited by Robert S. Wallerstein. A variety of insightful perspectives on Erikson; includes a selection of photographs.

Tribe, Carol. *Profile of Three Theories: Erikson, Maslow, Piaget.* Dubuque, Iowa: Kendall/Hunt, 1982. Examines the work of Erik Erikson, Abraham Maslow, and Jean Piaget.

Joseph C. LaVoie

See also:

Child and Adolescent Psychiatry; Divorce and Separation: Children's Issues; Juvenile Delinquency; Midlife Crises; Psychotherapy: Children; Teenage Suicide.

Insomnia

Type of psychology: Consciousness
Fields of study: Sleep

Insomnia is a complaint of poor, insufficient, or nonrestorative sleep; it may be experienced for a few nights or for a lifetime. Daytime functioning is often affected. Insomnia may be caused by an underlying physiological or psychological disorder, or by substance abuse, but it can also occur independently of these factors.

Principal terms

CHRONOTHERAPY: the systematic adjustment of an individual's sleep-wake cycle to align it with the person's circadian rhythm
CIRCADIAN RHYTHM: a rhythm, such as the human sleep-wake cycle, that follows a roughly twenty-four-hour pattern
PERSISTENT PSYCHOPHYSIOLOGICAL INSOMNIA (PPI): behavioral insomnia that may be caused by sleep-incompatible behaviors (such as stimulant intake) or by chronic anxiety or stress
POLYSOMNOGRAPHY: a technique employed in a sleep laboratory to monitor the electrical activity, respiration, heart rate, and movements of the body during sleep
TRANSIENT INSOMNIA: a period of insomnia lasting no more than three weeks

Causes and Symptoms

Insomnia is defined as a person's perception that his or her sleep is inadequate or abnormal. It may include difficulty initiating sleep, short sleep time, frequent awakenings from sleep, and sleep that is nonrestorative. The daytime symptoms of insomnia include fatigue, excessive daytime sleepiness, mood changes, and impaired mental as well as physical functioning. Insomnia can be caused by conditions such as stress, anxiety, depression, substance abuse, medical illness, or other sleep disorders, but it may stand alone in some patients, separate from any known underlying disorders. The occurrence of insomnia increases with age; one study estimates that approximately 50 percent of persons between the ages of sixty-five and seventy-nine experience trouble sleeping.

The Association of Sleep Disorders Centers (ASDC) recognizes that there are two general types of insomnia. Classified on the basis of the duration of the period in which the person experiences insomnia, these two types are transient insomnia and primary insomnia. Transient insomnia is seen when persons have had a history of normal sleep but experience a period of insomnia which lasts less than three weeks; the patient returns to normal sleep after the insomnia period. The insomnia period is usually tied to a specific experience or situation, and it is believed that there are two common processes that are involved in transient insomnia. The first involves central nervous system arousal and any condition which may cause such arousal, whether it is psychological or environmental. There is no clear physiological disorder associated with this condition, but some research suggests that individuals who are likely to be aroused by stress may be more vulnerable to this type of insomnia than other people. Some sleep researchers indicate that emotional disturbance may play a role in up to 80 percent of transient insomnia cases.

A second process involved in transient insomnia results from persons having a sleep-wake schedule that is not aligned with their own circadian (twenty-four-hour) rhythms. Biological rhythms control many bodily functions, such as blood pressure, body temperature, hormonal activity, and the menstrual cycle, as well as the sleep-wake cycle. Insomnia can be caused by a sleep-wake cycle which is misaligned with the circadian rhythm, such as that which occurs when persons travel across many time zones or engage in shift work. Circadian rhythm disorders can last for periods of more than six months, in which case the problem would be considered chronic.

Primary insomnia is diagnosed when the patient's insomnia is not secondary to problems such as depression, anxiety, pain, or some other sleep disorder, and it lasts for a period longer than three weeks. Two types of primary insomnia are persistent psychophysiological insomnia (PPI) and insomnia complaints without objective findings. PPI is commonly known as learned, or behavioral, insomnia, as it is caused or maintained by maladaptive learning—that is, by the occurrence of sleep-incompatible behaviors, such as caffeine intake before bedtime. PPI is diagnosed when the patient demonstrates sleep difficulties which are verified in a sleep laboratory and are then traced to their behavioral causes. Figures vary, but approximately 15 percent of those patients diagnosed as having insomnia probably have PPI. One common feature of PPI is excessive worrying about sleep problems. Great efforts are made to fall asleep at night, which are unsuccessful and lead to increased sleep difficulty; however, the patient may fall asleep quite easily when not trying to fall asleep.

One theory concerning how persistent psychophysiological insomnia can develop suggests that some people have a poor sleep-wake system, which makes it more difficult for them to overcome sleep-inhibiting behavior. For example, it is possible for persons to become so anxious concerning their poor sleep that even the thought of their own bedroom causes them stress, which further increases their sleep problems and creates a cycle of increasingly difficult sleep. This cycle would eventually end for persons with normal sleep cycles, but it is much easier for these events to disrupt those who already have the poor sleep-wake cycle suggested by this theory. Although PPI may begin in response to stress or an emotional situation, it should again be noted that in PPI this type of learning or behavior plays the major role in the insomnia complaint.

Most insomnia patients will exhibit irregular sleep patterns or polysomnographic findings when tested in a sleep laboratory; however, there are those who complain of insomnia yet show no irregular sleep patterns. In the past, these people were viewed as having "pseudoinsomnia," and they were even thought of as possibly using poor sleep as an excuse for being lazy. Those who have insomnia complaints without objective findings do not show any physiological or psychological disorder and do not exhibit any sleep-incompatible behaviors, yet they commonly respond to treatment of their insomnia as would a verified insomnia patient.

One study found that insomnia was associated with anxiety, depression, psychiatric distress, and medical illness in 47 percent of the cases. The medical and psychiatric disorders, as well as the pharmacological substances, that can cause insomnia are too numerous to list here. James Walsh and Roger Sugerman note three theories which attempt to explain the occurrence of insomnia in psychiatric disorders that may prove helpful in understanding the process. The first suggests that insomnia results from a psychological disturbance that goes unresolved and leads to arousal that prevents sleep. The second states that neurochemical abnormalities may be the cause of insomnia in psychiatric disorders. The final theory asserts that affective (emotional) disorders may disturb the biological rhythms that control sleep.

The trouble that many people face when trying to get a good night's rest is not the only problem caused by insomnia. Insomnia may have drastic effects on behavior during the day. As stated previously, fatigue, excessive daytime sleepiness, mood changes, and impaired mental and physical functioning are all frequently caused by insomnia. Difficulties in the workplace, as well as increased health problems, are also associated with complaints of insomnia, though they are not necessarily caused by insomnia. Insomnia is not a problem that the individual faces only at night.

Diagnosis of insomnia depends on an accurate evaluation of the circumstances surrounding the complaint. The clinician must take many things into account when diagnosing each particular case, as insomnia may be the result of any number of factors in the patient's life. Questions concerning behavior should be asked to determine if the insomnia is caused by sleep-incompatible behaviors. Polysomnographic testing in a sleep laboratory may be necessary in order to determine which type of insomnia the patient has.

Treatment and Therapy

Once properly diagnosed, insomnia may be treated in a number of ways, all of which are dependent on the type of insomnia with which the clinician is faced. While the classical treatment for sleeping problems in the past has been "sleeping pills," and treatment of transient insomnia today may still involve small doses of a short-acting drug (such as benzodiazepines) when necessary, merely counseling or educating patients concerning situations that may increase their sleep problems is frequently found to be effective. If the transient insomnia is caused by disrupting sounds in the sleeping environment (such as snoring or traffic noise), devices that mask the noise may be used; earplugs and placing a fan in the room to mask the noise are two simple examples of this method. If the sleep disturbance is associated with misaligned circadian rhythms, the person's bedtime may be systematically adjusted toward either an earlier or later hour, depending on what time they presently go to sleep. Strict adherence to the adjusted sleep-wake schedule is then necessary in order for the individual to remain on a regular schedule. This method is referred to as chronotherapy.

Peter Hauri suggests that treatment of persistent psychophysiological insomnia will typically involve aspects of three "domains": sleep hygiene, behavioral treatment, and the use of hypnotics. Methods involving sleep hygiene focus on educating the patient concerning proper sleep habits. Hauri states that the goal is for the patient to avoid all thoughts that may stimulate or arouse the patient. This is done by focusing on or engaging in monotonous or nonstimulating behaviors at bedtime such as reading or listening to pleasant music.

Behavioral methods include relaxation therapy, limiting sleep time to a few hours per night until the patient is able to use the time in bed as "true" sleeping time, and using "stimulus control" therapy. This method requires the patient to get out of bed whenever she or he is not able to sleep. The process is aimed at reducing the association between the bedroom and the frustration with trying to go to sleep. Finally, the use of hypnotic medications is indicated in patients who have such a need for sleep that they "try too hard" and thus become aroused by their efforts. As with transient insomnia, a small dose of a short-acting drug is suggested in order to break this cycle of frustration. The treatment for patients who exhibit no objective polysomnographic findings is similar to that for patients with any other type of insomnia. Such patients also tend to respond to behavioral, educational, and pharmacological methods.

Perspective and Prospects

The importance of a greater understanding of the mechanisms of sleep and insomnia can be appreciated by everyone. Anyone knows that when one feels truly sleepy, it is difficult to concentrate, perform simple tasks, or maintain patience with other people. If this situation were to last for a week, a month, or several years, one would at least wish for it to end and at most find it nearly intolerable.

A National Institute of Mental Health survey reported that approximately 17 percent of a nationally representative sample had experienced "serious" trouble sleeping in the year prior to the survey. Other research suggests that as many as 38 percent of adults in the United States experience trouble sleeping. It is likely that at some time in their lives, nearly everyone has experienced some difficulty sleeping.

The discovery of the methods used to monitor electrical activity in the human brain during the late 1920's essentially ushered in the modern era of sleep research. With this development, sleep stages were discovered, which eventually led to a greater understanding of what takes place in both normal and abnormal sleep.

A. Michael Anch, Carl Browman, Merrill Mitler, and James Walsh write in *Sleep: A Scientific Perspective* (1988) that most insomnia research prior to 1980 treated insomniacs as one group, with little attention paid to differences such as duration or causal factors in the subject's insomnia. While this limits the ability to generalize the earlier findings, these authors concede that the inclusion of different types of insomnia in studies eventually came to increase knowledge of the psychology of sleep and insomnia.

With regard to the treatment of insomnia, much has been learned that allows doctors and psychologists to treat the different types of this disorder more effectively. The myth of the "cure-all" sleeping pill has been replaced with a more sophisticated approach, which includes educational and behavioral practices. Medications are still used, but treatment options have increased so that clinicians are not as limited as they once were.

As the study of sleep disorders has developed in terms of scientific sophistication, researchers have been able to learn the importance that sleep holds in day-to-day functioning. They have also discovered how detrimental sleep loss or disruption of the sleep-wake cycle can be. Aiding in the discoveries have been scientific developments in neurobiology, behavioral medicine, physiology, and psychiatry that allow analysis of the mechanisms in normal and abnormal sleep. It is hoped that as scientists gain a further understanding of insomnia through research, they will also understand, more generally, the true purpose of sleep.

Bibliography
Anch, A. Michael, Carl P. Browman, Merrill M. Mitler, and James K. Walsh. *Sleep: A Scientific Perspective*. Englewood Cliffs, N.J.: Prentice Hall, 1988. A comprehensive work on the field of sleep disorders that also provides a concise history of the science. Chapter 9 covers insomnia, but the entire book is noteworthy for its broad coverage of historical as well as modern research and treatment of sleep and its disorders. A very helpful work for those interested in learning about any aspect of sleep.

Dement, William C. *Some Must Watch While Some Must Sleep*. San Francisco: W. H. Freeman, 1974. A classic book by a scientist who many consider to be the leading authority in the field of sleep studies. Easily readable by high school or college students. Very informative; provides an excellent starting point for further study.

DiGeronimo, Theresa Foy, and Frank Dimaria. *Insomnia: Fifty Essential Things to Do*. New York: Plume, 1997. Diagnoses the kinds and causes of insomnia, explains which foods and environments promote good sleep, and presents a step-by-step approach to remedies from homeopathy to prescription drugs.

Kryger, Meir H., Thomas Roth, and William C. Dement, eds. *Principles and Practice of Sleep Medicine*. 2d ed. Philadelphia: W. B. Saunders, 1994. An extremely thorough collection of articles written by many of the leaders in sleep research and treatment. It is an advanced work to some extent, but is written in a style that allows the novice reader to understand many technical concepts with little difficulty. Deals with insomnia and includes further information on many subclassifications of insomnia as well as on the medical and psychiatric illnesses commonly associated with insomnia.

Mendelson, W. B. *Human Sleep: Research and Clinical Care*. New York: Plenum Medical Book Company, 1987. Provides an overview of research and treatment practices for a number of sleep disorders. Recommended for the college student, but may be understood by those having a basic knowledge of sleep.

Nicholson, Anthony N., and John Marks. *Insomnia: A Guide for Medical Practitioners*. Boston: MTP Press, 1983. Though the title may sound imposing to those who are new to the study of insomnia, this book is quite easily understood by those with a limited knowledge of sleep disorders. The entire work is devoted to insomnia, and it provides information on diagnosis and treatment of various types.

Zammit, Gary, and Jane A. Zanca. *Good Nights: How to Stop Sleep Deprivation, Overcome Insomnia, and Get the Sleep You Need.* Kansas City, Mo.: Andrews and McMeel, 1997. Provides answers to overcoming insomnia, ending sleep deprivation, and getting the proper amount of sleep to stay alert. Includes an index.

Alan K. Gibson

See also:

Anxiety Disorders; Biofeedback and Relaxation; Depression; Post-traumatic Stress; Sleep Apnea Syndromes and Narcolepsy; Stress: Behavioral and Psychological Responses; Stress: Physiological Responses.

Jealousy

Type of psychology: Social psychology
Fields of study: Interpersonal relations

Jealousy is the experience of perceiving that one's relationship is threatened; it is influenced by cultural expectations about relationships, personal self-esteem, and feelings of possessiveness. Jealousy is a common source of conflict, and it can have a destructive impact on relationships.

Principal terms

DISPOSITIONAL: relating to disposition or personality
DYADIC: pertaining to a couple
PATRILINEAGE: the tracing of ancestry through fatherhood
POSSESSIVENESS: the desire to maintain and control a resource, object, or person
SOCIALIZATION: the process of learning and internalizing social rules and standards

Causes and Symptoms

Jealousy is not a single emotion; it is most likely a complex of several emotions. Their central theme is the fear of losing to someone else what rightfully belongs to one. In personal relationships, jealousy focuses on fear of losing the partner; the partner is seen as a possession whose ownership is in jeopardy. Whether the threat is real or imaginary, it endangers the jealous person's self-esteem as well as the relationship. Theorists argue that three elements are central to the emotional experience of jealousy: an attachment between two people; valued resources that are exchanged between them; and an intrusion on this attachment by a third person seen to be supplanting the giver or receiver of resources.

Early theories of jealousy suggested that the jealous person fears losing possession; later conceptualizations, however, have specified that jealousy is a fear not of loss of possession but of loss of control. The intrusion of a third party also threatens the cohesiveness of the attachment, dividing partners into opponents. Insofar as the relationship has been integrated into each partner's identity, the intruder threatens not only what the jealous person has but also who he or she is. Most researchers conclude that the experience of jealousy is itself a damaging and destructive relationship event. Emotional bonds are reduced to property rights; jealousy involves the manipulation of feelings and behaviors, and it can erupt in anger or cause depression. The positive aspects of jealousy are few, but they are identifiable: It intensifies feelings, provides information about the partners, can trigger important discussions between them, and can enhance the jealous person's self-concept.

Jealousy is more likely when a relationship is intensely valued by someone; the more important it is, the more dangerous would be its loss. Social norms do not support the expression of some forms of jealousy; for example, most cultures do not tolerate expressing jealousy of one's own children. Inexpressible jealousies may be displaced onto the more tolerated forms, such as a couple's sexual relationship. Sexual attraction or behavior is often the focus of jealousy, even though sexual interaction may not be the most valued aspect of a relationship. For example, one gender difference that has been identified in the experience of jealousy (in heterosexual relationships) is that while men focus on sexual infidelity or intrusion, women express greater jealousy about the emotional attachment between a partner and a rival.

Dispositional factors in jealousy include feelings of personal insecurity, a poor self-image, and deficient education. Jealous people appear to be unhappy even before they identify a target for their dissatisfaction. Describing oneself as "a jealous person" is related to a negative attributional style; a self-described jealous person sees his or her jealous reaction as stable and uncontrollable, and thus as less likely to change. Developmental research suggests that jealous emotions originate in childhood when the child's exclusive attachment to the mother outlives the mother's intense bond to the child. Childhood jealousy also manifests itself in rivalry with one's other parent or with siblings, implying that jealousy assumes that love is a finite resource that cannot be shared without diminishment. A common theme in jealousy research is the jealous person's sense of dependence on the threatened relationship, as well as the conviction that he or she is somehow lacking. Before an intrusion appears or is imagined, therefore, a jealous person may already feel inadequate, insecure, and threatened.

Jealousy is also related to possessiveness—the desire to maintain and control a person or resource. Thus the central issue of relationship jealousy is not love but power and control. Relatively powerful people (in most societies, men rather than women) feel less possessive because they feel less powerless. Circumstances can trigger possessiveness: In all types of relationships studied, one partner feels more possessive when he or she fears that the other might have a meaningful interaction with a third person.

Cultural and subcultural norms determine the forms and incidences of jealousy. For both men and women, jealousy is related to the expectation of exclusiveness in a relationship. For men in particular, jealousy is related to gender-role tradition-alism (adherence to traditional standards of masculinity) and dependence on partners' evaluations for self-esteem. For women, jealousy is related to dependence on the relationship. With these gender-role expectations, individuals decide whether they are "obligated" to feel jealous when the circumstances indicate a threat to self-esteem or intimacy.

Cultures vary widely in the standards and degree of jealousy attached to sexual relationships. Jealousy is rare in cultures that place few restrictions on sexual gratification and do not make marriage or progeny important to social recognition. In contrast, high-jealousy cultures are those that place great importance on control of sexual behavior and identification of patrilineage. Cultural researchers conclude that jealousy is not inborn but learned through socialization to what is valued in one's culture. For example, a cultural norm commonly associated with jealousy is monogamy. In monogamous cultures, alternative liaisons are condemned as wrong, and jealousy is seen as a reasonable, vigilant response. In such contexts a double standard is promoted, separating jealousy from envy, a covetous feeling about material property. While envy and greed are considered unacceptable, jealousy is justified as a righteous defense of intimate territory.

Despite the negative form and consequences of jealousy in most relationships, it is popularly associated with intensity of romantic commitment. Researchers have found that individuals who score high in measures of romanticism believe that jealousy is a desirable reaction in a partner. Perhaps because jealousy is mistakenly believed to strengthen intimacy (although research indicates that it has the opposite effect), some individuals may seek to induce jealousy in their partners. Researchers have found that women are more likely than men to induce jealousy with an expectation of renewed attention or greater control of the relationship. Five jealousy-inducement techniques have been identified: exaggerating a third person's appeal, flirting with others, dating others, fabricating another attachment, and talking about a previous partner. Theorists speculate that the gender difference in jealousy inducement reflects the imbalance of power in male-female relationships. Provoking jealousy may be an attempt to redress other inequities in the relationship.

Reactions to jealousy vary by age, gender, and culture. Young children may express rage in tantrums or attack the interloping sibling. Research has identified six common responses made by jealous children: aggression, identification with the rival (for example, crying or acting cute like a new baby), withdrawal, repression or feigning apathy, masochism (exaggerating pain to win attention), and creative competition (with the possible outcome of greater self-reliance).

Gender differences in jealous reactions include self-awareness, emotional expression, focus of attention, focus of blame, and restorative behavior. When jealous, men are more likely to deny such feelings, while women more readily acknowledge them. Men express jealousy in rage and anger, while women experience depression and fear (that the relationship may end). Men are more likely to blame the third party or the partner, while women blame themselves. Men engage in confrontational behavior and focus on restoring self-esteem. Women intensify possessiveness and focus on strengthening the relationship. In general, these gender differences reflect different sources of jealousy and different emotional and social implications. For most men, a relationship is regarded as a personal possession or resource to be protected with territorial aggression. For most women, a relationship is an extension of the self, a valued opportunity but not a personal right, whose loss is feared and defended with efforts to secure the bonds of attachment. The focus of postjealousy behavior is guided by the resource that is most damaged or threatened by the episode: For men, this is the role of the relationship in supporting self-esteem; for women, it is the health and security of the relationship.

Cultural differences in reacting to jealousy range from extreme violence to dismissive inattention. A jealous Samoan woman might bite her rival on the nose, while a New Mexican Zuñi wife might refuse to do her straying husband's laundry. Cultures may overtly or tacitly condone violence incited by jealous passion. Jealousy has been cited as a justifying factor in many forms of social violence: family murder and suicide, spouse abuse, divorce, depression, and criminal behavior. Despite cultural stereotypes of woman as more prone to jealousy, a review of murders committed in a jealous rage has revealed women to be the perpetrators in fewer than 15 percent of the cases.

Treatment and Therapy

Researchers have identified positive, constructive approaches to managing jealous experiences. Three broad coping strategies have been identified: self-reliance, self-image improvement, and selective devaluing of the loved one. In the first case, self-reliance involves controlling expressions of sadness and anger, and forging a tighter commitment with one's partner. In the second, one's self-image can be enhanced by making positive social comparisons and identifying and developing one's good qualities. Finally, jealousy can be reduced and the threat eliminated if one convinces oneself that the loved person is not so important after all. These approaches are all popular, but they are not equally effective. Researchers comment that self-reliance works best, selective devaluing is less effective, and self-bolstering does not appear to be effective at all.

Perspective and Prospects

Research on jealousy has several origins. Anthropologists have long observed the dramatic cultural variations in the causes and expressions of jealousy. Psychologists have noted that jealousy has no consistent emotional expression or definition: For some people, jealousy is a version of anger; for others, it resembles sadness, depression, or fear. When research on close relationships began to develop in the 1960's and 1970's, jealousy was found to help explain the dynamics of power and conflict in intimacy. Early research produced the counterintuitive findings that jealousy hinders rather than enhances romantic relationships, and that its roots are not in intimacy but possessiveness. Jealousy was eventually found to be an aspect of self-esteem and defensiveness rather than a quality of intimacy or dyadic communication.

Jealousy has also gained attention as a social problem because of its implications in criminal behavior and domestic violence. Increases in the rate of domestic assault and murder have warranted a closer examination of the cultural assumptions and stereotypes that support jealous rage and depression. Educational programs to address self-esteem, especially in young children and adolescents, are focusing on jealousy as a symptom of pathology rather than a normal or healthy emotional experience.

Consistent discoveries of cultural differences in patterns of jealous experience have supported the view that jealousy, like many other "natural" relationship phenomena, is learned and acquired through socialization and experience. Thus, jealousy research is contributing to the "demystification" of close relationships— attraction and attachment are not seen as mysterious or fragile processes, but as learned behavior patterns that can be both understood and modified. Jealous individuals can be taught to derive their sense of self-esteem or security from more stable, self-controlled sources. Jealousy can be explained as the unhealthy symptom of a treatable complex of emotions, beliefs, and habits. Its contributions to relationship conflict and personal distress can be reduced, and its lessons applied to developing healthier attitudes and behaviors.

Bibliography

Brehm, Sharon S. *Intimate Relationships*. 2d ed. New York: Random House, 1992. This excellent text devotes one chapter to jealousy, reviewing research and putting jealousy in the context of other relationship experiences.

Clanton, Gordon, and Lynn G. Smith, eds. *Jealousy*. Englewood Cliffs, N.J.: Prentice-Hall, 1977. A short, readable, and interesting edited collection reviewing gender differences, cultural factors, and other issues in jealousy research.

Malakh-Pines, Ayala. *Romantic Jealousy: Causes, Symptoms, Cures*. New York: Routledge, 1998. Draws on case studies from clinical practice, jealousy workshops, and research with more than one hundred individuals and couples. Explores the many facets of this complex emotion.

Pines, Ayala M., and Elliot Aronson. "Antecedents, Correlates, and Consequences of Sexual Jealousy." *Journal of Personality* 51 (1983): 108-136. An easy-to-read, clarifying review of the causes, symptoms, and outcomes of jealousy in romantic relationships.

Salovey, Peter, and Judith Rodin. "The Heart of Jealousy." *Psychology Today* 19 (September, 1985): 22-29. This engaging article reviews research findings and suggests practical applications.

White, Gregory L., and Paul E. Mullen. *Jealousy: Theory, Research, and Clinical Strategies*. New York: Guilford Press, 1989. This well-written academic book includes chapters on romantic jealousy; the origins of jealousy in sociobiology, personality, and culture; gender effects in jealousy; pathological and violent jealousy; and strategies for assessing and managing jealousy.

Ann L. Weber

See also:

Anxiety Disorders; Borderline, Histrionic, and Narcissistic Personalities; Couples Therapy; Divorce and Separation: Adult Issues; Domestic Violence; Midlife Crises; Neurosis; Obsessive-Compulsive Disorder; Paranoia; Sibling Rivalry.

Juvenile Delinquency

Type of psychology: Developmental psychology; social psychology
Fields of study: Adolescence; aggression; substance abuse

Juvenile delinquency refers to crime or status offenses by juveniles; the adult criminal typically began as a juvenile delinquent.

Principal terms

CRIME: activity defined as illegal by authorized officials, such as the legislature, and having punishment spelled out for violations

DELINQUENCY: violation of the law, or proof of violation of the law

JUVENILE: one below the legally established age of adulthood

PARENTAL NEGLECT: failure of parents to show proper concern for their child; failure to provide a child with such things as food, shelter, and psychological support

STATUS OFFENSE: violation of rules which the state holds to govern juvenile conduct, such as curfews, school attendance, or obeying parents

Causes and Symptoms

Juvenile delinquency may be defined in either of two ways. It refers either to crime or to status offenses by a person defined as not yet being an adult. The age of adulthood varies somewhat from state to state. For example, one is an adult in California at age eighteen, while one becomes an adult under Louisiana law at seventeen years of age. A crime is anything which the criminal laws of the state define as illegal. This is what most people think of when they hear the term "juvenile delinquency." There is a second category of juvenile delinquency, however, known as status offenses. These are actions for which the state holds the youth responsible, although they would not be illegal if the person were an adult. Examples include not attending school, staying out too late at night, and defiance of parents.

A juvenile can be sent to a juvenile prison for a status offense. For example, in one instance a youth was sent to a juvenile prison for status offense, fell in with more criminally oriented youth, and participated in the burglary of the home of a woman who did volunteer work with the prisoners. It was rumored that she was well-to-do, although this was apparently not really the case. The youths did not find the money, but in the process of the crime they confronted and killed the woman. Thus, a youth sent to a juvenile facility for a status offense was charged with murder for his part in the affair.

Studies of juvenile delinquents often try to explain why the youth became a criminal. In many cases, especially with youths from the lower socioeconomic classes but also sometimes with middle-class or upper-class youths, the finding is that the family unit is dysfunctional. That is, the youth does not come from a normal healthy home but from a home in which there is considerable aggression among family members, either verbal or physical. Often the parents are not very

James Dean played a young man labeled a "juvenile delinquent" in the 1955 film Rebel Without a Cause. *The motion picture reflected society's concerns about the behavior and changing attitudes of teenagers in the 1950's.* (The Museum of Modern Art, Film Stills Archive)

supportive of the children but instead show either indifference or constant criticism. Youths who murder have often been physically and psychologically abused by their parents. For example, there is a case of a young murderer who shot and killed a female boarder in his home when he was fifteen years old. The youth had received beatings from a series of stepfathers. He said that the psychological abuse he suffered was even worse than the physical abuse. He gave an example in psychotherapy of one of his stepfathers telling him, "You are no better than the dog. You can go sleep outside in the doghouse tonight." With that, the adult forced him out of the house.

Many juvenile delinquents have suffered parental physical, sexual, or psychological abuse when growing up, and turning to crime seems to be one way of responding to these abuses. Too few people see the various kinds of abuse as a possible causal factor in choosing a life of crime. There is, however, increasing research supporting this notion. This leads to the idea that early intervention into the home may be a preventive, in that stopping some of this abuse may save some juveniles from becoming criminals. Yet not everyone who suffers such abuse becomes a criminal, so there must be many causes of crime. Some people grow up to be fairly normal despite the abuse, while others suffer various degrees of mental illness instead of becoming criminals or growing up to be normal.

In the instances where there is no obvious physical, sexual, or psychological abuse leading to juvenile delinquency, one often finds that the parents themselves are antisocial. Thus, in a sense, the child grows up following rules of socialization, but in these cases the child is socialized to antisocial choices. For example, parents may violate certain laws, often in a flagrant fashion, such as using cocaine in their child's presence. The child learns that this is the normal, approved way within his or her household, and adopts the parents' values. Thus, the road is set for the child to become a juvenile delinquent. When one thinks of crime, one may think of lower-class people, and indeed prisons are primarily filled with people from the lower socioeconomic classes, including many minorities. Middle- or upper-class youths may also be delinquent, but they are more likely to avoid going to prison, either through preferential treatment or by having better attorneys.

A totally different view of crime from the one presented thus far puts the blame squarely on the shoulders of the offender. According to this view, people have free will and commit crimes because they choose to do so. They are not seen as victims of family background but as bad people who do bad things. A slightly modified version of this approach would be that there is something in the offender that predisposes him or her toward committing crimes. It could, for example, possibly be brain chemistry which makes a person oriented toward thrill-seeking behavior. Perhaps some people have such a strong need for sensation-seeking that ordinary excitements do not satisfy them, and under the right circumstances, such as a group which encourages them, they will commit crimes. Yet another view which places the responsibility primarily on the individual would be approaches suggesting that many criminals suffer from brain damage or other physical problems which interfere with good judgment.

All these explanations focus on the individual as being responsible and shy away from seeing the social setting, including the family, as having much to do with the juvenile becoming delinquent. An attempt to explain crime by saying that many criminals possess an extra Y chromosome, thus putting the cause on a genetic basis, has been shown to be inadequate. Most criminals do not possess an extra Y chromosome, and those who do seem to have low intelligence. They apparently do not become criminals because of their chromosomal abnormality.

Treatment and Therapy

Given that society thinks of some juveniles as delinquent, there are two general approaches to the problem. First, society needs some way of controlling those juveniles who disobey the law. Here one has the whole criminal justice system: police, juvenile courts, probation officers, prisons, and so on. Second, people can try to help the juvenile via treatment. Some would say that prison or probation is treatment, but what is meant here is the kind of intervention that a social worker, psychologist, or psychiatrist might make.

There are three kinds of prevention. Primary prevention occurs when something bad is prevented from happening before the person shows any signs of a problem. Drug education in the early school grades would be an example. Secondary prevention occurs when professionals work with an at-risk population. For example, helping a youth who lives in a high-crime area where drugs are sold and laws are often violated, but who himself or herself is not delinquent, would be secondary prevention. He or she is at risk of becoming a delinquent, given the environment, but has not become delinquent yet. Tertiary prevention occurs when the problem has already occurred and then something is done. Treating a disease after a person has become sick is tertiary prevention; so is doing psychotherapy with people who already are mentally ill, or performing some kind of intervention with someone who is already a delinquent.

Unfortunately, most of society's preventive attempts are tertiary prevention, whereas primary prevention would seem to be the most effective, followed by secondary prevention. Psychologists and psychiatrists are typically called upon for tertiary prevention. Social workers are as well, but some of the time they may intervene in a primary or secondary fashion, as when they do home visits to assess the problems in a home and devise some strategy for improving the situation. Psychologists and psychiatrists can do primary and secondary prevention, and sometimes they do, especially if they work with some agency, such as a school, and try to prevent problems before they occur. It may be too late to change most juvenile delinquents once they reach about sixteen years of age. Primary or secondary preventive efforts would seem the most effective approach. By the time an offender is sixteen, he or she may have a long history of crime and may be dedicated to an antisocial lifestyle. Some sixteen-year-olds can be helped, certainly, especially if they are fairly new to crime. Many juvenile delinquents have no sense of how they could be other than a criminal. Treatment efforts need to provide them with alternatives and with the skills, via education or job training, to meet these alternatives.

Once the juvenile has been tried and convicted in a juvenile court (or in a regular adult court, if tried as an adult, as sometimes occurs in very serious cases), the court has three major dispositions it can make. The convicted juvenile may be placed on probation, ordered to make restitution if money was stolen or property damaged, or incarcerated. One would hope that fairness would prevail and that the sentences handed down from jurisdiction to jurisdiction would be similar for similar offenses. Such, unfortunately, is not always the case.

The criminal justice system is plagued with the problem of sentencing disparity. This affects juvenile and adult offenders alike. In other words, if an offender is convicted in one court, the sentence may be very different from that which is handed down in another court for the same offense, and for a juvenile with the same history. History here means that the court, legitimately, takes into account the previous arrest and conviction record of the juvenile in determining sentence. In one look at sentences given to juveniles by courts in six different sites (five different states and Washington, D.C.), all the offenders were repeat offenders convicted of serious crimes. The sentences handed down in the different sites should have been about the same. They were not. In one jurisdiction, most of the convicted juvenile offenders were incarcerated and none received probation. In the other sites, incarceration was very unlikely, and probation or restitution were frequently employed. Thus, what sentence one received depended upon where one was convicted. This is hardly an equitable application of the law. The one jurisdiction which typically used incarceration may be overly harsh, while the other jurisdictions may be overly lenient. Sometimes probation or restitution makes sense in order to give the offender another chance, while sometimes incarceration is necessary for the protection of society. The sentences should fit the needs of society and of the offender, but at times they seem to reflect the bias of the community for either harsh or lenient treatment of convicted juveniles.

Perspective and Prospects
The idea that juveniles should be treated differently from adults is a fairly modern one. For example, in the Middle Ages people had quite a different conception of childhood. Their art often shows babies who look like small adults. Until quite recently, juveniles were often placed in prison with adults, where they were sometimes subject to rape or other abuse. Some states still place juveniles in adult prisons. Thinking of someone as a juvenile delinquent, instead of simply as a delinquent (criminal), often means that the juvenile receives what are supposed to be special considerations. For example, the juvenile may not be "convicted of a crime" but instead may have a "sustained petition" declaring him or her delinquent. The penalties may be much less than if an adult had committed the crime.

Since juveniles are treated differently, it once was held that the juvenile court was not really a court in the adult sense but a place where the judge's function was to help the youth. One consequence of this thinking was that the adult right to have an attorney was not granted universally to juveniles. Thus, those charged with juvenile delinquency would face the possibility of being convicted and sent to prison but might not have a lawyer during their trial. The United States Supreme Court changed that in 1967 in a case known as *In re Gault*, in which it ruled that juveniles are entitled to adultlike protections, including having an attorney. No longer would juveniles be tried and convicted without legal counsel.

It was previously noted that juveniles may receive lesser penalties for crimes than adults; sometimes, however, the penalties are worse. Two examples are status offenses, wherein the offense, such as disobeying parents, would not even be a crime if the juvenile were an adult, and instances where the juvenile may be confined in a juvenile prison until he or she becomes an adult. In the second case, an adult male who breaks into a warehouse may receive a three-year sentence, while a fourteen-year-old boy may be confined until he is eighteen or perhaps even until he is twenty-one. In this case, the person would have received a shorter sentence had he been an adult. The use of status offenses as a basis for charging or imprisoning juveniles has received much criticism from social scientists as unfair. Those who favor retaining it see it as an effective social control mechanism for what they consider criminal tendencies.

Bibliography
Alloy, Lauren B., Neil S. Jacobson, and Joan Acocella. *Abnormal Psychology: Current Perspectives*. 8th ed. New York: McGraw-Hill, 1998. A very readable abnormal psychology text. Deals with problems of drug dependence. Crime is

related to drugs in various ways. The authors cover the topics of psychological disturbance and criminal law, civil commitment, patients' rights, and power and the mental health profession.

Bartollas, Clemens. *Juvenile Delinquency*. 5th ed. Boston: Allyn & Bacon, 1999. A book popular with undergraduate students. Provides a sociological examination of delinquency. This edition includes new chapters on social reaction theories and female delinquency.

Brown, Stephen E., F. A. Esbensen, and Gilbert Geis. *Criminology: Explaining Crime and Its Context*. Cincinnati: Anderson, 1991. An excellent text that gives a good overview of crime and its various explanations. While not specifically focused on juvenile crime, the book does give a good general explanation of crime from a variety of standpoints, including such things as robbery, the impact of gambling, different theories of crime, and the goals of the criminal justice system. Everything from abortion to marijuana is covered.

Eisenman, Russell. *From Crime to Creativity: Psychological and Social Factors in Deviance*. Dubuque, Iowa: Kendall/Hunt, 1991. Discusses causes of crime and makes the important point that most theories of crime are really theories of lower-class crime. The American view of the criminal, juvenile or adult, tends to be that of a person from the lower socioeconomic class, which does not allow an understanding of middle-class and upper-class crime. Both lower-class and white-collar crime are discussed. Juvenile delinquency is explored; the negative family backgrounds of juvenile delinquents are discussed.

Glueck, Sheldon, and Eleanor Glueck. *Unraveling Juvenile Delinquency*. Cambridge, Mass.: Harvard University Press, 1951. This book is one of the early classics. The Gluecks, a husband-and-wife team of researchers, use psychological and sociological concepts to try to understand why youth become delinquent. It makes sense, they hold, to look at both the personality of the offender and the social background, such as family and neighborhood.

Hunter, Mic, ed. *The Sexually Abused Male*. 2 vols. Lexington, Mass.: D. C. Heath, 1990. Since many juvenile delinquents have suffered sexual abuse, it may be that this abuse helps cause them to become criminals. Some sexually abused children do not become criminals, so this is obviously only a partial explanation. These two volumes deal extremely well with various aspects of abuse, including, but not limited to, how the abused child may go on to become a sex offender.

Sharp, Paul M., and Barry W. Hancock, eds. *Juvenile Delinquency: Historical, Theoretical, and Societal Reactions to Youth*. 2d ed. Upper Saddle River, N.J.: Prentice Hall, 1998. A comprehensive collection of original readings in juvenile delinquency. Combines historical pieces and classic and contemporary theoretical articles. Includes bibliographical references.

Siegel, Larry J., and Joseph J. Senna. *Juvenile Delinquency: Theory, Practice, and Law*. 7th ed. Belmont, Calif.: Wadsworth, 1999. This comprehensive, best-selling text provides an in-depth analysis of theories of delinquency, environmental issues, juvenile justice issues, and the juvenile justice system.

Yablonsky, Lewis. *Juvenile Delinquency: Into the Twenty-first Century*. Belmont,

Calif.: Wadsworth/Thomson Learning, 2000. A practical approach to controlling and preventing juvenile delinquency and a systematic analysis of the juvenile delinquency problem in the United States.

Russell Eisenman

See also:

Abnormality: Family Models; Abnormality: Legal Models; Addictive Personality and Behaviors; Aggression: Definitions and Theoretical Explanations; Aggression: Reduction and Control; Antisocial Personality; Child Abuse; Child and Adolescent Psychiatry; Identity Crises; Psychotherapy: Children.

LEARNING DISABILITIES

Type of psychology: Language; memory
Fields of study: Childhood and adolescent disorders; cognitive processes; social perception and cognition

This variety of disorders involves the failure to learn an academic skill despite normal levels of intelligence, maturation, and cultural and educational opportunity. Estimates of the prevalence of learning disabilities in the general population range between 2 and 20 percent.

Principal terms

ACHIEVEMENT TEST: a measure of an individual's degree of learning in an academic subject, such as reading, mathematics, and written language
DYSLEXIA: difficulty in reading, with an implied neurological cause
INTELLIGENCE TEST: a psychological test designed to measure an individual's ability to think logically, act purposefully, and react successfully to the environment; yields intelligence quotient (IQ) scores
NEUROLOGICAL DYSFUNCTION: problems associated with the way in which different sections and structures of the brain perform tasks, such as verbal and spatial reasoning and language production
NEUROLOGY: the study of the central nervous system, which is composed of the brain and spinal cord
PERCEPTUAL DEFICITS: problems in processing information from the environment, which may involve distractibility, impulsivity, and figure-ground distortions (difficulty distinguishing foreground from background)
STANDARDIZED TEST: an instrument used to assess skill development in comparison to others of the same age or grade

Causes and Symptoms

An understanding of learning disabilities must begin with the knowledge that the definition, diagnosis, and treatment of these disorders have historically generated considerable disagreement and controversy. This is primarily attributable to the fact that people with learning disabilities are a highly diverse group of individuals with a wide variety of characteristics. Consequently, differences of opinion among professionals remain to such an extent that presenting a single universally accepted definition of learning disabilities is not possible. Definitional differences most frequently center on the relative emphases that alternative groups place on characteristics of these disorders. For example, experts in medical fields typically describe these disorders from a disease model and view them primarily as neurological dysfunctions. Conversely, educators usually place more emphasis on the academic problems that result from learning disabilities. Despite these differences, the most commonly accepted definitions, those developed by the United States Office of Education in 1977, the Board of the Association for Children and Adults

POSSIBLE SIGNS OF LEARNING DISABILITIES IN CHILDREN

❖ difficulty understanding and following instructions

❖ trouble remembering what someone just told him or her

❖ failing to master reading, writing, and/or math skills, and thus failing schoolwork

❖ difficulty distinguishing right from left, for example, confusing 25 with 52, "b" with "d," or "on" with "no."

❖ lacking coordination in walking, sports, or small activities such as holding a pencil or tying a shoelace

❖ easily losing or misplacing homework, schoolbooks, or other items

❖ not understanding the concept of time; confused by "yesterday," "today," and "tomorrow."

with Learning Disabilities in 1985, and the National Joint Committee for Learning Disabilities in 1981, do include some areas of commonality.

Difficulty in academic functioning is included in the three definitions, and virtually all descriptions of learning disabilities include this characteristic. Academic deficits may be in one or more formal scholastic subjects, such as reading or mathematics. Often the deficits will involve a component skill of the academic area, such as problems with comprehension or word knowledge in reading or difficulty in calculating or applying arithmetical reasoning in mathematics. The academic difficulty may also be associated with more basic skills of learning that influence functioning across academic areas; these may involve deficits in listening, speaking, and thinking. Dyslexia, a term for reading problems, is the most common academic problem associated with learning disabilities. Because reading skills are required in most academic activities to some degree, many view dyslexia as the most serious form of learning disability.

The presumption of a neurological dysfunction as the cause of these disorders is included, either directly or indirectly, in each of the three definitions. Despite this presumption, unless an individual has a known history of brain trauma, the neurological basis for learning disabilities will not be identified in most cases because current assessment technology does not allow for such precise diagnoses. Rather, at least minimal neurological dysfunction is simply assumed to be present in anyone who exhibits characteristics of a learning disorder.

The three definitions all state that individuals with learning disabilities experience learning problems despite possessing normal intelligence. This condition is referred to as a discrepancy between achievement and ability or potential.

Finally, each of the three definitions incorporates the idea that learning disabilities cannot be attributed to another handicapping condition such as mental retardation, vision or hearing problems, emotional or psychiatric disturbance, or social, cultural, or educational disadvantage. Consequently, these conditions must be excluded as primary contributors to academic difficulties.

Reports on the prevalence of learning disabilities differ according to the definitions and identification methods employed. Consequently, statistics on prevalence range between 2 and 20 percent of the population. Many of the higher reported percentages are actually estimates of prevalence that include individuals who are presumed to have a learning disorder but who have not been formally diagnosed. Males are believed to constitute the majority of individuals with learning disabilities, and estimated sex ratios range from 6:1 to 8:1. Some experts believe that this difference in incidence may reveal one of the causes of these disorders.

A number of causes of learning disabilities have been proposed, with none being universally accepted. Some of the most plausible causal theories include neurological deficits, genetic and hereditary influences, and exposure to toxins during fetal gestation or early childhood.

Evidence to support the assumption of a link between neurological dysfunction and learning disabilities has been supported by studies using sophisticated brain imaging techniques such as positron emission tomography (PET) and computed tomography (CT) scanning and magnetic resonance imaging (MRI). Studies using these techniques have, among other findings, indicated subtle abnormalities in the structure and electrical activity in the brains of individuals with learning disabilities. The use of such techniques has typically been confined to research; however, the continuing advancement of brain imaging technology holds promise not only in contributing greater understanding of the nature and causes of learning disabilities but also in treating the disorder.

Genetic and hereditary influences also have been proposed as causes. Supportive evidence comes from research indicating that identical twins are more likely to be concordant for learning disabilities than fraternal twins and that these disorders are more common in certain families.

A genetic cause of learning disabilities may be associated with extra X or Y chromosomes in certain individuals. The type and degree of impairment associated with these conditions vary according to many genetic and environmental factors, but they can involve problems with language development, visual perception, memory, and problem solving. Despite evidence to link chromosome abnormalities to those with learning disabilities, most experts agree that such genetic conditions account for only a portion of these individuals.

Exposure to toxins or poisons during fetal gestation and early childhood can also cause learning disabilities. During pregnancy nearly all substances the mother takes in are transferred to the fetus. Research has shown that mothers who smoke, drink alcohol, or use certain drugs or medications during pregnancy are more likely to have children with developmental problems, including learning disabilities. Yet not all children exposed to toxins during gestation will have such problems, and the consequences of exposure will vary according to the period when it occurred, the amount of toxin introduced, and the general health and nutrition of the mother and fetus.

Though not precisely involving toxins, two other conditions associated with gestation and childbirth have been linked to learning disabilities. The first, anoxia or oxygen deprivation, occurring for a critical period of time during the birthing process has been tied to both mental retardation and learning disabilities. The second, and more speculative, involves exposure of the fetus to an abnormally large amount of testosterone during gestation. Differences in brain development are proposed to result from the exposure causing learning disorders, among other abnormalities. Known as the embryological theory, it may account for the large number of males with these disabilities, since they have greater amounts of testosterone than females.

The exposure of the immature brain during early childhood to insecticides, household cleaning fluids, alcohol, narcotics, and carbon monoxide, among other toxic substances, may also cause learning disabilities. Lead poisoning resulting from ingesting lead from paint, plaster, and other sources has been found in epidemic numbers in some sections of the country. Lead poisoning can damage the brain and cause learning disabilities, as well as a number of other serious problems.

The number and variety of proposed causes not only reflect differences in experts' training and consequent perspectives but also suggest the likelihood that these disorders can be caused by multiple conditions. This diversity of views also carries to methods for assessing and providing treatment and services to individuals with learning disabilities.

Treatment and Therapy

In 1975, the U.S. Congress adopted the Education for All Handicapped Children Act, which, along with other requirements, mandated that students with disabilities, including those with learning disabilities, be identified and provided appropriate educational services. Since that time, much effort has been devoted to developing adequate assessment practices for diagnosis and effective treatment strategies.

In the school setting, assessment of students suspected of having learning disabilities is conducted by a variety of professionals, including teachers specially trained in assessing learning disabilities, school nurses, classroom teachers, school psychologists, and school administrators. Collectively, these professionals are known as a multidisciplinary team. An additional requirement of this educational legislation is that parents must be given the opportunity to participate in the assessment process. Professionals outside the school setting, such as clinical psychologists and independent educational specialists, also conduct assessments to identify learning disabilities.

Because the definition of learning disabilities in the 1975 act includes a discrepancy between achievement and ability as a characteristic of the disorder, students suspected of having learning disabilities are usually administered a variety of formal and informal tests. Standardized tests of intelligence, such as the third edition of the Wechsler Intelligence Scale for Children, are administered to determine ability. Standardized tests of academic achievement, such as the Woodcock-Johnson Psychoeducational Battery and the Wide Range Achievement Test, also are administered to determine levels of academic skill.

Whether a discrepancy between ability and achievement exists to such a degree to warrant diagnosis of a learning disability is determined by various formulas comparing the scores derived from the intelligence and achievement tests. The precise methods and criteria used to determine a discrepancy vary according to differences among state regulations and school district practices. Consequently, a student diagnosed with a learning disability in one part of the United States may not be viewed as such in another area using different diagnostic criteria. This possibility has been raised in criticism of the use of the discrepancy criteria to identify these disorders. Other criticisms of the method include the use of intelligence quotient (IQ) scores (which are not as stable or accurate as many assume), the inconsistency of students' scores when using alternative achievement tests, and the lack of correspondence between what students are taught and what is tested on achievement tests.

In partial consequence of these and other problems with standardized tests, alternative informal assessment methods have been developed. One such method that is frequently employed is termed curriculum-based assessment (CBA). The CBA method uses materials and tasks taken directly from students' classroom curriculum. For example, in reading, CBA might involve determining the rate of words read per minute from a student's textbook. CBA has been demonstrated to be effective in distinguishing among some students with learning disabilities, those with other academic difficulties, and those without learning problems. Nevertheless, many professionals remain skeptical of CBA as a valid alternative to traditional standardized tests.

Other assessment techniques include vision and hearing tests, measures of language development, and tests examining motor coordination and sensory perception and processing. Observations and analyses of the classroom environment may also be conducted to determine how instructional practices and a student's behavior contribute to learning difficulties.

Based on the information gathered by the multidisciplinary team, a decision is made regarding the diagnosis of a learning disability. If a student is identified with one of these disorders, the team then develops an individual education plan to address identified educational needs. An important guideline in developing the plan is that students with these disorders should be educated to the greatest extent possible with their nonhandicapped peers, while still being provided with appropriate services. Considerable debate has occurred regarding how best to adhere to this guideline.

Programs for students with learning disabilities typically are implemented in self-contained classrooms, resource rooms, or regular classrooms. Self-contained classrooms usually contain ten to twenty students and one or more teachers specially trained to work with these disorders. Typically, these classrooms focus on teaching fundamental skills in basic academic subjects such as reading, writing, and mathematics. Depending on the teacher's training, efforts may also be directed toward developing perceptual, language, or social skills. Students in these programs usually spend some portion of their day with their peers in regular education meetings, but the majority of the day is spent in the self-contained classroom.

The popularity of self-contained classrooms has decreased significantly since the 1960's, when they were the primary setting in which students with learning disabilities were educated. This decrease is largely attributable to the stigmatizing effects of placing students in special settings and the lack of clear evidence to support the effectiveness of this approach.

Students receiving services in resource rooms typically spend a portion of their day in a class where they receive instruction and assistance from specially trained teachers. Students often spend one or two periods in the resource room with a small group of other students who may have similar learning problems or function at a comparable academic level. In the elementary grades, resource rooms usually focus on developing basic academic skills, whereas at the secondary level time is more typically spent in assisting students with their assignments from regular education classes.

Resource room programs are viewed as less restrictive than self-contained classrooms; however, they too have been criticized for segregating children with learning problems. Other criticisms center on scheduling difficulties inherent in the program and the potential for inconsistent instructional approaches and confusion over teaching responsibilities between the regular classroom and resource room teachers. Research on the effectiveness of resource room programs also has been mixed; nevertheless, they are found in most public schools across the United States.

Though they remain a minority, increasing numbers of students have their individual education plans implemented exclusively in a regular classroom. In most schools where such programs exist, teachers are given assistance by a consulting teacher with expertise in learning disabilities. Supporters of this approach point to the lack of stigma associated with segregating students and the absence of definitive research supporting other service models. Detractors are concerned about the potential for inadequate support for the classroom teacher, resulting in students receiving poor quality or insufficient services. The movement to provide services to educationally handicapped students in regular education settings, termed the Regular Education Initiative, has stirred much debate among professionals and parents. Resolution of the debate will greatly affect how individuals with learning disabilities are provided services.

No one specific method of teaching these students has been demonstrated to be superior to others. A variety of strategies have been developed, including perceptual training, multisensory teaching, modality matching, and direct instruction. Advocates of perceptual training believe that academic problems stem from underlying deficits in perceptual skills. They use various techniques aimed at developing perceptual abilities before trying to remedy or teach specific academic skills. Multisensory teaching involves presenting information to students through several senses. Instruction using this method may be conducted using tactile, auditory, visual, and kinesthetic exercises. Instruction involving modality matching begins with identifying the best learning style for a student, such as visual or auditory processing. Learning tasks are then presented via that mode. Direct instruction is based on the principles of behavioral psychology. The method involves developing precise educational goals, focusing on teaching the exact skill of concern, and providing frequent opportunities to perform the skill until it is mastered.

With the exception of direct instruction, research has generally failed to demonstrate that these strategies are uniquely effective with students with learning disabilities. Direct instruction, on the other hand, has been demonstrated effective but has also been criticized for focusing on isolated skills without dealing with the broader processing problems associated with these disorders. More promisingly, students with learning disabilities appear to benefit from teaching approaches that have been found effective with students without learning problems when instruction is geared to ability level and rate of learning.

Perspective and Prospects

Interest in disorders of learning can be identified throughout the history of medicine. The specific study of learning disabilities, however, can be traced to the efforts of a number of physicians working in the first quarter of the twentieth century who studied the brain and its associated pathology. One such researcher, Kurt Goldstein, identified a number of unusual characteristics, collectively termed perceptual deficits, which were associated with head injury.

Goldstein's work influenced a number of researchers affiliated with the Wayne County Training School, including Alfred Strauss, Laura Lehtinen, Newell Kephart, and William Cruickshank. These individuals worked with children with learning problems who exhibited many of the characteristics of brain injury identified by Goldstein. Consequently, they presumed that neurological dysfunction, whether it could specifically be identified or not, caused the learning difficulties. They also developed a set of instructional practices involving reduced environmental stimuli and exercises to develop perceptual skills. The work and writings of these individuals through the 1940's, 1950's, and 1960's were highly influential, and many programs for students with learning disabilities were based on their theoretical and instructional principles.

Samuel Orton, working in the 1920's and 1930's, also was influenced by research into brain injury in his conceptualization of children with reading problems. He observed that many of these children were left-handed or ambidextrous, reversed letters or words when reading or writing, and had coordination problems. Consequently, he proposed that reading disabilities resulted from abnormal brain development and an associated mixing of brain functions. Based on the work of Orton and his students, including Anna Gilmore and Bessie Stillman, a variety of teaching strategies were developed which focused on teaching phonics and using multisensory aids. In the 1960's, Elizabeth Slingerland applied Orton's concepts in the classroom setting and they have been included in many programs for students with learning disabilities.

A number of other researchers have developed theories for the cause and treatment of learning disabilities. Some of the most influential include Helmer Mykelbust and Samuel Kirk, who emphasized gearing instruction to a student's strongest learning modality, and Norris Haring, Ogden Lindsley, and Joseph Jenkins, who applied principles of behavioral psychology to teaching.

The work of these and other researchers and educators raised professional and public awareness of learning disabilities and the special needs of individuals with the disorder. Consequently, the number of special education classrooms and programs increased dramatically in public schools across the United States in the 1960's and 1970's. Legislation on both the state and federal level, primarily resulting from litigation by parents to establish the educational rights of their children, also has had a profound impact on the availability of services for those with learning disabilities. The passage of the Education for All Handicapped Children Act in 1975 not only mandated appropriate educational services for students with learning disabilities but also generated funding, interest, and research in the field. The Regular Education Initiative has since prompted increased efforts to identify more effective assessment and treatment strategies and generated debates among professionals and the consumers of these services. Decisions resulting from these continuing debates will have a significant impact on future services for individuals with learning disabilities.

Bibliography

Bender, William N. *Learning Disabilities: Characteristics, Identification and Teaching Strategies*. 4th ed. Boston: Allyn & Bacon, 2000. Focuses on characteristics of students with learning disabilities and classroom-tested instructional strategies. Topics include medical aspects of learning disabilities, cognition and language, personality and social characteristics, placement, services, and educational treatments.

Cordoni, Barbara. *Living with a Learning Disability*. Rev. ed. Carbondale: Southern Illinois University Press, 1990. Written by a professor of special education and the mother of two children with learning disabilities, this book focuses on the social skill problems associated with these disorders. Offers suggestions to parents and professionals regarding effective counseling, teaching, and coping strategies. Included is a helpful explanation of the laws governing education for students with learning disabilities.

Hallahan, Daniel P., James M. Kauffman, and John Wills Lloyd. *Introduction to Learning Disabilities*. Boston: Allyn & Bacon, 1996. This text addresses different learning disabilities and the education of the learning disabled. Includes a bibliography and indexes.

Lovitt, Thomas. *Introduction to Learning Disabilities*. Needham Heights, Mass.: Allyn & Bacon, 1989. This book is exceptionally well written and comprehensive in its review of topics associated with learning disabilities, including assessment and treatment issues, the history of these disorders, and recommendations for future efforts in the field. Provides balanced coverage of alternative views regarding the controversial aspects of learning disabilities.

MacCracken, Mary. *Turnabout Children: Overcoming Dyslexia and Other Learning Disabilities*. Boston: Little, Brown, 1986. Written by an educational therapist, this publication includes case histories of children with learning disabilities who have been successful in adapting to the unique difficulties that they face. Includes descriptions of assessment instruments and effective remedial techniques.

Scheiber, Barbara, and Jeanne Talpers. *Unlocking Potential*. Bethesda, Md.: Adler & Adler, 1987. This practical publication provides a step-by-step method for individuals with learning disabilities wishing to pursue postsecondary education. Advice is provided for selecting, gaining admission to, and successfully completing college, vocational, and trade school programs. Provides an excellent overview of how these disorders are diagnosed and what services are available. Includes a listing of postsecondary programs that have special accommodations for students with learning disabilities.

Snowling, M. J., and M. E. Thomson, eds. *Dyslexia: Integrating Theory and Practice*. London: Whurr, 1991. This publication includes selected papers from the second International Conference of the British Dyslexia Association, held in 1991. Chapters include detailed descriptions of theoretical and practical aspects of reading disabilities and reviews of treatment strategies for individuals from early childhood to adulthood.

Sternberg, Robert J., and Louise Spear-Swerling, eds. *Perspectives on Learning Disabilities*. Boulder, Colo.: Westview Press, 1999. Brings together experts from biological, cognitive, educational, sociological, and interactive perspectives to discuss the nature of learning disabilities, their origins, diagnosis, and treatment.

Wong, Bernice Y. L. *Learning About Learning Disabilities*. San Diego: Academic Press, 1998. Gives equal attention to the intellectual, conceptual, and practical aspects of learning disabilities. Covers assessment of attention disorders, memory, language, vision, socialization, reading, writing, and mathematics.

Paul F. Bell

See also:

Aphasias; Attention-Deficit Disorder; Autism; Brain Disorders; Child and Adolescent Psychiatry; Down Syndrome; Dyslexia; Mental Retardation.

LOBOTOMY

Type of psychology: Psychotherapy
Fields of study: Aggression; anxiety disorders; biological treatments

*Lobotomy is a psychosurgical treatment in which portions of the brain are discon-
nected or removed by surgical methods in order to treat psychiatric problems such
as aggression, anxiety disorders, and schizophrenia; it was used mostly between
1935 and the 1960's, until psychoactive drugs and more targeted psychosurgery
began to replace it.*

Principal terms

AFFECTIVE: pertaining to or resulting from emotion or feeling rather than from
thought

CENTRUM OVALE: a portion of the frontal lobes of the cerebrum, rich in nerve fibers
and lacking major blood vessels

CEREBRUM: The large, rounded brain structure that occupies most of the cranial
cavity; it is divided into two cerebral hemispheres by a deep groove and is joined
at the bottom by the corpus callosum

FRONTAL LOBE: the largest part of the anterior portion of the cerebral cortex

PSYCHOSIS: a severe mental disorder characterized by the deterioration of normal
intellectual and social function and by withdrawal from reality

SCHIZOPHRENIA: a group of psychotic conditions characterized by withdrawal
from reality and accompanied by highly variable affective, behavioral, and
intellectual disturbances

THALAMUS: a large ovoid mass of gray matter that is connected to the cerebrum
and relays sensory stimuli to the cerebral cortex

Overview

According to Elliot S. Valenstein, in *Great and Desperate Cures: The Rise and
Decline of Psychosurgery and Other Radical Treatments for Mental Illness* (1986),
"Between 1948 and 1952 tens of thousands of mutilating brain operations were
performed on men and women around the world." By 1960, however, Valenstein
states, the practice had fallen off drastically. "Not only had chlorpromazine and
other psychoactive drugs provided a simple and inexpensive alternative, but it was
discovered that these operations were leaving in their wake many seriously brain
damaged people."

Why, then, was lobotomy pursued by reputable members of the medical profession, both on indigent patients in publicly supported institutions and on the wealthy
in expensive private hospitals and at universities? The answer is quite complex; it
includes the powerful proponents of the method in the medical community, the
state of knowledge of the brain at the time, the extensive overcrowding of mental
hospitals, and the ministrations of the popular press, which lauded the method with
uncritical and uninformed enthusiasm.

Two main figures in lobotomy were António Egas Moniz, the Portuguese neurologist who initiated lobotomy operations—and later won a Nobel Prize for his work—and Walter Freeman, the well-known American neuropathologist and neuropsychiatrist who roamed the world and convinced many others to carry out these operations. No evil was intended by these well-known physicians; they were driven by compassion for the mentally ill at a time when the mentally ill lived horrible lives under degrading conditions in understaffed asylums that were likened to hell by many observers. As Valenstein pointed out, "into the fourth decade of the twentieth century. . . conditions in the institutions for the incurably insane had advanced but little. . . . Patients were beaten, choked, and spat on by attendants. They were put in dark, damp, padded cells." Very little could be done to cure them.

There were, at the time, two opposing theories of mental illness: the somatic or organic theory that mental disease was of biological origin, and the functional theory, which supposed that life experiences caused mental problems. The somatic theory was shaped mostly by Emil Kraepelin, a prominent authority during the early twentieth century. Kraepelin distinguished more than twenty types of mental disorder, including dementia praecox (schizophrenia) and manic-depressive disorder (bipolar disorder). Kraepelin and his colleagues viewed these diseases as being genetically determined, and practitioners of psychiatry developed complex physical diagnostic schemas that supposedly identified people with the various types of psychoses. In contrast, Sigmund Freud was the main proponent of the functional theory.

Attempts to help mental patients included electroconvulsive therapy; various water treatments; and surgical treatment by removal of tonsils, sex organs, and portions of the digestive system. These and many other attempted cures had widely varied success rates. By the 1930's, the most generally effective curative procedures were believed to be several types of shock treatments and lobotomy.

The first lobotomy was performed on November 12, 1935, at a hospital in Lisbon, Portugal. A neurosurgeon drilled two holes into the skull of a female mental patient and injected ethyl alcohol directly into the frontal lobes of her brain to destroy nerve cells. After several more such operations, the tissue-killing procedure was altered in that an instrument called a leucotome was used. After its insertion into the brain, the knifelike instrument was rotated, like an apple corer, to destroy chosen areas of the lobes.

The already well-known neurologist who devised the operation, António Egas Moniz, initially named it prefrontal leucotomy. Within a year, the psychosurgery (a term also coined by Egas Moniz) had spread through Europe. It was widely reported—though denied by Egas Moniz—that the idea for the procedure came when Egas Moniz noted that removal of the frontal lobes of chimpanzees (not by Egas Moniz) had made them less emotional and more docile. The main justifications for wide use of the procedure were the absence of any other effective somatic treatment and the emerging concept that the frontal lobes of the cerebrum are the site of both intellectual activity and mental problems.

Selection of the target site for the leucotomy was reportedly based on two considerations: finding the position in the frontal lobes where nerve fibers (not nerve cells) were most concentrated, and avoiding damage to large brain blood vessels. Therefore, Egas Moniz used as his target the centrum ovale of the frontal lobes, which contains few blood vessels. With the surgical site chosen, the first subject, a sixty-three-year-old woman suffering from severe anxiety and paranoia, was operated on. The operation, overseen by Egas Moniz, was carried out by his neurosurgeon colleague, Pedro Almeida Lima. Egas Moniz and Lima continued with more of the operations, and after eight operations—half on schizophrenics—they asserted that their cure rates were good. Several other psychiatric physicians, however, disagreed strongly.

After twenty operations, it became fairly clear that the new psychosurgery was most effective on mental patients suffering from anxiety and depression; schizophrenics did not benefit very much. The main effect of the leucotomy surgery appeared to be a calming down of patients; it made them much more docile. Retrospectively, it is believed that Egas Moniz's evidence for serious improvement in many cases was very sketchy; however, many psychiatrists and neurologists of the time were impressed with the procedure, and the stage was set for its wide dissemination.

Applications

The second great proponent of Egas Moniz's leucotomy—the physician who renamed it lobotomy and then greatly modified the methodology used—was Walter Freeman, a professor of neuropathology at George Washington University Medical School. He is reported to have come upon Egas Moniz's first paper in 1936, tested the procedure on preserved brains from the medical school morgue, and set out to replicate Egas Moniz's efforts.

After six lobotomies, Freeman and his associate, James Winston Watts, became optimistic that the method was useful for treating patients exhibiting apprehension, anxiety, insomnia, and nervous tension. They were quick to point out, however, that the words "recovery" and "cure" could not be applied to mental problems "until after a period of five years."

As Freeman and Watts continued to operate, they began to notice problems: These included a relapse to the original abnormal state of mind in many patients and the need for repeated surgery in others; the inability of lobotomized patients to resume any jobs that required the use of reasoning power; and deaths from hemorrhage after the surgery. This led them to develop a more precise technique that involved the use of landmarks on the skull to identify where to drill the entry holes into it, cannulation to ensure that the lobar penetration depth obtained was not dangerous to the patient, and the use of a knifelike spatula to make the actual lobotomy cuts. The extent of surgery was also varied depending upon whether the patient involved was suffering from an affective psychological disorder or from schizophrenia. Their methodology, which became known as the "routine Freeman-Watts lobotomy procedure," became popular throughout the world.

Another method used for prefrontal lobotomy was that of J. G. Lyerly, who designed a procedure in which the brain was opened enough that the psychosurgeon involved could look into it and see exactly what was being done to the frontal lobes being operated on. This technique also became popular and was used at many prestigious sites throughout the United States. Near the same time, in Japan, Mizuho Nakata of Niigata Medical College began to remove from the brain portions of one or both frontal lobes that were operated on.

The Freeman-Watts method became the most popular, however, because their 1942 book on the procedure constituted what a number of experts, including Elliot Valenstein, have called a "do-it-yourself manual" and "manifesto" for psychosurgery. As Valenstein also pointed out, Watts's book theorized that brain pathways between the cerebral frontal lobes and the thalamus regulate the "intensity of the emotions invested in ideas," and acceptance of this theory led to the "scientific justification of psychosurgery."

A final type of lobotomy that became fairly widespread was the transorbital method designed by Freeman (on the framework of a method originally used by the Italian physician Amarro Fiamberti), because of the shortcomings of his routine method and because he thought that the new method aided schizophrenics. This simple, very rapid—but frightening—procedure entailed driving icepicklike transorbital leukotomes through the eye sockets (orbits of the eyes) above the eyeballs and into the frontal lobes. Electroconvulsive shock treatment was used as the anesthetic method that rendered subjects unconscious, and the procedure was carried out before they woke up. Transorbital lobotomy reportedly alienated Freeman's collaborator, Watts. The charismatic Freeman gained many other converts to its use, however, and gruesome as the procedure may seem, the method produced much less brain damage than the other lobotomy procedures already described. It was widely used at state hospitals for the insane and received many laudatory comments from the popular press, including statements that many previously hopeless cases were immediately transformed by the procedure to quite normal states and that it was more useful with schizophrenics than other procedures were.

Perspective and Prospects

Lobotomy and other forms of psychosurgery might be defined as the disconnection or destruction of part of the brain to alleviate severe and otherwise untreatable psychiatric disease. Lobotomy is believed to have originated with the observation by early medical practitioners that severe head injuries could produce extreme changes in behavior. In addition, according to several sources, practitioners from the thirteenth to the sixteenth century reported that sword and knife wounds that penetrated into the skull could change both normal and abnormal behavior patterns.

In the late nineteenth and early twentieth centuries, several experimenters showed that removal of parts of the cerebral cortexes of animals profoundly altered their behavior. Then, Egas Moniz (who was also the founder of brain angiography) triggered the widespread use of lobotomy in 1935. His efforts and those of Freeman and Watts popularized the concept of lobotomy, though different styles of operation were used by these main proponents of this surgery, for which Freeman became the main spokesperson.

Largely because of the overcrowding of understaffed mental institutions and a lack of effective alternate methods for treating mental disorders, lobotomy was widely used between 1936 and 1955; Egas Moniz won the Nobel Prize in Physiology or Medicine in 1949. It is estimated by various sources that between 75,000 and 150,000 lobotomies were performed, worldwide, in this time period. The development of psychoactive drugs in the 1950's and growing concern about the damage done to lobotomized patients led to a rapid decrease in the number of patients operated on. For example, Valenstein has reported that from 1956 to 1977 the number of American lobotomies fell dramatically. Since then, the amount of such surgery has decreased still more.

There has been considerable criticism of lobotomy. Its opponents argue that tremendous damage was done to patients, that many studies were not compared to appropriate—or even any—controls, and that observations made about cures failed to take into account the fact that mental aberrations tend to fluctuate temporally. Even more moderate voices point out that whatever positive results came of lobotomies were too heavily weighted toward the elimination of behavior that was inconvenient to medical personnel and families of patients, without consideration being given to the quality of life of the patients themselves.

In addition, there has been eloquent support for the rights of disturbed persons, and legal decisions have upheld those rights. The use of psychosurgery has come to be limited to patients who are not helped by existing chemotherapeutic or psychoanalytical methodology. This number is small, but psychosurgical procedures are still highly controversial.

Bibliography

Freeman, Walter Jackson, and James Winston Watts. *Psychosurgery: Intelligence, Emotion, and Social Behavior Following Prefrontal Lobotomy for Mental Disorders*. Springfield, Ill.: Charles C Thomas, 1942. This book describes the results of eighty lobotomies; it provides case histories, explains the methodology of Freeman and Watts's standard operation, proposes the theory that interconnections between cerebral frontal lobes and the thalamus regulate the intensity of emotions associated with ideas, and virtually provides a "do-it-yourself manual" for doctors wishing to perform psychosurgery.

Fulton, John Farquhar. *Frontal Lobotomy and Affective Behavior: A Neuropsychological Analysis*. New York: W. W. Norton, 1951. This book, by a prominent member of the American medical profession of the time, is dedicated to a description of the work of Egas Moniz and Lima. It discusses both human and animal lobotomy; and it is of historical interest, because Fulton lauds both the achievements and the prospects of lobotomy. Contains many useful references and illustrations.

Pressman, Jack D. *Last Resort: Psychosurgery and the Limits of Medicine*. New York: Cambridge University Press, 1998. Challenges the previously accepted psychosurgery story and raises new questions about what should be considered its important lessons. Includes bibliographical references and an index.

Rodgers, Joann Ellison. *Psychosurgery: Damaging the Brain to Save the Mind*.

New York: HarperCollins, 1992. Explores the concept of modern psychosurgery, performed with much greater accuracy than in the past. Provides a detailed account of clinical practice, case histories, and quotes from physicians.

Sackler, Arthur M., et al., eds. *The Great Physiodynamic Therapies in Psychiatry: An Historical Reappraisal.* New York: Hoeber-Harper, 1956. This is a compilation of a number of selected articles on lobotomy and related areas, taken from several important biomedical journals. It includes Egas Moniz's article "How I Succeeded in Performing Prefrontal Leukotomy." A brief biographical sketch of Egas Moniz is included.

Shuman, Samuel I. *Psychosurgery and the Medical Control of Violence: Autonomy and Deviance.* Detroit: Wayne State University Press, 1977. Covers topics that include the meaning of psychosurgery; its legal, medical, and political implications; aspects of freedom of thought being affected; and the famous "Detroit psychosurgery case." Much useful and interesting information is provided.

Turner, Eric Anderson. *Surgery of the Mind.* Birmingham, England: Carmen Press, 1982. This brief book addresses the ethics of performing psychosurgery, its consequences, and its justifications. Topics include the function and operation of the brain, the selection of lobotomy patients, various types of psychosurgery, and a follow-up of almost five hundred psychosurgical operations.

Valenstein, Elliot S. *Great and Desperate Cures: The Rise and Decline of Psychosurgery and Other Radical Treatments for Mental Illness.* New York: Basic Books, 1986. This well-thought-out book describes the basis for the development, the rise, and the decline of psychosurgery. Its coverage includes the theories of mentation that led to psychosurgery, the endeavors and the methodology of its main proponents, and reasons for both its replacement and its present limited use. Many useful illustrations.

_____, ed. *The Psychosurgery Debate: Scientific, Legal, and Ethical Perspectives.* New York: W. H. Freeman, 1980. This valuable work is edited by Valenstein. Its topical content includes an overview of the history of, rationale for, and extent of psychosurgery; consideration of patient selection; evaluation of various methods used; description of legal and ethical issues involved; and an extensive bibliography.

Sanford S. Singer

See also:

Abnormality: Biomedical Models; Aggression: Reduction and Control; Anxiety Disorders; Electroconvulsive Therapy; Madness: Historical Concepts; Psychoactive Drug Therapy; Psychosurgery; Schizophrenia.

MADNESS
Historical Concepts

Type of psychology: Psychopathology
Fields of study: Models of abnormality

Throughout history and, it might be assumed, prehistory, human society has tried to explain the abnormal behavior of people with mental disorders. From ancient concepts of animism and demonology to modern biological and psychological explanations, these attempts have influenced the way society treats those who are labeled "mad."

Principal terms

COGNITION: that aspect of human functioning involving thought, decision making, perception, memory, and other basic mental functions

DEMONOLOGY: the belief that evil spirits inhabit the world and may actually "take over" a personality

LABELING: attaching a name to some aspect of a person which may influence how that person is perceived in almost all aspects of his or her life

LOBOTOMY: an operation on the frontal lobe of the brain which was used on some mental patients whose behavior was aggressive or uncontrollable

MORAL TREATMENT: a way of helping mentally ill patients which emphasized humane treatment, useful work, and ethical and religious teaching

PERCEPTION: the psychological process by which information which comes in through the sense organs is meaningfully interpreted by the brain

PHENOTHIAZINES: a group of drugs, some forms of which decrease or eliminate psychotic symptoms

PSYCHOSIS: a term which includes the most severe mental disorders such as the schizophrenias and manic-depressive (bipolar) disorder

Overview

In many ways, the history of madness is really the story of how society has understood and behaved toward those whom it considers to be "mad." Many anthropologists and historians believe that, throughout prehistory and up to fairly recent times, madness was almost universally believed to be the result of the possession of a person by evil spirits. The idea is by no means dead, even at the present time. Since animism and demonology were nearly universal ideas in prehistorical and (to some extent) medieval religion, an idea such as demoniacal possession seemed quite congruent with a point of view which tended to believe that all things were inhabited by souls or spirits which at times could be quite evil. This idea—that possession was responsible for the strange and incomprehensible behaviors of the mentally ill person—was for a long time the dominant theory of madness.

Benjamin Rush, one of the founders of the American Psychiatric Association, invented this "tranquillizing chair" in 1811 to help calm the mentally ill. (National Library of Medicine)

One of the terrible consequences of the belief in supernatural possession by demons was the inhumane treatment which often resulted. An example is found in the book of Leviticus in the Bible, which many scholars believe is a compilation of laws which had been handed down orally in the Jewish community for as long as a thousand years until they were written down, perhaps about 700 B.C.E. Leviticus 20:27, in the King James version, reads, "A man or a woman that hath a familiar spirit . . . shall surely be put to death: they shall stone him with stones." The term "familiar spirit" suggests demoniac possession, and the recommended treatment seems worse than the disease.

It is important to remember, however, that the mentally ill were often very difficult to deal with. There were no "cures," there was no real understanding, and undoubtedly there was often considerable fear—some based on the socially un-aceptable behavior of the "mad" person, some based on the fearsome unanswered questions raised by the very existence of these people.

There were exceptions to the possession theory and the inhumane treatment to which it often led. Hippocrates, who lived around 300 B.C.E. in Greece and who is regarded as the father of medicine, believed that mental illness had biological causes and could be explained by human reason through empirical study. Although his attempt to develop a natural understanding of mental illness did not result in a correct explanation, it did change attitudes toward the mentally ill. Hippocrates found no cure, but he did recommend that the mentally ill be treated with a general humane approach, as other ill people would be treated. Humane treatment of the mentally ill (which in the eighteenth century came to be known as the "moral treatment") was often the best that physicians and others could do; it has much to recommend it, even in the present.

The period of Western history that is sometimes known as the Dark Ages was particularly dark for the mentally ill. Folk myth, theology, and occult beliefs and practices of all kinds often led to terrible treatment of those persons with a mental illness or defect. Although some educated and thoughtful people, even in that period, held humane views toward the mentally ill, they were in the minority.

It was not until what could be considered the modern historical period, the end of the eighteenth century—the time of the French Revolution—that major changes took place in the treatment of the mentally ill. There was a change in attitudes toward the mentally ill, toward their treatment, and toward the causes of their strange behaviors. The man who, because of his courage, has become a symbol of this new attitude was the French physician Philippe Pinel (1745-1826). Appointed physician in chief of the Bicêtre Hospital in Paris in 1792, Pinel literally risked his neck at the guillotine. The Bicêtre was one of a number of "asylums" which had developed in Europe and in Latin America over several hundred years to house the mentally ill. Often started with the best of intentions, most of the asylums had become the epitome of inhumanity, more like prisons (or worse) than hospitals.

In the Bicêtre, patients were often chained to the walls of their cells and lacked even the most elementary amenities. Pinel insisted to a skeptical committee of the Revolution that he be permitted to remove the chains from the patients. In one of the great, heroic acts in human history, Pinel restored the "moral treatment" to the mentally ill, risking grave personal consequences if his humane experiment had turned out badly.

This change was occurring in other places at about the same time. A Quaker, William Tuke, started the York Retreat and fought the inhumane beliefs and practices prevalent in Great Britain. In America, Benjamin Rush, a founder of the American Psychiatric Association, applied the moral treatment from his Philadelphia hospital. Toward the middle of the nineteenth century, a crusader by the name of Dorothea Dix fought for the establishment of state mental hospitals for the mentally ill. Under the influence of Dix, some thirty-two states established at least one mental hospital. Dix had been influenced by the moral model, as well as by the medical sciences, which were so rapidly developing in the nineteenth century. Unfortunately, the state mental hospital, established under the most humanitarian of motives, soon tended to lose its character as a "retreat" for some of the victims of society. In 1946, a former mental patient named Mary Jane Ward published a book called *The Snake Pit*, whose very title suggests the negative image that many had of the large mental institution.

The nineteenth century was the first time in human history (with some exceptions already noted) when a number of scientists turned their attention to abnormal behavior. For example, the German psychiatrist Emil Kraepelin spent much of his life trying to develop a scientific classification system for psychopathology. Sigmund Freud attempted to develop a science of mental illness. Although many of Freud's specific points have not withstood empirical investigation, perhaps his greatest contribution was his insistence that scientific principles apply to mental illness. He believed that abnormal behavior is not caused by supernatural forces and does not arise in a chaotic, random way, but that it can be understood as serving some psychological purpose.

Many of the medical/biological treatments for mental illness in the first half of the twentieth century were frantic attempts to deal with very serious problems—

A "centrifugal bed" for spinning mental patients in 1818. (National Library of Medicine)

attempts made by clinicians who had few therapies to use. The attempt to produce convulsions (which often did seem to make people "better," at least temporarily) was popular for a decade or two. One example was insulin shock therapy, in which convulsions were induced in mentally ill people by insulin injection. Electroconvulsive (electric shock) therapy was also used. Originally it was primarily used with patients who had schizophrenia, perhaps the worst form of psychosis. Although it was not very effective with schizophrenia, it was found to be useful with patients who had resistant forms of depressive psychosis. Another treatment sometimes used, beginning in the 1930's, is prefrontal lobotomy. Many professionals today would point out that the use of lobotomy illustrates the almost desperate search for an effective treatment for the most aggressive or the most difficult psychotic patients. As originally used, lobotomy was merely an imprecise slashing of the frontal lobe of the brain.

The real medical breakthrough in the treatment of psychotic patients was associated with the use of certain drugs from a chemical family known as phenothiazines. Originally used in France as a tranquilizer for surgery patients, their potent calming effect attracted the interest of psychiatrists and other mental health workers. One drug of this group, chlorpromazine, was found to reduce or eliminate psychotic symptoms in many patients. This and similar medications came to be referred to as antipsychotic drugs. Although their mechanism of action is still not completely understood, there is no doubt that they worked wonders with many severely ill patients (although they did have severe side effects in some patients). The drugs allowed patients to function outside the hospital and often to lead normal lives. They enabled many patients to benefit from psychotherapy. The approval of the use of chlorpromazine as an antipsychotic drug in the United States in 1955 revolutionized the treatment of many mental patients. Individuals who, prior to 1955, might have spent much of their lives in a hospital could now control their illness effectively enough to live in the community, work at a job, attend school, and be a functioning member of a family.

In 1955, the United States had approximately 559,000 patients in state mental hospitals; seventeen years later, in 1972, the population of the state mental hospitals had decreased almost by half, to approximately 276,000. Although all of this cannot be attributed to the advent of the psychoactive drugs, they undoubtedly played a major role. The phenothiazines had finally given medicine a real tool in the battle with psychosis. One might believe that the antipsychotic drugs, combined with an up-to-date edition of the moral treatment, would enable society to eliminate madness as a major human problem. Unfortunately, good intentions go awry. The "major tranquilizers" can easily become chemical straitjackets; those who prescribe the drugs sometimes forget about the human beings they are treating. The makers of social policy saw what appeared to be the economic benefits of reducing the role of the mental hospital, but did not foresee the homeless psychotics who are often the end product of what is sometimes called "deinstitutionalization."

Applications

The twentieth century saw the exploration of many avenues in the treatment of mental disorders. Treatments ranging from classical psychoanalysis to cognitive and humanistic therapies to the use of therapeutic drugs were applied. Psychologists examined the effects of mental disorders on many aspects of life, including cognition and personality. These disorders affect the most essential of human functions, including cognition, which has to do with the way in which the mind thinks and makes decisions. Cognition does not work in "ordinary" ways in the person with a serious mental illness, making his or her behavior very difficult for family, friends, and others to understand. Another aspect of cognition is perception. Perception has to do with the way that the mind, or brain, interprets and understands the information which comes to a person through the senses. There is a general consensus among most human beings about what they see and hear, and perhaps to a lesser extent about what they touch, taste, and smell. The victim of "madness," however, often perceives the world in a much different way. The victim of mental illness may see objects or events that no one else sees, phenomena called hallucinations. The hallucinations may be visual—a frightening wild animal which is seen by no one else—or the person may hear a voice accusing him or her of terrible crimes or behaviors.

A different kind of cognitive disorder is delusions. Delusions are untrue and often strange ideas, usually growing out of psychological needs or problems of a person who may have only tenuous contact with reality. A woman, for example, may believe that other employees are plotting to harm her in some way when, in fact, they are merely telling innocuous stories around the water cooler. Sometimes people with mental illness will be disoriented, which literally means that they do not know where they are in time (what year, what season, or what time of day) or in space (where they live, where they are at the present moment, or where they are going).

In addition to the cognitively related functions which create so much havoc in mentally ill persons, these persons may also have emotional problems that go beyond the ordinary. For example, they may live on such an emotional "high" for weeks or months at a time that their behavior is exhausting both to themselves and to those around them. They may exhibit bizarre behavior in which, for example, they may talk about giving away vast amounts of money (which they do not have), or they may go without sleep for days until they literally drop from exhaustion. This emotional "excitement" which seems to dominate their lives is called mania. The word "maniac" comes from this terrible emotional extreme.

At the other end of the emotional spectrum is clinical depression. This does not refer to the ordinary "blues" of daily life, with all its ups and downs, but to an emotional emptiness in which the individual seems to have lost all emotional "energy." The individual often seems completely apathetic. The person may see nothing which makes life worth living and may have anhedonia, which refers to an inability to experience pleasure of almost any kind.

Anyone interacting with a person with these sorts of problems comes to think of him or her as being different from most other human beings. Their behavior is regarded, with some justification, as bizarre and unpredictable. They are often labeled with a term that sets them apart, such as "crazy" or "mad." There are many words in the English language that have been, or are, used to describe these persons—many of them quite cruel and derogatory. Since at least the eighteenth century, the preferred word among many behavioral and medical scientists to designate this individual has been the word "psychotic," which could be translated as suffering from a "sickness of the soul." Until recently, the term psychotic was used to differentiate those who had these severe cognitive/perceptual and emotional problems from those who had "neurosis" (literally, a disease of the nerves). Whether neurosis is always less disabling or disturbing than psychosis has been an open question. An attempt was made to deal with this dilemma in 1980, when the third edition of the *Diagnostic and Statistical Manual of Mental Disorders* (DSM-III) of the American Psychiatric Association officially dropped the term "neurosis" from the diagnostic terms.

Perspective and Prospects

The contemporary approach to "madness," at its best, emphasizes a humane approach to the cognitive and emotional dysfunctions which characterize mental illness. Psychology's best understandings of these behaviors—understandings which have arisen from knowledge in biological and medical science, psychological and social science—are incomplete. What psychologists do understand has often helped them to treat and to care for the human beings who exhibit these puzzling behaviors in ways that offer hope as well as healing.

In 1963, President John F. Kennedy signed the Community Mental Health and Retardation Act. The goal was to set up areas covering the United States which would offer services to mentally and emotionally disturbed citizens and their families, incorporating the best that had been learned and that would be learned from science and from common humanity. Outpatient services in the community, emergency services, "partial" hospitalizations (adult day care), consultation, education, and research were among the programs built into the act. Not perfect, it nevertheless demonstrated how far science had come from the days when witches were burned at the stake and the possessed were stoned to death.

When one deals with "madness," one is dealing with human behavior—both the behavior of the individual identified as having the problem and the behavior of the rest of society. If society is going to solve the problem, it must take into account both poles. How society deals with the mentally ill is crucial. D. L. Rosenhan, in a well-known 1973 study published under the title "On Being Sane in Insane Places," showed how easy it is to be labeled "crazy" and how difficult it is to get rid of the label. The real essence of the study is how one's behavior is interpreted and understood on the basis of the labels that have been applied. (The "pseudopatients" in the study had been admitted to a mental hospital and given a diagnosis—a label—of schizophrenia. Consequently, even their writing of notes in a notebook was regarded as evidence of their illness.) To understand madness is not merely to understand something that some people have, but also to understand social and cultural biases and the way in which a culture interprets behavior.

Bibliography

Bellenir, Karen, ed. *Mental Health Disorders Sourcebook: Basic Consumer Health Information About Anxiety Disorders, Depression, and Other Mood Disorders.* 2d ed. Detroit: Omnigraphics, 2000. A volume on mental illness in the health reference series. Includes a bibliography and an index.

Braginsky, Benjamin M., D. D. Braginsky, and Kenneth Ring. *Methods of Madness: The Mental Hospital as a Last Resort.* New York: Holt, Rinehart & Winston, 1969. A major critique of the mental hospital in the United States, with an interesting suggestion for improvement noted by a play on words in the book's title.

Dohrenwend, Bruce P., ed. *Adversity, Stress, and Psychopathology.* New York: Oxford University Press, 1998. Reviews and analyzes research on the nature of adversity and its relationship to major types of psychopathology, including schizophrenia, depression, alcoholism and other substance abuse, antisocial personality disorder, post-traumatic stress disorder, and nonspecific distress.

Dolnick, Edward. *Madness on the Couch: Blaming the Victim in the Heyday of Psychoanalysis.* New York: Simon & Schuster, 1998. Focuses on psychotherapy's fight against schizophrenia, autism, and obsessive-compulsive disorder in the 1950's and 1960's. Includes bibliographical references and an index.

Frankl, Viktor Emil. *Man's Search for Meaning.* New York: Simon & Schuster, 1962. A powerful book which serves as an example of many publications that emphasize what has been called "moral treatment." Frankl's book is partly autobiographical, based on his experiences as a Jew in a German concentration camp. The book then goes on to develop some ideas related to abnormal behavior. This book has been published in many paperback editions, which have a relatively complete bibliography of writings by and about Frankl and his ideas.

Freud, Sigmund. *New Introductory Lectures on Psychoanalysis.* Translated by W. J. H. Sprott. New York: W. W. Norton, 1933. Perhaps the most accessible of Freud's writing for the person who is interested in abnormal behavior in general and psychoanalysis in particular. For the most part, an interesting and quite comprehensible elaboration of Freud's general point of view; does not read at all like something only for a professional.

Robinson, Daniel N. *An Intellectual History of Psychology.* Rev. ed. New York: Macmillan, 1981. Although mental illness as such occupies a small part of this book, it is a genuinely important work in helping to understand the philosophical and intellectual currents which have played such a major role in the psychological and scientific understanding of mental illness. A sometimes demanding book to read, it is well worth the intellectual energy for one who wants to understand how various intellectual disciplines interact together.

Rosenhan, David L. "On Being Sane in Insane Places." *Science* 179 (January 19, 1973): 250-258. More of a "naturalistic illustration" than a scientific experiment, this article raises provocative questions and puts forth some controversial conclusions. Enjoyable reading that does not require much psychological background on the part of the reader.

James Taylor Henderson

See also:

Abnormality; Abnormality: Biomedical Models; Abnormality: Psychodynamic Models; Abnormality: Sociocultural Models; Lobotomy; Psychosurgery; Psychotherapy: Historical Approaches to Treatment; Schizophrenia.

Manic-Depressive Disorder

Type of psychology: Psychopathology
Fields of study: Depression

This recurrent affective (mood) illness is characterized either by alternating periods of extreme depression and extreme elation or, less often, by only one of these moods.

Principal terms

AFFECTIVE DISORDERS: a group of disorders characterized by a disturbance of mood accompanied by a full or partial manic or depressive syndrome that is not caused by any other physical or mental disorder
BIPOLAR: a manic-depressive course with both manias and depressions
DUAL DIAGNOSIS: when a patient receives the diagnosis of a substance use disorder and another major clinical syndrome, such as manic-depressive disorder
LITHIUM: a drug used in the treatment of manic depression
PSYCHOSIS: any mental disorder in which the personality is seriously disorganized
UNIPOLAR: a manic-depressive course with recurrent depression and no mania

Causes and Symptoms

Although the causes of manic-depressive illness (often called manic depression or bipolar disorder) are not known, research indicates that some persons may be genetically predisposed to respond readily with manic or depressive episodes to internal and external influences. It is believed that insufficient resolution of deep personality problems may also play a role. While changes in the metabolism of the brain are thought to be significant in the development of manic depression, both psychological and nonpsychological stresses are able to precipitate episodes. It is often not possible to find one precipitating factor, however, since there is presumably a complex interaction between the effects of internal and external influences in persons suffering from this disease.

Manic depression is an illness that occurs in attacks, or episodes. These may be attacks of mania (periods of extreme elation and increased activity) or attacks of depression (periods of abnormal sadness and melancholy). A patient may have both manias and depressions (a bipolar course) with varying levels of intensity for each type of episode. Occasionally, the disease presents a mixture of manic and depressive features; this condition is referred to as a "mixed state." The degree, type, and chronicity of cognitive, perceptual, and behavioral disorganization determine the subclassifications, or stages, of mania. In increasing order of severity, these stages are hypomania, acute mania, and delirious mania (severe mania with psychotic overtones). Recent work indicates that many variants of this disorder exist.

SYMPTOMS OF MANIA

* increased energy, activity, restlessness, racing thoughts and rapid talking
* denial that anything is wrong
* excessive "high" or euphoric feelings
* extreme irritability and distractibility
* decreased need for sleep
* unrealistic beliefs in one's ability and powers
* uncharacteristically poor judgment
* a sustained period of behavior that is different from the person's usual behavior
* increased sexual drive
* abuse of drugs, particularly cocaine, alcohol and sleeping medications
* provocative, intrusive, or aggressive behavior

Manic depression occurs in about one to two persons out of every hundred, at some time in life, of such severity that hospitalization is required. More women than men suffer from the disease. The onset of the disease frequently occurs between the ages of twenty and fifty, but it may appear for the first time at fifteen years of age and as late as sixty to seventy years. Manic and depressive episodes present themselves differently in different persons; they can even vary within a particular patient from one time to another. Although mania has characteristic features, not all features are present during each manic episode.

Prominent features of manic episodes are elation, easily aroused anger, and increased mental activity. The elation varies from unusual vigor to uninhibited enthusiasm. The anger most often takes the form of irritability. Manic patients become annoyed if other people are unable to keep up with their racing thoughts. Intellectual activity takes place with lightning speed, ideas race through the mind, speech flows with great rapidity and almost uninterruptedly, and puns alternate with caustic commentary.

During a manic episode, patients are often excessively self-confident and lacking in self-criticism. This produces a previously unknown energy, and when that energy is combined with racing thoughts, indefatigability, and lack of inhibition, the consequences are often disastrous. During manic episodes, patients may destroy their relationships, ruin their reputations, or create financial disasters. Manic patients usually sleep very little. They rarely feel tired and are usually kept awake by the rapid flow of ideas. Sexual activity may also be increased. Manic patients often neglect to eat and may lose weight. The combination of violent activity, decreased food intake, and an inadequate amount of sleep may lead to physical exhaustion.

Depressions are in many respects the opposite of manias. They are characterized by sadness, a lack of self-confidence, and decreased mental activity. The sadness may vary from a slight feeling of being "down" to the bleakest despair. Ideas are few, thoughts move slowly, and memory function is impaired. Frequently, depressed patients feel tired and emotionally drained; they feel the need to cry but are unable to do so. Weighed down by feelings of guilt and self-reproach, they may contemplate or even commit suicide. The depressed patient's courage and self-confidence are often eroded, and, as a result, the patient may withdraw socially, lack initiative and energy, feel that obstacles are insurmountable, and have difficulty making even trivial decisions. Because of their low self-esteem and feelings of inadequacy, patients suffering from depression often fear social interaction and become anxious, agitated, and restless in a crowd. Sleep disturbances are also frequent. Occasionally, there is an increased need for sleep, but more often patients have difficulty sleeping. Some patients find it difficult to fall asleep, others wake up frequently during the night, and others wake up early with feelings of anxiety. Depressed patients often experience variations in mood over the course of a day. They are, typically, depressed late at night and in the early morning. The desire to stay in bed is overwhelming, and the first hours of the day are difficult to get through.

Symptoms of Depression

* persistent sad, anxious, or empty moods
* feelings of hopelessness or pessimism
* feelings of guilt, worthlessness, or helplessness
* loss of interest or pleasure in ordinary activities, including sex
* decreased energy, a feeling of fatigue or of being "slowed down"
* difficulty concentrating, remembering, or making decisions
* restlessness or irritability
* sleep disturbances
* loss of appetite and weight, or weight gain
* chronic pain or other persistent bodily symptoms that are not caused by physical disease
* thoughts of death or suicide; including suicide attempts

Depressions are often accompanied by physical transformations. The muscles give the impression of being slack, the facial expression is static, and movement is slow. There may be constipation, menstruation may stop, and sexual interest and activity may decrease or disappear completely for a time. Appetite is reduced, and there is a resulting loss of weight. The cessation of depression is sometimes followed by a light and transient mania, which may be seen as a reaction to the depression or as a sign of relief that it is over.

In addition to manias and depressions, manic-depressive disease may present mixed states during which signs of mania and depression are present concurrently. Patients who experience mixed states may be sad and without energy but also irritable, or they may be manic and restless yet feel an underlying melancholy. Mixed states may occur as independent episodes, but they are seen more often during transitions from mania to depression or from depression to mania. During these periods of transition, the condition may alternate between mania and depression several times within the course of a day. During the intervals between episodes, the patients often enjoy mental health and stability.

Treatment and Therapy

Until the 1950's, manic-depressive illness had remained intractable, frustrating the best efforts of clinical practitioners and their predecessors. This long history ended abruptly with the discovery of the therapeutic effects of lithium. In an ironic turn of events, the pharmacologic revolution then initiated a renaissance in the psychotherapy of manic-depressive patients. Substantially freed from the severe disruptions of mania and the profound withdrawal of depression, patients, with the help of their therapists, focused on the many psychological issues related to the illness and confronted basic developmental tasks. Even a combination of drugs and psychotherapy, however, did not yield a completely satisfactory outcome for every patient. The treatment approaches that are available, however, do allow most manic-depressive patients to lead relatively normal lives.

Electroconvulsive therapy (ECT) is one alternative to medications in treating acute manic-depressive disorder. Although ECT may be used to treat severely manic patients, those who have proven unresponsive to drugs, and those in mixed states with a high risk of suicide, it is used primarily for severe depressions. In ECT, following narcosis (an unconscious state induced by narcotics), certain parts of the patient's brain are stimulated electrically through electrodes placed on the skin. This stimulation elicits a seizure, but since the drug relaxes the muscles, the seizure manifests as muscle twitching only. The patients do not feel the treatment, but during the hours following the treatment, they may have headaches and feel tenderness of the muscles. Transitory memory impairment may also occur. Treatment, which occurs two to four times a week for three to four weeks, leads to amelioration of symptoms in most patients. ECT may be given at a hospital or on an outpatient basis.

For treatment of manic agitation, the so-called neuroleptics are often used. These are sedative drugs such as chlorpromazine (Largactil, Thorazine) and haloperidol (Haldol). Neuroleptics exert a powerful tranquilizing effect on anxiety, restlessness, and tension. They also attenuate or relieve hallucinations and delusions. Neuroleptics are not specific for any single disease. They may be used, possibly in conjunction with lithium, in the treatment of mania, and they may be used in depressions that are accompanied by delusions. Neuroleptics may, however, produce side effects involving the muscles and the nervous system.

Antidepressants act, as the name indicates, on depression, but only on abnormal depression; they do not affect ordinary sadness or grief. They are drugs such as imipramine (Tofranil), amitriptyline (Elavil, Tryptizol), and fluoxetine (Prozac). The side effects of antidepressants may include tiredness, mouth dryness, tremor, constipation, difficulty in urinating, and a tendency to faint. Changes in heart rate and rhythm may also occur, and careful evaluation is necessary in patients with cardiac disease.

Treatment with antidepressants is often continued for some time after disappearance of the symptoms; for example, three to four months. Occasionally, antidepressant therapy precipitates episodes of mania, and patients with previous attacks of mania may have to discontinue antidepressants earlier than other patients. In patients with a bipolar course who require prophylactic (preventive) treatment, lithium is indicated. Patients with a unipolar course may be treated prophylactically with either lithium or antidepressants.

Lithium, a metallic element discovered by a Swedish chemist in 1818, is produced from lithium-containing minerals such as spodumene, amblygonite, lepidolite, and petalite. As a drug, lithium is always used in the form of one of its salts; for example, lithium carbonate or lithium citrate. It is the lithium portion of these salts that is effective medically. Lithium was introduced into medicine in

1850 for the treatment of gout, and during the following century many medical uses of the element were proposed. It was used, for example, as a stimulant, as a sedative, for the treatment of diabetes, for the treatment of infectious diseases, as an additive to toothpaste, and for the treatment of malignant growths. The efficacy of lithium in these conditions was not proved, however, and lithium treatment never became widespread.

In 1949, an Australian psychiatrist, John Cade, published an article that forms the basis of all later lithium treatment. The prophylactic action of lithium in manic-depressive illness was debated in the psychiatric literature for some years, but extensive trials in many countries have fully documented the efficacy of the drug. Its prophylactic action is exerted against both manic and depressive relapses and can be seen in unipolar as well as bipolar patients. One of the characteristic features of lithium is that it removes manic symptoms without producing sedation, unlike treatment with neuroleptics, which are also effective in the treatment of mania but which exert sedative action. Lithium may occasionally produce side effects, such as nausea, stomachache, tremor of the hands, and muscle weakness, but these symptoms are usually neither severe nor incapacitating. The greatest drawback of the treatment is that the full antimanic effect is usually not seen until after six to eight days of treatment, and sometimes it is necessary to supplement lithium with a neuroleptic drug.

In addition to being used in the treatment of manic episodes, lithium is also used in the prevention of manic-depressive illness; moreover, the drug's prophylactic effect is almost as beneficial in the treatment of depression as it is in the treatment of mania. While lithium may also be used to treat depressive episodes, this use is less widespread because treatment with antidepressants and electric convulsive therapy appear to be more effective in cases of depression.

Although prophylaxis denotes prevention, lithium is unable to prevent the development of manic-depressive illness. Lithium prophylaxis merely prevents relapse so that manic and depressive recurrences become less frequent or disappear during treatment. Thus, prophylactic lithium keeps the illness under control but does not cure it. If the patient's lithium therapy ceases, the disease is likely to reappear, exhibiting episodes as frequent and severe as those that occurred before therapy. Therefore, it is necessary that patients continue taking lithium during periods in which no signs of illness are present.

Manic-depressive illness is treated most effectively with a combination of lithium or other medications and adjunctive psychotherapy. Drug treatment, which is primary, relieves most patients of the severe disruptions of manic and depressive episodes. Psychotherapy can assist them in coming to terms with the repercussions of past episodes and in comprehending the practical implications of living with manic-depressive illness.

Although not all patients require psychotherapy, most can benefit from individual, group, and/or family therapy. Moreover, participation in a self-help group is often useful in supplementing or supplanting formal psychotherapy. Psychotherapeutic issues are dictated by the nature of the illness: Manifested by profound changes in perception, attitudes, personality, mood, and cognition, manic-depressive illness can lead to suicide, violence, alcoholism, drug abuse, and hospitalization. Although reactions vary widely, patients typically feel angry and ambivalent about both the illness and its treatment. They may deny its existence, its severity, or its consequences, and they are often concerned about issues such as relationships and the possibility of genetically transmitting the illness to their children.

No one technique has been shown to be superior in the psychotherapy of manic-depressive patients. The therapist is guided by knowledge of both the illness itself and its manifestation in the individual patient. In style and technique, the therapist must remain flexible in order to adjust to the patient's fluctuating levels of dependency and mood change, cognition and behavior. The therapist must be especially alert to the countertransference issues that commonly occur when working with manic-depressive patients. In addition, educating patients and their families is essential because it helps them to recognize new episodes.

Perspective and Prospects

Manic-depressive illness is among the most consistently identifiable of all mental disorders, and it is also one of the oldest; it is discernible in descriptions in the Old Testament, and it was recognized in clinical medicine almost two thousand years ago. The medical writers of ancient Greece (the Hippocratic school) conceived of mental disorders in terms that sound remarkably modern. They believed that melancholia was a psychological manifestation of an underlying biological distur-bance—specifically, a perturbation in brain function. Early conceptions of "mel-ancholia" and "mania" were, however, broader than those of modern times. These two terms, together with "phrenitis," which roughly corresponds to an acute organic delirium, comprised all mental illnesses throughout most of the ancient period.

As they did with other illnesses, the Hippocratic writers argued forcefully that mental disorders were not caused by supernatural or magical forces, as primitive societies had believed. Their essentially biological explanation for the cause of melancholia, which survived until the Renaissance, was part of the prevailing understanding of all health as an equilibrium of the four humors—blood, yellow bile, black bile, and phlegm—and all illness as a disturbance of this equilibrium. First fully developed in the Hippocratic work *Nature of Man* (c. 400 B.C.E.), the humoral theory linked the humors with the seasons and with relative moistness. An excess of black bile was seen as the cause of melancholia, a term that literally means "black bile." Mania, by contrast, was usually attributed to an excess of yellow bile.

Reflections on the relationship between melancholia and mania date back at least to the first century B.C.E. and Soranus of Ephesus. Aretaeus of Cappadocia, who lived in the second century C.E., appears to have been the first to suggest that mania was an end-stage of melancholia, a view that was to prevail for centuries to come. He isolated "cyclothymia" (an obsolete term for mild fluctuations of the manic-depressive type) as a form of mental disease presenting phases of depression alternating with phases of mania. Although Aretaeus included syndromes that in the twentieth century would be classified as schizophrenia, his clear descriptions of the spectrum of manic conditions are impressive even in modern times.

The next significant medical writer, Galen of Pergamon (131-201 C.E.), firmly established melancholia as a chronic condition. His few comments on mania included the observation that it can be either a primary disease of the brain or secondary to other diseases. His primary contribution was his all-encompassing elaboration of the humoral theory, a system so compelling that it dominated medical thought for more than a millennium.

Medical observations in succeeding centuries continued to subscribe to the conceptions of depression and mania laid down in classical Greece and Rome. Most authors wrote of the two conditions as separate illnesses yet suggested a close connection between them. Yet where mania and depression are considered in the historical medical literature, they are almost always linked.

The explicit conception of manic-depressive illness as a single disease entity dates from the mid-nineteenth century. Jean Pierre Falret and Jules Baillarger, French "alienists," independently and almost simultaneously formulated the idea that mania and depression could represent different manifestations of a single illness. In 1854, Falret described a circular disorder that he expressly defined as an illness in which the succession of mania and melancholia manifested itself with continuity and in an almost regular manner. That same year, Baillarger described essentially the same thing, emphasizing that the manic and depressive episodes were not two different attacks, but two different stages of the same attack. Despite the contributions of Falret, Jeanne-Étienne-Dominique Esquirol, and other observers, however, most clinical investigators continued to regard mania and melancholia as separate chronic entities that followed a deteriorating course.

It was left to the German psychiatrist Emil Kraepelin (1856-1926) to distinguish psychotic illnesses from one another and to draw the perimeter clearly around manic-depressive illness. He emphasized careful diagnosis based on both longitudinal history and the pattern of current symptoms. By 1913, in the eighth edition of Kraepelin's textbook of psychiatry, virtually all of melancholia had been subsumed into manic-depressive illness.

Wide acceptance of Kraepelin's broad divisions led to further explorations of the boundaries between the two basic categories of manic-depressive illness and dementia praecox, the delineation of their similarities, and the possibility that subgroups could be identified within two basic categories. Kraepelin's synthesis was a major accomplishment because it formed a solid and empirically anchored base for future developments.

During the first half of the twentieth century, the views of Adolf Meyer (1866-1950) gradually assumed a dominant position in American psychiatry, a position that they maintained for several decades. Meyer believed that psychopathology emerged from interactions between an individual's biological and psychological characteristics and his or her social environment. This perspective was evident in the label "manic-depressive reaction" in the first official American Psychiatric Association diagnostic manual, which was published in 1952. When the Meyerian focus, considerably influenced by psychoanalysis, turned to manic-depressive illness, the individual in the environment became the natural center of study, and clinical descriptions of symptoms and the longitudinal course of the illness were given less emphasis.

Eugen Bleuler (1857-1939), in his classic contributions to descriptive psychiatry, departed from Kraepelin by conceptualizing the relationship between manic-depressive (affective) illness and dementia praecox (schizophrenia) as a continuum without a sharp line of demarcation. Bleuler also broadened Kraepelin's concept of manic-depressive illness by designating several subcategories and using the term "affective illness." His subcategories of affective illness anticipated the principal contemporary division of the classic manic-depressive diagnostic group—the bipolar-unipolar distinction. The bipolar-unipolar distinction represents a major advance in the classification of affective disorders primarily because it provides a basis for evaluating genetic, pharmacological, clinical, and biological differences rather than representing a purely descriptive subgrouping. As research on this disorder continues, it is likely that the relationship of manic depression to substance use disorders will increase. In 1997, it was estimated that at least 50 percent of individuals affected by one are affected by the other. As such, common mechanisms of problems related to these two types of disorders may lead to more specific treatments designed to address situations when there is a dual diagnosis.

Bibliography

Basco, Monica Ramirez, and A. John Rush. *Cognitive-Behavioral Therapy for Bipolar Disorder*. Foreword by Robert M. Post. New York: Guilford Press, 1996. Presents useful cognitive-behavioral techniques for managing bipolar disorder. Describes the benefits of using an integrated approach to treating the disorder and discusses its diagnosis, course, and characteristics.

Goldberg, Joseph F., et al., eds. *Bipolar Disorders: Clinical Course and Outcome*. Washington, D.C.: American Psychiatric Press, 1999. Offers practical information on the prognosis, course, and potential complications of bipolar disorders. Includes bibliographical references and an index.

Goodwin, Frederick K., and Kay Redfield Jamison. *Manic Depressive Illness*. New York: Oxford University Press, 1990. Drawing on their extensive clinical and research experience, the authors have analyzed and interpreted the literature on manic-depressive illness and presented a unique synthesis of information for the acute and chronic management of manic-depressive patients. This 938-page work contains more than 100 pages of references.

Jamison, Kay Redfield. *An Unquiet Mind: A Memoir of Moods and Madness*. New York: Vintage Books, 1995. This book articulately describes the personal experiences of a prominent psychiatric researcher with her bipolar condition. The highs and lows of the condition are well illustrated, as is the importance of consistent medication with lithium.

Mondimore, Francis M. *Bipolar Disorder: A Guide for Patients and Families*. Baltimore: The Johns Hopkins University Press, 1999. Offers a comprehensive guide to symptoms, diagnosis, treatment, and causes. Includes bibliographical references and an index.

_____. *Depression: The Mood Disease*. Rev. ed. Baltimore: The Johns

Hopkins University Press, 1993. In this excellent scholarly work, the author discusses the biological basis of and medical treatment for depression, mood swings, and other affective disorders. Contains a bibliography.

Rosenthal, Norman E. *Seasons of the Mind.* New York: Bantam Books, 1989. An insightful popular account of depression. The author discusses the etiology of the "winter blues" and what can be done about it. Charting moods to obtain an objective pattern of moods and treatment responses is one useful technique suggested by Rosenthal. Contains a useful reading list.

Wolpert, Edward A., ed. *Manic Depressive Illness: History of a Syndrome.* New York: International Universities Press, 1977. This lengthy and scholarly work presents a collection of papers that are historically significant in the development of understanding of manic-depressive illness. The aim of demonstrating the developmental history of the idea embodied in the syndrome allows the reader to transcend an enumeration of symptoms and arrive at an understanding of the syndrome itself.

Genevieve Slomski
updated by Nancy A. Piotrowski

See also:

Abnormality: Biomedical Models; Anxiety Disorders; Depression; Electroconvulsive Therapy.

MEMORY LOSS

Type of psychology: Memory
Fields of study: Organic disorders

An impairment of memory which may be total or limited, sudden or gradual.

Causes and Symptoms

Memory impairment is a common problem, especially among older people. It occurs in various degrees and may be associated with other evidence of brain dysfunction. Amnesia is complete memory loss.

In benign forgetfulness, the memory deficit affects mostly recent events, and although a source of frustration, it seldom interferes with the individual's professional activities or social life. An important feature of benign forgetfulness is that it is selective and affects only trivial, unimportant facts. For example, one may misplace the car keys or forget to return a phone call, respond to a letter, or pay a bill. Cashing a check or telephoning someone with whom one is particularly keen to talk, however, will not be forgotten. The person is aware of the memory deficit, and written notes often are used as reminders. Patients with benign forgetfulness have no other evidence of brain dysfunction and maintain their ability to make valid judgments.

In dementia, the memory impairment is global, does not discriminate between important and trivial facts, and interferes with the person's ability to pursue professional or social activities. Patients with dementia find it difficult to adapt to changes in the workplace, such as the introduction of computers. They also find it difficult to continue with their hobbies and interests.

The hallmark of dementia is no awareness of the memory deficit, except in the very early stages of the disease. This is an important difference between dementia and benign forgetfulness. Although patients with early dementia may write themselves notes, they usually forget to check these reminders or may misinterpret them. For example, a man with dementia who is invited for dinner at a friend's house may write a note to that effect and leave it in a prominent place. He may then go to his host's home several evenings in succession because he has forgotten that he already has fulfilled this social engagement. As the disease progresses, patients are no longer aware of their memory deficit.

In dementia, the memory deficit does not occur in isolation but is accompanied by other evidence of brain dysfunction, which in very early stages can be detected only by specialized neuropsychological tests. As the condition progresses, these deficits become readily apparent. The patient is often disoriented regarding time and may telephone relatives or friends very late at night. As the disease progresses, the disorientation affects the patient's environment: A woman with dementia may wander outside her house and be unable to find her way back, or she may repeatedly ask to be taken back home when she is already there. In later stages, patients may not be able to recognize people whom they should know: A man may think that his son is his father or that his wife is his mother. This stage is particularly distressing to the caregivers. Patients with dementia may often exhibit impaired judgment. They may go outside the house inappropriately dressed or at inappropriate times, or they may purchase the same item repeatedly or make donations that are disproportional to their funds. Alzheimer's disease is one of the most common causes of dementia in older people.

Multiple infarct dementia is caused by the destruction of brain cells by repeated strokes. Sometimes these strokes are so small that neither the patient nor the relatives are aware of their occurrence. When many strokes occur and significant brain tissue is destroyed, the patient may exhibit symptoms of dementia. Usually, however, most of these strokes are quite obvious because they are associated with weakness or paralysis in a part of the body. One of the characteristic features of multiple infarct dementia is that its onset is sudden and its progression is by steps. Every time a stroke occurs, the patient's condition deteriorates. This is followed by a period during which little or no deterioration develops until another stroke occurs, at which time the patient's condition deteriorates further. Very rarely, the stroke affects only the memory center, in which case the patient's sole problem is amnesia. Multiple infarct dementia and dementia resulting from Alzheimer's disease should be differentiated from other treatable conditions which also may cause memory impairment, disorientation, and poor judgment.

Depression, particularly in older patients, may cause memory impairment. This condition is quite common and at times is so difficult to differentiate from dementia that the term "pseudodementia" is used to describe it. One of the main differences between depression that presents the symptoms of dementia and dementia itself is insight into the memory deficit. Whereas patients with dementia are usually oblivious of their deficit and not distressed (except those in the early stages), those with depression are nearly always aware of their deficit and are quite distressed. Patients with depression tend to be withdrawn and apathetic, given a marked disturbance of affect, whereas those with dementia demonstrate emotional blandness and some degree of lability. One of the problems characteristic of depressed patients is their difficulty in concentrating. This is typified by poor cooperation and effort in carrying out tasks with a variable degree of achievement, coupled with considerable anxiety.

Amnesia is sometimes seen in patients who have sustained a head injury. The extent of the amnesia is usually proportional to the severity of the injury. In most cases, the complete recovery of the patient's memory occurs, except for the events just preceding and following the injury.

Treatment and Therapy

Memory impairment is a serious condition which can interfere with one's ability to function independently. Every attempt should be made to identify the underlying condition because, in some cases, a treatable cause can be found and the memory loss reversed. Furthermore, it may soon be possible to arrest the progress of amnesia and memory loss and even to treat the dementias which now are considered as irreversible, such as Alzheimer's disease and multiple infarct dementia.

Bibliography

American College of Physicians, David R. Goldmann, and David A. Horowitz, eds. *Memory Loss and Dementia*. New York: DK, 2000. Offers guidelines for memory evaluation, tips for coping with an unreliable memory, and advice about when memory loss is a sign of something serious. Discusses dementia and its emotional impact.

Cummings, Jeffrey L., and D. Frank Benson. *Dementia: A Clinical Approach*. 2d ed. Boston: Butterworth-Heinemann, 1992. A comprehensive presentation of the clinical, diagnostic, therapeutic, and basic science aspects of the dementia syndromes. The role of computed tomography (CT), magnetic resonance imaging (MRI), positron emission tomography (PET), and single photon emission computed tomography (SPECT) is described.

Goldman, Robert M., Ronald Katz, and Lisa Berger. *Brain Fitness: Anti-Aging Strategies to Fight Alzheimer's Disease, Supercharge Your Memory, Sharpen Your Intelligence, De-Stress Your Mind, Control Mood Swings, and Much More*. New York: Doubleday, 1999. Offers the latest scientific research on how to retain mental powers throughout life and to strengthen and improve mind-power with age. Includes numerous self-tests, information charts, and quizzes.

Hamdy, Ronald C., et al., eds. *Alzheimer's Disease: A Handbook for Caregivers*. 2d ed. St. Louis: Mosby Year Book, 1994. Focuses on brain function; causes and diagnoses; patient care and behavior management; caregiver stress; and legal issues. Offers practical ideas and solutions for caregivers in finding support and community resources.

Terry, Robert D., ed. *Aging and the Brain*. New York: Raven Press, 1988. A review of the application of concepts in neurobiology and technology in the study of brain structure and function in normal elderly people and those with different types of dementia.

Terry, Robert D., and Robert Katzman, eds. *Alzheimer Disease*. 2d ed. Philadelphia: Lippincott/Williams & Wilkins, 1999. Discusses the clinical, epidemiological, structural, chemical, genetic, and molecular aspects of Alzheimer's disease. Includes bibliographical references.

Wang, Eugenia, and D. Stephen Snyder, eds. *Handbook of the Aging Brain*. San Diego: Academic Press, 1998. Presents a summary of research findings on the aging brain and its relation to learning and memory, language, cognition, and the effects of Alzheimer's and Parkinson's diseases and other brain disorders.

West, Robin L., and Jan D. Sinnott, eds. *Everyday Memory and Aging*. New York: Springer-Verlag, 1992. Examines the role of age factors in memory. Includes bibliographical references and indexes.

Ronald C. Hamdy, M.D.
Louis A. Cancellaro, M.D.

See also:

Alzheimer's Disease; Amnesia, Fugue, and Multiple Personality; Anxiety Disorders; Brain Disorders; Dementia; Depression; Forgetting and Forgetfulness; Geriatric Psychiatry.

MENTAL HEALTH PRACTITIONERS

Type of psychology: Psychotherapy
Fields of study: Behavioral therapies; cognitive therapies; psychodynamic therapies

Mental health practitioners are those professionals who are involved in the treatment of psychological and emotional disorders. They include clinical psychologists, counseling psychologists, psychiatrists, and psychiatric social workers; their professional preparations differ considerably, but their contributions are all essential.

Principal terms

ASSESSMENT: a process to determine the assets and liabilities of the patient through the use of interviews and a battery of psychological tests

BEHAVIORAL MEDICINE: the application of psychological knowledge to physical conditions such as ulcers, headaches, smoking, or obesity

DIAGNOSIS: the process of determining a person's condition or problem; psychologists use interview techniques and psychological tests to aid in this process

ELECTROCONVULSIVE THERAPY (ECT): a treatment for severe depression in which an electric current is passed through the brain of the patient

FORENSIC PSYCHOLOGY: the application of psychological skills in the legal profession—for example, in jury selection, sanity determination, and assessing competency to stand trial

NEUROPSYCHOLOGY: the branch of psychology that relates brain function with behavior

PSYCHOTHERAPY: the treatment of psychological or emotional disorders; the therapist usually meets with the patient weekly to deal with the patient's crises or stresses

Overview

Since the beginning of the twentieth century, there has been a growing concern about mental health. Studies have indicated that approximately one out of every five persons in the United States will at some time or another experience a psychological disorder severe enough to warrant professional help. Given the magnitude of this problem, the question emerges as to who will provide the kind and amount of treatment needed for this large number of individuals.

Mental health practitioners have emerged from different fields of endeavor. The field of medicine produced psychiatrists; the field of psychology produced clinical psychologists and counseling psychologists; and the field of social work produced psychiatric social workers. In some states, such as California, legislation created special mental health practitioners called marriage, family, and child counselors to fulfill the needs that were not met by these large professional groups. This article will look at the types of mental health practitioners and describe their professional preparation, their general activity, and their special competencies.

Psychiatrists are those individuals who have completed four years of college and four years of medical school, including one year of internship. After completion, they continue their studies in a residency in psychiatry for approximately three years and learn the skills of a practicing psychiatrist. This is generally done in a mental hospital or clinic, under the supervision of other psychiatrists. Upon completion, they may choose to take an examination which will award them the status of being certified. This status recognizes that a psychiatrist has demonstrated a level of competence that meets professional standards.

As a physician, the psychiatrist can perform all the medical functions that any physician can perform. In terms of the mental health setting, this means that the psychiatrist's activities can involve the administration of different types of drugs that are designed to alter the way a patient feels, thinks, or behaves. The psychiatrist conducts psychotherapy and is concerned about any physical conditions which might make the patient's psychological disposition more serious. The psychiatrist may use other biological treatments, such as electroshock therapy, in the treatment of severe depression and is qualified to supervise the care of patients requiring long-term hospitalization.

The clinical psychologist emerges from the tradition of psychology rather than that of medicine, with a background in theories of behavior and the ways in which behavior may be changed. After completing four years of undergraduate study, usually in psychology but not necessarily so, the student studies two more years to obtain a master's degree in psychology and complete a master's thesis, which provides evidence of research capabilities. This is followed by three more years working toward a Ph.D. degree and the completion of an internship in a mental health setting. After completion of these academic requirements, a psychologist is eligible to take the state licensing examination, which usually requires an oral and written test. In some states, such as California, the psychologist is required to complete an additional year of supervised experience after receiving a Ph.D. degree before becoming eligible for the licensing examination. After passing the examination for licensing, the psychologist is then able to offer services to the public for a fee. Many clinical psychologists choose to go into private practice, that is, to provide services to private patients in their own offices. About 23 percent of all psychologists in the United States list private practice as their primary setting of employment. Other clinical psychologists work in settings such as hospitals, mental health clinics, university counseling centers, or other human service agencies.

After five years of clinical experience, the psychologist may apply for certification by the American Psychological Association. Obtaining certification requires passing written and oral tests as well as an on-site peer examination of clinical skills. Those who succeed are awarded the title of Diplomate in Clinical Psychology. This same award is given in other areas, such as counseling psychology, school psychology, industrial and organizational psychology, and neuropsychology. Board certification clarifies for the general public that the psychologist has demonstrated better-than-average clinical skills and is recognized as such by his or her professional peers. Fewer than 10 percent of all clinical psychologists have been awarded the status of diplomate. This is a useful guide, therefore, for persons who are uncertain about who to see for therapy or assistance. Most telephone directories will designate the diplomate status of individuals, since the American Psychological Association requires that they identify themselves as such.

The counseling psychologist, much like the clinical psychologist, is required to obtain a Ph.D. degree and complete an internship in counseling psychology. Counseling psychologists work in the mental health profession by providing services to those individuals, or couples, who are under stress or crisis but who are continuing to be functional. These are individuals who have functioned well in their lives but are meeting particularly difficult situations and require professional help to adjust to or overcome the stresses of the moment. These situations could involve loss of job, marital conflict, divorce, separation, parent-child or other family conflicts, prolonged physical illnesses, or academic difficulties of high school and college students. Counseling psychologists may either be in private practice or be employed by a university counseling center, where they provide services exclusively to college students.

The fourth type of mental health worker is the psychiatric social worker. This person completes four years of undergraduate study in the social or behavioral sciences, then completes two additional years of study in a school of social work. Social workers may choose different areas of specialty; the mental health worker usually concentrates in psychiatric social work. This involves recognizing the social environment of the patient and altering it in ways that will reduce stress and help maintain the gains that the patient may have achieved in treatment. The social worker becomes involved with issues such as vocational placements, career choice, and family stresses and is the link between the patient and the outside world. Social workers who are licensed may have their own private practices and may offer counseling and psychotherapy as a form of treatment.

Applications

Surveys conducted by the American Psychological Association indicate that clinical psychologists spend most of their professional time providing therapy, diagnosis and assessment, and teaching and administration. These categories constitute approximately 70 percent of their daily activity. Additional activities involve research and consultation with other agencies or professionals. Forty percent of their daily activity, however, is devoted to providing direct clinical services to patients either through psychotherapy or psychological testing.

Almost all practicing clinical psychologists engage in some type of diagnosis or assessment. These assessments usually involve the administration of psychological tests, which include intelligence testing, vocational testing, personality tests, attitude tests, and behavioral repertoires. The purpose of the testing is to assess the patient's current status, to determine any disabling conditions, to assess the patient's psychological strengths that can be utilized in therapy, and to determine treatment recommendations that are specific to the particular problem the patient is presenting. Usually these results are discussed with the patient, and a plan of treatment or therapy is recommended by the psychologist and agreed upon by the patient.

Since there are more than two hundred forms of psychotherapy or behavioral interventions, it is the responsibility of the psychologist to determine which of these procedures is best for the patient, taking into consideration the patient's age, physical status, psychological and emotional condition, and the length of time the disorder has been present. Psychologists should have a good knowledge of the research literature, which would tell them which of these many therapeutic approaches is best for the particular clients with whom they are working at the time.

In the course of private clinical work, the clinical psychologist is likely to meet a variety of different types of cases. These clients may be referred for treatment by other mental health workers, hospitals, insurance plans, ministers, or, very often, by word-of-mouth recommendation from prior patients.

Clients vary as to the severity of their disorders. Some are very seriously disturbed, such as schizophrenic adults who are not receiving treatment in the community and are homeless. They often require hospitalization which provides a complete plan of treatment. Clients with drug or alcohol problems who have had long-standing difficulties with these substances may also require partial hospitalization. The clinical psychologist often acts as the principal or cooperating therapist who plans and participates in the treatment program. Since many clinical psychologists have hospital privileges that allow them to admit their patients to a hospital facility, this procedure is utilized with severely disturbed persons who are a danger to themselves or to others.

Those psychologists who work principally in private practice tend to see clients who have problems adjusting but who do not require hospitalization. These clients often experience excessive symptoms of anxiety, depression, or intrusive thoughts that affect their daily life. They seek therapy for the reduction of these symptoms so that their daily living can be more enjoyable. Other clients seek help in relationships with others, in solving marital, parent-child, employee-supervisor, or sexual conflicts. The clinical psychologist in private practice meets the needs of these clients by providing the best means of resolving these conflicts.

Because psychologists deal with human behavior, they are often involved in many other facets of human activity that require their expertise. For example, psychologists are called upon to testify in court, on questions of sanity, in custody cases, and, occasionally, as expert witnesses in criminal cases. Other psychologists are involved in sports psychology, helping athletes to develop the best psychological and emotional conditions for maximum performance. Still others work in the area of neuropsychology, which deals with patients who have experienced head injuries. Psychologists are asked to assess the extent of the injury and to find those areas that could be used to help the patient recover lost skills. Other psychologists specialize in the treatment of children who have been sexually or physically abused, in drug or alcohol counseling, in working in prisons with juvenile delinquents, or in working with patients who have old-age disorders.

Some psychologists are involved in full-time or part-time teaching at a university. These clinical psychologists not only continue their own clinical practice but also help prepare undergraduate and graduate students through direct classroom instruction or through supervision of their intern or field experiences.

Perspective and Prospects

The field of psychology that deals mainly with emotional and psychological adjustment is called clinical psychology. This field began to take root during World War I, when psychologists were asked to screen military recruits for emotional problems and to assess intellectual abilities so that recruits could be placed in various military positions. During World War II, clinical psychologists assumed an even greater role by developing psychological tests that were used in the selection of undercover agents. They were also asked to provide psychotherapy for soldiers who had emotional or neurological disorders.

Following World War II, clinical psychologists became heavily involved in the development and construction of psychological tests to measure intelligence, interest, personality, and brain dysfunction. Psychologists also became more involved in providing psychotherapy. Today, more psychologists spend their time providing psychotherapy than performing any other single activity.

Clinical psychology today regards itself as an independent profession, separate from the field of psychiatry, and sees itself rooted in the discipline of general psychology with the added clinical skills that make its practitioners uniquely capable of providing services to the general public. It is likely that clinical psychologists will continue to move in the direction of independent practice, focusing on new areas such as behavioral medicine, neuropsychology, and forensic psychology.

Bibliography

American Psychological Association. *Graduate Study in Psychology and Associated Fields*. Washington, D.C.: Author, 1990. Presents more than five hundred programs of graduate study in psychology in the United States and abroad that lead to a master's or doctorate degree in any field of psychology. Lists the requirements for admission for each school, financial assistance available, degree requirements, and the procedures for submitting applications. Most helpful to any student considering graduate study in psychology.

_____. *Psychology as a Health Care Profession*. Washington, D.C.: Author, 1979. A seventeen-page pamphlet covering psychology in its professional role. Discusses how psychological methods are applied to the health care profession; what psychologists do in various settings; the question of how cost-effective their contributions are; and ways that psychologists have affected public policy in health care issues. Single issues of this pamphlet are available at no cost from the American Psychological Association.

Kaplinski, Elizabeth, ed. *Careers in Psychology*. Washington, D.C.: American Psychological Association, 1986. Provides information to students who may be interested in psychology as a career. Defines psychology and describes what psychologists do. Also describes the procedure for preparation to become a psychologist. Single copies of this pamphlet are free upon request from the American Psychological Association.

Routh, Donald K. *Clinical Psychology Since 1917: Science, Practice, and Organization.* New York: Plenum Press, 1994. A chronology of clinical psychology, followed by studies of personalities and such topics as basic science and psychopathology, research and scholarly activities, education and training, credentials for practitioners, and the economics of the field.

Saccuzzo, Dennis P., and Robert M. Kaplan. *Clinical Psychology.* Boston: Allyn & Bacon, 1984. A textbook in clinical psychology providing a broad introduction to this field. Covers the historical foundation, the acquisition of clinical skills, theoretical models, psychotherapy, psychological testing, community psychology, and behavioral medicine. A useful introduction to the field of clinical psychology which includes a valuable chapter on the way it relates to other branches of psychology such as learning, motivation, perception, and biological factors.

Walker, C. Eugene, ed. *Clinical Practice of Psychology: A Guide for Mental Health Professionals.* New York: Pergamon Press, 1981. Intended as an introduction to psychology interns or students who are beginning their work in clinical psychology. Discusses the history of this field and professional issues such as supervision, interviewing skills, ethics, and various forms of treatment. While not intended for the general public, the book will provide a good overview of the field of clinical psychology for someone who is considering entering it.

Wierzbicki, Michael. *Introduction to Clinical Psychology: Scientific Foundations to Clinical Practice.* Boston: Allyn & Bacon, 1999. Discusses the scientific foundations of clinical psychology; theories of personality and psychopathology; clinical assessment; assessment of psychological ability; behavioral assessment; personality assessment; psychoanalytic therapy; humanistic therapy; cognitive and behavioral therapies; biological treatment; child, family, and group therapy; and the training and professional roles of clinical psychologists.

Gerald Sperrazzo

See also:

Analytical Psychotherapy; Aversion, Implosion, and Systematic Desensitization Therapies; Behavioral Assessment and Personality Rating Scales; Behavioral Family Therapy; Child and Adolescent Psychiatry; Cognitive Behavior Therapy; Cognitive Therapy; Community Psychology; Geriatric Psychiatry; Gestalt Therapy; Group Therapy; Modeling Therapies; Music, Dance, and Theater Therapy; Operant Conditioning Therapies; Person-Centered Therapy; Play Therapy; Psychiatry; Psychoactive Drug Therapy; Psychoanalysis; Psychotherapy: Children; Psychotherapy: Effectiveness; Psychotherapy: Goals and Techniques; Psychotherapy: Historical Approaches to Treatment; Rational-Emotive Therapy; Reality Therapy; Strategic Family Therapy; Transactional Analysis.

MENTAL RETARDATION

Type of psychology: Psychopathology
Fields of study: Cognitive processes; organic disorders

Mental retardation involves significant subaverage intellectual development and deficient adaptive behavior accompanied by physical abnormalities.

Principal terms

EDUCABLE MENTALLY RETARDED (EMR): individuals with mild-to-moderate retardation; they can be educated with some modifications of the regular education program and can achieve a minimal level of success

IDIOT: an expression which was formerly used to describe a person with profound mental retardation; such an individual requires custodial care

INBORN METABOLIC DISORDER: an abnormality caused by a gene mutation which interferes with normal metabolism and often results in mental retardation

MENTAL HANDICAP: the condition of an individual classified as "educable mentally retarded"

MENTAL IMPAIRMENT: the condition of an individual classified as "trainable mentally retarded"

NEURAL TUBE DEFECTS: birth defects resulting from the failure of the embryonic neural tube to close; usually results in some degree of mental retardation

TRAINABLE MENTALLY RETARDED (TMR): individuals with moderate-to-severe retardation; only low levels of achievement may be reached by such persons

Causes and Symptoms

Mental retardation is a condition in which a person demonstrates significant subaverage development of intellectual function, along with poor adaptive behavior. Diagnosis can be made fairly easily at birth if physical abnormalities also accompany mental retardation. An infant with mild mental retardation, however, may not be diagnosed until problems arise in school. Estimates of the prevalence of mental retardation vary from 1 to 3 percent of the world's total population.

Diagnosis of mental retardation takes into consideration three factors: subaverage intellectual function, deficiency in adaptive behavior, and early-age onset (before the age of eighteen). Intellectual function is a measure of one's intelligence quotient (IQ). Four levels of retardation based on IQ are described by the American Psychiatric Association. An individual with an IQ between 50 and 70 is considered mildly retarded, one with an IQ between 35 and 49 is moderately retarded, one with an IQ between 21 and 34 is severely retarded, and an individual with an IQ of less than 20 is termed profoundly retarded.

A person's level of adaptive behavior is not as easily determined as an IQ, but it is generally defined as the ability to meet social expectations in the individual's own environment. Assessment is based on development of certain skills: sensory-motor, speech and language, self-help, and socialization skills. Tests have been developed to aid in these measurements.

To identify possible mental retardation in infants, the use of language milestones is a helpful tool. For example, parents and pediatricians will observe whether children begin to smile, coo, babble, and use words during the appropriate age ranges. Once children reach school age, poor school achievement may identify those who are mentally impaired. Psychometric tests appropriate to the age of the children will help with diagnosis.

Classification of the degree of mental retardation is never absolutely clear, and dividing lines are often arbitrary. There has been debate about the value of classifying or labeling persons in categories of mental deficiency. On the one hand, it is important for professionals to understand the amount of deficiency and to determine what kind of education and treatment would be appropriate and helpful to each individual. On the other hand, such classification can lead to low self-esteem, rejection by peers, and low expectations from teachers and parents.

There has been a marked change in the terminology used in classifying mental retardation from the early days of its study. In the early twentieth century, the terms used for moderate, severe, and profound retardation were "moron," "imbecile," and "idiot." In Great Britain, the term "feeble-minded" was used to indicate moderate retardation. These terms are no longer used by professionals working with the mentally retarded. "Idiot" was the classification given to the most profoundly retarded until the middle of the twentieth century. Historically, the word has changed in meaning, from William Shakespeare's day when the court jester was called an idiot, to an indication of psychosis, and later to define the lowest grade of mental deficiency. The term "idiocy" has been replaced with the expression "profound mental retardation."

Determining the cause of mental retardation is much more difficult than might be expected. More than a thousand different disorders that can cause mental retardation have been reported. Some cases seem to be entirely hereditary, others to be caused by environmental stress, and others the result of a combination of the two. In a large number of cases, however, the cause cannot be established. The mildly retarded make up the largest proportion of the mentally retarded population, and their condition seems to be a recessive genetic trait with no accompanying physical abnormalities. From a medical standpoint, mental retardation is considered to be a result of disease or biological defect and is classified according to its cause. Some of these causes are infections, poisons, environmental trauma, metabolic and nutritional abnormalities, and brain malformation.

Infections are especially harmful to brain development if they occur in the first trimester of pregnancy. Rubella is a viral infection that often results in mental retardation. Syphilis is a sexually transmitted disease which affects adults and infants born to them, resulting in progressive mental degeneration.

Poisons such as lead, mercury, and alcohol have a very damaging effect on the developing brain. Lead-based paints linger in old houses and cause poisoning in children. Children tend to eat paint and plaster chips or put them in their mouths, causing possible mental retardation, cerebral palsy, and convulsive and behavioral disorders.

Traumatic environmental effects that can cause mental retardation include prenatal exposure to X rays, lack of oxygen to the brain, or a mother's fall during pregnancy. During birth itself, the use of forceps can cause brain damage, and labor that is too brief or too long can cause mental impairment. After the birth process, head trauma or high temperature can affect brain function.

Poor nutrition and inborn metabolic disorders may cause defective mental development because vital body processes are hindered. One of these conditions, for which every newborn is tested, is phenylketonuria (PKU), in which the body cannot process the amino acid phenylalanine. If PKU is detected in infancy, subsequent mental retardation can be avoided by placing the child on a carefully controlled diet, thus preventing buildup of toxic compounds that would be harmful to the brain.

The failure of the neural tube to close in the early development of an embryo may result in anencephaly (an incomplete brain or none at all), hydrocephalus (an excessive amount of cerebrospinal fluid), or spina bifida (an incomplete vertebra, which leaves the spinal cord exposed). Anencephalic infants will live only a few hours. About half of those with other neural tube disorders will survive, usually with some degree of mental retardation. Research has shown that if a mother's diet has sufficient quantities of folic acid, neural tube closure disorders will be rare or nonexistent.

Microcephaly is another physical defect associated with mental retardation. In this condition, the head is abnormally small because of inadequate brain growth. Microcephaly may be inherited or caused by maternal infection, drugs, irradiation, or lack of oxygen at birth.

Abnormal chromosome numbers are not uncommon in developing embryos and will cause spontaneous abortions in most cases. Those babies that survive usually demonstrate varying degrees of mental retardation, and incidence increases with maternal age. A well-known example of a chromosome disorder is Down syndrome (formerly called mongolism), in which there is an extra copy of the twenty-first chromosome. Gene products caused by the extra chromosome cause mental retardation and other physical problems. Other well-studied chromosomal abnormalities involve the sex chromosomes. Both males and females may be born with too many or too few sex chromosomes, which often results in mental retardation.

Mild retardation with no other noticeable problems has been found to run in certain families. It occurs more often in the lower economic strata of society and probably reflects only the lower end of the normal distribution of intelligence in a population. The condition is probably a result of genetic factors interacting with environmental ones. It has been found that culturally deprived children have a lower level of intellectual function because of decreased stimuli as the infant brain develops.

Treatment and Therapy
Diagnosis of the level of mental retardation is important in meeting the needs of the intellectually handicapped. It can open the way for effective measures to be

taken to help these persons achieve the highest quality of life possible for them.

Individuals with an IQ of 50 to 70 have mild-to-moderate retardation and are classified as "educable mentally retarded" (EMR). They can profit from the regular education program when it is somewhat modified. The general purpose of all education is to allow for the development of knowledge, to provide a basis for vocational competence, and to allow opportunity for self-realization. The EMR can achieve some success in academic subjects, make satisfactory social adjustment, and achieve minimal occupational adequacy if given proper training. In Great Britain, these individuals are referred to as "educationally subnormal" (ESN).

Persons with moderate-to-severe retardation generally have IQs between 21 and 49 and are classified as "trainable mentally retarded" (TMR). These individuals are not educable in the traditional sense, but many can be trained in self-help skills, socialization into the family, and some degree of economic independence with supervision. They need a developmental curriculum which promotes personal development, independence, and social skills.

The profoundly retarded (formerly called idiots) are classified as "totally dependent" and have IQs of 20 or less. They cannot be trained to care for themselves, to socialize, or to be independent to any degree. They will need almost complete care and supervision throughout life. They may learn to understand a few simple commands, but they will only be able to speak a few words. Meaningful speech is not characteristic of this group.

EMR individuals need a modified curriculum, along with appropriately qualified and experienced teachers. Activities should include some within their special class and some in which they interact with students of other classes. The amount of time spent in regular classes and in special classes should be determined by individual needs in order to achieve the goals and objectives planned for each. Individual development must be the primary concern.

For TMR individuals, the differences will be in the areas of emphasis, level of attainment projected, and methods used. The programs should consist of small classes that may be held within the public schools or outside with the help of parents and other concerned groups. Persons trained in special education are needed to guide the physical, social, and emotional development experiences effectively.

A systematic approach in special education has proven to be the best teaching method to make clear to students what behaviors will result in the successful completion of goals. This approach has been designed so that children work with only one concept at a time. There are appropriate remedies planned for misconceptions along the way. Progress is charted for academic skills, home-living skills, and prevocational training. Decisions on the type of academic training appropriate for a TMR individual is not based on classification or labels, but on demonstrated ability.

One of the most important features of successful special education is the involvement of parents. Parents faced with rearing a retarded child may find the task overwhelming and have a great need of caring support and information about their child and the implications for their future. Parental involvement gives the parents the opportunity to learn by observing how the professionals facilitate effective learning experiences for their children at school.

Counselors help parents identify problems and implement plans of action. They can also help them determine whether goals are being reached. Counselors must know about the community resources that are available to families. They can help parents find emotional reconciliation with the problems presented by their special children. It is important for parents to be able to accept the child's limitations. They should not lavish special or different treatment on the retarded child, but rather treat this child like the other children.

Placing a child outside the home is indicated only when educational, behavioral, or medical controls are needed which cannot be provided in the home. Physicians and social workers should be able to do some counseling to supplement that of the trained counselors. Those who offer counseling should have basic counseling skills and relevant knowledge about the mentally retarded individual and the family.

EMR individuals will usually marry, have children, and often become self-supporting. The TMR will live in an institution or at home or in foster homes for their entire lives. They will probably never become self-sufficient. The presence of a TMR child has a great impact on families and may weaken family closeness. It creates additional expenses and limits family activities. Counseling for these families is very important.

Sheltered employment provides highly controlled working conditions, helping the mentally retarded to become contributing members of society. This arrangement benefits the individual, the family, and society as the individual experiences the satisfaction and dignity of work. The mildly retarded may need only a short period of time in the sheltered workshop. The greater the degree of mental retardation, the more likely shelter will be required on a permanent basis. For the workshop to be successful, those in charge of it must consider both the personal development of the handicapped worker and the business production and profit of the workshop. Failure to consider the business success of these ventures has led to failures of the programs.

There has been a trend toward deinstitutionalizing the mentally retarded, to relocate as many residents as possible into appropriate community homes. Success will depend on a suitable match between the individual and the type of home provided. This approach is most effective for the mentally retarded if the staff of a facility is well trained and there is a fair amount of satisfactory interaction between staff and residents. It is important that residents not be ignored, and they must be monitored for proper evaluation at each step along the way. Top priority must be given to preparation of the staff to work closely with the mentally impaired and handicapped.

In the past, there was no way to know before a child's birth if there would be abnormalities. With advances in technology, however, a variety of prenatal tests can be done and many fetal abnormalities can be detected. Genetic counseling is important for persons who have these tests conducted. Some may have previously had a retarded child, or have retarded family members. Others may have something in their backgrounds that would indicate a higher-than-average risk for physical and/or mental abnormalities. Some come for testing before a child is conceived, others do not come until afterward. Tests can be done on the fetal blood and tissues that will reveal chromosomal abnormalities or inborn metabolic errors.

Many parents do not seek testing or genetic counseling because of the stress and anxiety that may result. Though most prenatal tests result in normal findings, if problems are indicated the parents are faced with what may be a difficult decision: whether to continue the pregnancy. It is often impossible to predict the extent of an abnormality, and weighing the sanctity of life in relation to the quality of life may present an ethical and religious dilemma. Others prefer to know what problems lie ahead and what their options are.

Perspective and Prospects

Down through history, the mentally retarded were first ignored, and then subjected to ridicule. The first attempts to educate the mentally retarded were initiated in France in the mid-nineteenth century. Shortly afterward, institutions for them began to spring up in Europe and the United States. These were often in remote rural areas, separated from the communities nearby, and were usually ill-equipped and understaffed. The institutions were quite regimented and harsh discipline was kept. Meaningful interactions usually did not occur between the patients and the staff.

The medical approach of the institutions was to treat the outward condition of the mentally retarded and ignore them as people. No concern for their social and emotional needs was shown. There were no provisions for children to play, nor was there concern for the needs of the family of those with mental handicaps.

Not until the end of the nineteenth century were the first classes set up in some U.S. public schools for education of the mentally retarded. The first half of the twentieth century brought about the expansion of the public school programs for individuals with both mild and moderate mental retardation. After World War II, perhaps in response to the slaughter of mentally handicapped persons in Nazi Germany, strong efforts were made to provide educational, medical, and recreational services for the mentally retarded.

Groundbreaking research in the 1950's led to the normalization of society's attitude about the mentally retarded in the United States. Plans to help these individuals live as normal a life as possible were made. The National Association for Retarded Citizens was founded in 1950 and had a very strong influence on public opinion. In 1961, President John F. Kennedy appointed the Panel on Mental Retardation and instructed it to prepare a plan for the nation, to help meet the complex problems of the mentally retarded. The panel presented ninety recommendations in the areas of research, prevention, medical services, education, law, and local and national organization. Further presidential commissions on the topic were appointed and have had far-reaching effects for the well-being of the mentally retarded.

A "Declaration of the Rights of Mentally Retarded Persons" was adopted by the General Assembly of the United Nations in 1971, and the Education for All Handicapped Children Act was passed in the United States in 1975, providing for the development of educational programs appropriate for all handicapped children and youth. These pieces of legislation were milestones in the struggle to improve learning opportunities for the mentally retarded.

Changes continue to take place in attitudes toward greater integration of the retarded into schools and the community, leading to significant improvements. The role of the family has increased in emphasis, for it has often been the families themselves that have worked to change old, outdated policies. The cooperation of the family is very important in improving the social and intellectual development of the mentally retarded child. Because so many new and innovative techniques have been used, it is very important that programs be evaluated and compared to one another to determine which methods provide the best training and education for the mentally retarded.

Bibliography

Baroff, George S., and J. Gregory Olley. *Mental Retardation: Nature, Cause, and Management.* 3d ed. Philadelphia: Brunner/Mazel, 1999. This edition retains the comprehensiveness and readability as its predecessors. Provides up-to-date material on the major dimensions of mental retardation—its nature, biological and psychological causes, and management.

Burack, Jacob A., Robert M. Hodapp, and Edward Zigler, eds. *Handbook of Mental Retardation and Development.* New York: Cambridge University Press, 1998. Reviews theoretical and empirical work in the developmental approach to mental retardation. Includes bibliographical references and an index.

Clarke, Ann M., Alan D. B. Clarke, and Joseph M. Berg. *Mental Deficiency: The Changing Outlook.* 4th ed. New York: Free Press, 1985. A classic text in the field of mental retardation which summarizes the tremendous amount of knowledge that has been amassed on the subject. Covers the genetic and environmental causes of mental retardation, prevention, help, intervention, and training.

Dudley, James R. *Confronting the Stigma in Their Lives: Helping People with a Mental Retardation Label.* Springfield, Ill.: Charles C Thomas, 1997. This book is written for anyone concerned about combating the negative effects of being labeled as having a mental disorder.

Gearheart, Bill R., and Freddie W. Litton. *The Trainable Retarded.* 2d ed. St. Louis: C. V. Mosby, 1979. An excellent text for students training to work with moderately to severely retarded individuals. Provides a history of work in the field and emphasizes the great strides taken in the mid-twentieth century. The topics covered include assessment, education and training, parental training, and alternatives in residential services.

Jakab, Irene, ed. *Mental Retardation.* New York: Karger, 1982. A clearly written text for training health professionals who work with the mentally retarded. Contains useful, practical information and emphasizes those things which can be done to improve the quality of life for the mentally retarded.

Matson, Johnny L., and Rowland P. Barrett, eds. *Psychopathology in the Mentally Retarded.* 2d ed. Boston: Allyn & Bacon, 1993. This book addresses an often-neglected topic: the psychological problems that may be found in mentally retarded individuals. Discusses special emotional problems of various types of mentally retarded persons based on the causation of their deficiency. Descriptions of major disorders and their treatments are given.

Zigler, Edward, and Dianne Bennett-Gates, eds. *Personality Development in Individuals with Mental Retardation*. New York: Cambridge University Press, 1999. Discusses the relationship of personality motivation and cognitive performance, learned helplessness, and expected success. Includes bibliographical references and an index.

Katherine H. Houp

See also:

Brain Disorders; Child and Adolescent Psychiatry; Down Syndrome; Learning Disabilities.

MIDLIFE CRISES

Type of psychology: Developmental psychology
Fields of study: Adulthood; coping

Midlife crisis describes the transition from early adulthood to middle age. It can be a stressful time of reevaluation, leading to both external and internal changes in a person's life.

Principal terms

CRISIS: a period of alienation and confusion during which one feels overwhelmed and dissatisfied with one's life

EMPTY NEST: transitional phase of parenting after the last child leaves the parents' home

GENERATIVITY: the desire to care for and contribute to further generations; desire to leave a legacy

LIFE STRUCTURE: the basic pattern of a person's life at a given time; both influences and is influenced by the person's relationship with the environment

OFF-TIME EVENTS: life events that occur at unexpected or unpredictable times

TRANSITION: a period of change and instability between one stage of development and the next

Overview

The term "midlife crisis" has become a part of the everyday vocabulary of most people and is often mentioned when explaining the cause of a variety of difficult changes during adulthood, ranging from depression to extramarital affairs. Most researchers describe the midlife crisis as a period of alienation, stress, and disequilibrium occurring immediately prior to the individual's entrance into middle age. The typical age reported for the midlife crisis varies depending on the researcher. Some claim that the midlife crisis may begin around age thirty-five and last until age forty, others have identified the late thirties and early forties as the most likely time for crisis, and still others claim that the midlife crisis occurs in the middle to late forties.

The notion of a midlife crisis being a predictable event in people's lives was popularized by Gail Sheehy's *Passages: Predictable Crises of Adult Life* (1976). Sheehy referred to the ages thirty-five to forty-five as the "deadline decade," emphasizing that this is the period during adulthood when people tend to start panicking about running out of time to accomplish the goals and dreams they established in their youth. The midlife crisis described by Sheehy is similar to Daniel Levinson and his coauthors' approach to adult development, outlined in their book *The Seasons of a Man's Life* (1978). Levinson's theory describes the changing "life structures" and transitional periods throughout an adult's development from entering early adulthood to entering late adulthood. During the midlife transition (ages forty to forty-five), Levinson claims that virtually all men experience a stressful period of crisis. Both Sheehy and Levinson, as well as other authors, emphasize the marked shift in time perspective that occurs during the transition into middle adulthood. The authors claim that this is the first time in people's lives when they fully realize that time is finite and that eventual death is a personal reality for them. Facing one's own mortality leads to considerable existential questioning about the meaning of life, one's identity, and one's role in life, somewhat similar to the questions that are first faced during adolescence.

The main reason that this growing awareness of mortality leads to a crisis is that people at this stage reevaluate their lives and tend to question virtually every major value and belief that they have held. Adults may reevaluate their previous decisions regarding career and marriage, question their satisfaction with these decisions, and subsequently make major changes in their lives. All this questioning and change can precipitate a crisis in people's lives because they often do not have sufficient strategies to cope with the changes and are unsure of who they are and what they stand for.

According to Levinson, there are three major psychological tasks that people in midlife must face. First, they must reappraise their past so that they can make the best use of their remaining time. During the process of reappraisal, people often come to realize that many of their assumptions about the world and their lives were idealistic illusions, and they then develop more realistic, balanced views. Another task is to modify their "life structure" by making both external and internal changes. External changes may include changes in family structure (possibly divorce and remarriage) or changes in career structure. Changes in personal outlook, values, and goals represent internal changes that occur during the midlife transition. Finally, the person must integrate into their personality those aspects of themselves that have previously been ignored or neglected. In particular, the polarities or opposites of being young versus old, destructive versus creative, masculine versus feminine, and attached versus separate must be integrated into the personality to form a broader, more balanced perspective.

Levinson's view that people inevitably experience a midlife crisis around age forty is shared by some experts in developmental psychology but is firmly disputed by others. Although most theorists agree that there is a transition between young and middle adulthood, many challenge the notion that the transition is experienced as a "crisis." Researchers such as Bernice Neugarten claim that life events, not birthdays, are the basis for crises. In particular, unpredictable or "off-time" events are more likely to bring on a crisis than events that are predictable and occur at the expected time. If people are prepared for a specific change during adulthood, such as having children leave home, then Neugarten suggests that the change, though stressful, does not set off a crisis.

The individual's personal approach to dealing with changes, as well as his or her attitude toward the change, influences whether the change will lead to a crisis. An event is more likely to be experienced as stressful if it is perceived as a negative event over which the person has no control. On the other hand, if the event is viewed as a challenge, the person is more likely to feel energized and optimistic about coping with any ensuing changes. Other factors that can influence how individuals deal with important life events are physical health, personality style (flexible versus inflexible, resilient versus vulnerable), their personal history of coping with previous stressful events, and the degree of social support they have from family, friends, coworkers, and community.

Applications

Neugarten suggests that important life events serve to mark the passage of time through one's lifetime. There are several such events that often occur during the transition to middle adulthood that can contribute to a midlife crisis. One of the main changes faced during this period are subtle but unmistakable signs of physical aging. Gray hairs become more abundant, wrinkles around the eyes and the rest of the face become more pronounced, and parents may find that their adolescent children can now regularly beat them in basketball, races, and other tests of athletic prowess in which the parents once were undisputed champions.

In addition to these physical changes, women entering midlife must face the eventual loss of their ability to have children with knowledge that the menopause is rapidly approaching. Even for women who do not wish to have children (or more children), the loss of choice on the matter can be disturbing. Men do not face the same loss of reproductive functioning, but they often do start to develop doubts about their "sex appeal"; consequently, a man may seek an affair with a younger woman in order to reaffirm his sense of sexual desirability.

The midlife transition is also a time when people's perspectives toward their careers often change. People begin to realize that their choice of career options has narrowed substantially. They also may have found that they have reached a plateau in their current career, as the important tasks and opportunities are frequently assigned to younger, more motivated employees. Finally, the limited time left before retirement may lead to a sense of disappointment when the middle-aged person realizes that he or she has not attained all the goals and dreams of youth.

Significant changes can also occur in the family during the midlife transition. Adults in their late thirties to early forties often have adolescent children who are most likely going through identity crises of their own. Two or more corresponding but separate crises occurring in the same family can interfere with communication and family harmony. Another change associated with having children is facing the "empty nest" when the grown children begin to leave home for college or to start families of their own. The departure of children from the home often involves a significant role loss for the mother and possibly a lost opportunity for a close relationship for the father. In addition, just as the children are leaving home, adults in midlife may suddenly find themselves saddled with the stress and responsibility of caring for frail, elderly parents. The caregivers (typically middle-age women) faced with the burden of caring for a dependent parent are referred to as the "sandwich" generation, because they are caught between the competing demands of their ailing parent, grown children, spouse, and their own desire finally to address their own personal needs and dreams. The increasing pressures at this time in life when people often expect to have more time to themselves can create a tremendous amount of stress.

Marital dissatisfaction during midlife is at an all-time high for many couples. The responsibilities of careers and rearing children keep many married couples busy and preoccupied during early adulthood. Once the children leave home and careers plateau, however, couples tend to take a more thorough look at their relationship and often wonder whether they want to maintain it. Not surprisingly, many divorces occur at this time in life.

Given all the important and difficult changes occurring during midlife, it should not be surprising that individuals' lives and perspectives are often qualitatively different after the midlife transition. According to Erik Erikson, people in middle adulthood struggle with opposing tendencies toward generativity and stagnation. Generativity refers to a desire to renew oneself through contributing to future generations. Ways that people typically contribute include rearing their own children, teaching, coaching, serving as a mentor, or making an artistic or creative contribution to society. People who are successful at generativity during this period are more likely to come through the midlife crisis with a stronger sense of identity and greater life satisfaction. On the other hand, those who stagnate at this stage and become self-absorbed tend to become increasingly narrow and rigid in perspective and bitter in attitude.

Another psychological change during this period has to do with the tendency for adults to exhibit characteristics typically associated with the opposite sex. Men who have primarily been aggressive and active in their careers may become more reflective, nurturing, and interested in building closer family relationships with their children and spouse. In contrast, women tend to become more assertive, self-confident, and oriented toward personal achievements at midlife, particularly once the responsibility of child rearing diminishes.

Perspective and Prospects

The idea of the midlife crisis can be traced back to the writings of Carl Jung in which he portrayed the second half of life as a time for balance and reflection. Jung claimed that the passing of youth at middle age is marked by psychological changes in the individual. Prominent aspects of the personality become less important and are even gradually replaced by opposite personality traits. In addition, Jung held that one of the primary changes of this period was a greater emphasis on exploration of one's inner self and a search for meaning in one's life. These changes are thought to pave the way for greater acceptance of one's eventual death.

Although Jung's work suggested that an important change occurred at midlife, the London psychoanalyst Elliott Jaques is credited with being the first author to use the term "midlife crisis." His article "Death and the Mid-Life Crisis" (1965) was based on his study of the lives of composers, writers, and artists. Jaques found that there was a marked shift in the themes and styles of these creators from the more straightforward and descriptive work of their early adult years to a much more tragic and philosophical approach during their middle-age years. Later in life, the themes of these writers and artists became more serene and calm. Jaques proposed that the shift in style at midlife was based on the individual's confrontation with his or her own mortality. Similarly, the eventual acceptance of their mortality led to a greater sense of peace in their later years, which was reflected in their work.

The writings of Jung and Jaques were significant in the field of psychology because they heralded a broader focus in the understanding of human development. Initially, the focus of developmental psychology was based solely on the physical, cognitive, and psychological changes during childhood and adolescence. It was assumed that people were finished with important development changes by puberty and that no further changes of significance occurred again in people's lives until the decline in functioning right before death. Regardless of whether one thinks of midlife as a transition or a crisis, the study of midlife changes has contributed much to the understanding of ongoing development during adulthood.

Future work in the area of midlife crisis is likely to lead to a greater understanding of the varied ways different people have of approaching and coping with stressors and changes in midlife. In particular, future research will probably focus on cultural differences in the experience of midlife as well as gender differences, as society's differential expectations and demands regarding gender continue to shift. Finally, changes in the expected age and duration of midlife crises may occur as the average human life span changes and the average age of the population as a whole continues to increase.

Bibliography

Baruch, Grace, and Jeanne Brooks-Gunn, eds. *Women in Midlife*. New York: Plenum Press, 1984. Provides a comprehensive review of a wide range of topics related to women in midlife. Topics include changing roles, psychological well-being, caring for aging parents, motherhood, health care, reproductive issues, sexuality, and cultural differences. Although some of the chapters are fairly technical and research focused, most are well written and highly informative.

Berglas, Charlotte. *Mid-Life Crisis*. Lancaster, Pa.: Technomic Publishing, 1983. Berglas's short book provides a very readable, nontechnical review of the struggles that many people encounter as they enter middle age. She focuses on issues such as physical, career, and family changes and illustrates her descriptions with examples of people she has encountered through her work as a nurse.

Farrell, Michael P., and Stanley D. Rosenberg. *Men at Midlife*. Boston: Auburn House, 1981. Based on surveys of three hundred men and in-depth interviews with twenty men and their families, the authors have developed an explanatory model for four different types of midlife experience for men. They challenge the notion that the midlife crisis is typical and emphasize the importance of family relationships. The book includes both research data and extensive case histories, which makes it accessible to the scholar and the general public.

Josselson, Ruthellen. *Revising Herself: Story of Women's Identity from College to Midlife*. New York: Oxford University Press, 1998. In 1972, Josselson selected thirty young women in their last year of college and followed their personal odysseys over the next twenty-two years, from graduation to midlife. She grouped them into the categories Guardians, Pathmakers, Searchers, and Drifters. By midlife, however, many reversals had occurred: Some Guardians were able to cut loose from earlier patterns, while many Drifters had found themselves.

Lachman, Margie E., and Jacquelyn Boone James, eds. *Multiple Paths of Midlife Development: Studies on Successful Midlife Development.* Chicago: University of Chicago Press, 1997. Leading researchers analyze the various changes involving the self and others that middle-aged adults experience in the realms of work, family, and health. Includes bibliographical references and an index.

Landau, Sol, and Joan Thomas. *Turning Points: Self-Renewal at Midlife.* Far Hills, N.J.: New Horizon Press, 1985. Landau, a retired rabbi turned counselor and educator, wrote this book as a guide for the general public for coping with midlife crisis. He discusses his own life history as well as some of the major theoretical explanations of midlife crisis. Uses real-life examples to illustrate midlife changes in areas such as marriage, sexuality, job burnout, and retirement. His writing is concise and includes many helpful tips for people experiencing a crisis in their own lives.

Levinson, Daniel J., et al. *The Seasons of a Man's Life.* New York: Alfred A. Knopf, 1978. Summarizes Levinson's influential theoretical approach to adult development, based on in-depth interviews with forty men, ages thirty-five to forty-five. He describes the life cycle from early adulthood through middle adulthood, pointing out the psychological tasks of each stage and transition. Case-study examples are included throughout. Most of the text can be understood without an extensive knowledge of technical terminology or psychological theory.

Sheehy, Gail. *Passages: Predictable Crises of Adult Life.* New York: E. B. Dutton, 1976. This widely read book describes the predictable crises of adulthood, including the midlife crisis. Sheehy includes many personal experiences and case examples to illustrate the stages of development. Intended for the general public; Sheehy's engaging writing style and clever chapter titles make the book readable and enjoyable for a wide range of audiences.

Stephanie Stein

See also:

Anxiety Disorders; Couples Therapy; Depression; Divorce and Separation: Adult Issues; Identity Crises; Jealousy; Stress; Stress: Coping Strategies; Stress: Prediction and Control.

MODELING THERAPIES

Type of psychology: Psychotherapy
Fields of study: Behavioral therapies; cognitive therapies

Modeling therapies are cognitive behavioral therapy techniques that are based on the principles of learning by observing; they are based on the idea that people can benefit from observing the behaviors of other people. These therapies have been applied successfully to a wide range of problems.

Principal terms

COPING MODEL: a model who is somewhat of a novice but who copes with the situation

COVERT MODELING: a modeling technique in which clients use their imaginations to visualize a given situation

LIVE MODELING: a modeling technique that involves observing a person directly, in the flesh

MASTERY MODEL: an expert who is very adept at the target behavior

SELF-AS-A-MODEL: a modeling technique in which clients watch themselves on videotape and in which the film is edited to include only appropriate examples of the behavior

SELF-MODELING: a modeling technique in which clients observe themselves on videotape and in which the film includes all behaviors, both appropriate and inappropriate

SYMBOLIC MODELING: a modeling technique in which clients observe a person indirectly, such as in films, on television, or through reading

TARGET BEHAVIOR: the behavior which the client desires to change through therapy

Overview

Much of what people know and how people behave they have learned through observing other people. From the child who learns how to tie shoelaces by having an adult demonstrate how to do it to the medical student who learns how to perform complicated surgery by watching expert physicians, all people learn from observing the behaviors of those around them. This process of learning has been given many different names, including imitation, copying, mimicry, vicarious learning, observational learning, and modeling.

Often, people are aware when this process of learning by observing others is occurring. That is, they are consciously paying attention to the behavior of another person in order to learn a new behavior. For example, when people first learn to ski, they will closely watch someone who already knows how to do it. In this way, they will learn how they are supposed to behave and what to do on the skis. This process of learning by observation most often occurs, however, without the learner even being aware of it. The child who watches a parent or other adult perform some task and then tries to do it like the adult is not usually thinking about wanting to learn that new behavior. For example, the young boy who tries to shave just like his father is not trying consciously to learn how to shave; he is simply imitating the adult. Yet the child is learning a new behavior through this observing and practicing process. So pervasive is this learning process in everyone's life that it has been estimated by some that at least 70 percent of human behavior can be accounted for by this learning process.

The principles behind modeling are used throughout society. In education, learning by observation is an essential aspect of all teaching. For example, an instructor could not teach a foreign language without first demonstrating the words for the student to learn. In industry and business, modeling techniques are used to train employees in the skills necessary to function in their jobs. In advertising, modeling is the primary basis by which consumers are manipulated to buy certain products. Consumers learn through advertisements that by driving certain automobiles, they will become popular. These are but a few examples of how observational learning, or modeling, occurs on a daily basis.

While the process of learning by observation is pervasive and has occurred throughout human history, the scientific exploration of the process and subsequent therapeutic application began with Albert Bandura's work in the 1960's. During this time, Bandura was conducting experiments with children and their reaction to "Bobo" dolls, which are large stuffed dolls often used for punching and kicking. In these now-famous studies, it was found that children would act in a more aggressive manner after watching other children punching and kicking the Bobo doll. In subsequent studies, Bandura and associates demonstrated the same learning process in children observing violent television shows. Children who observed aggressive television shows would subsequently behave with greater aggression.

Bandura's research did much to stimulate interest in the process of learning through observation and helped inspire the development of therapy techniques based on modeling. While there are many different types of modeling therapies, they are all based on the principle that learning will occur as a result of observation.

Modeling therapies are used primarily in cognitive behavioral and other behavioral therapy approaches. The types of modeling therapies that exist include symbolic modeling, live modeling, covert modeling, and cognitive modeling. Symbolic modeling involves the client observing some indirect representation of the behavior being demonstrated. This might mean watching television or a motion picture, reading a book, or being told about the behavior. In contrast to symbolic modeling, live modeling involves the client directly observing the behavior that is being demonstrated by another person. Typically, this will be the therapist demonstrating the desired behavior. Covert modeling involves the client being directed by the therapist to imagine himself or herself or someone similar to the client demonstrating the desired behavior. In cognitive modeling, therapists tell clients what to say to themselves when they are performing a certain task.

With the advent of video technology, other forms of modeling have become possible and readily accessible. Two approaches that use this new technology are self-modeling and the self-as-a-model technique. In both of these approaches, rather than observing another person perform a target behavior, clients serve as their own models. The client is videotaped demonstrating the target behavior, and this videotape is then used by the client either to gain or increase mastery of the target behavior or to eliminate a particular behavior. In self-modeling, clients watch all the examples of the behavior, both appropriate and inappropriate. In self-as-a-model, concurrently developed by Ray Hosford and Peter Dowrick, clients also observe their own behavior; however, in this approach, only appropriate examples of the behavior are left on the videotape, while the inappropriate examples are deleted.

Applications

Modeling therapies have been used successfully to treat a wide variety of problems. In fact, these techniques have considerable usefulness across the full spectrum of problems that clients present to therapists. They have been used to help clients acquire new skills, strengthen existing skills, eliminate problem behaviors, and decrease fears and phobias.

In examining how the various types of modeling therapies would be applied to an actual client, one could look at a case example of a nineteen-year-old male client who lacks assertive behavior when dealing with his coworkers. The first step in helping this client would be to get as much specific information as possible about the behaviors that need to be changed and the situations in which the problem arises. Having gained this information, the therapist would then be ready to implement a therapeutic strategy to help the client become more assertive.

Choosing symbolic modeling, the therapist might show the client films or videotapes of other people demonstrating assertive behavior, or have the client read a book about the topic. After the videotape has been viewed, the client would then have an opportunity to practice the assertive behavior in the presence of the therapist, who will observe and give feedback.

The use of live modeling is very similar to that of symbolic modeling, except that the client would observe the person in the flesh. In the case of the nonassertive client, the therapist and client might act out a possible scene involving the client and the coworkers. The therapist would first play the role of the client and demonstrate assertive behaviors in the situation. Then the therapist and client would switch roles, and the client would try out this new behavior. As with the prior approach, the therapist's role would be to give feedback to the client on the appropriateness of the behavior and, as necessary, repeat the behavior while the client observes. This example presents the primary elements of modeling therapies: observation of the model, practice, feedback, additional modeling, and further practice and feedback.

If covert modeling is chosen, the therapist would direct the client to imagine himself, or someone who is similar, behaving in an assertive manner. Perhaps the therapist would slowly describe a scene in which the client is behaving in an assertive manner with his coworkers. While the therapist is describing the scene, the client would be imagining the scene actually occurring.

With cognitive modeling, the therapist shows the client what to say to himself while performing the assertive behavior. The therapist would first demonstrate the behavior while speaking aloud the appropriate "self-talk." For example, the therapist would act assertively while saying aloud, "I'm doing fine; I have the right to express my opinions; I'm proud of myself for acting this way." Then the client would perform the same behavior while the therapist gave instructions on what to say aloud. After this, the client would practice the behavior while following the instructions on what self-talk to be using.

Finally, if self-modeling or self-as-a-model is selected, the client would first perform the behavior while being videotaped. The therapist's role would be to help direct this performance to optimize the client's appropriate behavior. With both self-modeling and self-as-a-model, the client would then watch the videotape and imagine himself performing the behavior. (Again, in self-modeling, the videotape would include all demonstrations of the behavior; in self-as-a-model, the videotape would have been edited to include only positive examples of the behavior.)

As shown in this case example, when modeling therapies are used, they are typically only one component of a more comprehensive therapy approach. Therapy will usually consist of many different techniques to help a client create a change in behavior. In the case example, the therapist would probably use, in addition to modeling, relaxation techniques to help reduce the client's anxiety in the situation, cognitive restructuring to facilitate a reduction in the client's negative self-talk, and homework to have the client practice the desired behavior.

While modeling therapies are effective in a variety of situations, there are a number of factors that will influence how well the intervention will work. Some of these factors have to do with the characteristics of the model (the therapist), and some with the characteristics of the observer (the client). For example, observers will learn more from models whom they perceive to be attractive, rewarding, prestigious, competent, powerful, or similar in ethnicity. Further, some observers will learn better from a mastery model, that is, from a person who is very skilled in the target behavior, while others will learn better from a coping model, that is, from a person who is somewhat of a novice at the behavior but who is managing to cope. One factor that affects which model will work best for a given individual is the observer's level of self-confidence.

The previous case example of assertiveness training is only one brief example of how modeling therapies can be used. These therapies are also used to help clients eliminate undesirable behaviors such as angry outbursts, decrease fears such as snake or height phobias, and strengthen existing skills such as public speaking. As people learn much of what they know and do from observational learning, so too can they change their behavior and learn new skills with the help of modeling used in therapy.

Perspective and Prospects
While psychologists, sociologists, and anthropologists have long known about the phenomenon of imitation learning, it was not until the 1960's that scientific investigation into observational learning began in earnest. Albert Bandura's early, pioneering work in this area was influenced by a growing societal concern over the potentially negative impact that television has on children, specifically over the

possible effects of violence on television. From these early investigations, in which Bandura and his associates demonstrated the presence of observational learning of aggressiveness in children, Bandura further elaborated on the theoretical principles behind the phenomenon of observational learning. These writings and work by many other psychologists led to the development of a variety of modeling therapies.

When first developed, modeling techniques were primarily used in behavioral approaches to therapy. The modeling approaches generally involved observation of the model and subsequent practice by the observer; that is, the focus of the modeling therapies was strictly on overt behavior. With the development of cognitive techniques and their subsequent incorporation into the behavioral approaches to therapy, new forms of modeling therapies came into existence. Two of these new approaches were cognitive modeling and covert modeling, in which clients use their thoughts to help create behavior change. As a result of the use of cognitive approaches, the range of modeling therapies increased, as did the range of therapists using modeling therapies.

With increases in video technology, the range of modeling therapies was further expanded, as was their use and effectiveness. The growing availability of videotape equipment has allowed a greater use of self-modeling and self-as-a-model. With the use of video equipment, it became feasible for clients to observe themselves performing a given behavior. These opportunities for self-observation have allowed clients to serve as their own model and, with the assistance of a therapist, make changes in their behavior.

While it is primarily thought of as a cognitive behavioral therapy approach, modeling, it should be noted, is a part of every form of therapy. In many forms of therapy it may not be called modeling, but it occurs nevertheless. In virtually every therapy approach, the therapist demonstrates appropriate behaviors and the client learns from these demonstrations; this is observational learning, or modeling, no matter what it is called by the therapist.

Bibliography

Bandura, Albert. *Principles of Behavior Modification.* New York: Holt, Rinehart and Winston, 1969. Provides a detailed description of various behavior therapy approaches, including modeling therapies. Includes case examples as well as summaries of the literature supporting the techniques.

_____. *Psychological Modeling: Conflicting Theories.* Chicago: Aldine-Atherton, 1971. Provides a thorough review of the principles of modeling as well as the research demonstrating its existence. Discusses various theories developed to explain the phenomenon and presents Bandura's explanation for observational learning. Written for those with background knowledge in learning theories.

Bergin, Allen E., and Sol L. Garfield, eds. *Handbook of Psychotherapy and Behavior Change.* 3d ed. New York: John Wiley & Sons, 1986. A standard reference book for professionals that covers many issues in psychotherapy. Several chapters, including one on modeling therapies written by Albert Bandura, describe various therapeutic approaches.

Dowrick, Peter W., and Simon J. Biggs, eds. *Using Video: Psychological and Social Applications*. New York: John Wiley & Sons, 1983. Provides information on how video equipment can be used to help clients create behavior changes. Included are chapters on self-modeling and self-as-a-model, with detailed descriptions of applications of these techniques.

Krumboltz, John D., and Carl E. Thoresen, eds. *Behavioral Counseling: Cases and Techniques*. New York: Holt, Rinehart and Winston, 1969. Short chapters use case examples to illustrate specific applications of various psychotherapy techniques, including several modeling techniques.

Martin, Garry, and Joseph Pear. *Behavior Modification—What It Is and How to Do It*. 6th ed. Upper Saddle River, N.J.: Prentice Hall, 1998. Offers readers personal, hands-on experience with the principles of behavior modification and their application to everyday concerns. Includes bibliographical references and an index.

Meichenbaum, Donald. *Cognitive Behavior Modification: An Integrative Approach*. New York: Plenum Press, 1977. Provides detailed descriptions of the use of cognitive approaches in therapy. Brief case descriptions illustrate various techniques including the use of cognitive approaches in modeling. Gives the reader an overview of how a client's self-talk can be used to help create behavior change through a variety of methods.

Sarafino, Edward P. *Principles of Behavior Change: Understanding Behavior Modification Techniques*. New York: John Wiley & Sons, 1997. Intended for students. Provides a thorough, up-to-date presentation of major issues, theories, concepts, and research in behavior modification. Includes bibliographical references and indexes.

Mark E. Johnson

See also:

Behavioral Family Therapy; Cognitive Behavior Therapy; Cognitive Therapy; Operant Conditioning Therapies; Psychotherapy: Goals and Techniques.

MUSIC, DANCE, AND THEATER THERAPY

Type of psychology: Psychotherapy
Fields of study: Psychodynamic therapies

Music, dance, and theater therapies utilize various media such as movement and creative expression to accomplish the desired therapeutic goals; these therapies reflect a focus on the therapeutic value of artistic experiences and expression.

Principal terms

ADAPTIVE PATTERNS: the behaviors an individual employs to utilize the environment and its demands while satisfying needs

CREATIVITY: a basic component in music, dance, and theater; it involves imagination and expression

DEVELOPMENTAL TASK: the process of learning an age-appropriate or sequential behavior

IMPROVISATION: a performance or construction from whatever material is available without previous preparation

MOVEMENT THERAPY: a means of enabling an individual, through movement, to develop and organize behavioral patterns that satisfy personal needs

Overview

Music, dance, and theater therapies employ a wide range of methods to accomplish the goal of successful psychotherapy. Psychotherapy is a general term for the wide variety of methods psychologists and psychiatrists use to treat behavioral, emotional, or cognitive disorders. Music, dance, and theater therapies are not only helpful in the observation and interpretation of mental and emotional illness but also useful in the treatment process. Many hospitals, clinics, and psychiatrists or therapists include these types of therapy in their programs. They are not limited to hospital and clinical settings, however; they also play important roles in a wide variety of settings, such as community mental health programs, special schools, prisons, rehabilitation centers, nursing homes, and other settings.

Music, dance, and theater therapies share a number of basic characteristics. The therapies are generally designed to encourage expression. Feelings that may be too overwhelming for a person to express verbally can be expressed through movement, music, or the acting of a role. Loneliness, anxiety, and shame are typical of the kinds of feelings that can be expressed effectively through music, dance, or theater therapy. These therapies share a developmental framework. Each therapeutic process can be adapted to start at the patient's physical and emotional level and progress from that point onward.

Music, dance, and theater therapies are physically integrative. Each can involve the body in some way and thus help develop an individual's sense of identity. Each therapy is inclusive and can deal with either individuals or groups, and with verbal or nonverbal patients in different settings. Each is applicable to different age groups (children, adolescents, adults, the elderly) and to different diagnostic categories, ranging from mild to severe. While music, dance, and theater therapies share these common characteristics, however, they also differ in important respects.

Dance therapy does not use a standard dance form or movement technique. Any genre, from ritual dances to improvisation, may be employed. The reason for such variety lies in the broad spectrum of persons that undergo dance therapy: neurotics, psychotics, schizophrenics, the physically disabled, and geriatric populations can all benefit from different types of dance therapy. Dance therapy may be based on various philosophical models. Three of the most common are the human potential model, the holistic health model, and the medical model. The humanistic and holistic health models have in common the belief that individuals share responsibility for their therapeutic progress and relationships with others. By contrast, the medical model assumes that the therapist is responsible for the treatment and cure.

Dance therapy is not a derivative of any particular verbal psychotherapy. It has its own origin in dance, and certain aspects of both dance and choreography are important. There are basic principles involving the transformation of the motor urge and its expression into a useful, conscious form. The techniques used in dance therapy can allow many different processes to take place. During dance therapy, the use of movement results in a total sensing of submerged states of feeling that can serve to eliminate inappropriate behavior. Bodily integration is another process that can take place in dance therapy. The patient may gain a feeling of how parts of the body are connected and how movement in one part of the body affects the total body. The therapist can also help the patient become more aware of how movement behavior reflects the emotional state of the moment or help the patient recall earlier emotions or experiences. Dance therapy produces social interaction through the nonverbal relationships that can occur during dance therapy sessions.

Music therapy is useful in facilitating psychotherapy because it stimulates the awareness and expression of emotions and ideas on an immediate and experiential level. When a person interacts musically with others, he or she may experience (separately or simultaneously) the overall musical gestalt of the group, the act of relating to and interacting with others, and his or her own feelings and thoughts about self, music, and the interactions that have occurred. The nonverbal, structured medium allows individuals to maintain variable levels of distance from intrapsychic (within self) and interpersonal (between people) processes. The abstract nature of music provides flexibility in how people relate to or take responsibility for their own musical expressions. The nonverbal expression may be a purely musical idea, or it may be part of a personal expression to the self or to others.

After the activity, the typical follow-through is to have each client share what was seen, heard, or felt during the musical experience. Patients use their musical experiences to examine their cognitive and affective reactions to them. It is then the responsibility of the music therapist to process with the individual the reactions and observations derived from the musical experience and to help the person generalize them—that is, determine how they might be applied to everyday life outside the music therapy session. Group musical experiences seem to stimulate verbal processing, possibly because of the various levels of interaction available to the group members.

Theater therapy, or drama therapy, uses either role playing or improvisation to reach goals similar to those of music and dance therapy. The aims of the drama therapy process are to recognize experience, to increase one's role repertoire, and to learn how to play roles more spontaneously and competently.

The key concepts of drama therapy are the self and roles. Through role taking, the processes of imitation, identification, projection, and transference take place. Projection centers on the concept that inner thoughts, feelings, and conflicts will be projected onto a relatively ambiguous or neutral role. Transference is the tendency of an individual to transfer his or her feelings and perceptions of a dominant childhood figure—usually a parent—to the role being played.

Applications

The goal of theater or drama therapy is to use the universal medium of theater as a setting for the psychotherapeutic goals. Opportunities for potential participants include forms of self-help, enjoyment, challenge, personal fulfillment, friendship, and support. The theater setting helps each individual work with issues of control, reality testing, and stress reduction.

David Johnson and Donald Quinlan have conducted substantial research into the effects of drama therapy on populations of schizophrenics. Their research addresses the problem of the loss of the self and the potential of drama therapy in recovering it. They found that paranoid schizophrenics create more rigid boundaries in their role playing, while nonparanoid schizophrenics create more fluid ones. They concluded that improvisational role playing is an effective means to assess boundary behaviors and differentiate one diagnostic group of schizophrenics from another.

Dance therapy has been found to be extremely useful in work with autistic children, as well as children with minimal brain dysfunction (MBD). The MBD child's symptoms may range from a behavioral disorder to a learning disability. Though the symptoms vary, and some seem to vanish as the child matures, the most basic single characteristic seems to be an inability to organize internal and external stimuli effectively. By helping the MBD child to reexperience, rebuild, or experience for the first time those elements upon which a healthy body image and body scheme are built, change can be made in the areas of control, visual-motor coordination, motor development, and self-concept.

The goals of dance therapy with the MBD child are to help the child identify and experience his or her body boundaries, to help each child master the dynamics of moving and expressing feelings with an unencumbered body, to focus the hyperactive child, to lessen anxiety and heighten ability to socialize, and to strengthen the self-concept.

Music therapy has been used successfully with patients who have anorexia nervosa, an eating disorder which has been called "self-starvation." Anorexia nervosa represents an attempt to solve the psychological or concrete issues of life through direct, concrete manipulation of body size and weight. Regardless of the type or nature of the issues involved, which vary greatly among anorectic clients, learning to resolve conflicts and face psychological challenges effectively without the use of weight control is the essence of therapy for these clients. To accomplish this, anorectics must learn to divorce their eating from their other difficulties, stop using food as a tool for problem solving, face their problems, and believe in themselves as the best source for solving those problems. Music therapy has provided a means of persuading clients to accept themselves and their ability to control their lives, without the obsessive use of weight control, and to interact effectively and fearlessly with others.

Many health professionals have acknowledged the difficulty of engaging the person with anorexia in therapy, and music has been found to work well. Because of its nonverbal, nonthreatening, creative characteristics, music can provide a unique, experiential way to help clients acknowledge psychological and physical problems and resolve personal issues.

Perspective and Prospects
The interdisciplinary sources of dance, music, and drama therapies bring a wide range of appropriate research methodologies and strategies to the discipline of psychology. These therapies tend to defy conventional quantification. Attempts to construct theoretical models of these therapies draw on the disciplines of psychology, sociology, medicine, and the arts. There is no unified approach to the study and practice of these therapies.

Dance therapy has its roots in ancient times, when dance was an integral part of life. It is likely that people danced and used body movement to communicate long before language developed. Dance could express and reinforce the most important aspects of a culture. Societal values and norms were passed down from one generation to another through dance, reinforcing the survival mechanism of the culture.

The direct experience of shared emotions on a preverbal and physical level in dance is one of the key influences in the development of dance or movement therapy. The feelings of unity and harmony that emerge in group dance rituals provide the basis of empathetic understanding between people. Dance, in making use of natural joy, energy, and rhythm, fosters a consciousness of self. As movement occurs, body sensations are often felt more clearly and sharply. Physical sensations provide the basis from which feelings emerge and become expressed. Through movement and dance, preverbal and unconscious material often crystallizes into feeling states of personal imagery. It was the recognition of these elements, inherent in dance, that led to the eventual use of dance or movement in psychotherapy.

Wilhelm Reich was one of the first physicians to become aware of and utilize body posturing and movement in psychotherapy. He coined the term "character armor" to describe the physical manifestation of the way an individual deals with anxiety, fear, anger, and similar feelings. The development of dance into a therapeutic modality, however, is most often credited to Marian Chace, a former dance teacher and performer. She began her work in the early 1940's with children and adolescents in special schools and clinics. In the 1950's and 1960's, other modern dancers began to explore the use of dance as a therapeutic agent in the treatment of emotional disturbances.

There is a much earlier history of music therapy; the use of music in the therapeutic setting dates back to the 1700's. Early research showed music therapy useful for helping mental patients, people with physical disabilities, children with emotional, learning, or behavioral problems, and people with a variety of other difficulties.

Bibliography

Boxill, Edith Hillman. *The Miracle of Music Therapy*. Gilsum, N.H.: Barcelona, 1997. A self-help book promoting the use of music therapy. Includes a bibliography.

Jones, Phil. *Drama as Therapy: Theatre as Living*. New York: Routledge, 1996. Introduces the concept of drama therapy. Provides a historical overview, defines therapeutic factors, and offers information about assessment, recording, and evaluation. Includes bibliographical references and indexes.

Landy, Robert J. *Drama Therapy: Concepts, Theories, and Practices*. 2d ed. Springfield, Ill.: Charles C Thomas, 1994. Particularly valuable in identifying the relationship between drama therapy and other psychotherapies. Contains numerous examples and illustrations of drama therapy as it has been used to address various psychological problems.

Mason, Kathleen Criddle, ed. *Dance Therapy*. Washington, D.C.: American Alliance for Health, Physical Education, and Recreation, 1974. Particularly good in identifying the special groups for which dance therapy is useful. Each chapter explores a special application of dance therapy to a particular audience or treatment population.

Newham, Paul. *Using Voice and Movement in Therapy: The Practical Application of Voice Movement Therapy*. London: Jessica Kingsley, 1999. Examines how massage, manipulation, and dance, combined with vocal expression, can alleviate certain emotional, psychosomatic, and psychological symptoms. Includes bibliographical references and an index.

Schneider, Erwin H., ed. *Music Therapy*. Lawrence, Kans.: National Association for Music Therapy, 1959. One of a series of annual publications of the proceedings of the National Association for Music Therapy. While somewhat old, this volume covers a wide variety of applications and settings of music therapy through case studies. A classic in the field.

Siegel, Elaine V. *Dance-Movement Therapy: Mirror of Our Selves*. New York: Human Sciences Press, 1984. Strong theoretical framework and applied theory of dance and psychotherapy. This is a very scholarly investigation of dance therapy; includes movement as well.

Wiener, Daniel J., ed. *Beyond Talk Therapy: Using Movement and Expressive Techniques in Clinical Practice*. Washington, D.C.: American Psychological

Association, 1999. Discusses the use of action-centered methods such as art, dance, yoga, drama, and ritual with traditional psychotherapy.

Robin Franck

See also:

Abnormality: Psychodynamic Models; Anorexia Nervosa and Bulimia Nervosa; Autism; Group Therapy; Person-Centered Therapy; Play Therapy; Psychotherapy: Children; Psychotherapy: Goals and Techniques; Schizophrenia.

NEUROSIS

Type of psychology: Psychotherapy
Fields of study: Anxiety disorders; depression; sexual disorders; substance abuse

Neurosis is a chronic mental disorder characterized by distressing and unacceptable anxiety.

Principal terms

ADDICTION: the use of substances or self-defeating behaviors to fulfill one's need for love instead of loving self or another person

ANXIETY: a generalized anxious affect which is pervasive and without a known cause

COMPULSION: a repetitively performed behavior that bears little relation to a person's needs

DEPRESSION: a mood of sadness, unhappiness, hopelessness, loss of interest, difficulty concentrating, and lack of a sense of self-worth

HYSTERIA: the presence of somatic symptoms resembling those of a physical disease without actual physical illness

OBSESSION: a recurrent thought that is foreign or intrusive

PHOBIA: an abnormal fear that arises because an inner fear is displaced onto an object or situation outside the individual

PSYCHOSOMATIC DISORDER: an organic illness caused by psychological distress

Causes and Symptoms

A neurosis is experienced at a level of severity that is less than psychotic but significant enough to impair a person's functioning. The term "neurosis" includes nine psychological states: hysteria, obsessions and compulsions, phobias, some depressions, some traumatic reactions, addictions, psychosomatic disorders, some sexual disorders, and anxiety. A person tends to continue suffering from one of the recurrent and continuing reactions noted above, if not treated for the neurosis.

Hysteria features somatic symptoms resembling those of a physical disease without actual physical illness (for example, a headache without organic cause). Phobias are abnormal fears that arise because an inner fear is displaced onto an object or situation outside the individual (for example, impotence to deal with fear of intimacy). Obsessions (recurrent thoughts) and compulsions (repetitively performed behaviors) bear little relation to the person's needs and are experienced by the person as foreign or intrusive (for example, repeated hand washing). Depression is a mood of sadness, unhappiness, hopelessness, loss of interest, difficulty concentrating, and lack of a sense of self-worth. Addictions are the use of substances or self-defeating behaviors to fulfill one's need for love instead of loving self or another person (for example, addiction to gambling). Psychosomatic disorders are organic illnesses caused by psychological distress (for example, peptic ulcer). Sexual disorders are the avoidance of developing adult sexual competency by immature sexual behavior (for example, exhibitionism). Traumatic reactions in the past delay or impair normal development in the present (for example, childhood sexual abuse leads to difficulty with intimacy as an adult). Anxiety is experienced as a generalized anxious affect which is pervasive and without a known cause (for example, a person chronically worrying that "something bad will happen").

Austrian physician Alfred Adler, who claimed that neurotic persons project their rigid thought process onto the world.

Treatment and Therapy
All the forms of neuroses listed above need treatment to be resolved. All have the potential to become borderline or overtly psychotic disorders under stress. Treat-

ment involves entering psychotherapy to understand better and therefore manage neurotic symptoms. It often can require the use of psychoactive medications for the treatment of anxieties, depressions, obsessions, and addictions. Treatment can be received from family physicians and general internists at the first level of intervention. Patients refer to psychiatrists, psychologists, social workers, and substance counselors for more advanced interventions.

Perspective and Prospects
Sigmund Freud (1856-1939), Alfred Adler (1870-1937), Carl Jung (1875-1961), and Karen Horney (1885-1952) all made major contributions toward understanding neuroses. All four were Austrian-born physicians who helped invent modern psychology, eventually leaving Austria to work in either Great Britain or America.

Freud founded psychoanalysis with his work on the causes and treatment of neurotic and psychopathic states. The methods that he developed form the root of all "talking therapies." Freud proposed that psychological conflicts produce neuroses according to the following pattern. Inner conflicts are produced by fears or guilt around one's emerging sexual drives. The conflicts, if not resolved on a conscious level, are repressed on the unconscious level, where they drive a person to act according to one or more of the various neurotic symptoms.

Adler was one of the four original members of Freud's psychoanalytic school. With his emphasis on the person as a whole being and on the importance of willpower, he created an individual psychology for the twentieth century. Adler said that neurotic persons form a rigid way of thinking about themselves and others. They then project that rigid thought process onto the world. They proceed to operate as though the world accepted their rigid thinking as real. This tendency is at the basis of the neurotic thought processes of sadism, hatred, intolerance, envy, and irresponsibility.

Jung was the only member of Freud's inner circle who was formally trained as a psychiatrist. He founded analytic psychology, which studies mental behavior as complexes of behavior, emotion, thought, and imagery. He opened up psychology to religious and mystical experiences. Jung wrote that neuroses are a dissociation of the personality caused by splitting. A person has a conscious set of values or beliefs which conflict with an opposite set of feelings. The person, rather than resolving the problem, maintains the rational-emotive split as one or more of the forms of neuroses.

Horney developed a psychoanalytic theory of humans who evolve within their culture, family, and environment. She was sensitive to the negative effects of a male-dominated psychology, attempting to explain women's experiences. Horney believed that neuroses are disturbances in the relationship of self-to-self and self-to-other. If one's development in childhood is disturbed from its normal pattern, the adult will use one of three neurotic coping styles: compliance, aggressiveness, or detachment.

These four psychologists agreed that neuroses are a childhood developmental defect which impairs the adult's rational-emotional integration, appearing as one or more of the indirect symptoms of anxiety.

Bibliography

Cleve, Jay. *Out of the Blues*. Minneapolis: CompCare, 1989. Presents methods of coping with neurotic depression, stemming from Alfred Adler's belief that neurosis comes from overly rigid thinking.

Fenichel, Otto. *The Psychoanalytic Theory of Neurosis*. New York: W. W. Norton, 1995. The fiftieth anniversary edition sets psychoanalytic theory up as a broad framework, with each theorist adding a novel perspective or elucidating finer points in the broad theory of neurosis.

Lindesay, James, ed. *Neurotic Disorders in the Elderly*. Oxford, England: Oxford University Press, 1995. Addresses neuroses in old age, including possible complications. Provides a bibliography and an index.

Rapoport, Judith. *The Boy Who Couldn't Stop Washing*. New York: Penguin Group, 1989. A classic description of the neurosis of obsessive-compulsive behaviors. Based upon Sigmund Freud's understanding of neurosis as an illness.

Roth, Geneen. *When Food Is Love*. New York: Plume, 1991. Reviews the neurotic abuse of foods as an addiction. Roth's work reflects Carl Jung's understanding of the importance of love and spirit for each person.

Sheehy, Gail. *Passages*. New York: E. P. Dutton, 1976. Presents an explanation of how and why neuroses are developmental. Sheehy's classic work is a follow-up to Karen Horney's theories of neurosis.

Wurmser, Leon. *The Power of the Inner Judge: The Psychodynamic Treatment of the Severe Neuroses*. Northvale, N.J.: Jason Aronson, 1999. Describes in detail how to treat severely ill but not psychotic patients, by careful psychotherapeutic work on the defenses and the superego. Includes bibliographical references and an index.

Gerald T. Terlep

See also:

Addictive Personality and Behaviors; Agoraphobia and Panic Disorders; Anxiety Disorders; Depression; Hypochondriasis, Conversion, Somatization, and Somatoform Pain; Manic-Depressive Disorder; Midlife Crises; Obsessive-Compulsive Disorder; Paranoia; Phobias; Psychoanalysis; Psychosis; Psychosomatic Disorders; Stress.

OBSESSIVE-COMPULSIVE DISORDER

Type of psychology: Psychopathology
Fields of study: Anxiety disorders

This anxiety disorder is characterized by intrusive and unwanted but uncontrollable thoughts, by the need to perform ritualized behavior patterns, or both. The obsessions and/or compulsions cause severe stress, consume an excessive amount of time, and greatly interfere with a person's normal routine, activities, or relationships.

Principal terms

ANAL STAGE: the stage of psychosexual development in which a child derives pleasure from activities associated with elimination

ANXIETY: an unpleasant feeling of fear and apprehension

BIOGENIC MODEL: the theory that every mental disorder is based on a physical or physiological problem

MAJOR AFFECTIVE DISORDER: a personality disorder characterized by mood disturbances

MONOAMINE OXIDASE INHIBITORS: antidepressant compounds used to restore the balance of normal neurotransmitters in the brain

PHOBIA: a strong, persistent, and unwarranted fear of a specific object or situation

TOURETTE'S SYNDROME: a childhood disorder characterized by several motor and verbal tics that may develop into the compulsion to shout obscenities

TRICYCLICS: medications used to relieve the symptoms of depression

Causes and Symptoms

Obsessive-compulsive disorder (OCD) is an anxiety disorder that is characterized by intrusive and uncontrollable thoughts and/or by the need to perform specific acts repeatedly. Obsessive-compulsive behavior is highly distressing because one's behavior or thoughts are no longer voluntarily controlled. The more frequently these uncontrolled alien and perhaps unacceptable thoughts or actions are performed, the more distress is induced. A disturbed individual may have either obsessions (which are thought-related) or compulsions (which are action-related), or both. At various stages of the disorder, one of the symptoms may replace the other.

OCD affects 1 to 2 percent of the population; most of those afflicted begin suffering from the disorder in early adulthood, and it is often preceded by a particularly stressful event such as pregnancy, childbirth, or family conflict. It may be closely associated with depression, with the disorder developing soon after a bout of depression or the depression developing as a result of the disorder. OCD is more likely to occur among intelligent, upper-income individuals, and men and women are equally affected. A fairly high proportion (as much as 50 percent) do not marry.

Obsessions generally fall into one of five recognized categories. Obsessive doubts are persistent doubts that a task has been completed; the individual is unwilling to accept and believe that the work is done satisfactorily. Obsessive thinking is an almost infinite chain of thought, targeting future events. Obsessive impulses are very strong urges to perform certain actions, whether they be trivial or serious, that would likely be harmful to the obsessive person or someone else and that are socially unacceptable. Obsessive fears are thoughts that the person has lost control and will act in some way that will cause public embarrassment. Obsessive images are continued visual pictures of either a real or an imagined event.

Four factors are commonly associated with obsessive characteristics, not only in people with OCD but in the general population as well. First, obsessives are unable to control mental processes. Practically, this means the loss of control over thinking processes, such as thoughts of a loved one dying or worries about hurting someone unintentionally. Second, there may be thoughts and worries over the potential loss of motor control, perhaps causing impulses such as shouting obscenities in church or school, or performing inappropriate sexual acts. Third, many obsessives are afraid of contamination and suffer irrational fear and worry over exposure to germs, dirt, or diseases. The last factor is checking behavior, or backtracking previous actions to ensure that the behavior was done properly, such as checking that doors and windows are shut, faucets are turned off, and so on. Some common obsessions are fear of having decaying teeth or food particles between the teeth, fear of seeing fetuses lying in the street or of killing babies, worry about whether the sufferer has touched vomit, and fear of contracting a sexually transmitted disease.

Compulsions may be either mild or severe and debilitating. Mild compulsions might be superstitions, such as refusing to walk under a ladder or throwing salt over one's shoulder. Severe compulsions become fixed, unvaried ritualized behaviors; if they are not practiced precisely in a particular manner or a prescribed number of times, then intense anxiety may result. Even these strange behaviors may be rooted in superstition; many of those suffering from the disorder believe that performing the behavior may ward off danger. Compulsive acts are not ends in themselves but are "necessary" to produce or prevent a future event from occurring. Although the enactment of the ritual may assuage tension, the act does not give the compulsive pleasure.

Several kinds of rituals are typically enacted. A common ritual is repeating; these sufferers must do everything by numbers. Checking is another compulsive act; a compulsive checker believes that it is necessary to check and recheck that everything is in order. Cleaning is a behavior in which many compulsives must engage; they may wash and scrub repeatedly, especially if the individual thinks that he or she has touched something dirty. A fourth common compulsive action is avoiding; for certain superstitious or magical reasons, certain objects must be avoided. Some compulsives experience a compelling urge for perfection in even the most trivial of tasks; often the task is repeated to ensure that it has been done correctly. Some determine that objects must be in a particular arrangement; these individuals are considered "meticulous." A few sufferers are hoarders; they are unable to throw away trash or rubbish. All these individuals have a constant need for reassurance; for example, they want to be told repeatedly that they have not been contaminated.

No cause for OCD has been isolated. Therapists even disagree over whether the obsessions increase or decrease anxiety. Three theories exist that attempt to explain the basis of OCD psychologically: guilt, anxiety, and superstition. Sigmund Freud first proposed that obsessive thoughts are a replacement for more disturbing thoughts or actions that induce guilt in the sufferer. These thoughts or behaviors, according to Freud, are usually sexual in nature. Freud based his ideas on the cases of some of his young patients. In the case of a teenage girl, for example, he determined that she exchanged obsessive thoughts of stealing for the act of masturbation. The thoughts of stealing produced far fewer guilt feelings than masturbation did. Replacing guilt feelings with less threatening thoughts prevents one's personal defenses from being overwhelmed. Other defense mechanisms may be parlayed into OCD. Undoing, one of these behaviors, is obliterating guilt-producing urges by undergoing repetitive rituals, such as handwashing. Since the forbidden urges continue to recur, the behavior to replace those urges must continue. Another mechanism is reaction formation. When an unacceptable thought or urge is present, the sufferer replaces it with an exactly opposite behavior. Many theorists believe that both obsessive and compulsive behaviors arise as a consequence of overly harsh toilet training. Thus the person is fixated at the anal stage and, by reaction formation, resists the urge to soil by becoming overly neat and clean. A third mechanism is isolation, the separation of a thought or action from its effect. Detachment or aloofness may isolate an individual from aggressive or sexual thoughts.

Although there is disagreement among therapists regarding the role of the anxiety associated with OCD, some theorize that OCD behaviors develop to reduce anxiety. Many thought or action patterns emerge as a way of escape from stress, such as daydreaming during an exam or cleaning one's room rather than studying for a test. If the stress is long-lasting, then a compulsive behavior may ensue. This theory may not answer the problem of behaviors such as handwashing. If this theory is always viable, then washers should feel increased anxiety at touching a "contaminated" object and washing should relieve and reduce those feelings. While this does occur in some instances, it does not explain the origin of the disorder.

The superstition hypothesis proposes a connection between a chance association and a reinforcer that induces a continuation of the behavior. Many theorists believe that the same sequence is involved in the formation of many superstitions. A particular obsessive-compulsive ritual may be reinforced when a positive outcome follows the behavior; anxiety results when the ritual is interrupted. An example would be a student who only uses one special pencil or pen to take exams, based on a previous good grade. In actuality, there is seldom a real relationship between the behavior and the outcome. This hypothesis, too, fails to explain the development of obsessions.

A fourth theory is accepted by those who believe that mental disorders are the result of something physically or physiologically amiss in the sufferer, employing data from brain structure studies, genetics, and biochemistry. Indeed, brain activity is altered in those suffering from OCD; and they experience increased metabolic activity. Whether the activity is a cause or an effect, however, is unclear. Studies of genetics in families, at least in twins, reinforce the idea that genetics may play a small role in OCD because there appears to be a higher incidence of the disorder in identical twins than in other siblings. Yet these results may be misleading: Because all the studies were carried out on twins who were reared together, environment must be considered. Relatives of OCD sufferers are twice as likely as unrelated individuals to develop the same disorder, indicating that the tendency for the behavior could be heritable.

Treatment and Therapy

While obsessional symptoms are not uncommon in the general population, a diagnosis of OCD is rare. Perhaps between five thousand and ten thousand Americans are affected by this mental disorder, although many sufferers are too horrified to admit to their symptoms.

Diagnostic techniques evaluating OCD have not changed much since the nineteenth century. There may be confusion about whether the patient is actually suffering from schizophrenia or a major affective disorder. When depression is also noted, it is important to determine whether the OCD is a result of the depression or the depression is a result of the OCD. If such a determination is not possible, both disorders must be treated.

In cases where differentiation between OCD and schizophrenia is necessary, the distinction can be made by determining the motive behind the ritualized behavior. Stereotyped behaviors are symptomatic of both disorders. In the schizophrenic, however, the behavior is triggered by delusions rather than by true compulsions. People suffering from true delusions cannot be shaken from them; they do not resist the ideas inundating the psyche and even rituals may not decrease the feelings associated with these ideas. On the other hand, obsessive people may be absolutely certain of the need to perform their ritual while other aspects of their thinking and logic are perfectly clear. They generally resist the ideas that enter their minds and realize the absurdity of the thoughts. As thoughts and images intrude into the obsessive person's mind, the person may appear to be schizophrenic.

Other disorders having symptoms in common with OCD are Tourette's syndrome and amphetamine abuse. What seems to separate the symptoms of these disorders from those experienced with OCD is that the former are organically induced. Thus, the actions of a sufferer from Tourette's syndrome may be mechanical since they are not intellectually dictated or purposely enacted. In the case of the addict, the acts may bring pleasure and are not resisted.

"Normal" people also have obsessive thoughts; in fact, the obsessions of normal individuals are not significantly different from the obsessions of those with OCD.

The major difference is that those with the disorder have longer-lasting, more intense, and less easily dismissed obsessive thoughts. The importance of this overlap is that mere symptoms are not a reliable tool to diagnose OCD, since some of the same symptoms are experienced by the general population.

Assessment of OCD separates the obsessive from the compulsive components so that each can be examined. Obsessional assessment should determine the triggering fears of the disorder, both internal and external, including thoughts of unpleasant consequences. The amount of anxiety that these obsessions produce should also be monitored. The compulsive behaviors then should be examined in the same light.

The greatest chance for successful treatment occurs with patients who experience mild symptoms that are usually obsessive but not compulsive in nature, with patients who seek help soon after the onset of symptoms, and with patients who had few problems before the disorder began. Nevertheless, OCD is one of the most difficult disorders to treat. Types of treatment fall into four categories: psychotherapy, behavioral therapy, drug therapy, and psychosurgery.

When psychotherapy is attempted, it usually begins with psychoanalysis. Whether psychoanalysis will be successful is often determined by the stressor or inducer of the thought or action and the personality of the patient. The major goal of this psychoanalytical approach is to find and then remove an assumed repression so that the patient can deal honestly and openly with whatever is actually feared. Some analysts believe that focusing on the present is most beneficial, since delving into the past may strengthen the defensive mechanism (the compulsive behavior). If the patient attempts to "return" to the mitigating event, the analyst should intervene directly and actively and bring the patient back to the present by encouraging, pressuring, and guiding him or her.

The most effective treatment for controlling OCD is the behavioral approach, in which the therapist aids the patient in replacing the symptoms of the obsession or compulsion with preventive or replacement actions. Aversive methods may include a nonvocal, internal shout of "stop!" when the obsessive thoughts enter the mind, the action of snapping a rubber band on the wrist, or physically restraining oneself if the compulsive action begins. This latter approach may be so uncomfortable and disconcerting to the patient that it may work only under the supervision supplied by a hospital.

Behavioral therapy may also help by breaking the connection between the stimulus (what induces the compulsion or obsession) and anxiety. Response prevention involves two stages. First, the patient is subjected to flooding, the act of exposing the patient to the real and/or imagined stimuli that cause anxiety. This process begins with brief exposure to the stressors while the therapist assesses the patient's thoughts, feelings, and behaviors during the stimulus period. In the second stage, the patient is flooded with the stimuli but restrained from acting on those stressors. Although flooding may produce intense discomfort at first, the patient is gradually desensitized to the stimuli, causing the resulting anxiety to decrease. The therapist must expend considerable time preventing the response, discussing the anxiety as it appears, and supporting the patient as the anxiety abates. To be effective, treatment must also occur in the home with the guidance and support of family members who have been informed about how best to interact with the patient. While behavioral treatment can help to control OCD, it does not generally "cure" the disorder. If the patient is also depressed, successful treatment with behavioral therapy is even less likely.

Drugs commonly used to treat OCD that have met with some success include antidepressants, tricyclics, monoamine oxidase inhibitors, LSD, and tryptophan. Although a psychiatrist may prescribe tranquilizers to reduce the patient's anxiety, these drugs are usually not adequate to depress the frequent obsessive thoughts or compulsive actions. Antidepressants may occasionally benefit those who are suffering from depression as well as OCD; as depression is lifted, some of the compulsive behavior is also decreased. Monoamine oxidaseinhibitors (MAOIs) are used most effectively in treating OCD associated with panic attacks, phobias, and severe anxiety. When medication is halted, however, the patient often relapses into the previous obsessive-compulsive state.

Some psychosurgeons may resort to psychosurgery to relieve a patient's symptoms. The improvement noted after surgery may simply be attributable to the loss of emotion and dulling of behavioral patterns found in any patient who has undergone a lobotomy. Because such surgery may result in a change in the patient's intellect and emotional response, it should be considered only in extreme, debilitating cases. Newer surgical techniques do not destroy as much of the cerebral cortex as they once did. These procedures separate the frontal cortex from lower brain areas in only an 8-centimeter square area.

Perspective and Prospects

Descriptions of OCD behavior go back to medieval times; a young man who could not control his urge to stick out his tongue or blurt out obscenities during prayer was reported in the fifteenth century. Medical accounts of the disorder and the term "obsessive-compulsive" originated in the mid-1800's. At this time obsessions were believed to occur when mental energy ran low. Later, Freud stated that OCD was accompanied by stubbornness, stinginess, and tidiness. He attributed the characteristics to a regression to early childhood, when there are perhaps strong urges to violence or to dirty and mess one's surroundings. To avoid acting on these tendencies, he theorized, an avoidance mechanism is employed, and the symptoms of obsession and/or compulsion appear. Other features related to this regression are ambivalence, magical thinking, and a harsh, punitive conscience.

An unpleasant consequence of OCD behavior is the effect that the behavior has on the people who interact with the sufferer. The relationships with an obsessive person's family, schoolmates, or coworkers all suffer when a person with OCD takes up time with uncontrollable and lengthy rituals. These people may feel not only a justifiable concern but also resentment. Some may feel guilt over the resentful feelings because they know the obsessive-compulsive cannot control these actions. An obsessive-compulsive observing these conflicting feelings in others may respond by developing depression or other anxious feelings, which may cause further alienation.

Although not totally disabling, OCD behaviors can be strongly incapacitating. A famous figure who suffered from OCD was millionaire and aviator Howard Hughes (1905-1976). A recluse after 1950, he became so withdrawn from the public that he only communicated via telephone and intermediaries. His obsession-compulsion was the irrational fear of germs and contamination. At first, it began by his refusal to shake hands with people. If he had to hold a glass or open a door, he covered his hand with a tissue. He would not abide any of his aides eating foods that gave them bad breath. He disallowed air conditioners, believing that they collected germs. Because Hughes acted on his obsessions, they became compulsions.

Most parents will agree that children commonly have rituals to which they must adhere or compulsive actions they carry out. A particular bedtime story may be read every night for months on end, and children's games involve counting or checking rituals. It is also not atypical for adults without psychiatric disorders to experience some mild obsessive thoughts or compulsive actions, as seen in an overly tidy person or in group rituals performed in some religious sects. Excessively stressful events may trigger obsessional thoughts as well. Some behaviors commonly called compulsions are not truly compulsive in nature. For example, gambling, drug addiction, or exhibitionism are not clinically compulsive because these addictive behaviors bring some pleasure to the person. The anxiety ensuing from these addictive behaviors is appropriate by society's standards; compulsive behavior produces anxiety that is considered inappropriate to the situation.

Bibliography

American Psychiatric Association. *Diagnostic and Statistical Manual of Mental Disorders, Fourth Edition (DSM-IV)*. 4th ed. Washington, D.C.: Author, 1994. The bible of the psychiatric community, this is a compendium of descriptions of disorders and diagnostic criteria widely embraced by clinicians. Included is an extensive glossary of technical terms, making this volume easy to understand.

Barlow, David H., ed. *Clinical Handbook of Psychological Disorders*. 2d ed. New York: Guilford Press, 1993. This collection defines and describes psychological disorders and uses case histories as illustrations for treatment. The chapter on OCD provides a series of tests that can be given to determine the presence and severity of this disorder.

Davison, Gerald C., and John M. Neale. *Abnormal Psychology*. 8th ed. New York: John Wiley & Sons, 2000. This college text addresses the causes of psychopathology and treatments commonly used to treat various disorders. The book is well organized, readable, and interesting. An extensive reference list and a glossary are included.

De Silva, Padmal, and Stanley Rachman. *Obsessive-Compulsive Disorder: The Facts*. New York: Oxford University Press, 1998. For patients and their families. Includes information about assessment and evaluation; treatment; effect on family, work, and social life; practical advice; and the relationship of OCD to other disorders.

Dumont, Raeann. *The Sky Is Falling: Understanding and Coping with Phobias, Panic, and Obsessive-Compulsive Disorders*. New York: W. W. Norton, 1996. A popular work on common anxiety-causing conditions. Includes bibliographical references and an index.

Frances, Allen, John P. Docherty, and David A. Kahn. "Treatment of Obsessive-Compulsive Disorder." *Journal of Clinical Psychiatry* 58 (1997): 5-72. This article offers recommendations for treating obsessive-compulsive disorder. It may be particularly useful to individuals or family members of individuals seeking treatment.

Koran, Lorrin M. *Obsessive-Compulsive and Related Disorders in Adults: A Comprehensive Clinical Guide*. New York: Cambridge University Press, 1999. Discusses the diagnosis, clinical picture, and pharmacotherapeutic and psychotherapeutic treatments for obsessive-compulsive disorder and for disorders traditionally included in the same spectrum, such as Tourette's syndrome and certain sexual disorders.

Sue, David, Derald Sue, and Stanley Sue. *Understanding Abnormal Behavior*. 6th ed. Boston: Houghton Mifflin, 2000. Recognized disorders of the mind and common successful treatments of these disorders are discussed in this college text. Well organized and understandable.

Swinson, Richard P., et al., eds. *Obsessive-Compulsive Disorder: Theory, Research, and Treatment*. New York: Guilford Press, 1998. A comprehensive overview of OCD. Explores the latest research and developments. Covers psychopathology, assessment, and treatment.

Iona C. Baldridge

See also:

Addictive Personality and Behaviors; Agoraphobia and Panic Disorders; Anorexia Nervosa and Bulimia Nervosa; Anxiety Disorders; Aversion, Implosion, and Systematic Desensitization Therapies; Depression; Eating Disorders; Manic-Depressive Disorder; Neurosis; Paranoia; Phobias; Psychoanalysis; Schizophrenia; Stress.

OPERANT CONDITIONING THERAPIES

Type of psychology: Psychotherapy
Fields of study: Behavioral and cognitive models; behavioral therapies

Operant conditioning therapies are based on the assumption that operant behavior is shaped by its consequences; therapists use reinforcement, extinction, punishment, and discrimination training to overcome behavioral problems. Operant conditioning techniques have been applied to individual and group behavior in a variety of settings, including hospitals, prisons, schools, businesses, and homes.

Principal terms

AVERSIVE STIMULUS: a painful or unpleasant event
DISCRIMINATION TRAINING: reinforcing a response in the presence of one stimulus and extinguishing the response in the presence of other stimuli
EXTINCTION: a procedure used to eliminate a previously reinforced response by withholding the reinforcer following the response
NEGATIVE PUNISHMENT: a procedure used to decrease the frequency of a response by removing a positive reinforcer following the response
OPERANT CONDITIONING: a form of learning in which voluntary behavior is modified by its consequences
POSITIVE PUNISHMENT: a procedure used to decrease the frequency of a response by presenting an aversive stimulus following the response
POSITIVE REINFORCEMENT: a procedure used to increase the frequency of a response by presenting a favorable consequence following the response
SUCCESSIVE APPROXIMATIONS: responses that more and more closely resemble the desired response

Overview

Behavior therapy uses principles of learning to modify human behavior. One orientation within behavior therapy is the operant conditioning approach, also called behavior modification. This approach modifies operant behavior by manipulating environmental consequences. The term "operant" refers to voluntary or emitted behavior that operates on the environment to produce consequences. The basic premise of operant conditioning is that operant behavior is controlled by its consequences. What happens to an individual after he or she performs some behavior determines the likelihood of that behavior being repeated. Pleasant or reinforcing consequences strengthen behavior, while unpleasant or punishing consequences weaken behavior.

Several characteristics distinguish the operant approach to therapy. One is the manner in which clinical problems are conceptualized and defined. Traditional psychotherapy tends to view disturbed behavior as a symptom of an internal psychological conflict; the goal of therapy is to help the individual gain insight into this inner problem. Therapists with an operant orientation, however, view maladaptive behavior as the problem itself. They believe that, just as normal or adaptive behavior is shaped by environmental consequences, so too is abnormal or maladaptive behavior. Therefore, by carefully arranging events in the client's environment, it should be possible to modify maladaptive behavior and help the client learn more appropriate ways of behaving.

The behavior therapist defines problems in terms of specific behaviors that can be observed and quantified. Behavioral excesses involve too much of a specific behavior that can be specified in terms of frequency, intensity, or duration. Chain-smoking, overeating, and physically abusing another person are examples of behavioral excesses. The opposite difficulty is a behavioral deficit. In the case of a behavioral deficit, a behavior either does not occur or occurs at an extremely low rate. An adult who cannot feed or dress himself and a child who rarely talks to other

Operant conditioning therapies evolved from the laboratory research of B.F. Skinner, who derived its basic principles by studying the effects of environmental consequences on lever-pressing behavior in rats. (Alfred A. Knopf)

children exhibit behavioral deficits. Still other behaviors are problematic because they are inappropriate when performed in a particular setting. Taking one's clothes off in public or laughing during a solemn funeral service illustrates behavioral inappropriateness.

Behavioral monitoring is an integral component of operant conditioning therapies. The problem behavior is first observed and recorded as it naturally occurs in a variety of settings, and no attempt is made to modify the behavior. The therapist, a parent, a teacher, a spouse, a peer, or the client may conduct the observation and record the behavior. This part of the behavior-modification program, which is called baseline observation, provides a record of where and when the behavior occurred as well as information about its topography or form, such as duration and intensity. Behavioral measures are often plotted on a graph to provide a visual record of behavior. The baseline data are used to define the problem or target behavior as precisely as possible. The client and therapist also define the desired changes in this target behavior and set up specific behavioral goals to be met during treatment.

Operant techniques that are appropriate for modifying the target behavior are then selected. Therapists begin by selecting the least intrusive and restrictive procedures demonstrated to be effective for treating a specific problem. Since these techniques are based on years of experimental research and evaluation, it is possible for therapists to define explicitly their methods and their rationale to the client. This degree of precision, rarely found in traditional psychotherapy, makes it easier for clients and those working with clients to understand and implement therapeutic procedures.

Behavioral observation continues throughout the treatment phase of the modification program. Behavior is monitored on a regular basis, and changes from the baseline level are recorded. Examination of this ongoing record of behavioral progess allows both therapist and client to evaluate the effectiveness of the treatment at any given time. If behavior is not changing in the desired direction or at the desired pace, the treatment program can be altered or adjusted.

Behavior modifiers often include a follow-up phase as part of the modification program. After termination of treatment, the client may be contacted on a periodic basis to assess whether treatment gains are being maintained. Behavior therapists have discovered that generalization of behavior changes from the therapeutic setting to the natural environment does not occur automatically. An increasing emphasis is being placed on incorporating procedures to facilitate behavior transfer into modification programs. Some therapists have reduced their reliance on tangible reinforcers, such a food or toys, and have stressed the use of social and intrinsic reinforcers, such as positive attention from others and personal feelings of pride and mastery. These are the kinds of reinforcers that are likely to maintain positive behavioral changes in the client's natural setting. Therapists also devote attention to training individuals who will interact with the client after the termination of treatment in the effective use of operant procedures.

Ethical guidelines are followed when conducting a behavior-modification program. Since behavior therapists insist on explicit definition of problem behaviors and treatment methods, this approach facilitates public scrutiny of ethical conduct. Educating the client in the rationale and application of procedures greatly reduces the possibility that operant conditioning techniques will be used in an exploitive or harmful fashion.

Applications

The treatment of behavioral deficits typically involves the application of positive-reinforcement techniques. Positive reinforcement increases the frequency of a response by immediately following the response with a favorable consequence. If the desired behavior does not occur at all, it can be developed by using the shaping procedure. In shaping, successive approximations of the desired behavior are reinforced. Wayne Isaacs, James Thomas, and Israel Goldiamond provided an impressive demonstration of the use of shaping to reinstate verbal behavior in a schizophrenic patient who had been mute for nineteen years. Chewing gum was used as the positive reinforcer, and gum delivery was made contingent first upon eye movements in the direction of the gum, then upon lip movements, then upon any vocalization, and finally upon vocalizations that increasingly approximated actual words. Within six weeks, the patient was conversing with the therapist.

Positive reinforcement is also used to strengthen weak or low-frequency behaviors. Initially, the desired behavior is placed on a continuous reinforcement schedule in which each occurrence of the behavior is followed by reinforcer delivery. Gradually, an intermittent schedule can be introduced, with several responses or a time interval required between successive reinforcer deliveries.

Since people get tired of the same reinforcer and different people find different commodities and activities reinforcing, a token economy system provides another means of programming positive reinforcement. A system that delivers tokens as rewards for appropriate behaviors can be used with a single individual or a group of individuals. Tokens are stimuli such as check marks, points, stickers, or poker chips, which can be accumulated and later exchanged for commodities and activities of the individual's choosing. Tokens can be delivered on a continuous or intermittent schedule of reinforcement and are often accompanied by praise for the desired behavior. Ultimately, the goal of the program is to fade out the use of tokens as more natural social and intrinsic reinforcers begin to maintain behavior.

Extinction and punishment procedures are used to treat behavioral excess. If the reinforcer that is maintaining the excessive behavior can be identified, an extinction program may be effective. Extinction is a procedure that is used to eliminate a response by withholding the reinforcer following performance of the response. A classic demonstration of extinction is a study by Carl Williams designed to eliminate intense tantrum behavior at bedtime in a twenty-one-month-old child. Observation revealed that parental attention was reinforcing tantrums, so the parents were instructed to put the child to bed, close the bedroom door, and not return to the child's room for the rest of the night. This extinction procedure eliminated tantrums in seven nights. Tantrums were then accidentally reinforced by the child's aunt, and a second extinction procedure was instituted. Tantrums were reduced to a zero level by the ninth session, and a two-year follow-up revealed that no further tantrums had occurred.

Punishment procedures decrease the frequency of a response by removing a reinforcing stimulus or by presenting an aversive stimulus immediately following the response. Removal of a positive reinforcer contingent upon performance of the target behavior is called negative punishment or response cost. Some token economy systems incorporate a response cost component, and clients lose tokens when specified inappropriate behaviors are performed. In another form of negative punishment, time-out or sit-out, an individual is moved from a reinforcing environment to one that is devoid of positive reinforcement for a limited amount of time. For example, a child who misbehaves during a classroom game might be seated away from the other children for a few minutes, thereby losing the opportunity to enjoy the game.

The most intrusive behavior-reduction technique is positive punishment, which involves the presentation of an aversive stimulus contingent upon performance of the undesirable behavior. This procedure is used only when other procedures have failed and the behavioral excess is injurious to the client or to others. Thomas Sajwaj and his colleagues employed a positive punishment procedure to reduce life-threatening regurgitation behavior in a six-month-old infant. Within a few minutes of being fed, the infant would begin to bring up the milk she had consumed, and regurgitation continued until all the milk was lost. Treatment consisted of filling the infant's mouth with lemon juice immediately following mouth movements indicative of regurgitation. Regurgitation was reduced to a very low level after sixteen lemon-juice presentations.

Extinction and punishment techniques can produce side effects that include aggressive behavior and fear, escape, and avoidance responses. These can be reduced by combining behavior-reduction procedures with a program of positive reinforcement for desirable alternative behaviors. In this way, the behavioral excess is weakened and the client is simultaneously learning adaptive, socially approved behaviors.

Behaviors that are labeled as inappropriate because of their place of occurrence may be treated using stimulus-discrimination training. This involves teaching the client to express a behavior in the presence of some stimuli and not express the behavior in the presence of other stimuli. For a preschooler who takes his clothes off in a variety of public and private places, discrimination training might involve praising the child when he removes his clothes in his bedroom or the bathroom and using extinction or punishment when clothing removal occurs in other settings. Verbal explanation of the differential contingencies also helps the client learn discrimination.

Perspective and Prospects

Operant conditioning therapies evolved from the laboratory research of B. F. Skinner. In 1938, Skinner published *The Behavior of Organisms*, which outlined the basic principles of operant conditioning that Skinner had derived from the experimental study of the effects of environmental consequences on the lever-pressing behavior of rats. This work stimulated other psychologists to analyze operant behavior in many animal species.

Most early studies with human subjects were designed to replicate and extend this animal research, and they served to demonstrate that operant techniques exerted similar control over human behavior. A literature of operant principles and theory began to accumulate, and researchers referred to this approach to learning as the experimental analysis of behavior.

Some of these human demonstrations were conducted in institutional settings with patients who had not responded well to traditional treatment approaches. The results of such studies suggested that operant procedures could have therapeutic value. In 1959, Teodoro Ayllon and Jack Michael described how staff members could use reinforcement principles to modify the maladaptive behaviors of psychiatric patients. In the 1960's, Sidney Bijou pioneered the use of operant procedures with mentally retarded children and Ivar Lovaas developed an operant program for autistic children.

The 1960's also saw applications in noninstitutional settings. Operant techniques were introduced into school classrooms, university teaching, programs for delinquent youth, marriage counseling, and parent training. Universities began to offer coursework and graduate training programs in the application of operant principles. By the late 1960's, the operant orientation in behavior therapy became known by the terms "behavior modification" and "applied behavior analysis."

During the 1970's, many large-scale applications were instituted. Psychiatric hospitals, schools, prisons, and business organizations began to apply operant principles systematically to improve the performances of large groups of individuals. Another important trend that began in the 1970's was an interest in the self-modification of problem behaviors. Numerous books offered self-training in operant procedures to deal with difficulties in such areas as smoking, drug abuse, nervous habits, stress management, sexual dysfunction, time management, and weight control.

Since the 1980's, operant conditioning therapies have become an integral component of behavioral medicine. Reinforcement techniques are being used in the treatment of chronic pain, eating and sleeping disorders, cardiovascular disorders, and neuromuscular disorders. Operant procedures are also effective in teaching patients adherence to medical instructions and how to make healthy lifestyle changes.

Behavior modifiers continue to direct attention toward public safety and improvement of the physical environment. Therapists are evaluating the effectiveness of operant procedures to combat crime, reduce traffic accidents, and increase the use of seat belts, car pools, and public transportation. Programs are being designed to encourage energy conservation and waste recycling.

Throughout the history of its development, behavior modification has emphasized the use of operant conditioning principles to improve the quality of life for individuals and for society as a whole. Behavior therapists actively support efforts to educate the public in the ethical use of operant techniques for social betterment.

Bibliography

Karoly, Paul, and Anne Harris. "Operant Methods." In *Helping People Change: A*

Textbook of Methods, edited by Frederick H. Kanfer and A. P. Goldstein. New York: Pergamon Press, 1986. A concise and easy-to-follow description of operant methods. Each technique is accompanied by illustrative case studies and recommendations for effective use.

Kazdin, Alan E. *Behavior Modification in Applied Settings*. 5th ed. Pacific Grove, Calif.: Brooks/Cole, 1994. An introduction to behavior modification that can be understood by the high school or college student. Operant techniques are clearly described, with the emphasis on how they are applied in a wide range of settings. Excellent discussion of recent developments in the field.

Lattal, Kennon A., and Michael Perone. *Handbook of Research Methods in Human Operant Behavior*. New York: Perseus, 1998. Describes methods used to study basic behavioral processes. Provides detailed information on specific research problems and more general information about the experimental analysis of human behavior.

Martin, Garry, and Joseph Pear. *Behavior Modification—What It Is and How to Do It*. 6th ed. Upper Saddle River, N.J.: Prentice Hall, 1998. Offers readers personal, hands-on experience with the principles of behavior modification and their application to everyday concerns. Includes bibliographical references and an index.

Rusch, Frank R., Terry Rose, and Charles R. Greenwood. *Introduction to Behavior Analysis in Special Education*. Englewood Cliffs, N.J.: Prentice-Hall, 1988. Intended for students contemplating a teaching career, this book provides a readable introduction to the use of operant techniques with individuals who have learning difficulties. Numerous examples illustrate the educational applications of operant technology.

Sherman, William M. *Behavior Modification*. New York: HarperCollins, 1990. An accessible introduction in which operant techniques are clearly defined and illustrated with case studies. Includes discussion of cognitive behavior modification and behavioral medicine as well as consideration of problems encountered in the implementation of modification programs.

Smith, Terry L. *Behavior and Its Causes: Philosophical Foundations of Operant Psychology*. San Diego: Kluwer Academic, 1994. Defines the place of behavioral psychology within the broader field. Concludes that operant psychology and cognitive psychology complement each other.

Watson, David L., and Roland G. Tharp. *Self-Directed Behavior: Self-Modification for Personal Adjustment*. 7th ed. Pacific Grove, Calif.: Brooks/Cole, 1997. This do-it-yourself guide to behavior changes makes extensive use of principles of reinforcement to help the lay reader improve behaviors in areas such as time management, smoking, overeating, assertiveness, insomnia, budgeting, and social behavior.

Linda J. Palm

See also:

Abnormality: Behavioral Models; Aversion, Implosion, and Systematic Desensitization Therapies; Behavioral Family Therapy; Cognitive Behavior Therapy; Modeling Therapies.

Paranoia

Type of psychology: Psychopathology
Fields of study: Personality disorders; schizophrenias

Paranoia is a pervasive distrust and suspiciousness of others and a tendency to interpret others' motives as malevolent.

Principal terms

DELUSION: a faulty belief involving the misinterpretations of events
ELECTROCONVULSIVE THERAPY: the use of electric shocks to induce seizure as a form of treatment
PARANOID SCHIZOPHRENIA: a chronic mental disorder characterized by delusions and auditory hallucinations
PERSONALITY DISORDER: a disorder in which personality traits are rigid and maladaptive and produce considerable impairment or distress for the individual
PHARMACOTHERAPY: the use of drugs for treatment
PROJECTION: a defense mechanism involving the attribution of aggressive and or sexual feelings to others or to the outside world in order to avoid guilt or anxiety

Causes and Symptoms

Paranoia is characterized by suspiciousness, heightened self-awareness, self-reference, projection of one's ideas onto others, expectations of persecution, and blaming of others for one's difficulties. Conversely, though paranoia can be problematic, it can also be adaptive. In threatening or dangerous situations, paranoia might instigate proactive protective behavior, allowing an individual to negotiate a situation without harm. Thus, paranoia must be assessed in context for it to be understood fully.

Paranoia can be experienced at varying levels of intensity in both normal and highly disordered individuals. As a medical problem, paranoia may take the face of a symptom, personality problem, or chronic mental disorder. As a symptom, it may be evidenced as a fleeting problem; an individual might have paranoid feelings that dissipate in a relatively brief period of time once an acute medical or situational problem is rectified.

As a personality problem, paranoia creates significant impairment and distress as a result of inflexible, maladaptive, and persistent use of paranoid coping strategies. Paranoid individuals often have preoccupations about loyalties, overinterpret situations, maintain expectations of exploitation or deceit, rarely confide in others, bear grudges, perceive attacks that are not apparent to others, and maintain unjustified suspicions about their relationship partner's potential for betrayal. They are prone to angry outbursts, aloof, and controlling, and they may demonstrate a tendency toward vengeful fantasies or actual revenge.

Finally, paranoia may be evidenced as a chronic mental disorder, most notably as the paranoid type of schizophrenia. In paranoid schizophrenia, there is a tendency toward delusions (faulty beliefs involving misinterpretations of events) and auditory hallucinations. Additionally, everyday behavior, speech, and emotional responsiveness are not as disturbed as in other variants of schizophrenia. Typically, these individuals are seen by others as anxious, angry, and aloof. Their delusions usually reflect fears of persecution or hopes for greatness, resulting in jealousies, odd religious beliefs (such as persecution by God, thinking they are Jesus Christ), or preoccupations with their own health (such as the fear of being poisoned or of having a medical disorder of mysterious origin).

Paranoia may best be understood as being determined by a combination of biological, psychological, and environmental factors. It is likely, for example, that certain basic psychological tendencies must be present for an individual to display paranoid feelings and behavior when under stress, as opposed to other feelings such as depression. Additionally, it is likely that certain physical predispositions must be present for stressors to provoke a psychophysiological response.

Biologically, there are myriad physical and mental health conditions that may trigger acute and more chronic paranoid reactions. High levels of situational stress, drug intoxication (such as with amphetamines or marijuana), drug withdrawal, depression, head injuries, organic brain syndromes, pernicious anemia, B vitamin deficiencies, and Klinefelter's syndrome may be related to acute paranoia. Similarly, certain cancers, insidious organic brain syndromes, and hyperparathyroidism have been related to recurrent or chronic episodes of paranoia.

In terms of the etiology of chronic paranoid conditions, such as paranoid schizophrenia and paranoid personality disorder, no clear causes have been identified. Some evidence points to a genetic component; the results of studies on twins and the greater prevalence of these disorders in some families support this view. More psychological theories highlight the family environment and emotional expression, childhood abuse, and stress. In general, these theories point to conditions contributing toward making a person feel insecure, tense, hungry for recognition, and hypervigilant. Additionally, the impact of social, cultural, and economic conditions contributing to the expression of paranoia is important. Paranoia cannot be interpreted out of context. Biological, psychological, and environmental factors must be considered in the development and maintenance of paranoia.

Treatment and Therapy

Three major types of therapies are available to treat paranoia: pharmacotherapies, community-based therapies, and cognitive behavioral therapies. For acute paranoia problems and the management of more chronic, schizophrenia-related paranoia, pharmacotherapy (the use of drugs) is the treatment of choice. Drugs that serve to tranquilize the individual and reduce disorganized thinking, such as phenothiazines and other neuroleptics, are commonly used. With elderly people who cannot tolerate such drugs, electroconvulsive therapy (ECT) has been used for treatment.

Community-based treatment, such as day treatment or in-patient treatment, is also useful for treating chronic paranoid conditions. Developing corrective and instructional social experiences, decreasing situational stress, and helping individuals to feel safe in a treatment environment are primary goals.

Finally, cognitive behavioral therapies focused on identifying irrational beliefs contributing to paranoia-related problems have demonstrated some utility. Skillful therapists help to identify maladaptive thinking while unearthing concerns but not agreeing with the individual's delusional ideas.

Perspective and Prospects

Certain life phases and social and cultural contexts influence behaviors that could be labeled as paranoid. Membership in certain minority or ethnic groups, immigrant or political refugee status, and more generally, language and other cultural barriers may account for behavior that appears to be guarded or paranoid. As such, one can make few assumptions about paranoia without a thorough assessment.

Clinically significant paranoia is notable across cultures, with prevalence rates at any point in time ranging from 0.5 to 2.5 percent of the population. It is a problem manifested by diverse etiological courses requiring equally diverse treatments. Increased knowledge about the relationship among paranoia, depression and other mood disorders, schizophrenia, and the increased prevalence of paranoid disorders in some families will be critical. As the general population ages, a better understanding of more acute paranoid disorders related to medical problems will also be necessary. Better understanding will facilitate the development of more effective pharmacological and nonpharmacological treatments that can be tolerated by the elderly and others suffering from compromising medical problems.

Bibliography

Bellenir, Karen, ed. *Mental Health Disorders Sourcebook: Basic Consumer Health Information About Anxiety Disorders, Depression, and Other Mood Disorders.* 2d ed. Detroit: Omnigraphics, 2000. A volume on mental illness in the health reference series. Includes a bibliography and an index.

McKay, Matthew, Peter D. Rogers, and Judith McKay. *When Anger Hurts: Quieting the Storm Within.* Oakland, Calif.: New Harbinger, 1989. An in-depth exploration of anger, its consequences and alternatives.

Munro, Alistair. *Delusional Disorder: Paranoia and Related Illnesses.* New York: Cambridge University Press, 1999. Provides a comprehensive review of delusional disorder. Begins with the emergence of the concept of delusional disorder and then details its manifold presentations, differential diagnosis, and treatment. Illustrated with case histories.

Robbins, Michael. *Experiences of Schizophrenia.* New York: Guilford Press, 1993. Arranged in five parts: "The Groundwork," "Cases: The Extremes of Outcome," "Viewpoints on Schizophrenia: A Pluralistic Model," "The Treatment of Schizophrenia," "Cases: The Middle Range of Outcome," and "Conclusion." Includes bibliographical references and indexes.

Shapiro, David. *Neurotic Styles.* New York: Basic Books, 1999. Originally published in 1965. A classic study of four kinds of neuroses—obsessive-compulsive, paranoid, hysterical, and impulsive—and the special characteristics of each. A landmark work in clinical psychology used as required reading in many courses.

Siegel, Ronald K. *Whispers: The Voices of Paranoia*. New York: Crown, 1994. Draws on actual case studies to shed light on the terrifying implications of this disease. Lets readers experience the suspicion, terror, and rage that possess the mind of the paranoid.

Nancy A. Piotrowski

See also:

Anxiety Disorders; Cognitive Behavior Therapy; Cognitive Therapy; Neurosis; Schizophrenia.

PERSON-CENTERED THERAPY

Type of psychology: Psychotherapy
Fields of study: Humanistic therapies

Person-centered therapy is based on a philosophy that emphasizes an inherent human tendency for growth and self-actualization. Psychologist Carl Rogers developed and described person-centered therapy as a "way of being."

Principal terms

CONGRUENCE: the consistency or correspondence among thoughts, experience, and behavior

EMPATHY: the focusing of the therapist's attention on the needs and experience of the client; also refers to the therapist's ability to communicate an understanding of the client's emotional state

GENUINENESS: a characteristic in which the therapist does not act out a professional role but instead acts congruently with his or her own sensory and emotional experience

PHENOMENOLOGY: a method of exploration in which subjective and/or experiential data are accepted without any need for further analysis

SELF: an existing picture of oneself; perceptions of "I" or "me" either in relationships with others or by oneself

SELF-ACTUALIZATION: a biologically and culturally determined process involving a tendency toward growth and full realization of one's potential

UNCONDITIONAL POSITIVE REGARD: the attempt by a therapist to convey to a client that he or she genuinely cares for the client

Overview

Psychologist Carl R. Rogers (1902-1987) was the leading figure in the development of phenomenological therapy, and his name has been used synonymously ("Rogerian" therapy) with person-centered therapy. Phenomenological theory is a method of exploration that emphasizes all aspects of human experience. In particular, it highlights the importance of an individual's creative power, in addition to genetics and environment. Moreover, this theory focuses primarily on a person's subjective experience (opinions, viewpoints, and understandings) and defines therapy on the basis of a good human-to-human relationship.

Rogers remained primarily concerned with the conditions for personal growth rather than with the development of personality theory; he focused on personality functioning rather than on personality structures. He did, however, offer formal conceptions of personality. The central concepts and key formulations of person-centered therapy were published in Rogers's *Counseling and Psychotherapy: Newer Concepts in Practice* (1942), *On Becoming a Person* (1961), and his

landmark book *Client-Centered Therapy* (1951). Rogers presented nineteen propositions about personality development. These propositions included the following
concepts: Each individual exists in a continually changing world in which he or
she is the center. Individuals react to the world as they experience and perceive it;
thus, "reality" is defined by the person's phenomenal field. Behavior is basically
the goal-directed attempt of the organism to satisfy its needs as experienced in the
phenomenal field. Each individual has a unique perspective—his or her own
private world—and to comprehend a person one must assume a frame of reference
from the person's perspective. Emotion facilitates goal-directed behavior. The
structure of the self is formed as a result of evaluative interactions with others; the
self is an organized, fluid, yet consistent pattern of perceptions about oneself.

The phenomenal field refers to everything experienced by an individual at any
given time. The term "internal frame of reference" refers to the process by which
therapists attempt to perceive clients' experiences and "reality" as closely as they
can. An individual's reality is essentially that which the person perceives. Moreover, it is the person's subjective experience and perceptions that shape the
person's understanding of reality and guide behavior. Events are significant for an
individual if the individual experiences them as meaningful. In treatment, therapists strive to understand clients by understanding their views of themselves and
the environment in which they live.

A central concept within phenomenological theory is the "self" (a structure
derived from experiences involving one's own body or resulting from one's own
actions). The self (or self-concept), then, is a self-picture or self-awareness. It is a
changing process that incorporates the individual's meaning when he or she refers
to the characteristics of "I" or "me" in isolation or in relationships with others. The
concept of self is also considered to be an organized, consistent, and learned
attribute composed of thoughts about self. Rogers views the need for positive
regard to be universal. The self-concept depends, in large part, on the "conditions
of worth" that a child has learned through interactions with significant others.
According to Rogers, the child's need to maintain the love of parents inevitably
results in conflict with his or her own needs and desires. For example, as young
children assert greater autonomy, a growing awareness of individuality and uniqueness follows. Quite often, the young child demonstrates a negativistic pattern
wherein conflicts become more common as the child's needs are in conflict with
parent desires.

Maladjustment occurs when there is a lack of consistency between one's concept
of self and one's sensory and visceral experiences. If the self-concept is based on
many conditions of worth and includes components of failure, imperfection, and
weakness, then a lack of positive self-regard will be evident. When such incongruence occurs, individuals are viewed as being vulnerable to psychological
problems. Of particular importance is self-esteem (feelings about self), which is
often negative or problematic in clients. Poor self-esteem occurs when the phenomenal self is threatened. A threat for one person is not necessarily a threat for
another. A person will experience threat whenever he or she perceives that the
phenomenal self is in danger. For example, if a well-adjusted athlete misses the

final shot at the buzzer in a close basketball game, he or she will not blame the referees or claim physical illness, but instead will examine this experience and perhaps revise his or her self-concept.

Other key principles that underlie person-centered theory involve the processes of self-direction and self-actualization. According to Rogers, humans have an innate tendency to maintain and enhance the self. In fact, all needs can be summarized as the urge to enhance the phenomenal self. Although the process of self-actualization may become disrupted by a variety of social, interpersonal, and cultural factors (determined in large part by the actions of parents, teachers, and peers), Rogers states that the positive growth tendency will ultimately prevail. This actualizing tendency is what produces the forward movement of life, the primary force upon which therapists rely heavily in therapy with clients. Self-actualization refers to the concept that unhampered individuals strive to actualize, enhance, and reach their full potential.

Via self-actualization, a person becomes a fully functioning individual. The qualities of a fully functioning person include being open to experience all feelings while being afraid of none; demonstrating creativity and individual expression; living in the present without preoccupation with past or future; being free to make choices and act on those choices spontaneously; trusting oneself and human nature; having an internal source of evaluation; demonstrating balance and realistic expressions of anger, aggression, and affection; exhibiting congruence between one's feelings and experience; and showing a willingness to continue to grow.

"Congruence" is the term used by Rogers and others to imply the correspondence between awareness and experience. If a client is able to communicate an awareness of feelings that he or she is currently experiencing, the behavior is said to be congruent or integrated. On the other hand, if an individual attempts to communicate a feeling (love, for example) to another person while experiencing incongruence (hostility toward that person), the recipient of that individual's expression of feelings may experience an awareness of miscommunication.

Person-centered theory and therapy have evolved since the 1940's. When Rogers published *Counseling and Psychotherapy* (1942), the predominant view among mental health professionals was that the therapist should act as an expert who directs the course of treatment. Rogers, however, described counseling as a relationship in which warmth, responsiveness, and freedom from coercion and pressure (including pressure from the therapist) are essential. Such an approach to treatment emphasized the client's ability to take positive steps toward personal growth. This phase, from 1940 to 1950, has been referred to as Rogers's nondirective period. The second phase, reflective psychotherapy, spanned the years from 1950 to 1957. During this period, Rogers changed the name of his approach to "client-centered counseling" and emphasized the importance of reflecting (paraphrasing, summarizing, and clarifying) the client's underlying feelings.

The third phase, experiential psychotherapy, has been described as lasting from 1957 to 1970. During this phase, Rogers focused on the conditions that would be necessary and sufficient for change to occur. Results of his studies demonstrated that the most successful clients were those who experienced the highest degree of accurate empathy, and that client ratings, rather than therapist ratings, of the quality of the therapeutic relationship were most closely associated with eventual success or failure. Also evident during this phase of development was his de-emphasis of psychotherapy techniques, such as reflection. Instead, Rogers focused more on the importance of basic therapist attitudes. By so doing, a wider range of therapist behaviors was encouraged in order to establish the essential relationship components of empathy, positive regard, and congruence. Therapists were encouraged to attend to their own experiences in the session and express their immediate feelings in the therapy relationship.

In 1974, Rogers changed the name of his approach to person-centered therapy. Rogers believed that person-centered therapy more appropriately described the human values that his approach incorporates. Since the 1970's, an additional phase of person-centered therapy, incorporating a more eclectic approach to treatment, has evolved. Specifically, person-centered therapists frequently employ strategies that focus on thoughts, feelings, and values from other schools of psychotherapy within the framework of a productive, accepting relationship. Person-centered approaches have been successfully incorporated into teaching and educational curricula, marriage programs, and international conflict-resolution situations.

Applications

Person-centered therapy aims to increase the congruence, or matching, between self-concept and organismic experience. As Rogers described it, psychotherapy serves to "free up" the already existing capacity in a potentially competent individual, rather than consisting of the expert manipulation of techniques designed to change personality. The primary mechanism for reintegration of self and experience is the interpersonal relationship between therapist and client. In fact, the therapeutic relationship is viewed as being of primary importance in promoting healing and growth. Thus, it is this relationship in and of itself that produces growth in the client. Rogers argues that the process of therapy is synonymous with the experiential relationship between client and therapist; change occurs primarily as a result of the interaction between them.

As described by N. J. Raskin and Rogers (1989), the most fundamental concept in person-centered therapy is trust—that is, trust in clients' growth tendency toward actualization, and trust in clients' ability to achieve their own goals and run their own lives. Similarly, it is important that the therapist be seen as a person in the relationship (not as a role), and that the therapist be appreciated and regarded with trust. Rogers stated that clients enter treatment in a state of incongruence, often resulting in vulnerability and anxiety. For treatment to be effective, he identified three necessary and sufficient ingredients for constructive change: The counselor experiences empathic understanding of the client's internal frame of reference, the counselor experiences unconditional positive regard for the client, and the counselor acts congruently with his or her own experience, becoming genuinely integrated into the relationship with the client. It is also essential to the therapy process that the counselor succeed in communicating unconditional positive regard, genuineness, and empathic understanding to the client.

Of particular importance is empathy. Empathy reflects an attitude of interest in the client's thoughts, feelings, and experiences. Moreover, Rogers describes empathy as "a way of being" that is powerfully curative because of its nonevaluative and accepting quality. In fact, the process of conveying accurate empathic understanding has been described as the most important aspect of the therapeutic endeavor. Therapists who convey this form of sensitivity to the needs, feelings, and circumstances of the client can in essence climb inside the client's subjective experience and attempt to understand the world as he or she does. Empathy facilitates a process through which clients assume a caring attitude toward themselves. Moreover, empathy allows clients to gain a greater understanding of their own organismic experiencing, which in turn, facilitates positive self-regard and a more accurate self-concept.

In perhaps all of their previous relationships, clients have learned that acceptance is conditional upon acting in an acceptable manner. For example, parents typically accept children if they do as they are told. In therapy, however, Rogers argued that no conditions of worth should be present. Acceptance of the client as a fallible yet essentially trustworthy individual is given without ulterior motives, hidden causes, or subtle disclaimers. The primary challenge of the therapist's unconditional positive regard comes with clients whose behavior and attitude run strongly counter to the therapist's beliefs. A sex offender, an abusive parent, or a lazy client can test a therapist's level of tolerance and acceptance. Rogers's position is that every individual is worthy of unconditional positive regard.

Genuineness refers to the characteristic of being congruent—the experience of therapists who appropriately express the behavior, feelings, and attitudes that the client stimulates in them. For example, a person does not laugh when sad or angry. Similarly, acting congruently with one's own emotional experience does not mean hiding behind a mask of calm when a client makes upsetting statements. Rogers believed that, in the long run, clients would respond best to a "real person" who is dedicated to the client's welfare and acts in an honest and congruent manner.

In person-centered treatment, sessions are usually scheduled once or twice a week. Additional sessions and telephone calls are typically discouraged in order to avoid dependency on the therapist that will stifle personal growth. Rogers has described the general process of therapy as involving a series of seven steps. Step one is an initial unwillingness to reveal self and an avoidance of feelings; close relationships may be perceived as threatening or dangerous. In step two, feelings are described briefly, but the person is still distant from his or her own personal experience and externalizes issues; the person begins to show recognition that conflicts and difficulties exist. In step three, describing past feelings becomes unacceptable; there is more self-disclosure and expression, and the client begins to question the validity of his or her constructs and beliefs.

Step four involves the description of personal feelings as owned by the self and a limited recognition that previously denied feelings may exist; there is an increasing expression of self-responsibility. Step five involves the free expression and acceptance of one's feelings, an awareness of previously denied feelings, a recognition of conflicts between intellectual and emotional processes, and a desire to be who one really is. In step six, there is an acceptance of feelings without the need for denial and a willingness to risk being oneself in relationships with others. In step seven, the person is comfortable with his or her self, is aware of new feelings and experiences, and experiences minimal incongruence.

Perspective and Prospects

As Carl Rogers began his career during the late 1930's, psychoanalysis was the primary approach to psychotherapy and the dominant model in personality theory. Though Rogers was subjected to traditional psychoanalytic influences, his perspective was nearly the exact opposite of Sigmund Freud's theory; Rogers tended to reject the notion of unconscious processes. Instead, he was strongly influenced by the therapeutic approach of psychoanalyst Otto Rank (and his followers at the University of Pennsylvania School of Social Work), the relationship therapy of social worker Jessie Taft, and the feeling-focused approach of social worker Elizabeth Davis. Rank believed that clients benefit from the opportunity to express themselves in session, exhibit creativity in treatment, and even dominate the therapist. Taft emphasized that there are key components to the therapeutic relationship (including a permissive therapeutic environment and a positive working relationship between the therapist and client) which are more important than psychoanalytic explanations of the client's problems. Davis focused almost exclusively on the feelings being expressed in treatment by her clients. From his association with Davis, Rogers developed the therapy component referred to as reflection of feelings. Rogers believed strongly that no individual has the right to run another person's life. Thus, his therapeutic approach was generally permissive and accepting, and he generally refused to give advice to clients.

Person-centered approaches have made major contributions to therapy, theory, and empirical research. In fact, Rogers was responsible for the first systematic investigations of the therapeutic process. He was the first to employ recordings of therapy sessions to study the interactive process and to investigate its effectiveness. Although the use of such recordings is now commonplace in most training programs, Rogers's willingness to open his approach to such scrutiny was unusual for its time.

Person-centered therapy has generated numerous research contributions. A 1971 review of research on "necessary and sufficient" conditions concluded that counselors who are accurately empathic, genuine, and nonpossessively warm tend to be effective with a broad spectrum of clients regardless of the counselors' training or theoretical orientation. The authors also concluded that clients receiving low levels of such conditions in treatment showed deterioration. Many researchers have questioned the "necessary and sufficient" argument proposed by Rogers, however; they suggest that the therapeutic conditions specified by Rogers are neither necessary nor sufficient, although such therapeutic approaches are facilitative.

Although Rogers's approach was developed primarily for counseling clients, the person-centered approach has found many other applications. Person-centered approaches are frequently used in human relations training, including paraprofessional counselors, Young Women's Christian Association (YWCA) and Young

Men's Christian Association (YMCA) volunteers, crisis center volunteers, Peace Corps and VISTA workers, and charitable organization workers. Small group therapy programs and personal growth groups also make frequent use of person-centered approaches.

Bibliography

Farber, Barry A., Debora C. Brink, and Patricia M. Raskin, eds. *The Psychotherapy of Carl Rogers: Cases and Commentary*. Foreword by Maria Villas-Boas Bowen. New York: Guilford Press, 1996. An in-depth examination of the work of this pioneer. Presents ten sessions representing a range of client difficulties and therapeutic responses from Rogers. Analyzes the strengths and weaknesses of each interaction.

Raskin, N. J., and Carl R. Rogers. "Person-Centered Therapy." In *Current Psychotherapies*, edited by Raymond J. Corsini and Danny Wedding. 4th ed. Itasca, Ill.: F. E. Peacock, 1989. One of the last projects that Rogers worked on prior to his death in 1987. Raskin knew Rogers for forty-seven years, and in this chapter he summarizes many of the key principles and concepts associated with person-centered therapy.

Rogers, Carl R. *Client-Centered Therapy*. Boston: Houghton Mifflin, 1951. A landmark text wherein Rogers highlights many of the key components of his evolving approach. The book describes aspects of the therapeutic relationship and the process of therapy.

_____. *Counseling and Psychotherapy: Newer Concepts in Practice*. Boston: Houghton Mifflin, 1942. Rogers's first book-length description of his approach to therapy. This book is of historical significance because it presents a revised version of Rogers's address at the University of Minnesota on December 11, 1940, at which time client-centered therapy was "officially" born.

_____. *On Becoming a Person*. Boston: Houghton Mifflin, 1961. One of Rogers's best-known and most highly regarded books. Presents valuable insight into Rogers, his approach, and the uses of client-centered approaches in education, family life, and elsewhere.

_____. *A Way of Being*. Boston: Houghton Mifflin, 1980. Rogers wrote this book as a follow-up to *On Becoming a Person*, and in it he updates his theory and therapeutic approach. An excellent bibliography is also included.

Silverstone, Liesl. *Art Therapy the Person-Centered Way: Art and the Development of the Person*. 2d ed. Philadelphia: J. Kinsley, 1997. An enlarged edition of the first book published on person-centred art therapy. Demonstrates that by bringing the person-centred facilitative approach to images expressed in art form, healing and growth can occur at every level of development.

Gregory L. Wilson

See also:

Abnormality: Behavioral Models; Abnormality: Cognitive Models; Abnormality: Humanistic-Existential Models; Abnormality: Psychodynamic Models; Analytical Psychotherapy; Cognitive Behavior Therapy; Cognitive Therapy; Psychoanalysis; Psychotherapy: Goals and Techniques.

PERSONALITY
Psychophysiological Measures

Type of psychology: Personality
Fields of study: Personality assessment

Psychophysiological studies comparing individuals with different personality traits have sought to determine the physical characteristics of particular behavioral characteristics. Such research can provide information that helps clarify the importance of various personality types with regard to risk of psychological and physical disorders.

Principal terms

ANXIETY SENSITIVITY: the tendency to fear sensations associated with anxiety because of beliefs that anxiety may cause illness, embarrassment, or additional anxiety

HARDINESS: a constellation of behaviors and perceptions thought to buffer the effects of stress; characterized by perceptions of control, commitment, and challenge

LOCUS OF CONTROL: individual perception of the world and evaluation of the amount of control the individual has over his or her own successes and failures

PERSONALITY: a relatively enduring set of behaviors that characterize the individual

PSYCHOPHYSIOLOGY: the scientific study of cognitive, emotional, and behavioral phenomena as related to and revealed through physiological principles and events

TYPE A BEHAVIOR PATTERN: a constellation of behaviors—competitiveness, time urgency, and hostility—thought to place the individual at risk for disease, particularly heart disease

Overview

A broad definition of personality typically includes the dimensions of stability, determinism, and uniqueness. That is, personality changes little over time, is determined by internal processes and external factors, and reflects an individual's distinctive qualities. Personality also can be thought of as unique, relatively stable patterns of behavior, multiply determined over the course of an individual's life. There are many theories for understanding the development of these patterns of behavior.

Twin studies have provided evidence that biological factors help to shape personality; such studies support Hans Eysenck's theory that personality is inherited. The psychodynamic perspective holds that personality is determined primarily by early childhood experiences. Some of the most influential contributions to this perspective came from Sigmund Freud. He argued that unconscious forces govern behavior and that childhood experiences strongly shape adult personality via coping strategies people use to deal with sexual urges. B. F. Skinner, founder of modern behavioral psychology, assumed that personality (or behavior) is determined solely by environmental factors. More specifically, he believed that consequences of behavior are instrumental in the development of unique, relatively stable patterns of behavior in individuals. According to Albert Bandura's social learning perspective, models have a great impact on personality development. That is, patterns of behavior in individuals are influenced by the observation of others. Finally, the humanistic perspective of Carl Rogers suggests that personality is largely determined by the individual's unique perception of reality in comparison to his or her self-concept.

Assessment of personality can be accomplished from three domains: subjective experience, behavior, and physiology. Traditional means for assessing personality have included objective and projective paper-and-pencil or interview measurements that tap the domain of subjective experience. Behavioral assessment techniques such as direct observation of behavior, self-monitoring (having the individual record occurrences of his or her own behavior), self-report questionnaires, role-play scenarios, and behavioral avoidance tests (systematic, controlled determination of how close an individual can approach a feared object or situation) tap the domains of subjective experience and objective behavior. These techniques have been used in clinical settings to aid in the diagnosis and treatment of deviant or abnormal behavior patterns.

Although psychophysiological measurement of personality has not gained popular use in clinical settings, it complements the techniques mentioned above and contributes to understanding the nature and development of psychological and physical disorders. Just as patterns of responding on traditional personality tests can indicate the possibility of aberrant behavior, so too can tests of physiological patterns. Typical measures taken during this type of assessment include heart rate, blood pressure, muscle tension (measured via electromyography), brain-wave activity (measured via electroencephalography), skin temperature, and palmar sweat gland or electrodermal activity. These measures of physiological activity are sensitive to "emotional" responses to various stimuli and have been instrumental in clarifying the nature of certain psychological and physical conditions. One of the fundamental assumptions of psychophysiology is that the responses of the body can help reveal the mechanisms underlying human behavior and personality.

Physiological responsivity can be assessed in a number of different ways. Two primary methodologies are used in the study of the relations between personality and physiology. The first method simply looks at resting or baseline differences of various physiological measures across individuals who either possess or do not possess the personality characteristic of interest. The second method also assesses individuals with or without the characteristic of interest, but does this under specific stimulus or situational conditions rather than during rest. This is often referred to as measuring reactivity to the stimulus or situational condition. Resting physiological measures are referred to as tonic activity (activity evident in the absence of any known stimulus event). It is postulated that tonic activity is relatively enduring and stable within the individual while at rest, although it can be influenced by external factors. It is both of interest in its own right and important in determining the magnitude of response to a stimulus. On the other hand, phasic activity is a discrete response to a specific stimulus. This type of activity is suspected to be influenced to a much greater extent by external factors and tends to be less stable than tonic activity. Both types of activity, tonic and phasic, are important in the study of personality and physiology.

Standard laboratory procedures are typically employed to investigate tonic activity and phasic responses to environmental stimuli. For example, a typical assessment incorporating both methodologies might include the following phases: a five-minute baseline to collect resting physiological measures, a five-minute presentation of a task or other stimulus suspected to differentiate individuals in each group based on their physiological response or change from baseline, and a five-minute recovery to assess the nature and rate of physiological recovery from the task or stimulus condition. Investigations focusing on the last phase attempt to understand variations in recovery as a response pattern in certain individuals. For example, highly anxious individuals tend to take much longer to recover physiologically from stimulus presentations that influence heart rate and electrodermal activity than individuals who report low levels of anxiety.

Studies of physiological habituation—the decline or disappearance of response to a discrete stimulus—also have been used to investigate personality differences. Physiological responses to a standard tone, for example, eventually disappear with repeated presentations of the tone. The rate at which they disappear varies across individuals; the disappearance generally takes longer in individuals who tend to be anxious. Thus, individuals who tend to have anxious traits may be more physiologically responsive, recover from the response less rapidly, and habituate to repeated stimulation more slowly than those who tend to be less anxious. Such physiological differences may be an important characteristic that determines anxious behavior and/or results from subjective feelings of anxiousness.

Applications

Research has demonstrated that there is considerable variability across individuals in their physiological response patterns, both at rest and in response to various situational stimuli or laboratory manipulations. Evidence indicates that part of this variability across individuals may in some cases be attributable to certain personality traits or characteristic patterns of behavior. Furthermore, research suggests that these personality traits may also be related to the development of psychological or physical disorders. Although the causal links are not well understood, a growing body of research points to relations among personality, physiological measures, and psychopathology/health.

Examples of these relationships are evident in the field of psychopathology, or the study of abnormal behavior. Hans Eysenck proposed that the general characteristics of introversion and extroversion lead individuals to interact very differently with their environment. Some psychophysiological studies support this notion and suggest that the behaviors characteristic of these traits may be driven by physiological differences. Anxiety sensitivity and locus of control are two personality traits that some suggest are related to the development of anxiety disorders and depression, respectively. To varying degrees, anxiety disorders and depression have been investigated in the psychophysiology laboratory and have been found to differentiate individuals with high and low levels of the personality trait, based on their physiological responses.

Introversion describes the tendency to minimize interaction with the environment; extroversion is characterized by the opposite behaviors, or the tendency to interact more with the environment. Eysenck proposed that such traits reflect physiological differences that are genetically determined and reflected in the individual's physiology. Introverted individuals are thought to be chronically physiologically hyperaroused and thus seek to minimize their arousal by minimizing external stimulation. Extroverted individuals are believed to be chronically physiologically underaroused and thus seek a more optimal level of arousal through increased environmental stimulation. It should be easy to confirm or disprove such a theory with psychophysiological studies of resting physiological activity in introverts and extroverts. Electroencephalograph (EEG) studies have produced contradictory evidence about the validity of Eysenck's theory, however; problems in EEG methodology, experimental design, and measurement of the traits themselves have led to considerable confusion about whether the traits actually do have a physiological basis.

Anxiety sensitivity describes the tendency for individuals to fear sensations they associate with anxiety because of beliefs that anxiety may result in harmful consequences. Research in the development and assessment of this construct was pioneered by Steven Reiss and his associates in the late 1980's. They developed a sixteen-item questionnaire, the Anxiety Sensitivity Index (ASI), to measure anxiety sensitivity and found it to be both reliable and valid. Anxiety sensitivity has been most closely related to panic disorder, an anxiety disorder characterized by frequent, incapacitating episodes of extreme fear or discomfort. In fact, as a group, individuals with panic disorder score higher on the ASI than individuals with any other anxiety disorder. Furthermore, some researchers have demonstrated that individuals scoring high on the ASI are five times more likely to develop an anxiety disorder after a three-year follow-up.

Research investigating responses to arithmetic, caffeine, and hyperventilation challenge in the laboratory has demonstrated that individual differences in anxiety sensitivity levels are probably more closely related to the subjective experience of anxiousness than to actual physiological changes. Individuals high and low on anxiety sensitivity, however, have exhibited differential heart-rate reactivity to a mental arithmetic stressor. That is, individuals high on anxiety sensitivity show a greater acceleration in heart rate than individuals low on anxiety sensitivity when engaging in an arithmetic challenge. Individuals scoring high on the ASI also more accurately perceive actual changes in their physiology when compared with their low-scoring counterparts. Such heightened reactivity and sensitivity to physiological change may partially explain how anxiety sensitivity influences the development of anxiety disorders. Individuals high in anxiety sensitivity may be more reactive to environmental threat; therefore, their increased sensitivity may have a physiological basis. They also may be more likely to detect changes in their physiology, which they are then more likely to attribute to threat or danger.

On a more general note, cardiovascular and electrodermal measures can differentiate between anxiety patients and other people at rest. The differences become greater under conditions of stimulation. Delayed habituation rates in anxiety patients are also part of the pattern of physiological overarousal typically seen in individuals with heightened anxiety. Indeed, heightened physiological arousal is one of the hallmark characteristics of anxiety.

Locus of control, made popular by Julian Rotter in the 1960's, refers to individuals' perceptions of whether they have control over what happens to them across situations. This personality construct has been related to the development of depression. Specifically, it is believed that individuals who attribute failures to internal factors (self-blame) and successes to external factors (to other people or to luck) are more susceptible to developing feelings of helplessness, often followed by despair and depression. Locus of control also is hypothesized to have implications in the management of chronic health-related problems.

In oversimplified categorizations, individuals are labeled to have an "internal" or "external" locus of control. "External" individuals, who believe they have little control over what happens to them, are said to be more reactive to threat, more emotionally labile, more hostile, and lower in self-esteem and self-control. Psychophysiological assessment studies have revealed heart-rate acceleration and longer electrodermal habituation for "externals" in response to the presentation of tones under passive conditions. When faced with no-control conditions in stress situations such as inescapable shock, "internals" show elevated physiological arousal, while findings for "externals" are mixed. Thus, the locus of control has varying effects on physiology, depending on the circumstances. Such effects may play a role in psychological disorders such as depression and anxiety. Heightened physiological reactivity may also inhibit recovery from acute illness or affect the course of chronic health problems such as hypertension.

In addition to the relevance of personality to physiological reactivity and psychopathology, research has demonstrated that certain personality types may be risk factors or serve protective functions with regard to physical health. Type A behavior pattern and hardiness are two examples. Type A behavior pattern is characterized by competitiveness, time urgency, and hostility. It has been identified as a potential risk factor for the development of coronary heart disease. Psychophysiological studies have suggested that, under certain laboratory conditions, males who exhibit the Type A pattern are more cardiovascularly responsive. This reactivity is the proposed mechanism by which Type A behavior affects the heart. More recent research has suggested that not all components of the Type A pattern are significantly associated with heightened cardiovascular reactivity. Hostility seems to be the most critical factor in determining heightened reactivity. Males who respond to stress with hostility tend to show greater heart-rate and blood-pressure increases than individuals low in hostility. It is unclear whether hostility is a risk factor for heart disease in women.

In contrast to hostility, hardiness is proposed to buffer the effects of stress on physiology. Hardy individuals respond to stressors as challenges and believe that they have control over the impact of stressors. They also feel commitment to their life, including work and family. Psychophysiological studies have supported the buffering effect of hardiness. Individuals who are more hardy tend to be less physiologically responsive to stressors and to recover from stressors more rapidly. Again, the construct of hardiness seems to be more relevant for males, partially because males have been studied more often.

These studies show that various personality types can be distinguished to varying degrees by psychophysiological measurement. The implications of such findings include possible physiological contributions to the development of various psychological problems, and personality contributions to the development or course of physical disease.

Perspective and Prospects

Although the sophisticated techniques and instruments that have enabled psychologists to study physiological events were not developed until the twentieth century, the notion that physiology and psychology (body and mind) are linked dates back as far as ancient Greece. Hippocrates, for example, described four bodily humors or fluids thought to influence various psychological states such as melancholy and mania. Although the link between mind and body has received varying degrees of importance in scientific thinking across the centuries, it regained prominence in the mid-1900's with the development of the field of psychosomatic medicine along with the widespread influence of Sigmund Freud's theories of personality. Psychosomatic medicine embraced the notion that personality and physiology are intertwined. Psychosomatic theorists believed that certain diseases, such as diabetes, asthma, and hypertension, were associated with particular personality characteristics. They suggested that personality influenced the development of specific diseases. Although much of this theorizing has been disproved, these theorists did return the focus to investigating the interactive nature of a person's psychological and physiological makeup.

Psychophysiologists acknowledge the influence of personality characteristics on physiology and vice versa, and they are working to characterize these relationships. Future work will better measure particular personality constructs and will clarify the interaction of gender with personality and physiology. Psychophysiologists also must be concerned with the external validity of the data they obtain in the laboratory. It has not been satisfactorily demonstrated that physiological responses measured in a given individual in the laboratory are at all related to that individual's response in the natural environment. Thus, in order to establish fully the usefulness of laboratory findings, psychophysiologists must also study individuals in their natural environments. Recent technological advances will enable ongoing physiological measurement, which should achieve this goal and further establish the relations among personality, physiology, and behavior.

Bibliography

Andreassi, John L. *Psychophysiology: Human Behavior and Physiological Response*. Mahwah, N.J.: Lawrence Erlbaum Associates, 2000. A comprehensive overview to psychophysiology. Provides information on the anatomy and physiology of various body systems, methods of recording their activity, and ways in which these measures relate to human behavior.

Eysenck, Hans J. *The Biological Basis of Personality*. Springfield, Ill.: Charles C Thomas, 1967. This older book provides a thorough, in-depth discussion of Eysenck's theories of the relations between neuroticism, introversion, and extroversion with physiology.

Hugdahl, Kenneth. *Psychophysiology: The Mind-Body Perspective*. Cambridge, Mass.: Harvard University Press, 1995. Illustrates the importance of psychophysiology as a research and clinical tool and highlights its many contributions to the assessment and diagnosis of physical disorders.

Kohnstamm, Geldolph A., and Mary K. Rothbart, eds. *Temperment in Childhood*. New York: John Wiley & Sons, 1997. Addresses major topics in childhood temperament in such areas as concepts and measures, biological bases of individual differences in temperament, developmental issues, applications of temperament research in clinical and educational settings, and sociocultural and other group factors.

Pennebaker, James W. *The Psychology of Physical Symptoms*. New York: Springer-Verlag, 1982. Pennebaker discusses his theories about the influence of individual differences in the experience of health and illness. He also provides an overview of some of the research that supports his views.

Stern, Robert Morris, William J. Ray, and Christopher M. Davis. *Psychophysiological Recording*. New York: Oxford University Press, 1980. The authors provide an excellent, readable introduction to basic principles of psychophysiology. Part 2, the main body of the text, covers physiology of and recording procedures for the brain, muscles, eyes, respiratory system, gastrointestinal system, cardiovascular system, and skin. Illustrations depicting typical recordings and a glossary of psychophysiological terms are helpful additions.

Surwillo, Walter W. *Psychophysiology for Clinical Psychologists*. Norwood, N.J.: Ablex, 1990. This text provides basic knowledge of psychophysiology and highlights some areas of application. Surwillo also incorporates helpful diagrams and relevant references for research in the area.

Weiten, Wayne, Margaret A. Lloyd, and R. L. Lashley. "Theories of Personality." In *Psychology Applied to Modern Life: Adjustment in the 90's*. Pacific Grove, Calif.: Brooks/Cole, 1991. This text, written for undergraduate students, provides the reader with a very readable chapter on personality and theories of personality development. Other chapters highlight the dynamics of adjustment, interpersonal factors, developmental transitions, and the impact that personality and styles of coping can have on psychological and physical health.

Virginia L. Goetsch
Lois Veltum

See also:

Abnormality: Behavioral Models; Addictive Personality and Behaviors; Antisocial Personality; Behavioral Assessment and Personality Rating Scales; Borderline, Histrionic, and Narcissistic Personalities; Codependent Personality; Projective Personality Traits; Type A Behavior Pattern.

PHOBIAS

Type of psychology: Psychopathology
Fields of study: Anxiety disorders

Phobias are excessive fears of certain objects, people, places, or situations.

Principal terms

AGORAPHOBIA: a flight reaction caused by the fear of places and predicaments outside a sphere of safety

DESENSITIZATION: a behavioral technique of gradually removing anxiety associated with certain situations by associating them with a relaxed state

SIMPLE PHOBIAS: fears directed toward specific things, animals, phenomena, or situations

SOCIAL PHOBIAS: fears of being watched or judged by others in social settings

Causes and Symptoms

Phobias can induce a state of anxiety or panic, often debilitating sufferers, restricting them from full freedom of action, career progress, or sociability. For example, a heterosexual person who fears talking with the opposite sex will have problems dating and progressing socially.

Phobias are caused by perceived dangerous experiences, both real and imagined. Sometimes, it is gradual: A worker may develop anxiety reactions to a boss over several weeks. Likewise, a single moment of terror can cause a lifetime of avoidance: A dog attack can generate cynophobia (fear of dogs) in a child. Children are especially susceptible to phobias, most of which are caused by fear of injury. The death of a close relative is difficult for children to understand and requires a delicate, sensitive, and honest explanation. Questions and expressions of feelings (often resentment) by the child should be encouraged and discussed. It is repression, unanswered questions, lack of supportive people, and guilt feelings that can lead to morbid attitudes and fantasies, by which phobias develop. Experiences in the past and associated fears remain dormant, to recur and be relived.

Anticipatory fears can also cause phobias. Driving trainees and beginning drivers often have phobic reactions, dreading possible accidents. Students, often the best or most conscientious ones, may spend sleepless nights worrying about the next day's examination. They fear experiences that may never occur, irrationally magnifying the consequences of their performance to one of absolute success or utter doom. Concentration produces positive results (that is, good grades), but obsession may cause paralyzing fear and pressure, even suicide. Several other theories exist regarding the cause of phobias.

Phobias can be classified into three primary groupings: simple phobias, social phobias, and agoraphobia. Simple phobias are directed toward specific things, animals, phenomena, or situations. Rodents, cats, dogs, and birds are common objects of fear. A swooping gull or pigeon may cause panic. Insects, spiders, and bugs can provoke revulsion. Many cultures have a fear of snakes. A phobia exists, for example, when a house is inspected several times each day for snakes; a phobic person may vacate a rural home for an urban dwelling in order to avoid them. Blood, diseased people, or hospital patients have caused fainting. Some vegetarians dread meat because of traumatic observations

POSSIBLE SYMPTOMS OF SOCIAL PHOBIA

- ❖ viewing of small mistakes as more exaggerated than they really are
- ❖ finding blushing to be painfully embarrassing
- ❖ feeling that all eyes are on you
- ❖ fear of speaking in public, dating, or talking with persons in authority
- ❖ fear of using public restrooms or eating out
- ❖ fear of talking on the phone or writing in front of others

of slaughter. Fear of heights, water, enclosed spaces, and open spaces involve imagined dangers of falling, drowning, feeling trapped, and being lost in oblivion, respectively. These feelings are coupled with a fear of loss of control and harming oneself by entering a dangerous situation. Sometimes, a specific piece of music, building, or person triggers reactions; the initial trauma or conditioning events are not easily remembered or recognized as such.

Social phobias are fears of being watched or judged by others in social settings. For example, in a restaurant, phobics may eat in rigid, restrictive motions to avoid embarrassments. They may avoid soups, making noises with utensils, or food that requires gnawing for fear of being observed or drawing attention. Many students fear giving speeches because of the humiliation and ridicule resulting from mistakes. Stage fright, dating anxiety, and fear of unemployment, divorce, or other forms of failure are also phobic conditions produced by social goals and expectations. The desire to please others can exact a terrible toll in worry, fear, and sleepless nights.

Agoraphobia is a flight reaction caused by the fear of places and predicaments outside a sphere of safety. This sphere may be home, a familiar person (often a parent), a bed, or a bedroom. Patients retreat from life and remain at home, safe from the outside world and its anticipated perils. They may look out the window and fear the demands and expectations placed on them. They are prisoners of insecurity and doubt, avoiding the responsibilities, risks, and requirements of living. Many children are afraid of school, and some feign illness to remain safely in bed. Facing the responsibilities of maturation causes similar reactions.

Treatment and Therapy
Different schools of psychology espouse different approaches to the treatment of phobias, but central themes involve controlled exposure to the object of fear. Common core fears include fear of dying, fear of going crazy, fear of losing control, fear of failure, and fear of rejection.

The most effective approach to treating these disorders is a cognitive behavioral strategy. With this approach, dysfunctional thinking is identified and changed through collaborative efforts between the patient and therapist. Additional dysfunctional behavior is identified and changed through processes involving conditioning and reinforcement.

Through an initial minimal exposure to the feared object or situation, discussion, and then progressively greater controlled contact, patients experience some stress at each stage but not at a level sufficient to cause a relapse. They will proceed to become desensitized to the object in phases. Therapists may serve as role models at first, demonstrating the steps that patients need to complete, or they may provide positive feedback and guidance. In either case, the role of the patient is active, and gradual exposure occurs. In the process, patients learn to adapt to stress and become more capable of dealing with life.

Other supervised therapies exist, some involving hypnosis, psychoanalysis, drugs, and reasoning out of one's fears. In dealing with phobics, it must be recognized that anyone can have a phobia. Patience, understanding, supportiveness, and professional help are needed. Telling someone simply to "snap out of it" increases stress and guilt.

Perspective and Prospects

Fear serves an important and necessary function in life. It keeps one from putting a hand in a flame or walking into oncoming traffic. The fear of death and the unknown is commonplace; it causes many to dislike, even dread, passing by cemeteries, even though there is no logical reason. While many forms of fear are normal, if they occur out of context, in socially unacceptable manners, too severely, or uncontrollably then the diagnosis is a phobia.

Many different phobias have been cited in the literature and have specific terms in dictionaries, constructed by prefixing the word "phobia" with Greek or Latin terms (such as acrophobia or claustrophobia). While their enumeration is an interesting pastime, phobias are serious conditions and should be treated by professional psychologists.

Bibliography

Beidel, Deborah C., and Samuel M. Turner. *Shy Children, Phobic Adults: Nature and Treatment of Social Phobia*. Washington, D.C.: American Psychiatric Press, 1998. Draws from the clinical, social, and developmental literatures as well as direct clinical experience to illustrate the impact of developmental stage on the phenomenology, diagnosis, assessment, and treatment of phobias.

Bourne, Edmond J. *The Anxiety and Phobia Workbook*. Oakland, Calif.: New Harbinger, 1995. A practical guide that offers help to anyone struggling with panic attacks, agoraphobia, social fears, generalized anxiety, obsessive-compulsive behaviors, or other anxiety disorders.

Davey, Graham, ed. *Phobias: A Handbook of Theory, Research, and Treatment*. New York: John Wiley & Sons, 1997. Describes the symptoms, prevalence, case histories, and etiology of phobias. Explores treatment options. Includes bibliographical references and indexes.

Dumont, Raeann. *The Sky Is Falling: Understanding and Coping with Phobias, Panic, and Obsessive-Compulsive Disorders*. New York: W. W. Norton, 1996. A popular work on common anxiety-causing conditions. Includes bibliographical references and an index.

Lindemann, Carol, ed. *Handbook of the Treatment of the Anxiety Disorders.* 2d ed. Northvale, N.J.: Jason Aronson, 1996. A revision of *The Handbook of Phobia Therapy* (1989). Includes bibliographical references and an index.

Marks, I. M. *Fears, Phobias, and Rituals.* New York: Oxford University Press, 1987. Offers a detailed discussion of the clinical aspects of fear-related syndromes and a broad exploration of the sources and mechanisms of fear and defensive behavior.

John Panos Najarian
updated by Nancy A. Piotrowski

See also:

Agoraphobia and Panic Disorders; Anxiety Disorders; Child and Adolescent Psychiatry; Cognitive Behavior Therapy; Neurosis; Psychosomatic Disorders; Stress; Stress: Behavioral and Psychological Responses.

PLAY THERAPY

Type of psychology: Psychotherapy
Fields of study: Humanistic therapies; psychodynamic therapies

Play therapy is a method of treating children who have emotional problems, psychological difficulties, or mental disorders. It is conducted in a room specifically equipped for this purpose with toys and activity materials to aid the child in solving problems and to enhance mental health. It most commonly involves one child and one therapist, though it can be conducted with groups of children.

Principal terms

COMMUNICATION: the sharing of information with other people, either through language or through other ways of interacting

EMPATHY: the ability to figure out how another person feels in certain situations or with different people and to communicate that understanding

INTERPERSONAL MATRIX: the environment and the relationship between two or more people who spend time together, along with all the occurrences within it

LIMIT SETTING: imposing rules or regulations upon another person and then enforcing them in a predictable way

NONDIRECTIVENESS: allowing another person to set the tone and pace of an interaction, as well as letting that person choose the topic and materials to be used

SYMBOLISM: the use of indirect means to express inner needs or feelings; a way of sharing oneself without doing so directly or in words

Overview

Children of all ages learn about their environment, express themselves, and deal with relationships with others through their play activity. Play is an integral part of childhood, an activity that must be allowed to a child to facilitate the child's development. In fact, play is seen as such an important aspect of a child's life that the United Nations made the right to play an inalienable right for children across the world. Some adults have labeled play a child's "work," and this may be an appropriate way of looking at children's play. Just as work fosters self-esteem for adults, so does play enhance the self-esteem of children. Just as adults learn to solve problems through their work, so do children learn to cope with and invent solutions to problems through their play. Just as adults spend a bulk of their time in work activity, so do children spend most of their waking hours engaged in play.

Through play, children grow in a number of ways. First, they grow emotionally; children learn to express their feelings, understand their feelings, and control their emotions. A child may hit a "Bobo" doll in an angry manner, then become very friendly and peaceful. The activity of hitting the doll helped the child act out her or his feeling of anger and then turn to more positive emotions. Through play, children grow cognitively. They learn to count in efforts to master sharing with other children; they learn about different functions of the same object; they learn that things can break and be repaired; they learn to think in symbols; and they learn language. Children also learn morality. They act out rules and regulations in play with other children; they learn to share; they learn that some things hurt other people and should therefore not be done; and they realize that rules often serve a purpose of protection or safety. All these growth processes are extremely important by-products of play, but perhaps the most important aspect of play is that of communication. Children tell about themselves and their lives through play. Even when they do not yet have the language, they possess the ability to play.

Psychiatrists Anna and Sigmund Freud. Anna Freud developed play therapy methods based on psychoanalytic theories that had been proposed by her famous father. (Library of Congress)

This aspect of communication through play is perhaps the most important ingredient of play therapy. In play therapy, a therapist uses a child's play to understand the child and to help the child solve problems, feel better about herself or himself, and express herself or himself better. Children often have difficulty telling adults what they feel and experience, what they need and want, and what they do not want and do not like. Often they lack the language skills to do so, and sometimes they are too frightened to reveal themselves for fear of punishment.

In play therapy, however, the therapist is an adult who is empathic, sensitive, and—above all—accepting and nonthreatening. The child is made to feel comfortable in the room with this adult and quickly recognizes that this person, despite being quite old (at least from the child's perspective), understands the child and accepts her or his wishes and needs. Children learn to play in the presence of this therapist, or even with the therapist, and through this play communicate with the therapist. They reveal through their activity what they have experienced in life, how they feel, what they would like to do, and how they feel about themselves.

The toys and activities that therapists use vary significantly, though they take great care to equip the room in which they work with the child in such a way as to allow maximum freedom and creativity on the child's part. Therapists generally have puppets, clay, paints, dolls, dollhouses, and building blocks in the room. All these materials share several important traits: They all foster creativity; they have many different uses; they are safe to play with; and they can be used easily by the child for communication. On the other hand, therapists rarely have things such as board games, Slinkies, or theme toys (for example, television "action" heroes), because these toys have a definite use with certain rules and restrictions, are often used merely to re-create stories observed on television, or are not very handy for getting the child to express herself or himself freely. Most of the time, the toys are kept in an office that is specifically designed for children, not a regular doctor's office. As such, the room generally has a child-size table and chairs but no adult-size desk. It usually has no other furniture but may have some large cushions that child and therapist can sit on if they want to talk for a while. Often the room has a small, low sink for water play, and sometimes even a sandbox. Floor and wall coverings are such that they can be easily cleaned so that spills are not a problem. The room is basically a large play area; children generally like the play therapy room because it is unlike any other room they have ever encountered and because it is equipped specifically with children in mind.

Applications

There are many reasons a child may be seen in play therapy. For example, a referral may come from a teacher who is concerned about a drop in the child's academic performance; from day care personnel who are concerned about the child's inability to relate to other children; from the child's pediatrician, who believes the child is depressed but cannot find a physical cause; or from parents who think the child is aggressive. Whatever the reason, therapy begins with an intake interview. The intake is a session during which the therapist meets not only with the child but also with the parents and siblings in an attempt to find out as much about the child as possible to gain an understanding of what is wrong. Once the therapist knows what is happening with the child, recommendations for treatment are made. Sometimes the recommendation is for the entire family to be seen in family therapy. Sometimes the recommendation is for the parents to be seen. Sometimes the recommendation is for play therapy for the child.

Once a child enters play therapy, she or he will meet with the therapist once weekly for fifty minutes (sometimes, for very young children, sessions can be as short as thirty minutes) for several weeks or months. During the sessions, the child decides what is played with and how, and the therapist is there to understand the child, help the child solve problems, and facilitate growth and self-esteem for the child. Often, while the child is seen, her or his parents are seen in some type of therapy as well. Children's problems often arise because of problems in the family, which is why it is rare that only the child is in treatment. Parents are often seen to work on their relationship either with each other or with the whole family, or to learn parenting skills.

The first thing that happens in play therapy is that the therapist and the child get to know each other and develop a positive relationship. Once the child begins to trust the therapist, she or he starts to reveal concerns and problems through play. The therapist observes and/or interacts with the child to help work out problems, deal with strong feelings, accept needs, and learn to deal with often difficult family or environmental circumstances. All this work is done through the child's play in much the same way as children use play while growing up. In addition to using play activity, however, the therapist also uses the trusting relationship with the child.

The process of play therapy is best demonstrated by an example of an actual play therapy interaction between a child and therapist. A nine-year-old boy was referred by his teacher because he was very depressed and frightened, had difficulty making friends, and was not able to trust people. In the intake interview, the therapist found out that the boy had been severely physically abused by his father and that he was abandoned by his birth mother at age two. His stepmother had brought three children of her own into the blended family and did not have much time for this child. In fact, it appeared as though he was left to his own devices most of the time. The family had a number of other problems but refused family therapy. Thus, the child was seen in play therapy. He had considerable difficulty starting to trust the therapist and showed this reluctance in his play. He would often start to play, then check with the therapist for approval, and then stop before he became too involved in any one activity. After six weeks, he realized that the therapist was there to help him, and he began to communicate about his family through play.

The following exchange is a good example of what happens in play therapy. One day, the boy picked up a large wooden truck and two small ones. He proceeded to smash the large truck into the small red one over and over. He took the other small truck and put it between the large one and the small red one, as though to protect the red truck from being hit by the large one. In the process, the blue small truck was hurt badly and had to retreat. The boy repeated this activity several times. The therapist picked up a toy truck of her own and drove between the large truck and both of the small trucks, indicating that she had a truck that was tough enough to stop the large truck from hurting the small ones. The child was visibly relieved and turned to another activity.

What had happened? Before the session, the therapist had received a call from the child's social worker, who told her that the night before, the boy's father was caught sexually abusing his four-year-old stepdaughter, who shared this boy's room. The boy had awakened and unsuccessfully tried to stop his father. He ran to a neighbor's house, and this woman called the police. The father was arrested but threatened to get revenge on both children before he was taken away. The boy had playacted this entire scene with the toy trucks. The father was the large truck; the red truck, his sister; the blue one, himself. The relief sensed by the boy after the therapist intervened is understandable, as her truck communicated to the boy that he would be protected from his father.

Perspective and Prospects

Children use their play in play therapy not only to communicate but also to solve problems and deal with overwhelming feelings. How this happens has been explained and described by many different therapists and theorists since play came to be viewed as an acceptable means of conducting therapy in the early 1930's, based upon the work of Melanie Klein and Anna Freud. These women developed play therapy methods that were based upon earlier psychoanalytic theories proposed by Sigmund Freud. In this approach, free play was considered most important, and the therapist did not generally become engaged at all in the child's play. The therapist merely reflected back to the child what was seen and occasionally interpreted to the child what the play may have meant.

In the 1940's, Virginia Axline developed her approach to play therapy, which was similar to Klein and Freud's. Axline also believed in free play and did not play with the child. She interpreted and emphasized an environment that put no limits or rules upon the child. She introduced the idea that children in play therapy need to experience unconditional acceptance, empathic concern, and a nondirective atmosphere. In other words, Axline's approach to play therapy was to sit and observe and not be involved with the child.

Since then, the lack of limit setting, as well as the lack of active involvement with children in play therapy, has been criticized by play therapists. Nowadays, play therapists are more likely to get involved in play and to respond to children through play activity (as in the example above), as opposed to using language to communicate with them. There are two major groups of therapists who use play therapy. Traditional psychoanalytic or psychodynamic therapists who are followers of Klein or Axline make up one group; however, even within this group, there is much diversity with regard to how involved the therapist becomes with the child's play. The second group is composed of therapists who focus on the human interaction that takes place—that is, humanistic therapists.

Regardless of which group a play therapist belongs to, however, the primary ingredients that were proposed many years ago remain intact. As such, free play is still deemed important, and empathy is stressed in the relationship with the child. Many therapists believe that the interpersonal matrix that exists between the child and the therapist is critical to changes noted in the child. Further, a primary focus remains on the symbolism and metaphor expressed by children through play. It is unlikely that the nature of play therapy will change much in the next decades. Play therapy has become one of the most accepted modes of treating children and is likely here to stay.

Bibliography

Axline, Virginia Mae. *Dibs: In Search of Self.* New York: Ballantine Books, 1971. Written for the layperson, this book represents a case-study example of a successful play therapy sequence. Outlines the treatment of a severely disturbed boy, providing an excellent example of what happens in a child therapy room.

_____. *Play Therapy: The Inner Dynamics of Childhood.* Boston: Houghton Mifflin, 1947. Provides a thorough look at play therapy from a very nondirective perspective. Written in the 1940's but has survived as an important reference for therapists who work with children in play therapy. The writing style is accessible to the layperson.

Dodds, J. B. A. *Child Psychotherapy Primer*. New York: Human Sciences, 1985. Provides very practical suggestions and guidelines for persons who are beginning to work with children in a therapy context. Relatively brief (150 pages). A good first resource or overview of the topic.

James, O'Dessie Oliver. *Play Therapy: A Comprehensive Guide*. Northvale, N.J.: Jason Aronson, 1997. Reviews the literature on theoretical, technical, and practical considerations of play therapy. Includes bibliographical references and an index.

Landreth, G. L. *Play Therapy*. Muncie, Ind.: Accelerated Development, 1991. Provides a fairly detailed look at the practical aspects of child psychotherapy from a humanistic, person-centered perspective. Easy to read, even for the layperson, despite having been written primarily for the professional or the student of psychology.

Nemiroff, M. A., and J. Annunziata. *A Child's First Book About Play Therapy*. Washington, D.C.: American Psychological Association, 1990. Written for children who may be in need of treatment. A great introduction to the principles of play therapy, best used by parents to read to their children before seeing a child therapist. A picture storybook that holds children's attention well.

Schaefer, Charles E., and S. E. Reid. *Game Play*. New York: John Wiley & Sons, 1986. While traditional play therapists use toys, these authors introduce the use of children's games for therapeutic reasons. Written for the professional but also has implications for parents with regard to making choices of games for children; for example, discusses games that can be used to enhance a child's self-esteem. Somewhat long and perhaps a bit complicated; a good choice for someone who has already read another book on the topic.

Sweeney, Daniel S., and Linda E. Homeyer, eds. *The Handbook of Group Play Therapy: How to Do It, How It Works, Whom It's Best For*. San Francisco: Jossey-Bass, 1999. Written by the top twenty-five authors in the field. Widely embraced as the definitive guide on the subject.

Christiane Brems

See also:
Abnormality: Family Models; Child Abuse; Child and Adolescent Psychiatry; Divorce and Separation: Children's Issues; Music, Dance, and Theater Therapy; Psychotherapy: Children; Psychotherapy: Goals and Techniques; Strategic Family Therapy.

POST-TRAUMATIC STRESS

Type of psychology: Psychopathology
Fields of study: Anxiety disorders

After an extreme psychological trauma, people tend to respond with stress symptoms that include reexperiencing the trauma through nightmares or unwanted thoughts, avoiding reminders of the traumatic event, loss of interest in daily life, and increased arousal; these symptoms can range from mild and temporary to very severe, chronic, and psychologically disabling.

Principal terms

FLASHBACK: a type of traumatic reexperiencing in which a person becomes detached from reality and thinks, feels, and acts as if a previous traumatic experience were happening again

HYPERAROUSAL: a set of symptoms of post-traumatic stress disorder that includes difficulty falling or staying asleep, irritability or angry outbursts, difficulty concentrating, extreme vigilance, and an exaggerated startle response

NATIONAL VIETNAM VETERANS READJUSTMENT STUDY: a large-scale federally funded study completed in the late 1980's that surveyed the mental and physical health of Vietnam veterans

POST-TRAUMATIC STRESS DISORDER: a disorder recognized by the American Psychiatric Association involving symptoms of stress and reexperiencing a traumatic event

REEXPERIENCING: the central symptom of post-traumatic stress disorder; it involves having nightmares, unwanted thoughts, or flashbacks of a traumatic event

TRAUMATIC EVENT: an event that is beyond the range of usual human experience and that would cause distress to almost anyone

Causes and Symptoms

It is common knowledge that there are psychological aftereffects from experiencing an intense psychological trauma. This discussion of post-traumatic stress symptoms will be organized around post-traumatic stress disorder (PTSD), one of the diagnostic categories of anxiety disorders recognized by the American Psychiatric Association. It should be realized at the outset, however, that it is normal for people to experience at least some of these symptoms after suffering a psychological trauma. The first step in understanding PTSD is to know its symptoms.

The first criterion for PTSD is that one has suffered a trauma. The American Psychiatric Association's definition of PTSD states that the trauma must be something that "is outside the range of usual human experience and that would be markedly distressing to almost anyone." It is not so much the objective event as one's perception of it that determines the psychological response. For example, the death of one's parents is not "outside the range of usual human experience," but it can result in some of the symptoms described later. Some of the traumatic experiences deemed sufficient to cause PTSD include threat to one's own life or the life of a close relative or friend, sudden destruction of one's home or community, seeing another person violently injured or killed, or being the victim of a violent crime. Specific experiences that often cause PTSD include combat, natural or man-made disasters, automobile accidents, airplane crashes, rape, child abuse, and physical assault. In general, the more traumatic the event, the worse the post-traumatic symptoms. Symptoms of stress are often more severe when the trauma is sudden and unexpected. Also, when the trauma is the result of intentional human action (for example, combat, rape, or assault), stress symptoms are worse than if the trauma is a natural disaster (flood or earthquake) or an accident (automobile crash). It has been found that combat veterans who commit or witness atrocities are more likely to suffer later from PTSD.

Post-traumatic stress disorder is common in combat veterans; it was called "shell shock" during World War I and "battle fatigue" during World War II. (Digital Stock)

The central symptom of post-traumatic stress disorder is that the person reexperiences the trauma. This can occur in a number of ways. One can have unwanted, intrusive, and disturbing thoughts of the event or nightmares about the trauma. The most dramatic means of reexperiencing is through a flashback, in which the person acts, thinks, and feels as if he or she were reliving the event. Another way in which experiencing might be manifested is intense distress when confronted with situations that serve as reminders of the trauma. Vietnam War veterans with combat-related PTSD will often become very upset at motion pictures about the war, hot and humid junglelike weather, or even the smell of Asian cooking. A person with PTSD often will attempt to avoid thoughts, feelings, activities, or events that serve as unwanted reminders of the trauma.

Another symptom that is common in people with PTSD is numbing of general responsiveness. This might include the loss of interest in hobbies or activities that were enjoyed before the trauma, losing the feeling of closeness to other people, an inability to experience strong emotions, or a lack of interest in the future. A final set of PTSD symptoms involves increased arousal. This can include problems with sleeping or concentrating, irritability, or angry outbursts. A person with PTSD may be oversensitive to the environment, always on the alert, and prone to startle at the slightest noise.

The paragraphs above summarize the symptoms that psychologists and psychiatrists use to diagnose PTSD; however, other features are often found in trauma survivors that are not part of the diagnosis. Anxiety and depression are common in people who have experienced a trauma. Guilt is common in people who have survived a trauma in which others have died. People will sometimes use alcohol or tranquilizers to cope with sleep problems, disturbing nightmares, or distressing, intrusive recollections of a trauma, and they may then develop dependence on the drugs.

Post-traumatic stress disorder is relatively common in people who suffer serious trauma. In the late 1980's, the most extensive survey on PTSD ever done was undertaken on Vietnam combat veterans. It found that more than half of all veterans who served in the Vietnam theater of operations had experienced serious post-traumatic stress at some point in their lives after the war. This represents about 1.7 million veterans. Even more compelling was the fact that more than one-third of the veterans who saw heavy combat were still suffering from PTSD when the survey was done—about fifteen years after the fall of Saigon. Surveys of crime victims are also sobering. One study found that 75 percent of adult females had been the victim of a crime, and more than one in four of the victims developed PTSD after the crime. Crime victims were even more likely to develop PTSD if they were raped, were injured during the crime, or believed that their lives were in danger during the crime.

Symptoms of post-traumatic stress are common after a trauma, but they often decrease or disappear over time. A diagnosis of PTSD is not made unless the symptoms last for at least one month. Sometimes a person will have no symptoms until long after the event, when memories of the trauma are triggered by another negative life event. For example, a combat veteran might cope well with civilian life for many years until, after a divorce, he begins to have nightmares about his combat experiences.

Most of the theory and research regarding PTSD has been done on combat veterans, particularly veterans of the Vietnam War. One of the most exciting developments in this area, however, is that the theory and research are also being applied to victims of other sorts of trauma. This has a number of important implications. First, it helps extend the findings about PTSD beyond the combat-veteran population, which is mostly young and male. Second, information gathered from combat veterans can be used to assist in the assessment and treatment of anyone who has experienced a serious trauma. Because a large proportion of the general population experiences severe psychological trauma at some time, understanding PTSD is important to those providing mental health services.

An extended example will illustrate the application of theory and research findings on PTSD to a case of extreme psychological trauma. The case involves a woman who was attacked and raped at knifepoint one night while walking from her car to her apartment. Because of injuries suffered in the attack, she went to an emergency room for treatment. Knowledge about PTSD can help in understanding this woman's experience and could aid her in recovery.

First, research has shown that this woman's experience—involving rape, life threat, and physical injury—puts her at high risk for symptoms of post-traumatic stress. Risk is so great, in fact, that researchers have proposed that psychological counseling be recommended to all people who are the victims of this sort of episode. This suggestion is being implemented in many rape-recovery and crime-victim programs around the United States.

Knowing what symptoms are common following a traumatic event can help professionals counsel a victim about what to expect. This woman can expect feelings of anxiety and depression, nightmares and unwanted thoughts about the event, irritability, and difficulties in sleeping and concentrating. Telling a victim that these are normal responses and that there is a likelihood that the problems will lessen with time is often reassuring. Since research has shown that many people with these symptoms cope by using drugs and alcohol, it may also help to warn the victim about this possibility and caution that this is harmful in the long run.

One symptom of PTSD, psychological distress in situations that resemble the traumatic event, suggests why combat veterans who experience their trauma in a far-off land often fare better than those whose trauma occurs closer to home. Women who are raped in their home or neighborhood may begin to feel unsafe in previously secure places. Some cope by moving to a different house, a new neighborhood, or even a new city—often leaving valued jobs and friends. If an attack occurred after dark, a person may no longer feel safe going out after dark and may begin living a restricted social life. Frequently, women who are raped generalize their fear to all men and especially to sexual relations, seriously damaging their interpersonal relationships. Given the problems that these post-traumatic symptoms can cause in so many areas of one's life, it may not be surprising that one study found that nearly one in every five rape victims attempted suicide.

Treatment and Therapy

The main symptoms of post-traumatic stress are phobia-like fear and avoidance of trauma-related situations, thoughts, and feelings, and the most effective treatment for PTSD is the same as for a phobia. Systematic desensitization and flooding, which involve confronting the thoughts and feelings surrounding the traumatic event, are the treatments that appear to be most effective. It may seem paradoxical that a disorder whose symptoms include unwanted thoughts and dreams of a traumatic event could be treated by purposefully thinking and talking about the event; however, Mardi Horowitz, one of the leading theorists in traumatic stress, believes that symptoms alternate between unwanted, intrusive thoughts of the event and efforts to avoid these thoughts. Because intrusive thoughts always provoke efforts at avoidance, the event is never fully integrated into memory; it therefore retains its power. Systematic desensitization and flooding, which involve repeatedly thinking about the event without avoiding, allow time for the event to become integrated into the person's life experiences so that the memory loses much of its pain.

Another effective way to reduce the impact of a traumatic event is through social support. People who have a close network of friends and family appear to suffer less from symptoms of trauma. After a traumatic experience, people should be encouraged to maintain and even increase their supportive social contacts, rather than withdrawing from people, as often happens. Support groups of people who have had similar experiences, such as Vietnam veteran groups or child-abuse support groups, also provide needed social support. These groups have the added benefit of encouraging people to talk about their experiences, which provides another way to think about and integrate the traumatic event.

Psychotherapy can help trauma victims in many ways. One way is to help the patient explore and cope with the way the trauma changes one's view of the world. For example, the rape victim may come to believe that "the world is dangerous" or that "men can't be trusted." Therapy can help this person learn to take reasonable precautions without shutting herself off from the world and relationships. Finally, symptoms of overarousal are common with PTSD. A therapist can address these symptoms by teaching methods of deep relaxation and stress reduction. Sometimes mild tranquilizers are prescribed when trauma victims are acutely aroused or anxious.

Perspective and Prospects

The concept of post-traumatic stress is very old and is closely tied to the history of human warfare. The symptoms of PTSD have been known variously as "soldier's heart," "combat neurosis," and "battle fatigue." Stephen Crane's novel *The Red Badge of Courage*, first published in 1895, describes post-traumatic symptoms in the Civil War soldier. It was the postwar experiences of the Vietnam combat veteran, however, studied and described by scholars such as Charles Figley, that brought great attention to issues of post-traumatic stress.

It was not until 1980 that the American Psychiatric Association recognized "post-traumatic stress disorder" in its manual of psychiatric disorders. Since then there has been an explosion of published research and books on PTSD, the creation of the Society for Traumatic Stress Studies in 1985, and the initiation of the quarterly *Journal of Traumatic Stress* in 1988. Since these developments, attention has also been directed toward post-traumatic symptoms in victims of natural disasters, violent crime, sexual and child abuse; Holocaust survivors; and many other populations. Surveys have found that more than 80 percent of college students have suffered at least one trauma potentially sufficient to cause PTSD, and many people seeking psychological counseling have post-traumatic stress symptoms. Thus, it is fair to say that the attention garnered by Vietnam veteran readjustment problems and by the recognition of PTSD as a disorder by the American Psychiatric Association has prompted the examination of many important issues related to post-traumatic stress.

Because research in this area is relatively new, there are many important questions that remain unanswered. One mystery is that two people can have exactly the same traumatic experience, yet one will have extreme post-traumatic stress and one will have no problems. Some factors are known to be important; for example, young children and the elderly are more likely to suffer from psychological symptoms after a trauma. Much research is needed, however, to determine what individual differences will predict who fares well and who fares poorly after a trauma.

A second area of future development is in the assessment of PTSD. For the most part, it is diagnosed through a self-report of trauma and post-traumatic symptoms. This creates difficulty, however, when the person reporting the symptoms stands to gain compensation for the trauma suffered. Interesting physiological and cognitive methods for assessing PTSD are being explored. For example, researchers have found that Vietnam veterans with PTSD show high levels of physiological arousal when they hear combat-related sounds or imagine their combat experiences. Finally, the future will see more bridges built between post-traumatic stress and the more general area of stress and coping.

Bibliography

Figley, Charles R., ed. *Trauma and Its Wake: The Study and Treatment of Post-traumatic Stress Disorder*. New York: Brunner/Mazel, 1985. This edited book is one of the most often cited references in the field of PTSD and contains some of the most influential papers written on the subject. It is divided into sections on theory, research, and treatment; a second volume with the same title was published in 1986. It is part of the Brunner/Mazel Psychosocial Stress Series, the first volume of which was published in 1978; through 1990, this valuable series had published twenty-one volumes on many aspects of stress and trauma.

Figley, Charles R., and Seymour Leventman, eds. *Strangers at Home: Vietnam Veterans Since the War*. 1980. Reprint. New York: Brunner/Mazel, 1990. This edited book, containing chapters by psychologists, sociologists, political activists, historians, political scientists, and economists, presents a look at the experience of the Vietnam veteran from many different perspectives. Many of the authors were Vietnam veterans themselves, so the book gives a very personal, sometimes stirring view of its subject.

Grinker, Roy Richard, and John P. Spiegal. *Men Under Stress*. Philadelphia: Blakiston, 1945. Long before the term "post-traumatic stress disorder" was coined, this classic book described the stress response to combat in Air Force flyers. It is written in jargon-free language by men who had unusual access to the flight crews.

Horowitz, Mardi Jon. *Stress Response Syndromes*. New York: J. Aronson, 1976.

Horowitz is one of the leading psychodynamic theorists in the area of post-traumatic stress. In this readable book, he describes his theory and his approach to treatment.

Joseph, Stephen, Ruth Williams, and William Yule. *Understanding Post-traumatic Stress: A Psychosocial Perspective on PTSD and Treatment.* New York: John Wiley & Sons, 1997. Examines the latest developments in theory and research in post-traumatic stress disorder. Drawing on the literature exploring personality and social psychology, it presents an integrative model of psychosocial factors affecting adjustment following traumatic stressors.

Maercker, Andreas, Matthias Schützwohl, and Zahava Solomon, eds. *Posttraumatic Stress Disorder: A Lifespan Developmental Perspective.* Seattle: Hogrefe & Huber, 1999. Brings together recent findings on the course of post-traumatic stress disorder. Discusses methods of coping with PTSD at different stages of life.

Yule, William, ed. *Post-traumatic Stress Disorders: Concepts and Therapy.* New York: John Wiley & Sons, 1999. Emphasizes the cognitive behavioral approach to PTSD and integrates important perspectives from social psychology, experimental cognitive psychology, neuropsychology, and developmental psychology.

Scott R. Vrana

See also:

Anxiety Disorders; Aversion, Implosion, and Systematic Desensitization Therapies; Child Abuse; Domestic Violence; Phobias; Stress; Stress: Behavioral and Psychological Responses; Stress: Coping Strategies.

PROJECTIVE PERSONALITY TRAITS

Type of psychology: Personality
Fields of study: Personality assessment

Projective personality traits are often assessed by tests which present ambiguous material to the person being tested; all of behavior is included under the definition of personality, and responses to unstructured tests will reveal an individual's needs, wishes, and attitudes. It is assumed that the person will give responses which cannot or will not be given otherwise.

Principal terms

CLINICAL PERSONALITY ASSESSMENT: the use of tests and other techniques to obtain broad understanding of an individual for the planning and evaluation of treatment

DEFENSE MECHANISMS: a psychoanalytic concept of mechanisms that protect an individual from excessive anxiety; considered signs of psychopathology when they are excessive

OBJECTIVE PERSONALITY TESTS: self-report measures used for psychological assessment; include personality inventories and checklists which require paper-and-pencil responses to questions

PROJECTIVE METHOD: refers to any task that provides an open-ended response that may reveal aspects of one's personality; tasks or tests commonly include standard stimuli that are ambiguous in nature

PSYCHOPATHOLOGY: disorders of psychological functioning that include major as well as minor mental disorders and behavior disorders

Overview

The concept of projection goes back to Sigmund Freud, who introduced this term to describe certain psychopathological processes. It was described as a defense which permits one to be "unaware of undesirable aspects of one's personality by attributing aggressive and or sexual feelings to others or to the outside world." In that way, one can avoid being aware of those feelings in oneself. Projection is usually described as a defense mechanism whose purpose is to avoid feeling guilty or neurotically anxious. Freud's theory suggested that it was easier to tolerate punishment from the outside rather than to accept impulses inconsistent with one's self-concept and moral principles. Thus, it is simpler to accuse someone else of hating oneself than it is to admit hating the other person. Defense mechanisms are unconscious processes; one is not likely to admit consciously that one hates someone if one is neurotically anxious. In its extreme forms, Freud notes, distortion of reality can be of such major proportions that perception of the judgment of others takes the form of paranoia.

One of the best-known tests employing projective techniques are the inkblots developed by Hermann Rorschach.

Freud later extended the use of the term "projection" to include times when there is no conflict. He believed that as one goes through life, memories of past events influence the way one sees the present. Early life experiences shape the future so that, for example, the kind of experiences one had with a brother when growing up influences how one sees "brothers" relate to their families. This leads to the basic assumption that all present responses to one's environment are based, as Albert Rabin puts it, on personal needs, motivations, and unique tendencies. All of these are actually based on past experiences. Sheldon Korchin suggests that the weakening of the boundaries between self and others also occurs in empathy, which has been viewed as the opposite of projection. In empathy, one figuratively puts oneself in another person's shoes by accepting and experiencing the feelings of another person. Empathy, therefore, is an important part of establishing close and meaningful relationships with others and is an important aspect of personality.

Leopold Bellak sees projection as the term one uses to describe a greater degree of overall distortion. This is consistent with Freud's original use of the term. He differentiates this pathological and unconscious type of projection, which he calls inverted projection, from simple projection. Simple projection occurs all the time and is not of great clinical significance.

For example, suppose a woman wants to borrow her friend's hedge trimmer. As she walks down the block to her friend's house, she thinks about how she is going to ask for the hedge trimmer, since she knows that her friend is not overly enthusiastic about lending his garden tools. She begins to think that her friend might say that it took her a long time to return the trimmer the last time she borrowed it and perhaps that it needed maintenance after she used it. She answers this imagined comment by saying that it rained soon after she started and that she could not finish the job for three days.

She then imagines that her friend will say that she should have returned the trimmer and asked for it again later. She imagines answering that criticism by stating that she knew her friend had gone out of town and would not be back until later in the week. This imaginary conversation might continue until she arrives at her neighbor's house. Her neighbor is on the porch, and he greets her in a friendly manner. Nevertheless, she responds angrily by telling him that she would never want to borrow his old hedge trimmer anyway. Ballak would explain this incident by noting that the woman wants something from her neighbor but can recall his hesitancy to lend tools: He may turn her request down, which makes her angry. She then assumes that her friend is angry with her. Her response is to be angry with him because he is angry with her.

A discussion of projective personality traits would be incomplete without discussing the projective hypothesis on which projective tests are based. This hypothesis states that when one is confronted by an ambiguous stimulus, responses will reflect personal needs, wishes, and overall attitudes toward the outside world. This assumes that all of one's behavior, even the least significant aspects, is an expression of personality. As Anneliese Korner asserts, individuals who are presented with ambiguous material give responses that they cannot or will not give otherwise. The person who responds to projective techniques does not know what the presenter expects. The resistance to disclosing personal material (including wishes, fears, and aspirations) is diminished. In addition, Korner suggests that what is disclosed in response to projective techniques is not a chance event but is determined by previous life experiences.

Among the most widely known tests that use projective techniques are the Rorschach inkblot test and Henry Murray's Thematic Apperception Test (TAT). The Rorschach technique consists of ten standard inkblots to which a participant is asked to respond by telling the examiner what the blots look like. Murray's Thematic Apperception Test, on the other hand, consists of twenty pictures designed to include stories which can give important clues to a person's life and personality. The set is sufficiently clear to permit one to tell stories without great difficulty, yet the pictures are ambiguous enough (unstructured) so that individuals will differ in the kinds of stories they will tell.

Applications

John Exner raises the issue as to whether all responses to a projective technique such as the Rorschach test are necessarily aspects of projection. Is it true, he asks, that more ambiguous stimulus material produces more projection than does less ambiguous material? A simple example may be helpful. Suppose an individual is shown a glass container with sand flowing from one portion of the glass to the other and asked to give this object a name. Most people will call it an egg timer. Assume, however, that a thirty-five-year-old individual embellishes the description of the egg timer by stating that it represents the sands of time and is an indication that life is drawing to a close. That kind of response, in an individual of good health who is thirty-five years old, would seem to be an example of projection. Clearly, however, based on one response, it would be premature to build firm conclusions about this individual's attitudes toward life and death. Similarly, on the Rorschach, one response descriptive of aggression may not be particularly diagnostic, but there is evidence that those who give higher frequencies of aggression responses show more aggressive verbal and nonverbal behaviors than those who do not.

Exner, in reporting on other studies, points out that Rorschach interpretations can also be useful with children. He notes that children change over time in their responses to the inkblots and that younger children change more than older children. Further, as children move into mid- and late adolescence, more overall stability is noted in the responses. Finally, he points out that perceptual accuracy stabilizes early.

A third study asks the question whether patients in a hospital setting who have experienced a major loss differ from patients who have not suffered such a loss. Mary Cerney defined three categories of major loss: death or serious injury to individuals close to the patient (including parents, close relatives, or friends); loss as a function of physical or sexual abuse such as incest, torture, or rape; and the observation of violence to other individuals. Cerney found differences in the responses between individual patients who had experienced such loss and patients who had not. She concluded that in this study, patients who had experienced early trauma had distinguishing Rorschach profiles. She further noted, however, that one needed further investigations to determine whether there were factors other than traumatic loss which could contribute to this profile difference.

In a study designed to measure change in defense mechanisms following intensive psychotherapy, researchers compared two groups of individuals who were being treated in a small, long-term treatment facility with a psychoanalytic orientation. One group of patients was judged in advance to be prime users of such defense mechanisms as repression and denial, while the other group was judged to make much more use of projection. This categorization was based on a through evaluation six weeks after admission to the treatment center. After about fifteen months of intensive treatment, patients were evaluated again in a comprehensive manner. The use of defense mechanisms was established on the basis of responses to the Thematic Apperception Test. Results indicated that all patients showed a reduction in the total use of defense mechanisms; this was associated with a reduction in psychiatric symptoms. Interestingly, the patients who made use of projection as a defense showed a greater decline in the use of that defense mechanism after treatment. Along with the decrease in psychiatric symptoms, both groups also showed, as one might expect, improved relationships with others from both a qualitative and a quantitative perspective.

Freud also applied the concept of projection to everyday personality traits such as jealousy. He differentiated between normal jealousy, projected jealousy, and delusional jealousy. From a psychoanalytic view, he had little to say about normal jealousy; however, projected jealousy, he stated, came from two sources. Either it comes from actual unfaithfulness or from impulses toward unfaithfulness which have been pushed into one's unconscious. He speculated that married individuals are frequently tempted to be unfaithful. In view of that temptation, it is likely that one's conscience can be soothed by attributing unfaithfulness to one's partner.

Jealousy arising from such a projection can be so strong as to take on the quality of a delusion. Many people are aware of individuals who incorrectly suspect their committed partner to be unfaithful. Freud would argue that these inaccurate expectations are unconscious fantasies of one's own infidelities and can be so analyzed in psychoanalytic therapy.

Perspective and Prospects
The term "projection" was introduced by Sigmund Freud in 1894. Initially Freud viewed it as a defensive process, but by 1913 the concept was broadened to refer to a process that may occur even if there is no conflict. John Exner believes that Freud's description of projection is most applicable in the context of projective tests. Exner also suggests that Freud's concept of projection fits in well with Henry Murray's discussion of the Thematic Apperception Test. Murray's broadened explanation of projection included the idea that the ambiguity of responding to a social situation (the test materials) provides clues to that individual's personality makeup and its expression through responses to projective methods. Lawrence Frank further emphasized the connection between projective tests and the unique expression of an individual's personality by stating the projective hypothesis.

Applied psychology has been heavily involved with the study of intelligence and the development of tests to evaluate achievement, memory, motor skills, and other cognitive aspects of human functioning. The study of personality was more heavily focused on individual traits, such as extroversion versus introversion. Emphasis on test construction focused on group norms, and comparisons of individual scores on tests were based on their relationships to group data. According to Exner, early Rorschach research also attempted to focus on group norms. To some extent, the focus on determining the meaning of individual responses was probably a reaction to the more "scientific" behavioral and statistically based methods commonly used.

As Exner notes, initial work with the Rorschach inkblots emphasized attempts to quantify personality characteristics; there was relatively little interest in the actual content of the responses. As interest in psychoanalysis swept the country, clinical psychologists began to focus on individual responses to tests, in contrast to their prior emphasis on group comparisons. Projective tests were very controversial, however, and a dichotomy developed between projective tests and the so-called objective tests. The latter tests were ones that could be scored reliably and for which group norms existed. Concurrently, numerous scoring systems were developed for the Rorschach test as well as for other projective measures.

In the late 1970's, Exner developed a comprehensive scoring system for the Rorschach which incorporated many of the features of the existing systems and integrated them into one overall method. In addition, he collected normative data on children, adolescents, and adults that provide opportunities for group comparisons. His comprehensive system is now widely taught in colleges and universities and has provided a measure of unity to the Rorschach test, which is still the personality instrument most widely used by clinicians. The assessment of personality traits will probably continue to flourish, and there will probably be an increasing emphasis on both subjective and objective responses in order to assess personality. Furthermore, computerized scoring of responses is common for objective personality tests and is beginning to be used with projective personality measures; this is likely to influence the future of personality tests.

Bibliography

Aiken, Lewis R. *Assessment of Personality*. Boston: Allyn & Bacon, 1989. This textbook is designed to introduce the reader to concepts, methods, and instruments important in personality assessment. It provides a straightforward discussion of psychodynamic theory in the context of projective testing and provides constructive criticisms.

_____. *Psychological Testing and Assessment*. 10th ed. Boston: Allyn & Bacon, 2000. A textbook intended to improve the knowledge, understanding, and practices of persons who construct tests, take tests, or question the meaning and value of test scores. Includes bibliographical references and indexes.

Anastasi, Anne, and Susana Urbina. *Psychological Testing*. Upper Saddle River, N.J.: Prentice Hall, 1997. Chapter 15 covers projective techniques. Includes bibliographical references and indexes.

Cronbach, Lee J. *Essentials of Psychological Testing*. 5th ed. New York: Harper & Row, 1990. The measurement of personality traits by projective tests is discussed in chapter 16. Discussion questions are included to assist the reader to understand why projective measures encourage both positive and negative evaluations. This chapter can be understood by high school and college students.

Leiter, E. "The Role of Projective Testing." In *Clinical and Experimental Psychiatry*, edited by Scott Wetzler and Martin M. Katz. New York: Brunner/Mazel, 1989. Leiter discusses projective testing and includes major changes in psychiatry as related to projective techniques. He focuses on changes in current diagnosis and relates them to projective measures.

Nathanson, S. "Denial, Projection, and the Empathic Wall." In *Denial: A Clarification of Concepts and Research*, edited by E. L. Edelstein, Donald L. Nathanson, and Andrew M. Stone. New York: Plenum Press, 1989. Discusses denial and projection and gives clinical illustrations. The author integrates concepts with other theories and provides relevant examples of research with infants. There is also a discussion of empathy and its relationship to substance abuse.

Rabin, Albert I., ed. *Assessment with Projective Techniques: A Concise Introduction*. New York: Springer, 1998. Discusses personality assessment through the use of projection.

Walsh, W. Bruce, and Nancy E. Betz. *Tests and Assessments*. Englewood Cliffs, N.J.: Prentice-Hall, 1985. Of particular interest is the discussion on projective and behavioral assessment, which reviews the concepts behind projective testing and discusses types of projective techniques with specific examples.

Norman Abeles

See also:

Abnormality: Psychodynamic Models; Behavioral Assessment and Personality Rating Scales; Jealousy.

PSYCHIATRY

Type of psychology: Psychotherapy
Fields of study: Behavioral therapies; classic analytic themes and issues; cognitive therapies; group and family therapies; humanistic therapies; personality assessment; psychodynamic therapies

Psychiatry is a medical field concerned with the diagnosis, epidemiology, prevention, and treatment of mental and emotional problems.

Principal terms

ANXIETY DISORDERS: problems in which physical and emotional uneasiness, apprehension, or fear is the dominant symptom

BIPOLAR DISORDERS: problems marked by mania or mania with depression; historically known as manic-depressive disorders

DEMENTIAS: disorders characterized by a general deterioration of intellectual and emotional functioning, involving problems with memory, judgment, emotional responses, and personality changes

DEPRESSIVE DISORDERS: problems involving persistent feelings of despair, weight change, sleep problems, thoughts of death, thinking difficulties, diminished interest or pleasure in activities, and agitation or listlessness

PERSONALITY DISORDERS: pervasive, inflexible patterns of perceiving, thinking, and behaving that cause long-term distress or impairment, beginning in adolescence and persisting into adulthood

PSYCHOTIC: referring to a disabling mental state characterized by poor reality testing (inaccurate perceptions, confusion, disorientation) and disorganized speech, behavior, and emotional experience

PSYCHOTROPIC DRUGS: substances primarily affecting behavior, perception, and other psychological functions

SCHIZOPHRENIC DISORDERS: mental disturbances characterized by psychotic features during the active phase and deteriorated functioning in occupational, social, or self-care abilities

Overview

Psychiatrists receive training in biochemistry, community mental health, genetics, neurology, neuropathology, psychopathology, psychopharmacology, and social science. They complete medical school, a four-year residency in psychiatry, and two or more years of specialty residency. Specialty residencies focus on particular treatment methods (such as psychoanalysis) or methods of diagnosis and treatment for particular groups of clients (such as children, adolescents, or elders).

As diagnosticians and treatment providers, psychiatrists must be excellent observers of behavior and be knowledgeable about how nutritional, physical, and situational conditions can be related to mental or emotional problems. An ability to consult with other professionals is also important. Psychiatrists often receive patients from other professionals (general practitioners, psychologists, emergency room staff) and often request diagnostic, legal, case management, and resource advice from other professionals (psychologists, attorneys, social workers). In situations involving abuse, neglect, incompetency, and suicide, such consultation relationships are critical for appropriate referral and treatment.

Given this preparation, psychiatrists are able to diagnose and treat a wide variety of disorders. Some of the most common disorders treated in adult populations include disorders of anxiety (such as phobias, panic attacks, obsessive-compulsive behavior, acute and post-traumatic stress) and mood (such as depressive and bipolar problems). Personality, schizophrenic, substance abuse, and dementia-related disorders also are treated frequently by psychiatrists. Such conditions are described in detail in the American Psychiatric Association's *Diagnostic and Statistical Manual of Mental Disorders* (4th ed., 1994, DSM-IV).

Applications

A well-formulated psychiatric diagnosis facilitates treatment planning for mental and emotional disorders. Psychiatric diagnoses, however, are very complex. They are described in a system with five axes of information in order to give a comprehensive picture of how well a person is functioning in everyday life. Axis I pertains to clinical conditions diagnosed in infancy, childhood, or adolescence, as well as other primary mental problems experienced by adults, including cognitive, substance-related, psychotic, anxiety, mood, eating, sleep, impulse control, factitious, somatoform, dissociative, and adjustment disorders. Axis II summarizes problems related to personality and mental retardation. Axis III describes any general medical conditions that are related to a person's mental problems and that may also warrant special attention. Axis IV summarizes psychological, social, and environmental problems that may affect the diagnosis, prognosis, or treatment of a person's mental problems. Axis V is used to give a standardized, overall rating of how well the person has been functioning with his or her disorder.

Once a diagnosis is formulated, a treatment plan is composed. Usually, it involves some combination of medicinal and psychotropic drugs, bibliotherapy, dietary and behavior change recommendations, and psychotherapy for the affected individual or his or her entire family. Treatment compliance is critical, particularly when psychotropic drugs are involved. As such, psychiatric treatment often involves frequent initial contacts and an after-care plan of continued visits with the psychiatrist or a support group able to encourage follow-through on the treatment recommendations.

Perspective and Prospects

The concepts of mental health and illness have been in human cultures since ancient times. As early as 2980 B.C.E., priest-physicians were noted for their treatment of spirit possession involving madness, violence, mutism, and melancholy. In those times, such problems were thought to originate from external, supernatural forces. Later, during the rise of Greco-Roman philosophies in medicine, such states of mind began to be explored more as disturbances of the brain and less as the result of supernatural causes. As such, treatments began to develop greater reliance on methods such as vapors, baths, diets, and emetic and cathartic drugs.

Over time, the field of psychiatry has matured and taken on a major role in medicine. Research into the mind-body relationship has clarified how the mind can influence the healing of medical conditions, as well as how certain medical conditions are rooted in psychological, social, and environmental problems, rather than in a person's biology alone. Additionally, advances in the development of psychotropic drugs have played a major role in the treatment of disabling conditions long thought to be untreatable, such as schizophrenic and bipolar disorders.

In the future, psychiatry is expected to continue developing a broad variety of specialty areas. New techniques for working with children, adolescents, elders, and individuals with particular medical problems or of a particular gender or cultural background are developing rapidly. Finally, understanding the relationship between psychiatric disorders across the life span is likely to increase, as is the need to develop treatments for complex scenarios involving multiple diagnoses.

Bibliography

American Psychiatric Association. *Diagnostic and Statistical Manual of Mental Disorders, Fourth Edition (DSM-IV)*. 4th ed. Washington, D.C.: Author, 1994. This manual contains diagnostic criteria and many other useful facts about a wide variety of mental disorders.

Barry, Patricia D. *Mental Health and Mental Illness*. 6th ed. Philadelphia: Lippincott-Raven, 1998. A concise textbook and reference work for nursing students and beginning practitioners on the fundamentals of human behavior and the management of mental disorders.

Hales, Robert E., Stuart C. Yudofsky, and John A. Talbott, eds. *The American Psychiatric Press Textbook of Psychiatry*. 3d ed. Washington, D.C.: American Psychiatric Press, 1999. Stresses clinical aspects. This edition includes new chapters on psychiatry and managed care, primary care, practice guidelines, and neuropsychiatry.

Kass, Frederic I., John M. Oldham, and Herbert Pardes, eds. *The Columbia University College of Physicians and Surgeons Complete Home Guide to Mental Health*. New York: Henry Holt, 1995. Covers all aspects of mental health, with vital information on choosing the right therapy, advice on legal and ethical issues, and a directory of psychiatric drugs.

Kay, Jerald, Allan Tasman, and Jeffrey A. Lieberman. *Psychiatry: Behavioral Science and Clinical Essentials*. Philadelphia: W. B. Saunders, 2000. A companion to the authors' text *Psychiatry* (1996), a reference for practitioners and students on the principles and practice of psychiatry. Includes the following sections: "Approaches to the Patient," "Human Development," "Scientific Foundation of Psychiatry," "Evaluating Psychiatric Patients," "Adult Psychiatric Disorders," "The Treatment of the Psychiatric Patient," and "Special Clinical Settings and Problems."

Mazure, Carolyn, ed. *Does Stress Cause Psychiatric Illness?* Washington, D.C.:

American Psychiatric Press, 1995. Examines studies relating stress to psychiatric illness and using new models to differentiate types of stress, accounts for various responses, and addresses related topics in neuroscience.

Preston, John, and James Johnson. *Clinical Psychopharmacology Made Ridiculously Simple*. 4th ed. Miami: MedMaster, 2000. Reviews specific disorders, breakthrough symptoms, patient education, and common errors.

Tomb, David. *Psychiatry*. 6th ed. Baltimore: Williams & Wilkins, 1999. Part of the House Officer Series. Provides a concise, user-friendly guide to managing clinical problems with practical tips for history taking, examination, and treatment.

Nancy A. Piotrowski

See also:

Analytical Psychotherapy; Aversion, Implosion, and Systematic Desensitization Therapies; Behavioral Assessment and Personality Rating Scales; Behavioral Family Therapy; Child and Adolescent Psychiatry; Cognitive Behavior Therapy; Cognitive Therapy; Community Psychology; Electroconvulsive Therapy; Geriatric Psychiatry; Gestalt Therapy; Group Therapy; Mental Health Practitioners; Modeling Therapies; Music, Dance, and Theater Therapy; Operant Conditioning Therapies; Person-Centered Therapy; Play Therapy; Psychoactive Drug Therapy; Psychoanalysis; Psychotherapy: Children; Psychotherapy: Effectiveness; Psychotherapy: Goals and Techniques; Psychotherapy: Historical Approaches to Treatment; Rational-Emotive Therapy; Reality Therapy; Strategic Family Therapy; Transactional Analysis.

PSYCHOACTIVE DRUG THERAPY

Type of psychology: Psychotherapy
Fields of study: Biological treatments; nervous system

Psychoactive drug therapy is one approach to the treatment of various psycho-pathologies. The relationship between nervous system function and behavior enables the use of drugs intended to reduce symptoms associated with abnormal psychology. One major goal is to design drugs that will permanently reverse psychopathologies; this has been accomplished only rarely.

Principal terms

EFFICACY: a pharmacological term that addresses a drug's ability to perform an action or actions effectively

MEDICINAL CHEMISTRY: a division of organic chemistry in which drugs that have a potential for pharmacological activity are produced

NEUROTRANSMITTER: a chemical substance released from one nerve cell that communicates activity by binding to and changing the activity of another nerve cell

PSYCHOPHARMACOLOGY: the science that studies drugs that act on the nervous system and are capable of altering behavior

RECEPTOR: a molecule or molecular complex that binds with a drug, resulting in an interaction that leads to a pharmacological effect

THERAPEUTIC INDEX: a pharmacological parameter that indicates safety by comparing a drug's beneficial and adverse effects

TRANQUILIZER: technically, an antipsychotic drug; often misused to refer to a sedative-hypnotic drug

Overview

Humans have used drugs for a variety of purposes throughout the ages. The earliest records demonstrate well-developed systems for therapeutic drug use; it is not a farfetched extension to suggest that the medicinal use of drugs long preceded recorded history. Early humans recognized the availability of useful medicines in the natural world, particularly in plants, while also feeling the need to treat ailments, including those that are now recognized as being associated with problems in the nervous system. Ancient use probably reached its peak in Egypt, where a precursor to modern chemistry, medicinal alchemy, developed as a result of considerable interest in health, life, and the afterlife.

Although intellectual activity in general stagnated during the Dark Ages, alchemy was kept alive in the Arabic world, and it slowly worked its way into Europe. Alchemy is often associated with attempts to convert base metals such as lead into precious metals such as gold, but medicinal alchemy held an equal footing during the Middle Ages. These practices were probably prescientific in that experimentation was blended in a complex fashion with mystical events, but the development and use of medicines during that time laid a substantial foundation for the modern era of drug use.

The scientific revolution was in progress by the time any substantial deviation from the native and alchemical uses of drugs occurred. The real break came with the end of vitalistic beliefs—that is, the belief that living matter somehow contained special attributes beyond other matter. The end of vitalism ushered in the field of organic chemistry, in which chemical knowledge is focused upon carbon and its compounds, the building blocks of life. By the late nineteenth century, organic chemists were gaining expertise in synthesis, the practice of constructing new molecules from simpler building blocks. The power of synthetic chemistry is that molecules can be designed from natural models or that unique substances, unknown in nature, can be built. The twentieth century has been dominated by the proliferation of synthetic chemicals, including drugs synthesized by organic chemists.

Psychoactive drug therapy as a formal scientific discipline may date from the reintroduction of the natural product ephedrine from China and the subsequent synthesis of amphetamine, a closely related but more powerful stimulant of the central nervous system, in the early third of the twentieth century. Parallel developments over time in philosophical beliefs about mind, brain, and behavior led to changes in attitudes about the nature of mental illness. Slowly, people associated psychopathology less with evil possession and other undefinable processes and more with brain mechanisms that could be treated with components of the material world. Drugs are one example of material substances that can affect brain function. Psychoactive drug therapy thus has developed as a result of the convergence of scientific thought in psychology and pharmacology.

Modern practice finds drug use for therapeutic purposes in a wide range of areas. Chief among them are the sedative-hypnotic drugs, which are used for anxiety reduction; the antidepressants, which are applied to clinical depression; and the antipsychotics, which have revolutionized the medical treatment of schizophrenia and other severe psychoses. All drug use involves complex outcomes, ranging from extreme benefit, occasionally even cure, to severe adversity, including death. Cost-benefit analysis is the rigorous study of the continuum of effects associated with drug use, including therapy. Generally, scientific development of drugs has resulted in drugs that are more specific in achieving wanted, beneficial outcomes at the expense of nonspecific, unwanted, and adverse results. Accordingly, drug development produces drugs whose cost-benefit analyses fall more toward the benefit side.

As drugs evolve, previously important categories, such as amphetamine stimulants, fall from therapeutic favor as finer tools, such as antidepressants, are introduced. In a given family of drugs, such as the sedative-hypnotic family, one generation replaces another. The barbiturate sedative-hypnotics widely used in the 1940's and 1950's were moved aside by the benzodiazepines, such as diazepam (Valium), in the 1960's. Psychoactive drug therapy involves the systematic search for new categories of drugs that can be used to treat previously untreatable disorders and for refinements of existing categories in order to produce safer, more effective therapy. This article deals with this developmental edge, speculation about future drug therapy, and the traditionally useful classifications.

Applications

From the standpoint of revolutionary impact, no drugs hold a higher position in the psychotherapeutic realm than the antipsychotics. Until the mid-1950's, there were no efficacious drugs in this area. Standard approaches to treatment included chronic institutionalization, shock therapy (both electrical and insulin), and psychosurgery (lobotomy and lobectomy). All these regimens had serious limitations in both efficacy and adversity.

In the early 1950's, researchers introduced the drug reserpine (Serpasil) on the strength of its active properties in the cardiovascular and nervous systems. Reserpine's ability to reduce symptomology in schizophrenia and related psychoses triggered the breakthrough into the age of antipsychotic drugs. In a very short time, reserpine was superseded by chlorpromazine (Thorazine), the first of the phenothiazine antipsychotics, which have remained the primary drugs of choice. Thorazine's introduction in 1955 produced a remarkable outflow of patients from the world's mental institutions, since its palliative properties of reduction of emotionality, blockage of hallucination, and clearing of thought processes allowed thousands of people to resume relatively normal lives as outpatients.

It is important to recognize that the phenothiazines do not cure psychoses. Rather, the drugs have been shown to block the action of the neurotransmitter dopamine in the brain. Antagonizing dopamine reduces symptomology but does not end the disorder. Scientists are still struggling to find the causes of psychoses among genetic, psychological, neurochemical, and social factors. Additionally, phenothiazines are not without negative effects. Although the drugs show very high therapeutic indices, suggesting high safety, there are problems that must be considered prior to and during administration of the agents. Foremost is the extremely high probability that chronic users of phenothiazines will suffer from progressive, sometimes irreversible, degeneration in the basal ganglia, leading to Parkinson-like tardive dyskinesias (involuntary motor movements or facial twitches) and related problems in secondary motor control. Like the efficacy of these drugs, these problems also seem to be related to dopamine-blocking properties. Another problem, although of lesser frequency, is liver toxicity. Another category of antipsychotics, the butyrophenones, haloperidol (Haldol) being the prototype, is also frequently used. These drugs are often used to treat geriatric patients; overall, their general pharmacology is very similar to that of the phenothiazines.

From the standpoint of societal impact, the sedative-hypnotic drugs are by far the most important psychotherapeutic agents. Since the introduction of chlordiazepoxide (Librium) in 1962, the benzodiazepines have been the favored category of sedative-hypnotic drugs. Each year in the United States alone, hundreds of millions of dollars are spent on benzodiazepines, mostly for their anxiety-reducing properties. Diazepam (Valium), the best known of these drugs, shows a prototypical dose-related spectrum of activity from low-dose anxiety reduction to sedation, hypnosis, and eventually anesthesia and coma at higher doses. The major advantage of the benzodiazepines relative to older drugs such as the barbiturates—for example, phenobarbital—is that the newer drugs are much more specific in their actions. Consequently, the older drugs are much more depressive, have lower therapeutic indices, and are much more likely to lead to overdose death as a result of respiratory and cardiovascular arrest.

Sedative-hypnotic drugs are thought to act by means of complex interactions with gamma aminobutyric acid (GABA) receptors in the brain. Unfortunately, highly specific antagonists have not been available clinically. Development of high-affinity antagonists is a priority of research in this field, because overdose death, particularly with use of the older drugs, could be greatly reduced if appropriate agents existed. The agonists, such as Valium, are also used for their anesthetic, anticonvulsant, and muscle-relaxing properties. The sedative-hypnotic drugs, frequently called tranquilizers, are likely to be highly used for years to come. Development of even-higher-specificity agonists, perhaps working by means of different mechanisms, is a common goal in the drug industry.

In terms of drugs that are becoming increasingly important, the antidepressants lead the way. The first drugs that showed widespread efficacy are those known as tricyclic antidepressants; amitriptyline (Elavil) and imipramine (Tofranil) are well-known examples. They are often called first-generation antidepressants. Although they have long latencies (a few weeks to months), these drugs are rather effective in the general population of severely depressed individuals. The term "first generation" is a misnomer, because a group of drugs known as the monoamine oxidase inhibitors (MAOIs) actually came first. The MAOIs, however, such as tranylcypromine (Parnate), carry much greater toxicity, and are currently used in cases that are refractory to other drugs. Thus, the first-generation drugs were the first to have reasonable therapeutic indices.

A second generation of drugs became prominent in the 1980's. Highly utilized examples include trazodone (Desyrel) and fluoxetine (Prozac). Some controversy surrounds these drugs in terms of their differential efficacy (with respect to the first generation) and their safety. Broadly speaking, they are quite similar to the first generation. All the antidepressants appear to act through biogenic-amine mechanisms, with special emphasis on norepinephrine and serotonin. Some of the second-generation drugs may be more specific toward serotonin.

No discussion of psychoactive drug therapy is complete without mention of drugs used to treat bipolar disorders (manic-depressive disorders). Traditional antidepressants are not usually effective in bipolar disorders. Instead, lithium salts, usually lithium carbonate or lithium chloride, are used. Lithium is especially remarkable because its organic structure is so much smaller than the organic structures of most psychoactive drugs. Nevertheless, lithium is one of the only known treatments for bipolar disorders; it is reasonably safe, provided the dosage is carefully monitored and is not allowed to drift into the toxic range. Its mechanism is unknown, although biogenic-amine mechanisms are frequently mentioned, and its similarity to the sodium ion in neuroconduction has been recognized.

There are many other psychoactive drugs. Those agents outlined here, however, constitute the heart of the category. The hallucinogens (psychotomimetics and psychedelics), which are unusually potent and show a variety of neural and behavioral activities, are worthy of note. These drugs have not, however, been shown to be useful therapeutically. Another extremely important category is the opiate or narcotic group. These drugs are especially fascinating in a psychological sense, in that their great effectiveness in relieving severe pain is associated more with an individual's perception of pain severity than with actual blockage of painful stimuli.

Perspective and Prospects

Psychoactive drug therapy has become an important component of clinical medicine with the recognition that few disorders can be effectively addressed by means of a single therapeutic regimen. Multifaceted approaches involving parameters from the psychological, sociological, pharmacological, and cultural realms are the rule rather than the exception. The increased importance of drug therapy also mirrors two other important trends: the increasing emphasis in science generally to embrace, at least in part, materialistic philosophical trends; and the boom in medical chemistry, which has made available many new, useful drugs.

In the past, drugs such as strychnine, salts of arsenic, mercury, lead, and chloroform were vital pharmacotherapeutic agents. Today, these substances are considered to be poisons, common laboratory chemicals, or, at best, therapeutic drugs of dubious character. This is not to say that these substances had no value. In most cases, they did have value; however, they have been superseded by agents with greater specificity, higher therapeutic indices, and targets that are better known. Thus, such previously used drugs are said to be antiquated. It does not take a great leap of imagination to suggest that any psychoactive drug list may become antiquated. In fact, it is the hope of almost all workers in this field that currently favored drugs will be displaced. Broadly speaking, few (if any) drugs in use today are ideal. Most are not curative, many lack specificity, and more than a few have therapeutic indices that are lower than one would wish.

Two significant trends should revolutionize the psychoactive drug list during the twenty-first century. First, a greater understanding of psychopathologies will progressively refine the targets for drugs. This awareness will arise from a number of areas. Drugs themselves are extraordinary tools for gaining a better understanding of the nervous system. Additionally, the behavioral and cognitive approaches to psychology, the evolution of counseling techniques and theories, and developments in the social sciences will increasingly shed light on the etiology of psychopathologies.

Second, drug development is undergoing revolutionary changes. Traditional development has centered on what are known as structure-activity relationships. This approach has been productive, but the continuous alteration of structure to achieve greater activity with higher specificity is a long process that has clear limitations. Progress in molecular biology in the latter half of the twentieth century, coupled with powerful computer modeling tools for molecules, has led pharmacologists to examine drug receptors themselves. As these macromolecular receptors become better understood in a chemical and three-dimensional sense, drugs can be efficiently designed to interact with the receptors. It is quite realistic to propose that psychotherapeutic drug therapy will be much more effective, safer, and in many cases even curative in the decades ahead. This is encouraging for scientist, clinician, and patient alike.

Bibliography

Bloom, Floyd E., and Arlyne Lazerson. *Brain, Mind, and Behavior*. 2d ed. New York: W. H. Freeman, 1988. Beautifully illustrated and artfully written, this popular yet rigorous book probes current understanding of brain processes and their implications. Bloom, one of the world's leading neuropharmacologists, has an exceptional grasp of the diverse fields of neuroscience.

Hardman, Joel G., and Lee E. Limbird, eds. *Goodman and Gilman's the Pharmacological Basis of Therapeutics*. 9th ed. New York: McGraw-Hill, 1996. The world's most authoritative treatise on pharmacology, this volume provides comprehensive, technical summaries on all major drug groups, including psychoactive substances. It is almost always the best place to start when researching a drug's activity.

Julien, Robert M. *A Primer of Drug Action*. 8th ed. New York: W. H. Freeman, 1998. One of the best drug-education texts ever written, this book combines unusual knowledge of drug effects with great insight into psychological and sociological factors. Perfect for scientifically inclined high school and college students.

Katzung, Bertram G., ed. *Basic and Clinical Pharmacology*. 7th ed. Stamford, Conn.: Appleton & Lange, 1998. Although less technical than *Goodman and Gilman's the Pharmacological Basis of Therapeutics*, this book is in the same class. Occasionally gives a somewhat different slant on drug action. The chapter by Bourne and Roberts on receptors and pharmacodynamics is superb.

Kolb, Bryan, and Ian Q. Whishaw. *Fundamentals of Human Neuropsychology*. 4th ed. New York: W. H. Freeman, 1996. Quite naturally, the neuroscientist, pharmacologist, and psychologist look at the nervous system and drug action in slightly different ways. This book provides an important psychological perspective on these approaches.

Poling, Alan D. *A Primer of Human Behavioral Pharmacology*. New York: Plenum Press, 1986. Psychopharmacology places a special emphasis on drug action in operant-conditioning paradigms. This book provides a fine, relatively nontechnical introduction to this complex, emerging field.

Snyder, Solomon H. *Drugs and the Brain*. New York: Scientific American Books, 1986. Snyder, one of the world's leading neuroscientists, provides an authoritative, wonderfully illustrated look at drugs. Excellent reading for the beginner.

Keith Krom Parker

See also:

Abnormality: Biomedical Models; Addictive Personality and Behaviors; Anxiety Disorders; Depression; Insomnia; Manic-Depressive Disorder; Neuroses; Psychosis; Schizophrenia.

PSYCHOANALYSIS

Type of psychology: Psychotherapy
Fields of study: Classic analytic themes and issues; evaluating psychotherapy; psychodynamic therapies

Classical psychoanalysis, developed by Sigmund Freud, was first used to treat people with symptoms (such as hysterical paralyses) lacking an organic cause. Modern psychoanalysis is more widely applicable, including to those whom Freud considered untreatable by psychoanalysis, those who are particularly resistant to treatment, and those who have had disappointing experiences with previous therapy.

Principal terms

CLASSICAL PSYCHOANALYSIS: the method of treatment of psychological disorders that was developed by Sigmund Freud

COUNTERTRANSFERENCE: errors therapists make in response to the errors their clients make; clients may assume that the therapist is omniscient and omnipotent, for example, and therapists may see themselves as infallible

DEVELOPMENT: the course of change and growth that an individual follows throughout life

PSYCHOANALYST: a person who has completed psychoanalytic training, a specialized and comprehensive form of psychotherapeutic training

PSYCHOTHERAPIST: a person who may have had a range of psychotherapeutic training (much or little); a general term for practitioners of various types of therapy

TRANSFERENCE: the errors clients make when they view therapists; one example would be believing that therapists will be as punitive toward them as their original caregivers were

Overview

Psychoanalysis, a method of treating psychological disorders and a way of investigating why people do what they do, was formulated by Sigmund Freud around the beginning of the twentieth century. When psychoanalysts and others in the mental health field investigate the reasons individuals act in specific ways (for example, avoiding contact with others), they are exploring human motivations. People who have completed psychoanalytic training are called psychoanalysts. Psychoanalysis was originally the province of psychiatry because Freud was a physician (by definition, a licensed psychiatrist is also a licensed physician). Since then, however, the specialty has broadened to include psychologists, social workers, the clergy, nurses, teachers, administrators, artists, and scientists.

Classical psychoanalysis is intended to assist individuals who have entered treatment. Those people most in need, however, usually do not elect treatment; those who enter appear to be better off than those who avoid saying "I need help." The ways in which help is rendered derive from the concept of excavating:

Psychoanalysts "dig" for motivations of which clients may be unaware or less than fully aware; self-defeating patterns of thinking, feeling, or acting; and blocks to optimal functioning. Modern analysts share such conceptualizations. Both classical and modern analysts employ views of awareness ranging from conscious awareness through what Freud termed "preconscious" (accessible to awareness under the right conditions of preparation or growth) to "unconscious." Freud's is a tripartite schema, but what exists is a continuum between the polar extremes of full awareness and complete unawareness.

Sigmund Freud, the founder of psychoanalysis. (Library of Congress)

Freud developed the theory and technique that became classical psychoanalysis. It includes free association and the concepts of transference and resistance. Free association means that people in psychoanalytic treatment say whatever occurs to them, no matter how illogical, bizarre, or embarrassing their utterances may be. Free association has been called the "fundamental rule" of classical psychoanalysis. Transference constitutes the mistaken assumptions that a client makes about the analyst. For example, hope or magical thinking may generate the view that the analyst can and will fix everything without the person in therapy having to undertake any responsibilities for the treatment or for personal growth outside it. Pessimism (stemming, for example, from previous mistreatment) may be responsible for mistrust of the analyst or for an expectation that the analyst will be as condemnatory as others were.

Resistance refers to the many ways clients disregard requests to free-associate, refuse to observe other rules of treatment, or sabotage their own progress toward health. Resistance shows the analyst that the client is avoiding something that is difficult to confront and therefore important.

The person in analysis is not the only one who misperceives the other. The analyst is also a human being and is therefore vulnerable to countertransference. Analysts may find themselves succumbing to acting on these feelings, thereby helping the client to sabotage progress and avoid change. Experienced and talented psychoanalysts, however, can use countertransference to understand and help their clients.

Freud learned that the analyst must resist certain temptations in order for therapy to be most effective. When the client is free-associating, the analyst should resist the impulse to offer interpretations immediately. Interpretations are explanations such as, "The reason you are experiencing inappropriate fear is that the dread of your father, instilled in you when he treated you harshly, has generalized to include others who resemble your father in their authority over you." The technique of interpretation was conceived as the principal manner in which the insights deduced by the psychoanalyst were to be imparted to the patient. The analyst's task is to listen carefully and respectfully, enabling the client to broaden and deepen transferential distortions or denials of reality, before offering interpretations.

Modern psychoanalysis evolved for several reasons. First, clients who are especially vulnerable, only marginally functional, or clearly at risk display tremendous fears and intractable resistances. Until such time as substitute behaviors become available to them and they are able to relax and ultimately discard their defenses, their resistances (defenses manifested during sessions) should be respected, understood, and used by their therapists. Modern psychoanalysis attempts to do so. Second, vulnerable clients demonstrate exquisite sensitivity to attempts to direct their activities or even to provide suggestions. They have received insufficient practice in running their lives and need more autonomy, not less. They have received too many orders and need fewer directives. Modern analysts try to minimize directions or suggestions (even when these are requested or demanded), to limit what they say to the briefest and fewest interventions, to avoid confrontations if possible, and to refrain from providing interpretations until clients give evidence of having achieved the maturity to accept and profit from them. Many practitioners believe that when clients are able to use interpretations, the clients themselves are more likely to originate them.

Applications

The essential distinction between psychoanalysis (both classical and modern) and other modalities of psychotherapy (including psychoanalytically oriented ones) rests not upon frequency of sessions or whether the client uses the couch rather than sitting face-to-face with the therapist but upon whether the treatment employs free association, transference, and resistance (embracing the preconscious and unconscious) and is an ego-maturational process. Analytic clients are assisted in becoming aware of alternatives, including new ways of viewing life events.

Psychoanalysis tries to determine the ways clients avoid seeing and doing the things of which they are capable. Other therapies tend to be problem-oriented.

Modern psychoanalysis deals with a much wider spectrum of client pathologies than classical psychoanalysis and is prepared to work with clients whom current classical psychoanalysts regard as unsuitable for treatment. Modern analysts modify the fundamental rule of free association and ask clients to say whatever they wish, rather than demanding that they say everything. The objective of enabling clients to be able to say everything, however, remains the same. When the ego strength of clients permits, modern analysts say more, but they prefer asking questions to answering them or making statements.

Making statements tends to be regarded as objectionable either because unsolicited statements are interpreted by the client as being lectures (which is often true) or because they derive from the therapist's own insecurities. Self-initiated requests for help are considered evidence of progress. Questions asked by clients frequently conceal other questions they may have. Answering the original question makes it less likely that the other, more important questions will be unearthed.

Modern analysts attempt to reverse the direction of clients' self-injurious acts. Attacking oneself is conceptualized as the "narcissistic defense" intended to protect "the object" (Freud's term for the "other," the most typical example of which is the first object of the infant's rage, the nurturer). Anger is precipitated by frustration, unmodulated rage by abuse or neglect. Modern analysts offer themselves as legitimate objects of criticism. All communications of disapproval are accepted. Acts are discouraged, although intentions are unobjectionable and may be explored if the client can tolerate exploration. It is all right to *want* to destroy or hurt, but it is not all right to *do* either. Clients may be assisted to see such acceptable alternatives to destructive actions as hostile thoughts, negative feelings, and destructive fantasies. Clients are seen as engaging in the most harmful behaviors when they damage themselves—physically, psychologically (destroying their minds and requiring institutionalization), or both. Progress is demonstrated when clients start attacking others and diminish self-attacks. Further progress consists of their proceeding toward verbalization of their feelings, concerns, and wishes; diminishing ego-oriented attacks upon others even if expressed in words; and attempting to confine attacks solely to the analyst, who is expected to deal more constructively with them than laypersons are.

Attacks are difficult, even for professionals, especially when taken personally. Therapeutic work is made more tolerable, and even challenging, by personal analysis and supervision that enable practitioners to view the attacks as part of transference, a generalized phenomenon and a component of desirable progress. Analysts view abuse of themselves by clients, however (as opposed to verbal attacks), as harmful to both parties and as treatment-destructive. When one injures another, one injures oneself. Analysts insist that both they and their client or clients (partners in a dyad, or members of a family) be treated respectfully.

One significant difference between classical and modern psychoanalysis concerns the attitude toward, and use of, countertransference. Both classical and modern analysts recognize the inevitability and importance of countertransference.

Freud, recognizing its perils, urged that it be obliterated as completely as possible; this was unrealistic. Moreover, countertransference can be used productively. Modern analysts, in fact, regard countertransference as the most valuable source of information about their clients and as the key to the most effective treatment. The comprehension of objective countertransference (feelings induced in the analyst by a client's problems) permits the analyst to understand more fully what the client is experiencing and formulate a treatment strategy. The recognition and correction of subjective countertransference (preexisting personal problems) via personal analysis and supervision afford measures to prevent analysts' blindnesses, vulnerabilities, and irrational expectations from interfering with their responsibilities for the welfare of their clients.

Classical psychoanalysts tend to agree with Freud that persons with particular kinds of mental illness (such as schizophrenia or narcissistic disorders) are not analyzable. They also regard interpretations as one of the foundations of treatment. In contrast, modern analysts regard no one with a psychologically reversible disorder as untreatable. In treating more vulnerable and remote clients, they have learned that interpretations can be viewed as attacks by such clients. They refrain from employing such feedback until they are sure that interpretations can be tolerated by the client.

Modern psychoanalysts are aware that thoughts and feelings play important roles in causing, exacerbating, ameliorating, treating, and curing somatic (that is, physical or bodily) conditions. Modern analysts have sought ways of treating organic disease (such as cancer) psychoanalytically—in effect considering such conditions psychologically reversible disorders rather than disease entities that are unchangeable.

Modern analysts are aware that a client's failure to make progress with a certain analyst does not necessarily mean that the individual will never have success in therapy. It may simply mean that the client does not have a proper "fit" with the analyst. Working with a different analyst, the client may have quite a different experience. Again, the effects of countertransference are important; in a curative relationship, the analyst should be able to experience feelings induced by the client and return to the client the necessary therapeutic feelings—appropriately spaced and in correct dosages—that lead to progress and eventual recovery.

In both classical and modern psychoanalysis, the intensity of treatment (the number of sessions per week) is often the result of a number of variables. These may include the particular benefits the client hopes to receive, how rapidly progress is desired, the ability of the client to afford the practitioner's fees, and the time available to both. One exception to this rule would be that modern analysts prefer limiting sessions to once a week at the beginning of therapy in order to assess whether the ego strength of the client is adequate to cope with the more intense and unsettling regression that occurs with more frequent sessions. Fees, like session frequency and treatment length, vary considerably. Professionals often employ a "sliding scale" of fees to accommodate people's varying abilities to afford treatment.

Perspective and Prospects

Before Sigmund Freud developed his theory at the beginning of the twentieth century, methods of dealing with psychological interferences with functioning (what are now called neuroses, character disorders, borderline conditions, and even some schizophrenias) as well as with more severe conditions (such as psychoses, narcissistic disorders, and chronic schizophrenias) lacked coherence and effectiveness. Functional impairment was perceived as being physiologically caused, even if a precise cause could not be located; it was therefore seen as requiring physiological treatment. Impairments that were psychological went untreated, often even undetected. The care of the more serious mental illnesses was at best ineffectual and at worst cruel and inhumane.

Freud confronted people with the concept that, in the psychic realm, they are not masters but servants of hidden drives and desires. Irrationality was suddenly seen as a universal condition. Freud's patients were upper-middle-class people who came for treatment of such conditions as "hysteria," in which psychic conflict is converted into a curtailment of functioning, such as blindness or an inability to perform particular motor skills. Other conditions he treated included autonomous episodes (such as sleepwalking) and anatomic anomalies. One anatomic anomaly, for example, is glove anesthesia, in which a patient has no sense of feeling in an area roughly corresponding to that covered by a glove; since no local injury could cause such a loss of feeling, it is a symptom of a functional disorder, most likely hysteria. All of these lacked an organic explanation. Freud provided a blueprint for such mental disorders: the psychodynamic method of explaining them and the psychoanalytic method of treating them. He also furnished concepts of development (of both individuals and groups—even civilizations) and personality, as well as two explanations of why dreams occur. His work ultimately led to countless other ways of explaining people, the events in which they participate (history), and the artifacts they create (literature, art, and music).

Freud has had many critics, and for good reason. His view of females, for example, was clearly flawed; it reflected the male-dominated society of his day that subordinated women and underestimated their potentials for accomplishment and creativity. Nevertheless, Freud's impact has been substantial and pervasive, and most of his contributions are incorporated into theory and practice.

Bibliography

Forrester, John. *Dispatches from the Freud Wars: Psychoanalysis and Its Passions.* Cambridge, Mass.: Harvard University Press, 1997. Six essays on Freudian psychoanalysis and its cultural implications.

Freeman, Lucy. *The Story of Anna O.* New York: Walker, 1972. A popularly written examination of the psychoanalysis of the first analytic patient, with a description of her subsequent life (which was fascinating) and achievements; she became the first social worker in Germany and was responsible for many advances in the care of unwed mothers and their children. A particularly important accompaniment to the Freud and Breuer work.

Freud, Sigmund, and Josef Breuer. *Studies on Hysteria.* 1895. Reprint. New York:

Basic Books, 2000. Contains not only the original source for the theory of psychoanalysis ("Anna O.," the only case conducted by Josef Breuer) but also the other analyses Freud conducted and about which he wrote. The germinative work in psychoanalysis.

Galatzer-Levy, Robert M., et al., eds. *Does Psychoanalysis Work?* New Haven, Conn.: Yale University Press, 2000. Critically analyzes every major study of the efficacy of psychoanalytic treatment. Includes bibliographical references and an index.

Kearns, Katherine. *Psychoanalysis, Historiography, and Feminist Theory: The Search for Critical Method.* New York: Cambridge University Press, 1997. Includes the chapters "Oedipal Pedagogy: Becoming a Woman," "Strange Angels: Negation and Performativity," "Daddy: Notes upon an Autobiographical Account of Paranoia," and "Telling Stories: Historiography and Narrative."

Nye, Robert D. *Three Psychologies: Perspectives from Freud, Skinner, and Rogers.* 6th ed. Pacific Grove, Calif.: Brooks/Cole, 2000. A revised edition of a popular and critically acclaimed book. Presents the essential ideas of Sigmund Freud, B. F. Skinner, and Carl Rogers, three of the most important contributors to contemporary psychological thought.

Saguaro, Shelley, ed. *Psychoanalysis and Woman: A Reader.* New York: New York University Press, 2000. Collects important psychoanalytic writings on female sexuality and women from Freud's contemporaries through French feminism to postmodernism and postfeminism.

Spotnitz, Hyman. *Modern Psychoanalysis of the Schizophrenic Patient.* 2d ed. New York: Jason Aronson, 1998. The seminal work in modern psychoanalysis. More comprehensible than the first edition, it is still difficult reading because it requires some familiarity with the theory and (particularly) practice of modern psychoanalytic treatment.

_____. *Psychotherapy of Preoedipal Conditions: Schizophrenia and Severe Character Disorders.* Reprint. New York: Jason Aronson, 1996. Considerably easier reading than the other Spotnitz book. While it does not contain as much theory or as many practice issues, it presents them more clearly and enjoyably.

Spotnitz, Hyman, and Phyllis W. Meadow. *Treatment of the Narcissistic Neuroses.* Rev. ed. New York: Jason Aronson, 1995. A sound and important collaborative effort between the founder of modern psychoanalysis and the person (Phyllis W. Meadow) who spearheaded the movement's appearance and started, with others, the institution founded to advance the philosophy and techniques of modern psychoanalysis.

Elliott P. Schuman

See also:

Analytical Psychotherapy; Cognitive Behavior Therapy; Cognitive Therapy; Person-Centered Therapy; Psychotherapy: Effectiveness; Psychotherapy: Goals and Techniques; Psychotherapy: Historical Approaches to Treatment.

PSYCHOSIS

Type of psychology: Psychopathology
Fields of study: Cognitive processes; social perception and cognition

Psychosis is the most severe mental disorder, in which the individual loses contact with reality and suffers from such symptoms as delusions and hallucinations.

Principal terms

DELUSION: a false belief that is held despite strong evidence to the contrary
FUNCTIONAL PSYCHOSES: psychoses for which no organic causes can be found
HALLUCINATION: a false perception of one of the five senses that is held despite strong evidence to the contrary
ORGANIC PSYCHOSES: psychoses that can be attributed directly to a problem in the structure, functioning, or chemistry of the brain

Causes and Symptoms

The individual with a psychosis displays disordered thinking, emotion, and behavior. The individual fails to make sense of his or her surroundings, reacts inaccurately to them, and develops false thoughts or ideas about them. The resulting behavior can be described as peculiar, abnormal, or bizarre. Psychosis runs in families and most often first appears in late adolescence or early adulthood. There are medical and physical causes of some psychoses and some for which the cause is unknown. Psychosis describes a group of symptoms that can be part of several formal psychiatric diagnoses to include schizophrenia. Psychotic symptoms are characterized by delusions, hallucinations, disturbances of movement, and/or speech disturbances.

Delusions are false beliefs that are held despite strong evidence to the contrary. An example of an extreme delusion might be a man who believes that someone has planted a radio transmitter in his brain that sends signals to creatures on Mars. Hallucinations are false perceptions of the senses that, like delusions, are held despite strong evidence to the contrary. Hallucinations can involve any of the five senses. Examples of extreme hallucinations include feeling as if one is covered by ants; seeing green cows walking through the wall; hearing voices that do not exist; and smelling a constant odor when none is present.

Disturbances of movement can occur with psychoses. For example, a woman may become very exaggerated in her movements or, conversely, may become motionless for periods of time. These disturbances of movement are clearly bizarre and unnatural. Finally, speech disturbances are very common in psychoses. A man might speak in a way which is not understandable to others. He may carry on a conversation in which he believes that he is communicating normally but without making sense. Alternatively, speech might be clear but the individual shifts from one unrelated idea to another without being aware of doing so. Another psychotic symptom is severe emotional turmoil described as intense shifting moods with accompanying feelings of being confused.

Treatment and Therapy

The treatment of psychoses involves removing or correcting the causes of the psychosis when possible. Psychoses are often categorized as organic or functional, which provides a way to communicate the cause of the psychosis and thereby the appropriate treatment. Organic psychoses are attributable to disturbances in the brain. These psychoses can be attributed directly to a problem in the structure, functioning, or chemistry of the brain. Various physical conditions and abnormalities can lead to psychosis, including thyroid disorders, drug reactions, infections, epilepsy, tumors, and circulatory disorders (for example, strokes). The treatment of organic psychoses involves removing or correcting the causes of the psychosis. In the case of a psychosis caused by a disorder of the thyroid gland, the individual might be prescribed medications to correct the thyroid problem or have the gland surgically removed. Certain prescription and illegal drugs can cause a psychosis; these include cocaine, alcohol, heart medications, and pain medications. In these situations, the psychotic symptoms are often eliminated when the medication or drug is discontinued. Organic psychoses may be the result of deteriorating physical conditions, such as Alzheimer's disease. Such a psychosis is typically nonreversible and is treated with tranquilizing medications to decrease the individual's discomfort and disruptive behaviors.

Functional psychoses are those psychoses for which no organic causes can be found. Often the psychotic symptoms are part of a more traditional psychiatric condition such as schizophrenia or depression. The mainstay of the treatment of functional psychoses is medication therapy. As with the organic psychoses in deteriorating physical conditions, tranquilizers are the most appropriate first-line treatment for psychotic symptoms. The goal of therapy is to decrease the frequency and disruption of psychotic thoughts and behaviors.

Individual, group, and family psychotherapy are also a major part of treating individuals with functional psychosis or organic psychosis in deteriorating physical conditions. These therapies help to ensure compliance with the medication therapy, decrease the tendency for relapse, and can even lead to the reduction in the amount of medication required to relieve the individual's symptoms. The goal of psychotherapy is to help the individual maintain optimal functioning.

Occasionally, the patient with a psychosis may require inpatient hospitalization. The experience of hallucinations or delusions can be particularly distressing and can lead to a severe depression. Furthermore, these hallucinations and delusions might be of a homicidal or suicidal nature. While hospitalization is not required in treating individuals with psychosis, when individuals become a danger to themselves or to others, a brief inpatient hospitalization may be required to stabilize the patients and return them to a higher state of functioning. During hospitalization, patients are treated with medication therapy along with individual, group, or family therapy until they can be safely returned to their environments. Occasionally, patients with psychoses have multiple episodes during their lives requiring numerous inpatient hospitalizations.

Perspective and Prospects

Approximately 2 percent of all people in the world will develop a psychosis sometime during their lifetime. Although psychoses typically first appear in late adolescence or early adulthood, they may begin in middle to late life as well. The symptoms are apparently equally common in males and females. Because there is a strong family pattern to the psychoses, some have suggested a genetic predisposition, and such evidence has been found. Environmental factors, however, such as home environment, parenting, and traumatic life events may also play a role in some psychoses.

Bibliography

Amador, Xavier F., and Anthony S. David. *Insight and Psychosis*. New York: Oxford University Press, 1998. Divided into the following parts: "Phenomenology of Insight," "Neuropsychology of Insight," "Culture and Insight," "Insight and Behavior," and "Clinical Implications of Poor Insight."

American Psychiatric Association. *Diagnostic and Statistical Manual of Mental Disorders, Fourth Edition (DSM-IV)*. 4th ed. Washington, D.C.: Author, 1994. The bible of the psychiatric community, this is a compendium of descriptions of disorders and diagnostic criteria widely embraced by clinicians. Included is an extensive glossary of technical terms, making this volume easy to understand.

Anderson, Carol M., Douglas J. Reiss, and Gerard E. Hogarty. *Schizophrenia and the Family: A Practitioner's Guide to Psychoeducation and Management*. New York: Guilford Press, 1986. Books, articles, and pamphlets for relatives and new staff members. A volume in the Guilford Family Therapy series.

McGorry, Patrick D., and Henry J. Jackson, eds. *The Recognition and Management of Early Psychosis: A Preventive Approach*. New York: Cambridge University Press, 1999. Focuses on the preventive potential of early detection of psychosis and on the practicalities of treatment.

Torrey, E. Fuller. *Surviving Schizophrenia: A Manual for Families, Consumers, and Providers*. 3d ed. New York: HarperPerennial, 1995. An excellent book for the general reader on schizophrenia. It should be read by everyone interested in the disorder, including every mental health worker.

Oliver Oyama

See also:

Addictive Personality and Behaviors; Alcoholism; Dementia; Depression; Neurosis; Paranoia; Schizophrenia; Substance Abuse.

PSYCHOSOMATIC DISORDERS

Type of psychology: Psychopathology
Fields of study: Cognitive processes; organic disorders; stress and illness

Psychosomatic disorders are physical disorders produced by psychological factors such as stress, mental states, or personality characteristics. A variety of psychological or psychotherapeutic interventions have been developed to alter the individual's ability to cope with stressful situations and to change the personality or behavior of the individual.

Principal terms

BEHAVIOR MODIFICATION: therapeutic techniques based on operant conditioning methods employing rewards for desirable behaviors and nonreinforcement or punishment for undesirable behaviors
BIOGENIC: of biological or physical origin
BIOPSYCHOSOCIAL: combining biological, psychological, and social factors
COGNITIVE: having to do with thought processes, such as images, memories, thinking, and problem solving
PSYCHOGENIC: of psychological origin
TYPE A BEHAVIOR PATTERN: a pattern of personality characteristics which leads to behavior that is thought to contribute to coronary heart disease
TYPE C BEHAVIOR PATTERN: a pattern of personality characteristics thought to contribute to development of cancer

Causes and Symptoms

Psychosomatic disorders are physical disorders which are caused by, or exacerbated by, psychological factors. These psychological factors fall into three major groups: stress resulting from encounters with the environment, personality characteristics, and psychological states. It should be noted that psychosomatic disorders are different from two other conditions with which they are often confused. Psychosomatic disorders are real—that is, they are actual physical illnesses that have underlying psychological causes or that are made worse by psychological factors. In somatoform disorders (such as hypochondriasis), by contrast there is no physiological cause; another condition, malingering, is the faking of an illness.

Psychosomatic disorders can affect any of the organ systems of the body. Certainly, not all physical disorders or illnesses are psychosomatic disorders; in many cases, an illness or physical disorder is caused entirely by biogenic factors. In many other cases, however, there is no question about the importance of psychogenic factors. The American College of Family Physicians has estimated that 90 percent of the workload of doctors is the result of psychogenic factors.

There are many familiar and common psychosomatic disorders that can affect the body's various organ systems. Included among them are skin disorders, such as acne, hives, and rashes; musculoskeletal disorders, such as backaches, rheumatoid arthritis, and tension headaches; respiratory disorders, such as asthma and hiccups; and cardiovascular disorders, such as hypertension, heart attacks, strokes, and migraine headaches. Other disorders have also been related to psychological factors, including anemia, weakening of the immune system, ulcers, and constipation. Genitourinary disorders such as menstrual problems, vaginismus, male erectile disorder, and premature ejaculation are included among psychosomatic disorders, as are certain endocrine and neurological problems.

The relationship between the mind and the body has long been the subject of debate. Early societies saw a clear link between the mind and the body. Early Greek and Roman physicians believed that body fluids determined personality types and that people with certain personality types were prone to certain types of diseases. Beginning during the Renaissance period and continuing almost to today, the dominant line of thought held that there was little or no connection between the mind and the body. Illness was seen as the result of organic, cellular pathology. Destruction of body tissue and invasion by "germs," rather than personality type, were seen as the causes of illness.

Sigmund Freud's work with patients suffering from conversion hysteria began to demonstrate both the importance of psychological factors in the production of physical symptoms of illness and the value of psychological therapy in changing the functioning of the body. Research conducted in the 1930's and 1940's suggested that personality factors play a role in the production of a variety of specific illnesses, including ulcers, hypertension, and asthma.

Today, the ascending line of thought can be described as a biopsychosocial view of illness, which begins with the basic assumption that health and illness result from an interplay of biological, psychological, and social factors. A man who suffers a heart attack at age thirty-five is not conceptualized simply as a person who is experiencing the effects of cellular damage caused by purely biological processes that are best treated by surgery or the administration of drugs. The victim, instead, is viewed as a person who also has engaged in practices that adversely affected his health. In addition to drugs and surgery, therefore, treatment for this man might include changing his views on the relative value of work and family as well as emphasizing the importance of daily exercise and diet. If he smokes, he will be encouraged to quit smoking. He might receive training in stress management and relaxation techniques.

Few people today would argue with the proposition that stress is a fact of life. Most have far more experience with stressors—those events that humans find stressful—than they would willingly choose for themselves. Stress is one of the major causes of psychosomatic disorders. Stressors are often assumed to be external events, probably because stressful external events are so easily identified and recognized. Many stressors, however, come from within oneself. For example, one is often the only person who demands that one meet the strict standards that one has set for oneself, and frequently judges oneself more harshly than anyone else for failing to meet those standards. Especially since the late 1970's and early 1980's, cognitive psychologists have focused attention on the internal thinking processes, thoughts, values, beliefs, and expectations that lead people to put unnecessary pressure on themselves that results in the subjective sense of stress.

Another contribution made by cognitive psychologists was the realization that a situation can be a stressor only if the individual interprets it as stressful. Any event that people perceive as something with which they can cope will be perceived as less stressful than an event that taxes or exceeds their resources, regardless of the objective seriousness of the two events. In other words, it is the cognitive appraisal of the event, coupled with one's cognitive appraisal of one's ability to deal with the event, rather than the objective reality of the event, that determines the degree to which one subjectively experiences stress.

Continuing the tradition of the early Greek and Roman physicians, modern personality theorists have often noted that certain personality characteristics seem to be associated with a propensity to develop illness, or even specific illnesses. Other personality characteristics appear to reduce vulnerability to illness. One of the best-known examples of a case in which personality characteristics affect health is that of the Type A behavior pattern (or Type A personality). The person identified as a Type A personality typically displays a pattern of behaviors which include easily aroused hostility, excessive competitiveness, and a pronounced sense of time urgency. Research suggests that hostility is the most damaging of these behaviors. Type A personalities typically display hyperreactivity to stressful situations, with a corresponding slow return to the baseline of arousal. The hostile Type A personality is particularly prone to coronary heart disease. By contrast, the less-driven Type B personality does not display the hostility, competitiveness, and time urgency of the Type A personality, and is about half as likely to develop coronary heart disease.

Studies conducted in the 1970's, and especially in the 1980's, have led to the suggestion that there is a Type C, or cancer-prone, personality. It is well known that many natural and artificial substances produce cancer, but many researchers have also noted that people with certain personality characteristics are more likely to develop cancer, are more likely to develop fast-growing cancers, and are less likely to survive their cancers. These personality characteristics include repression of strong negative emotions, acquiescence in the face of stressful life situations, inhibition, depression, and hopelessness. Encounters with uncontrollable stressful events appear to be particularly related to the development of cancer. In addition, some research suggests that not having strong social support systems contributes to the likelihood of developing cancer.

Recent research has begun to focus on the possible interaction between risk factors for cancer. For example, depressed smokers are many more times likely to develop smoking-related cancers than are either nondepressed smokers or depressed nonsmokers. One theory suggests that the smoking provides exposure to the carcinogenic substance that initiates the cancer, and depression promotes its development.

It has been suggested that hardiness is a broad, positive personality variable that affects one's prospensity for developing stress-related illness. Hardiness is made up of three more specific characteristics: commitment (to become involved in things that are going on around oneself), challenge (accepting the need for change and seeing new opportunities for growth in what others see as problems), and control (a belief that one's actions determine what happens in life and that one can have an effect on the environment). It has been hypothesized that people who possess these characteristics are less likely to develop stress-related disorders because they view stressful situations more favorably than do other people. Commitment and control seem to be more influential in promoting health. Locus of control is a related concept which has received much attention.

Locus of control refers to the location where one believes control over life events originates. An external locus of control is outside oneself; an internal locus of control is within oneself. The individual who perceives that life events are the result of luck, or are determined by others, is assuming an external locus of control. The belief that one's efforts and actions control one's own destiny reflects an internal locus of control. Internalizers are thought to be more likely to assume responsibility for initiating necessary lifestyle changes, to employ more direct coping mechanisms when confronted with stressful situations, and to be more optimistic about the possibility of successfully instituting changes that are needed. This last characteristic is sometimes called self-efficacy. Self-efficacy refers to the belief that one is able to do what is needed and attain the intended effect.

Martin E. P. Seligman began to investigate the phenomenon of learned helplessness in 1964. In part, his interest was fueled by his observations of the life and fate of his father, who suffered a series of devastating strokes. Seligman found that when faced with a situation in which they can do nothing to prevent or escape from what is happening to them, both dogs and people often simply lie down and take it (literally or figuratively). They learn the attitude of helplessness. He also found that helplessness can be unlearned, but that it is usually difficult to do so because the individual has quit trying to escape or avoid the situation. A decade later, Seligman and his colleagues began to investigate the question of why some people (and dogs) did *not* become helpless. They concluded that people (and, presumably dogs) who adopt a pessimistic explanatory style become helpless when adversity is encountered, but that an optimistic explanatory style prevents the development of learned helplessness.

Seligman has described the chain of events by which the pessimistic explanatory style may lead to illness. Beginning with unfortunate experiences such as a serious loss, defeat, or failure, the person with a pessimistic explanatory style becomes depressed. The depression leads to depletion of a neurotransmitter substance called catecholamine, and the body increases the secretion of endorphins—the body's own naturally produced form of morphine. When receptors in the immune system detect the increased presence of the endorphins, the immune system begins to turn itself down. Any disease agents that are encountered while the immune system is weakened have a much greater likelihood of overwhelming the remaining defenses of the immune system. This process is very similar to the situation faced by the individual who contracts the human immunodeficiency virus (HIV) and develops acquired immunodeficiency syndrome (AIDS). When the immune system of the person with AIDS is unable to function effectively, opportunistic infections against which the body could normally defend itself are able to take over. It is those opportunistic infections that kill, rather than the HIV or AIDS itself.

Treatment and Therapy

Since the hyperreactivity of the Type A behavior pattern is thought to be at least partially genetically based, there are probably some limits on what can be done to reduce the incidence of coronary heart disease resulting from physiological hyperreactivity. There is, however, much that can be done in other areas. Persons who are prone to such disorders can be taught to exercise properly, eliminate unhealthy dietary practices, and reduce or quit smoking. Of particular interest to psychologists is the opportunity to help these individuals by teaching effective coping strategies, stress management, values training, behavior modification to control Type A behaviors, and cognitive control of depression and other negative emotions.

Studies by psychologists have demonstrated a wide range of interventions that can be helpful in reducing the danger of cardiovascular disease in Type A personalities. Exercise produces positive effects on physiological functioning, appears to improve general psychological functioning, and reduces Type A behaviors. Cognitive behavioral stress management techniques have been shown to reduce behavioral reactivity. Values training focusing on changing the person's perceptions of the importance of occupational success and competitiveness has enabled them to concentrate on more beneficial behaviors. Behavior modification techniques have been used to alter the kinds of behavior that appear to be most dangerous for the Type A person, substituting other behavioral responses in place of explosive speech and hostility. Cognitive control of emotions produces more rapid physiological recovery after stress.

Efforts by psychologists to help the Type C personality might focus on assertiveness training and altering the person's belief that it is not appropriate to display strong negative emotions, such as anger or frustration. Teaching the Type C person to fight back against stressful life situations, rather that acquiescing to them, might also be of benefit. Imagery therapy appears to be beneficial to some cancer patients, perhaps for that reason, but also because it promotes the development of learned optimism in place of learned pessimism. Promoting the development of effective social support systems is another means for psychologists to have a positive impact on the fight against cancer.

Perspective and Prospects

Psychosomatic disorders are not themselves considered mental disorders. While the psychological factors that cause the physical illness are unhealthy or abnormal from a psychiatric or psychological perspective, the psychosomatic disorder is a real, physical illness or condition controlled by real, physical processes.

Somatoform disorders, on the other hand, are mental disorders which manifest themselves through real or imagined physical symptoms for which no physical cause exists. These symptoms are not intentionally produced by the client. Conversion disorder is one of the somatoform disorders that laypeople often confuse with psychosomatic disorders. Unlike the case with psychosomatic disorders, there is no organic or physiological pathology that would account for the presence of the physical symptoms displayed by the person suffering from a conversion disorder. Hypochondriasis is the second somatoform disorder that is often confusing for laypeople. The person suffering from hypochondriasis fears or believes that he or she has the symptoms of a serious disease, but the imagined "symptoms" are actually normal sensations or body reactions which are misinterpreted as symptoms of disease.

Malingering is the third condition which is sometimes confused with psychosomatic disorders. The person who is malingering is faking illness, and is either reporting symptoms that do not exist at all or which are grossly exaggerated. The malingering is motivated by external goals or incentives.

By eliminating many of the diseases that used to be epidemic, especially those which killed people early in life, medical science has increased the average life expectancy of Americans by about thirty years since the beginning of the twentieth century. Eliminating the psychological factors that cause psychosomatic disorders holds promise for another increase in average life expectancy in the next few decades. Heart disease, cancer, and strokes are the top three killer diseases in the United States, and each has a powerful psychosomatic component. The reduction in human suffering and the economic benefits that can be gained by controlling nonfatal psychosomatic disorders is equally promising.

Cognitive and health psychologists have, particularly since the 1970's, tried to determine the degree to which cognitive psychotherapy interventions can boost immune system functioning in cancer patients. They have also used behavioral and cognitive therapy approaches to alter the attitudes and behaviors of people who are prone to heart disease and strokes with considerable success. In the near future, they can be expected to focus their efforts on two major fronts. The first will involve further attempts to identify the psychological factors which might increase people's propensity to develop psychosomatic disorders. The second will involve continuing efforts to develop and refine the therapeutic interventions intended to reduce the damage done by psychosomatic disorders, and possibly to prevent them entirely.

Bibliography

Chopra, Deepak. *Creating Health*. Boston: Houghton Mifflin, 1987. Chopra is a proponent of meditation, an approach that many American psychologists do not necessarily feel comfortable advocating. Nevertheless, this book is written by a practicing physician for the layperson. He covers a wide variety of psychosomatic disorders, suggests a variety of healthy habits, and presents the viewpoint that "health is our natural state."

Fava, G. A., and H. Freyberger, eds. *Handbook of Psychosomatic Medicine*. Madison, Conn.: International Universities Press, 1999. A volume in the Stress and Health series. Discusses fundamental, clinical, and treatment issues.

Finell, Janet Schumacher, ed. *Mind-Body Problems: Psychotherapy with Psychosomatic Disorders*. New York: Jason Aronson, 1997. Examines mind-body problems in contemporary psychotherapeutic practice, introducing both theoretical perspectives and clinical realities.

Reisner, Morton F., ed. *Organic Disorders and Psychosomatic Disorders*. Vol. 3 in *American Handbook of Psychiatry*. 2d ed., edited by Silvano Arieti. New York:

Basic Books, 1975. Heavy reading, but an authoritative source of information on the subject of psychosomatic disorders. Chapters 1, 21, 25, and 36 offer a particularly pertinent overview of the topic, and several chapters in part 2 focus on specific psychosomatic disorders.

Seligman, Martin E. P. *Learned Optimism*. New York: Alfred A. Knopf, 1991. Chapter 2 provides an especially interesting account of how two young upstart graduate students can blow a hole in one of the most basic assumptions of a well-entrenched viewpoint and promote the development of a new way of looking at things. Chapter 10 describes how explanatory styles might affect health and the mechanism by which this is thought to occur. A test developed to measure explanatory styles is included in chapter 3, and the last chapters focus on how to develop an optimistic orientation. A very readable book which examines a most interesting concept.

Simonton, O. Carl, Stephanie Matthews-Simonton, and James L. Creighton. *Getting Well Again*. New York: Bantam Books, 1980. Cancer researchers and therapists examine the mind-body connection, effects of beliefs, causes of cancer, effects of stress and personality, and effects of expectations on the development and progress of cancer. They describe a holistic approach to treatment, emphasizing relaxation and visual imagery, that is reported to produce cancer survival rates that are twice the national norm. A very readable book which is readily available in paperback.

Taylor, Shelley E. *Health Psychology*. 4th ed. New York: McGraw-Hill, 1999. A moderately high-level college textbook that comprehensively covers the general field of health psychology. As could be expected, many research studies are presented, and not all of them corroborate one another. The general reader should have no particular difficulty handling this material; the writing is reader-friendly.

John W. Nichols

See also:
Abnormality: Biomedical Models; Cognitive Behavior Therapy; Cognitive Therapy; Depression; Hypochondriasis, Conversion, Somatization, and Somatoform Pain; Stress; Stress: Coping Strategies; Stress: Physiological Responses.

PSYCHOSURGERY

Type of psychology: Psychotherapy
Fields of study: Biological treatments

Psychosurgery is a method for treating certain mental disorders by performing surgical operations on the brain, either by severing the connections between different parts of the brain or by destroying brain tissue in specific areas. Psychosurgery was popular from about 1935 to 1960; it has now largely been replaced by drugs. It remains a highly controversial procedure.

Principal terms

BIOETHICS: includes the study of the moral, ethical, and social issues posed by treating mental disorders by biological means, especially psychosurgery

BIOLOGICAL DETERMINISM: the belief that behavior is determined or caused by a corresponding set of conditions within the brain

BIOMEDICAL MODEL: the belief, similar to biological determinism, that mental illness is the result of dysfunction in certain areas of the brain

BIOMEDICAL TREATMENT: a therapy for mental disorders that is based on altering brain function; includes drugs, electroconvulsive shock, and psychosurgery

LOBOTOMY: the archetypical psychosurgical technique for destroying brain tissue; although it is but one of several methods, it was the first and most commonly performed and remains the most notorious

Overview

Psychosurgery, also referred to as psychiatric surgery, psychiatric neurosurgery, or functional neurosurgery, is a medical procedure intended to alleviate certain mental illnesses by destroying brain tissue in selected areas of the brain. Psychosurgery is based on the biomedical model of mental illness, which posits that mental states and ensuing behavior are the result of activity in the nervous system. That is, at the most fundamental level, human thoughts and actions are biologically determined by the functioning nervous system. Therefore, mental illness and abnormal behavior are caused by abnormalities in the nervous system: by the release of certain neurotransmitters and/or by abnormalities in brain structure. If it is assumed that the basis of a mental illness is an abnormality of the nervous system, the appropriate therapy is biomedical: The nervous system is treated directly to alleviate the problem. Biomedical treatments include psychosurgery, electroconvulsive shock, and drugs.

Contemporary psychosurgery was founded in 1935 by the Portuguese neurosurgeon António Egas Moniz. Egas Moniz attended a symposium in August, 1935, at which Carlyle Jacobsen reported anecdotally a marked change in the level of emotionality of a chimpanzee following destruction of a large part of the frontal lobe of the cerebral cortex. Formerly, the chimpanzee had been highly emotional and obstinate; following the operation, the chimpanzee appeared calm and coop-

Contemporary psychosurgery was founded in 1935 by the Portuguese neurosurgeon António Egas Moniz, who was awarded the Nobel Prize in Physiology or Medicine for his work. (©The Nobel Foundation)

erative. Egas Moniz inquired of Jacobsen whether the technique could be used to relieve anxiety states in humans; less than three months later, in November, 1935, Egas Moniz performed his first operation.

In these operations, two holes were drilled into the skull of mental patients. Initially, alcohol was injected through the holes directly into the frontal lobes. Commencing with the eighth operation, however, a scalpel-like instrument was inserted through the hole into the frontal lobes, and a wire loop was then extended from the scalpel and rotated, destroying whatever nerve tissues it contacted. Egas Moniz coined the term "psychosurgery" to describe this kind of treatment. He referred to his particular technique as prefrontal leucotomy (from the Greek *leuco*, meaning "white matter," or nerve fibers, and *tome*, meaning "knife"). The instrument he used was called a leucotome.

Egas Moniz's claims of success in alleviating extreme states of emotionality with this procedure stimulated worldwide interest, excitement, and practice. About thirty-five thousand operations were performed in the United States from 1936 through 1978, with perhaps double that number worldwide. Psychosurgery was seen as a quick and effective method for alleviating certain commonly occurring mental illnesses which could not be treated rapidly and effectively by any other means, as well as providing a partial solution to the problem of overcrowding in mental hospitals.

As other psychosurgeons began performing psychosurgery, new techniques were developed that were believed to be improvements. Egas Moniz's prefrontal leucotomy, which did not permit precise location of the area to be cut, was superseded by the prefrontal lobotomy, developed by the Americans Walter Freeman and James Watts in 1937. Larger holes were drilled into both sides of the skull, and a leucotome was inserted and precisely moved in a sweeping motion through the frontal lobe. In 1948, Freeman introduced the transorbital lobotomy. This procedure involved inserting an icepick-like knife through the top of the eye socket into the brain and then swinging it back and forth. This procedure was quick and efficient and could be performed as an office procedure. Freeman said that he could perform fifty operations in a day.

The lobotomy was handicapped, however, by two important limitations. Destruction of the frontal lobe usually produced a number of serious side effects. Although the lobotomy was perhaps more precise than the leucotomy, the psychosurgeon still could not know with certainty exactly what part of the brain was being excised. A considerable risk of damaging other areas of the brain or of inducing hemorrhaging was present.

Later technological innovations and increased understanding of the structure of the nervous system permitted more precise and less invasive surgical procedures. An apparatus called the stereotaxis allowed precise mapping of the brain. Using this instrument, Ernest Spiegel and Henry Wycis inserted electrodes into previously inaccessible parts of the brain and destroyed a small area of tissue with electricity. This procedure initiated surgery on small and precisely located areas of the brain other than the frontal lobes, thus minimizing side effects. Nevertheless, over its more than fifty-year history, the vast majority of psychosurgical operations have been lobotomies.

Applications

As John Kleinig observes in *Ethical Issues in Psychosurgery* (1985), nearly every brain structure has at some point been subject to a psychosurgical procedure.

Psychosurgery involving various brain structures has been performed in the belief that specific abnormal mental states and behaviors that are unaffected by other treatments can be alleviated through psychosurgery. According to Kleinig, psychosurgery has been used to treat many disorders.

Psychosurgery has not in general produced favorable results with schizophrenia. Drugs are the preferred biomedical procedure. Schizophrenia is still occasionally treated by psychosurgery, but only in those cases with a high emotional component—that is, with affective behaviors or mood states. Psychosurgery has been most commonly used with cases characterized by severe and disabling depression, obsessive-compulsive disorders, and acute tension and anxiety. The purpose is to even or level out the patient's feelings and emotions. As with schizophrenia, drugs are the preferred mode of treatment for these disorders; however, psychosurgery may be a consideration for those patients who do not respond appropriately to drugs and whose dysfunction is extremely severe.

Anorexia nervosa is the chronic refusal to eat sufficient food to maintain normal health. It has been viewed by some as an extreme compulsion which may be related to a disorder of the limbic system. Psychosurgery has been performed in extreme cases. Hyperactive syndrome, or attention-deficit hyperactivity disorder, in children has been viewed by some as a disorder that is a genetically based brain dysfunction, and psychosurgery has been performed when other treatments have failed. Uncontrollable rage and/or aggression is believed to be regulated by the amygdaloid body in the limbic system. Moderately favorable results have been reported with amygdalectomies performed on both adults and children.

Substance abuse and addictions can be viewed as analogues to compulsions. The purpose of psychosurgery is to reduce the strength of the desire of the addiction's object. Data indicate favorable outcomes for certain groups of alcoholics and drug addicts, but the efficacy of the procedure with obesity and compulsive gambling is lacking.

Psychosurgery has been performed on pedophiliacs (child molesters) and others who have engaged in violent sexual offenses, in order to remove the desire to perform such acts. The operation has focused on the hypothalamus, a structure in the limbic system. In some cases, the operation has succeeded, probably by producing a reduction of sexual desire in general.

The anterior angulate region of the limbic system, which is believed to be involved with the perception of pain, has been subjected to psychosurgery. Some favorable results have been obtained, which some believe are the result of the alleviation of depression or obsessive behaviors associated with intractable pain. Some pain specialists believe that psychosurgery is not appropriate in any instance.

It is apparent from this survey that psychosurgery has been employed for a wide variety of disorders and performed upon a wide variety of patient populations. With its introduction by Egas Moniz in the 1930's, and its vigorous advocacy by Egas Moniz in Europe and by Freeman and Watts in the United States, psychosurgery was received with great hope and expectation. It was seen as providing a fast, easy, and inexpensive way of treating certain mental illnesses that were unresponsive to any alternative treatments available at the time. In addition, if institutionalized patients could be successfully treated by psychosurgery, they could be released, thus simultaneously alleviating the abysmal overcrowding and intolerable conditions of mental institutions and returning the patients to a productive life in society. In fact, Egas Moniz won the Nobel Prize in Physiology or Medicine in 1949 in recognition of his work. The citation states: "Frontal leucotomy, despite certain limitations of the operative method, must be considered one of the most important discoveries ever made in psychiatric therapy, because through its use a great number of suffering people and total invalids have recovered and have been socially rehabilitated."

Perspective and Prospects

Egas Moniz's Nobel citation may be contrasted with David L. Rosenhan and Martin E. P. Seligman's assessment of lobotomy in the second edition of their book *Abnormal Psychology* (1989): "There is the danger that physicians and patients may become overzealous in their search for a quick neurological cure. . . . [T]he disastrous history of frontal lobotomies . . . should serve as a warning."

Although the biomedical model is a sound theory, and biological treatments have proved to be valuable and worthwhile, in retrospect, Rosenhan and Seligman were correct. Lobotomies were, in general, "disastrous," and their sorry history provides a textbook example of how not to bring a new medical procedure on-line. Irreversible destruction of brain tissue and side effects were produced by procedures of highly questionable effectiveness.

The goals and desires of the early psychosurgeons may have been laudable, but their methods were not. Within three months of hearing Jacobsen's anecdotal account, Egas Moniz was performing lobotomies, despite the lack of clear evidence from prior animal experimentation that might at least support the irreversible destruction of the brain tissue. Egas Moniz performed no animal experimentation himself. He declared the frontal lobes to be the area of the brain responsible for the mental disorders to be treated by psychosurgery. His reading of the scientific literature to support his beliefs, however, was spotty and selective, and contradictory evidence was ignored. Furthermore, there was present a large animal and human literature clearly demonstrating a range of serious side effects and deficits produced by lesions of the frontal lobes, such as apathy, retarded movement, loss of initiative, and mutism. Yet, with no supporting evidence, Egas Moniz insisted these side effects were only temporary. In fact, they could be permanent. Egas Moniz's initial report on twenty patients claimed a cure for seven, lessening of symptoms in six, and no effect on six. An impartial review of these cases by Stanley Cobb, however, concluded that only one of the twenty cases provided enough information to allow a judgment.

Mercifully, the introduction of psychoactive drugs and growing criticism of lobotomies effectively brought them to an end by the late 1950's. Psychosurgery is still occasionally performed; its advocates argue that newer techniques are used that avoid the frontal lobes, that the procedure is based upon a good understanding of how the nervous system functions, that side effects are minimal, that its use is much more strictly monitored and regulated, and that it is viewed only as a treatment of last resort. Nevertheless, psychosurgery still remains highly controversial. Many practitioners and scientists are skeptical about its effectiveness, arguing that destruction of any brain tissue can produce unavoidable side effects; psychosurgery is believed by these individuals to be an ethically and morally unacceptable procedure of dubious value.

Bibliography

Kleinig, John. *Ethical Issues in Psychosurgery*. London: Allen & Unwin, 1985. This informative book focuses on the bioethical problems raised by psychosurgery. Discusses psychiatric diagnosis, the use of experimental therapies, criteria for success, informed consent, medical priorities, safeguards, and the relation between personality and the brain.

Lader, Malcolm Harold, and Reginald Herrington. *Biological Treatments in Psychiatry*. 2d ed. New York: Oxford University Press, 1996. A reference work for psychiatric residents or practitioners on drug treatment in psychiatry. This expanded edition offers coverage of dementia and panic disorder and is updated to include newer drugs.

Marsh, Frank H., and Janet Katz, eds. *Biology, Crime, and Ethics*. Cincinnati: Anderson, 1984. Explores the relationship between biological factors (genetics, physiology) and criminal and aggressive behavior. Contains a section on psychosurgery and its appropriateness in treating violent and aggressive behavior.

Pressman, Jack D. *Last Resort: Psychosurgery and the Limits of Medicine*. New York: Cambridge University Press, 1998. Challenges the previously accepted psychosurgery story and raises new questions about what should be considered its important lessons. Includes bibliographical references and an index.

Rodgers, Joann Ellison. *Psychosurgery: Damaging the Brain to Save the Mind*. New York: HarperCollins, 1992. Explores the concept of modern psychosurgery, performed with much greater accuracy than in the past. Provides a detailed account of clinical practice, case histories, and quotes from physicians.

Valenstein, Elliot S. *Great and Desperate Cures*. New York: Basic Books, 1986. Highly recommended. A very interesting and readable treatment of psychosurgery and other extreme treatments for mental illness. Concentrates on psychosurgery and presents a thorough consideration of its history from its inception to the 1980's. Filled with many interesting photographs and anecdotes that collectively provide an intimate insider's view on psychosurgery.

_____, ed. *The Psychosurgery Debate*. San Francisco: W. H. Freeman, 1980. A wide-ranging discussion of various aspects of psychosurgery. Presentations include the rationale for psychosurgery, selection of patients, postoperative evaluation, techniques, evaluation, legal issues, and ethical issues.

Laurence Miller

See also:

Abnormality: Biomedical Models; Aggression: Reduction and Control; Anxiety Disorders; Electroconvulsive Therapy; Lobotomy; Madness: Historical Concepts; Psychoactive Drug Therapy; Schizophrenia.

PSYCHOTHERAPY
Children

Type of psychology: Psychotherapy
Fields of study: Behavioral therapies; group and family therapies; psychodynamic
therapies

Psychotherapy with children involves the use of psychological techniques in the treatment of children with behavioral, cognitive, or emotional disorders. The specific focus of treatment varies and may involve children only, parents only, or a combination of these individuals.

Principal terms

EXTERNALIZING DISORDERS: children's psychiatric disorders that are likely to disrupt the lives of individuals with whom they come in contact

FAMILY THERAPY: a type of psychotherapy that focuses on correcting the faulty interactions among family members that maintain children's psychological problems

INTERNALIZING DISORDERS: children's psychiatric disorders that are likely to cause greater internal distress to the children affected than to others

INTERPRETATION: therapists' comments regarding some aspect of children's behavior designed to promote insight into the causes of their psychological disorders

LEARNING THEORY: principles derived from extensive experimentation that explain the production and modification of behavior

PLAY THERAPY: a system of individual psychotherapy in which children's play is utilized to explain and reduce symptoms of their psychological disorders

WORKING THROUGH: a psychoanalytical term that describes the process by which children develop more adaptive behavior once they have gained insight into the causes of their psychological disorders

Overview

Various psychological techniques designed to treat children's behavioral, cognitive, or emotional problems are used in psychotherapy with children. The number of children with psychological disorders underscores the need for effective child psychotherapy: It is estimated that between 7 and 14 million, or between 5 and 15 percent, of America's children suffer from psychological disorders. It is believed that only one-fourth to one-third of all children who have psychological problems receive psychotherapeutic services.

Children, like adults, may experience many different kinds of psychological disorders. For example, in the *Diagnostic and Statistical Manual of Mental Disorders* (rev. 3d ed., 1987, DSM-III-R), published by the American Psychiatric Association, forty-seven separate disorders were listed which primarily affect children. This number does not include many disorders, such as major depressive disorder, which primarily affect adults but may also affect children. In general terms, children's disorders can be divided into two major categories: externalizing and internalizing disorders.

Externalizing disorders are those in which children engage in activities that are physically disruptive or are harmful to themselves or others. An example of this type of disorder is conduct disorder. Conduct disorder is characterized by children's involvement in a continued pattern of behavior that demonstrates a fundamental disregard for the safety or property of others. In contrast to externalizing disorders, internalizing disorders create greater emotional distress for the children themselves than for others around them. An example of an internalizing disorder is overanxious disorder. In overanxious disorder, the child experiences persistent, unrealistic anxiety regarding numerous situations and events such as being liked or school grades.

In response to the prevalence and variety of childhood disorders, many different treatments have been developed to address children's psychological problems. Historically, the earliest interventions for addressing these problems were based on psychoanalytic theory, developed by Sigmund Freud. Psychoanalysis is a type of psychotherapy based on the idea that individuals' unconscious processes, derived from early childhood experiences, are responsible for the psychological problems they experience as adults. One of the first therapists to adapt Freud's psychoanalysis to the treatment of children was Anna Freud, his daughter.

Psychoanalysis had to be modified for the treatment of children because of its heavy reliance on individuals' verbalizing their unconscious thoughts and feelings. Anna Freud realized that children would not be able to verbalize regarding their experiences to the extent necessary for effective treatment. Therefore, beginning in the 1920's, she created play therapy, a system of psychotherapy in which children's responses during play provided information regarding their hidden thoughts and feelings. Although play therapy had its roots in Sigmund Freud's psychoanalysis, this type of therapy came to be associated with other systems of psychotherapy. For example, Virginia Axline demonstrates her version of play therapy in the 1964 book *Dibs: In Search of Self*; her approach is based on Carl Rogers's person-centered therapy.

Also in the 1920's, Mary Cover Jones was applying the principles of behavior therapy developed by John B. Watson and others to the treatment of children's fears. Behavior therapy rests on the notion that all behavior, whether adaptive or maladaptive, is learned and thus can be unlearned. Jones's treatment involved reconditioning, a procedure in which the object of which the child is afraid is gradually associated with a pleasurable activity. By regularly associating the feared object with a pleasurable activity, Jones was able to eliminate children's fears.

Although early child analysts and behaviorally oriented psychologists attributed many children's problems to difficulties within their family environments, these treatment providers' primary focus was on treating the children, not their parents. In the early 1940's, however, Nathan Ackerman, a psychiatrist trained in the psychoanalytic tradition, began to treat children in conjunction with their families. His justification for seeing all family members in treatment was that families, like individuals, possess hidden conflicts that prevent them from engaging in healthy psychological functioning. Therefore, the role of the family therapist was to uncover these family conflicts, thus creating the possibility that the conflicts could be addressed in more adaptive ways. Once these family conflicts were properly handled, the causes of the child's psychological problems were removed. Ackerman's approach marked the beginning of the use of family therapy for the treatment of children's problems.

Another historical movement within child psychotherapy is behavioral parent training (BPT). BPT evolved from the recognition that parents are important in shaping their children's behavior and that they can be trained to eliminate many of their children's problems. Beginning in the late 1960's, researchers such as Gerald Patterson and Rex Forehand began to develop programs designed to target parents as the principal persons responsible for change in their children's maladaptive behavior. In this system of psychotherapy, parents were taught ways to assess and to intervene in order to correct their children's misbehavior. The role of the child was de-emphasized to the point that the child might not even be seen by the therapist during the treatment process.

It is estimated that more than two hundred different types of child psychotherapy exist; however, these specific types of therapy can be roughly divided into three larger categories of treatment based on the primary focus of their interventions. These three categories are children only, parents only, or children and parents combined.

Applications

Individual child psychotherapy, the first category of psychotherapy with children, focuses on the child alone because of the belief that the greatest amount of improvement can result when the child is given primary attention in treatment. An example of individual child treatment is psychodynamic play therapy. Originating from the work of Anna Freud, the basic goal of psychodynamic play therapy is to provide the child with insight into the internal conflicts that have caused his or her psychological disorder. Once the child has gained sufficient insight, he or she is guided in handling these conflicts in more adaptive ways. Play therapy can be divided into three basic phases: initial, interpretative, and working-through phases.

In the initial phase of play therapy, the major goal is to establish a cooperative relationship between the child and the therapist. The attainment of this goal may require considerable time for several potential reasons. These reasons include a child's unwillingness to participate in therapy, lack of understanding regarding the therapy process, and lack of a previous trusting relationship with an adult. The participation in play activities provides an opportunity for the therapist to interact with the child in a relaxed and interesting manner. The specific kinds of play utilized differ from therapist to therapist but may include competitive games (such as checkers), imaginative games involving different figures (hand puppets, for example), or cooperative games (playing catch).

Once a sufficient level of cooperation is established, the therapist can begin to make interpretations to the child regarding the play. These interpretations consist of the therapist identifying themes in the content or style of a child's play that may relate to a psychological problem. For example, in playing with hand puppets, a child referred because of aggressive behavior may regularly enact stories in which a larger puppet "beats up" a smaller puppet. The child's therapist may interpret this story as meaning that the child aggresses against others because he or she feels inadequate.

Once the child gains insight into the internal conflict that has caused his or her problematic behavior, the child is guided by the therapist to develop a more adaptive way of handling this conflict. This final process of therapy is called working through. The working-through phase may be the most difficult part of treatment, because it involves the child abandoning a repetitive and maladaptive manner of handling a conflict in favor of a new approach. In comparison to most other psychotherapies, this treatment process is lengthy, ranging from months to years.

The second category of child psychotherapy, parent training, focuses intervention on the parents, because they are viewed as potentially the most effective persons available to alleviate the child's problems. This assumption is based on several factors, including the great amount of time parents spend with their children, the parents' control over the child's access to desired reinforcers, and the parents' understanding of the child's behavior because of their past relationship with the child. Behavioral parent training (BPT) is the most common type of parent training program. In BPT, parents are taught ways to modify their children's environment in order to improve their behavior.

The initial phase of this treatment process involves instructing parents in the basics of learning theory. They are taught that all behavior, adaptive or maladaptive, is maintained because it is reinforced. The application of learning theory to the correction of children's misbehavior involves three principles. First, positive reinforcement should be withdrawn from children's maladaptive behavior. For example, a parent who meets the demands of his screaming preschooler, who throws a temper tantrum in the checkout line of the grocery store because she wants a piece of candy, is unwittingly reinforcing the child's screaming behavior. Second, appropriate behavior that is incompatible with the maladaptive behavior should be positively reinforced. In the case of the screaming preschooler, this would involve rewarding her for acting correctly. Third, aversive consequences should be applied when the problem behavior recurs. That is, when the child engages in the misbehavior, he or she should consistently experience negative costs. For example, the preschooler who has a temper tantrum in the checkout line should not be allowed money to purchase gum, which she had previously selected as a potential reward for good store behavior, as the cost for her tantrum. In order to produce the greatest effect, positive reinforcement and negative consequences should be administered as close as possible to the occurrence of the appropriate or inappropriate behavior.

The final category of child psychotherapy, family therapy, focuses intervention on both the child and the child's family. Family therapy rests on the assumption that the child's psychological problems were created and are maintained by interactions among different family members. In this model, attention is shifted away from the individual child's problems toward the functioning of the entire family. For example, in structural family therapy, a widely practiced type of family therapy, the boundaries between different family members are closely examined. Family boundaries represent the degree of separation between different family members or subsets of members (for example, the parent-versus-child subset). According to Salvador Minuchin, the originator of structural family therapy, families in which there is little separation between parents and children may cause certain children to misbehave as a way to gain increased emotional distance from their parents. On the other hand, families characterized by too much separation between parents and children may cause certain children to become depressed because of the lack of a confiding relationship with a parental figure. Regardless of the child's specific disorder, all family members, not the child or parents alone, are the focus of treatment.

Perspective and Prospects
The two large questions that can be asked regarding psychotherapy for children are whether it is effective and whether one type of treatment is more effective than others. The answer to the first question is very clear; psychotherapy is effective in treating the majority of children's psychological disorders. Two major studies in the 1980's reviewed the existing research examining the effects of child psychotherapy. The first of these studies was conducted by Rita Casey and Jeffrey Berman (1985), and the second was conducted by John Weisz, Bahr Weiss, Mark Alicke, and M. L. Klotz (1987). Both these studies found that children who received psychotherapy were better off than approximately 75 percent of the children who did not receive psychotherapy. Interestingly, Weisz and colleagues found that younger children (ages four to twelve) appeared to obtain more benefit from psychotherapy than older children (ages thirteen to eighteen). In addition, Casey and Berman found that girls tend to receive more benefit from psychotherapy than boys.

As one might expect, some controversy exists in attempting to answer the second question, regarding which treatment is the most effective. Casey and Berman concluded that all treatments were equally effective; however, Weisz et al. found that behavioral treatments were more effective than nonbehavioral treatments. Disagreement regarding which type of psychotherapy is most effective should not be allowed to obscure the general conclusion that psychotherapy for children is clearly beneficial. Many investigators would suggest that the common characteristics shared by all types of child psychotherapy are responsible for the relatively equivalent improvement produced by different treatments. For example, one of these common characteristics may be the therapist's and child's expectations that therapy will result in a reduction in the child's psychological problems. In spite of the treatments' apparent differences in rationale and method, it may be that this component, as well as other common elements, accounts for much of the similarity in treatment outcomes.

The number of psychotherapeutic approaches available to treat children's psychological disorders has exploded since their introduction in the 1920's. Recent research has clearly demonstrated the effectiveness of psychotherapy for children. Controversy still remains, however, regarding which treatment approach is the most effective; continued research is needed to address this issue. Of greater urgency is the need to provide psychotherapy to the approximately 5 to 10 million children with psychological disorders who are not being served. Perhaps even more cost effective, in terms of both alleviating human suffering and reducing costs, would be the development of programs to prevent children's psychological disorders.

Bibliography

Axline, Virginia. *Dibs: In Search of Self.* New York: Ballantine Books, 1964. This book, written for a general audience, presents Axline's play therapy, illustrated by the presentation of a clinical case. The two-year treatment process with Dibs, a seriously disturbed child, is described in detail. The book provides an excellent example of child-centered play therapy.

Gordon, Thomas. *Parent Effectiveness Training.* Rev. ed. New York: Three Rivers Press, 2000. Written primarily for parents interested in successfully handling parent-child interactions. The author utilizes behavioral parent training principles to address various topics which primarily relate to improving communication between parents and children as well as handling children's misbehavior.

Minuchin, Salvador. *Families and Family Therapy.* Reprint. Cambridge, Mass.: Harvard University Press, 1989. This book, first published in 1974 and largely intended for professionals, is widely cited by family therapy experts as one of the most pivotal works in the field. Minuchin outlines his views regarding the functioning of healthy and unhealthy families. Specifically, he addresses the maladaptive interactions among family members that create psychological disorders such as anorexia nervosa in children.

Monte, Christopher. "Anna Freud: The Psychoanalytic Heritage and Developments in Ego Psychology." In *Beneath the Mask: An Introduction to Theories of Personality.* 4th ed. Fort Worth, Tex.: Holt, Rinehart and Winston, 1991. In this textbook chapter, Monte describes Anna Freud's contributions to the field of child psychotherapy. The chapter traces Anna Freud's adaptation of her father's psychoanalytic therapy to her work with children. This is a valuable work because it describes Anna Freud's therapy in understandable terms—which is difficult, given the complexity of child psychoanalysis.

Nemiroff, Marc A., and Jane Annunziata. *A Child's First Book About Play Therapy.* Washington, D.C.: American Psychological Association, 1999. Children ages four to seven who are entering play therapy are the intended audience of this book. Uses frequent illustrations and simple words to communicate to children the purpose and process of children's play therapy. An excellent resource for parents whose children are about to enter play therapy.

Prout, H. Thompson, and Douglas T. Brown, eds. *Counseling and Psychotherapy with Children and Adolescents: Theory and Practice for School and Clinical Settings.* 3d ed. New York: John Wiley & Sons, 1999. Discusses the latest thinking and practices using the seven major approaches to counseling and psychotherapeutic interventions with children and adolescents. Includes bibliographical references and an index.

Schaefer, Charles E. *Short-Term Psychotherapy Groups for Children: Adopting Group Processes for Specific Problems*. Northvale, N.J.: Jason Aronson, 1999. Offers specific guidelines for conducting a wide range of psychotherapy groups and detailed descriptions of sixteen structured group interventions. These groups focus on such treatment issues as separation and divorce, alcoholism, bereavement, sexual abuse, fears and anxieties, anger management, weight loss, and bed-wetting.

Schaefer, Charles E., and Steven E. Reid, eds. *Game Play: Therapeutic Use of Childhood Games*. 2d ed. New York: John Wiley & Sons, 2000. An edited book in which numerous types of games and activities that may be used in play therapy are described. Discusses games which have been specifically designed for play therapy as well as familiar games, such as checkers, whose use may be modified for therapeutic work. The book is largely intended for child therapy professionals of various treatment orientations.

R. Christopher Qualls

See also:

Abnormality: Behavioral Models; Abnormality: Family Models; Abnormality: Psychodynamic Models; Behavioral Family Therapy; Child and Adolescent Psychiatry; Operant Conditioning Therapies; Play Therapy; Psychotherapy: Effectiveness; Psychotherapy: Goals and Techniques; Strategic Family Therapy.

PSYCHOTHERAPY
Effectiveness

Type of psychology: Psychotherapy
Fields of study: Evaluating psychotherapy

Psychotherapy is a rapidly expanding field; it has been estimated that there are more than four hundred psychotherapeutic approaches. Research evaluating the effectiveness of psychotherapy serves a primary role in the development and validation of therapeutic approaches. Studies have examined the effectiveness of psychotherapy on thousands of patients. Although such studies often produce contradictory and perhaps even disappointing findings, there is clear evidence that psychotherapy is effective.

Principal terms

CASE STUDY: an unsystematic report of treatment which is typically based on a therapist's opinions about the results

EMPATHY: the ability to convey an understanding of the client's emotional experiences

META-ANALYSIS: a set of quantitative (statistical) procedures used to evaluate a body of empirical literature

PLACEBO: a procedure designed to be inert or inactive; used frequently in research designs as a method of controlling certain variables

RANDOMIZATION: a procedure in which patients or treatments are selected without regard for particular variables; for example, flipping a coin to decide who goes first

RELAPSE: reexperiencing an earlier problem or returning to a previous level of functioning

SPONTANEOUS REMISSION: recovery from an illness; improvement without treatment

Overview

Although the roots of psychotherapy can be traced back to ancient times, the birth of modern psychotherapy is frequently targeted with the famous case of "Anna O." in 1882. Physician Josef Breuer, who was a colleague of Sigmund Freud, described Anna O. as a twenty-one-year-old patient with multiple symptoms including paralysis and loss of sensitivity in her limbs, lapses in awareness, problems in vision and speech, headaches, and dual personality. During treatment, Breuer found that if Anna discussed every occurrence of a symptom until she described its origin and vividly recalled its first appearance, the symptom would disappear. Hypnosis was also employed to help Anna O. eliminate the symptoms more rapidly. (Eventually, Breuer stopped working with this patient because of numerous difficulties, including his jealous wife and his patient's tendency to become hysterical.) Anna O., whose real name was Bertha Pappenheim, later became well known throughout Germany for her work with children, prostitutes, and Jewish relief organizations.

The case of Anna O. is not only important as perhaps representing the birth of modern psychotherapy but also characteristic of a method of investigation referred to as the case study or case report. A case report attempts to highlight descriptions of a specific patient and treatment approach, typically as reported by the therapist. Given the fact that most patients treated in psychotherapy are seen individually by a single therapist, it is not surprising that some of the most influential literature in the history of psychotherapy is based on case reports. Unfortunately, the vast majority of case reports are inherently problematic in terms of scientific merit and methodological rigor. Moreover, it is very difficult to determine which factors are most effective in the treatment of any particular patient. Thus, whereas case reports are common in the history of psychotherapy research, their value is generally limited.

The earliest psychotherapy outcome studies were conducted from the 1930's to the 1960's. These initial investigations were concerned with one primary question: "Does psychotherapy demonstrate positive effects?" Unfortunately, the research methodology employed in these studies was typically flawed, and interpretations proved ambiguous. The most common area of disagreement in the early investigations was the concept of "spontaneous remission." That is, psychotherapy was evaluated in comparison to the rates of improvement seen among patients who were not currently receiving treatment.

For example, British psychologist Hans Eysenck created a furor in the early 1950's, one which continued to trouble psychologists and mental health workers for several decades. Eysenck concluded, on the basis of his review of twenty-four studies, that psychotherapy produced no greater changes in individuals than did naturally occurring life events. Specifically, he argued that two-thirds of people with neurotic disorders improve over a two-year period with or without psychotherapy. Two particular problems with his review warrant comment, however; first, the studies that were included in his review rarely employed randomization, which raises significant concerns about subsequent interpretations. Second, later analyses of the same data set demonstrated that Eysenck's original estimates of improvements in the absence of treatment were inflated.

The manner in which research investigations were conducted (the research methodology) became more sophisticated in the 1970's. In particular, research designs included appropriate control groups to account for spontaneous improvements, randomly assigned experimental conditions, well-specified treatment protocols administered by well-trained therapists, and improved instruments and procedures to measure effectiveness. As a result, it became increasingly clear that many psychotherapies demonstrate statistically significant and clinically meaningful effects on patients. Not all patients reveal improvement, however, and many patients relapse following successful treatment.

In 1977, researchers Mary Smith and Gene Glass presented a review of 375 psychotherapy outcome studies via a newly devised methodology called "meta-analysis." Meta-analysis literally means "analysis of analyses" and represents a statistical procedure used to summarize collections of research data. Meta-analysis is frequently regarded as more objective and more sophisticated than traditional review procedures such as those employed by Eysenck. Smith and Glass revealed that most patients who entered outpatient psychotherapy showed noticeable improvement. In addition, the average therapy patient improved more than did 75 percent of comparable control patients.

The results reported by Smith and Glass were controversial, and they stimulated much productive debate. In particular, the authors were criticized for certain procedural steps (for example, excluding particular studies and including others). In response to such criticism, many researchers conducted additional meta-analytic investigations to examine the empirical effectiveness of psychotherapy. Of particular importance is the large follow-up investigation that was conducted by Smith, Glass, and Thomas Miller in 1980. The authors presented many detailed analyses of their results and expanded the data set from 375 studies to 475 studies involving approximately twenty-five thousand patients treated by seventy-eight therapies over an average of sixteen sessions. Smith, Glass, and Miller revealed that the average therapy patient was better off than 80 percent of the control group.

To date, numerous studies have provided evidence for the general effectiveness of psychotherapy to produce positive changes in targeted problem areas; however, psychotherapy is not a unitary procedure applied to a unitary problem. Moreover, many of the nearly four hundred psychotherapeutic approaches have yet to be systematically evaluated. Thus, it is important to understand the empirical evidence for specific treatment approaches with specific patient populations. It is similarly important to note that each therapist is a unique individual who provides his or her own unique perspective and experience to the psychotherapeutic process. Fortunately, positive effects are generally common among psychotherapy patients, and negative (deterioration) effects, which are also observed regularly, often appear related to a poor match of therapist, technique, and patient factors.

Applications

Recent research has focused on some of the factors associated with patient improvement, and several specific methods have been used to evaluate different treatments. Common research designs include contrasting an established treatment with a new treatment approach (for example, systematic desensitization versus eye-movement desensitization for anxiety) or therapeutic format (group depression treatment versus individual depression treatment), separating the components of an effective treatment package (such as cognitive behavioral treatment of anxiety) to examine the relative effectiveness of the modules, and analyzing the interactions between therapist and patient during psychotherapy (process research).

The results from studies employing these designs are generally mixed and reveal limited differences between specific therapeutic approaches. For example, in the largest meta-analytic studies, some analyses revealed that behavioral and cognitive therapies were found to have larger positive changes when compared to other types of psychotherapy (psychodynamic and humanistic), while other analyses did not. Similarly, several large comparative studies revealed considerable patient improvement regardless of treatment approach. Such results must be carefully evaluated, however, because there are numerous reasons for failing to find differences between treatments.

All psychotherapy research is flawed; there are no "perfect studies." Thus, studies should be evaluated along several dimensions, including rigor of methodology and adequacy of statistical procedures. Psychotherapy is both an art and a science, and it involves the complex interaction between a socially sanctioned helper (a therapist) and a distressed patient or client. The complexity of this interaction raises some significant obstacles to designing psychotherapy research. Thus, methodological problems can be diverse and extensive, and they may account for the failure to find significant differences between alternative psychotherapeutic approaches. Moreover, some researchers have argued that the combination of methodological problems and statistical limitations (such as research samples that are too small to detect differences between groups or inconsistency with regard to patient characteristics) plagued many of the comparative studies completed in the 1980's.

Still, the search for effective components of psychotherapy remains a primary research question focused on several key areas, including patient characteristics, therapist characteristics, treatment techniques, common factors across different psychotherapies, and the various interactions among these variables. As highlighted in Sol Garfield and Allen Bergin's edited book entitled *Handbook of Psychotherapy and Behavior Change* (1986), some evidence reveals that patient characteristics (such as amount of self-exploration and ability to solve problems and express emotions constructively) are of primary importance in positive outcomes. Therapist characteristics such as empathy, interpersonal warmth, acceptance toward patients, and genuineness also appear to play a major role in successful therapy. Treatment techniques seem generally less important than the ability of the therapist and patient to form a therapeutic relationship.

Additional studies have asked patients at the conclusion of psychotherapy to identify the most important factors in their successful treatment. Patients have generally described such factors as gradually facing their problems in a supportive setting, talking to an understanding person, and the personality of their therapist as helpful factors. Moreover, patients frequently conclude that their success in treatment is related to their therapist's support, encouragement, sensitivity, honesty, sense of humor, and ability to share insights. In contrast, other research has examined negative outcomes of psychotherapy in order to illuminate factors predictive of poor outcomes. These factors include the failure of the therapist to structure sessions and address primary concerns presented by the patient, poorly timed interventions, and negative therapist attitudes toward the patient.

Taken as a whole, psychotherapy research reveals some consistent results about many patient and therapist characteristics associated with positive and negative outcomes. Yet remarkably few differences have been found among the different types of treatment. This pattern of evidence has led many researchers to conclude that factors which are common across different forms of psychotherapy may account for the apparent equality among many treatment approaches. At the forefront of this position is psychiatrist and psychologist Jerome D. Frank.

In various books and journal articles, Frank has argued that all psychotherapeutic approaches share common ingredients that are simply variations of age-old procedures of psychological healing such as confession, encouragement, modeling, positive reinforcement, and punishment. Because patients seeking treatment are typically demoralized, distressed, and feeling helpless, all psychotherapies aim to restore morale by offering support, reassurance, feedback, guidance, hope, and mutual understanding of the problems and proposed solutions. Among the common factors most frequently studied since the 1960's, the key ingredients outlined by the client-centered school are most widely regarded as central to the development of a successful therapeutic relationship. These ingredients are empathy, positive regard, warmth, and genuineness.

Various factors should be considered when one chooses a therapist. To begin with, it may be wise to consider first one's objectives and motivations for entering treatment. A thoughtful appraisal of one's own goals can serve as a map through the maze of alternative treatments, therapy agencies, and diverse professionals providing psychotherapeutic services. In addition, one should learn about the professionals in one's area by speaking with a family physician, a religious adviser, or friends who have previously sought psychotherapeutic services. It is also important to locate a licensed professional with whom one feels comfortable, because the primary ingredients for success are patient and therapist characteristics. All therapists and patients are unique individuals who provide their own distinctive perspectives and contributions to the therapy process. Therefore, the most important factor in psychotherapeutic outcome may be the match between patient and therapist.

Perspective and Prospects

Although the roots of psychotherapy can be traced back to antiquity, psychotherapy research is a recent development in the field of psychology. Early evidence for the effectiveness of psychotherapy was limited and consisted of case studies and investigations with significant methodological flaws. Considerable furor among therapists followed psychologist Hans Eysenck's claims that psychotherapy is no more effective than naturally occurring life events are. Other disagreements followed the rapid development of many alternative and competing forms of psychotherapy in the 1960's and 1970's. Claims that one particular approach was better than another were rarely confirmed by empirical research. Still, psychotherapy research is a primary method in the development, refinement, and validation of treatments for diverse patient groups. Advancements in research methodology and statistical applications have provided answers to many important questions in psychotherapy research.

Rather than examining the question of whether psychotherapy works, researchers are designing sophisticated research programs to evaluate the effectiveness of specific treatment components on particular groups of patients with carefully diagnosed mental disorders. Researchers continue to identify specific variables and processes among patients and therapists that shape positive outcomes. The quality of interactions between patient and therapist appear to hold particular promise in understanding psychotherapy outcome.

To address the complexity of psychotherapy, research must aim to address at least two important dimensions: process ("how and why does this form of therapy work?") and outcome ("to what degree is this specific treatment effective for this particular client in this setting at this time?"). In addition, empirical comparisons between psychotherapy and medications in terms of effectiveness, side effects, compliance, and long-term outcome will continue to shape clinical practice for many years to come. As one example, the National Institutes of Mental Health (NIMH) sponsored a large comparative psychotherapy and drug treatment study of depression. In that investigation, the effectiveness of individual interpersonal psychotherapy, individual cognitive therapy, antidepressant medication, and placebo conditions were tested. While findings from initial analyses revealed no significant differences between any of the treatment conditions, secondary analyses suggested that severity of depression was an important variable. For the less severely depressed, there was no evidence for the specific effectiveness of active-versus-placebo treatment conditions. The more severely depressed patients, however, responded best to antidepressant medications and interpersonal therapy. Future reports from the NIMH team of researchers may reveal additional results which could further shape the ways in which depressed patients are treated.

Bibliography

Bergin, Allen E., and Sol L. Garfield, eds. *Handbook of Psychotherapy and Behavior Change*. 4th ed. New York: John Wiley & Sons, 1994. Provides a historical overview and synopsis of research studies concerned with the evaluation of psychotherapy. Patient and therapist variables are highlighted in terms of their importance in successful intervention. Additional topics include training therapeutic skills, medications and psychotherapy, and the effectiveness of treatment approaches with children, couples, families, and groups.

Beutler, Larry E., and Marjorie Crago, eds. *Psychotherapy Research: An International Review of Programmatic Studies*. Washington, D.C.: American Psychological Association, 1991. Reviews a variety of large-scale and small-scale research programs in North America and Europe. Presents a summary of research findings from studies investigating various aspects of psychotherapy including prevention of marital distress, process variables in psychotherapy, treatment of difficult patients, and inpatient hospitalization approaches.

Frank, Jerome David, and Julia B. Frank. *Persuasion and Healing: A Comparative Study of Psychotherapy*. 3d ed. Baltimore: The Johns Hopkins University Press, 1993. Provides an overview of Frank's position on psychotherapy. The significance of common treatment components shared by all forms of healing, including psychotherapy, continues to be an important consideration in treatment outcome work.

Friedman, Steven. *Time-Effective Psychotherapy: Maximizing Outcomes in an Era of Minimized Resources.* Boston: Allyn & Bacon, 1997. Written by a practicing family therapist at a managed care facility and based on a flexible, competency-based model of psychotherapy. Offers clinicians a set of practical ideas and useful strategies for providing time-effective therapy that meets the requirements of managed care.

Kazdin, Alan E. *Single-Case Research Designs: Methods for Clinical and Applied Settings.* New York: Oxford University Press, 1982. Provides an overview of various research methods used in psychotherapy research. In particular, this book presents information about case studies and single-case research designs. Single-case research has become increasingly common in psychotherapy research as an alternative approach to group designs.

Smith, Mary Lee, and Gene V. Glass. "Meta-Analysis of Psychotherapy Outcome Studies." *American Psychologist* 32, no. 9 (1977): 752-760. A classic in the field of psychotherapy research, this journal article represents a significant step in the manner in which knowledge is distilled from the scientific literature. This controversial article concluded that psychotherapy was effective.

Smith, Mary Lee, Gene V. Glass, and Thomas I. Miller. *Benefits of Psychotherapy.* Baltimore: The Johns Hopkins University Press, 1980. Presents many detailed analyses from 475 psychotherapy research studies that were systematically analyzed via meta-analysis. Provides a follow-up to many of the criticisms that were expressed about Smith and Glass's initial psychotherapy meta-analysis.

Spiegel, David, ed. *Efficacy and Cost-Effectiveness of Psychotherapy.* Washington, D.C.: American Psychiatric Press, 1999. Written by leading psychotherapists from around the world who describe their methods of assessment and treatment, as well as providing new evidence for the effectiveness of these interventions.

Gregory L. Wilson

See also:

Behavioral Family Therapy; Cognitive Behavior Therapy; Cognitive Therapy; Gestalt Therapy; Group Therapy; Psychotherapy: Children; Psychotherapy: Goals and Techniques; Psychotherapy: Historical Approaches to Treatment.

PSYCHOTHERAPY
Goals and Techniques

Type of psychology: Psychotherapy
Fields of study: Evaluating psychotherapy

The goals to be reached in the meetings between a psychotherapist and a client, or patient, and the techniques employed to accomplish them vary according to the needs of the client and the theoretical orientation of the therapist.

Principal terms

BEHAVIORAL THERAPY: an approach emphasizing how behaviors are controlled by stimuli that precede or follow them

DESENSITIZATION: a behavioral technique of gradually removing anxiety associated with certain situations by associating a relaxed state with these situations

HUMANISTIC THERAPY: an approach that emphasizes the innate capacity of people for positive change and ways of relating that encourage this change

INTERPRETATION: a psychodynamic technique in which the psychotherapist points out to a client patterns in behavior or the origin of these patterns

PSYCHODYNAMIC THERAPY: an approach emphasizing the influences of different parts of the mind on one another and the origins of these influences in childhood experience

RESISTANCE: the tendency of clients to avoid revealing themselves or attempting to change

SHAPING: a behavioral technique in which the psychotherapist rewards, usually through praise and attention, a client's gradual changes toward meeting psychotherapeutic goals

Overview

Psychotherapy is an interpersonal relationship in which clients present themselves to a psychotherapist in order to gain some relief from distress in their lives. It should be noted that although people who seek psychological help are referred to as "clients" by a wide range of psychotherapists, this term is used interchangeably with the term "patients," which is traditionally used more often by psychodynamically and medically trained practitioners. In all forms of psychotherapy, patients or clients must tell the psychotherapist about their distress and reveal intimate information in order for the psychotherapist to be helpful. The psychotherapist must aid clients in the difficult task of admitting difficulties and revealing themselves, since a client's desire to be liked and to be seen as competent can stand in the way of this work. The client also wants to find relief from distress at the least possible cost in terms of the effort and personal changes to be made, and, therefore, clients often prevent themselves from making the very changes in which they are interested.

This is termed resistance, and much of the work of the psychotherapist involves dealing with such resistance.

The goals of the client are determined by the type of life problems that are being experienced. Traditionally, psychotherapists make a diagnosis of the psychiatric disorder from which the client suffers, with different disorders presenting certain symptoms to be removed in order for the client to gain relief. The vast majority of clients suffer from some form of anxiety or depression, or from certain failures in personality development, which produce deviant behaviors and rigid patterns of relating to others called personality disorders. Relatively few clients suffer from severe disorders, called psychoses, which are characterized by some degree of loss of contact with reality. Depending on the particular symptoms involved in the client's disorder, psychotherapeutic goals will be set, although the client may not be aware of the necessity of these changes at first. In addition, the diagnosis allows the psychotherapist to anticipate the kinds of goals that would be difficult for the client to attain. Psychotherapists also consider the length of time they will likely work with the client. Therefore, psychotherapeutic goals depend on the client's wishes, the type of psychiatric disorder from which the client suffers, and the limitations of time under which the psychotherapy proceeds.

Another factor that plays a major role in determining psychotherapeutic goals is the psychotherapist's theoretical model for treatment. This model is based on a personality theory that explains people's motivations, how people develop psychologically, and how people differ from one another. It suggests what occurred in life to create the person's problems and what must be achieved to correct these problems. Associated with each theory is a group of techniques that can be applied to accomplish the goals considered to be crucial within the theory utilized. There are three main models of personality and treatment: psychodynamic therapies, behavioral therapies, and humanistic therapies. Psychodynamic therapists seek to make clients aware of motives for their actions of which they were previously unconscious or unaware. By becoming aware of their motives, clients can better control the balance between desires for pleasure and the need to obey one's conscience. Behavioral therapists attempt to increase the frequency of certain behaviors and decrease the frequency of others by reducing anxiety associated with certain behavior, teaching new behavior, and rewarding and punishing certain behaviors. Humanistic therapists try to free clients to use their innate abilities by developing relationships with clients in which clients can be assured of acceptance, making the clients more accepting of themselves and more confident in making decisions and expressing themselves.

Most psychotherapists use a combination of theories, and therefore of goals and techniques, in their practice. These "eclectic" therapists base their decisions about goals and techniques upon the combined theory they have evolved or upon a choice among other theories given what applies best to a client or diagnosis. It also appears that this eclectic approach has become popular because virtually all psychotherapy cases demand attention to certain common goals associated with the various stages of treatment, and different types of therapy are well suited to certain goals and related techniques at particular stages.

Applications

When clients first come to a psychotherapist, they have in mind some things about their lives that need to be changed. The psychotherapist recognizes that before this can be accomplished, a trusting relationship must be established with clients. This has been termed the "therapeutic alliance" or a "collaborative relationship." Establishing this relationship becomes the first goal of therapy. Clients must learn that the therapist understands them and can be trusted with the secrets of their lives. They must also learn about the limits of the therapeutic relationship: that the psychotherapist is to be paid for the service, that the relationship will focus on the clients' concerns and life experiences rather than the psychotherapist's, that the psychotherapist is available to clients during the scheduled sessions and emergencies only, and that this relationship will end when the psychotherapeutic goals are met.

The therapist looks early for certain recurring patterns in what the client thinks, feels, and does. These patterns may occur in the therapy sessions, and the client reports about the way these patterns have occurred in the past and how they continue. These patterns become the focal theme for the therapy and are seen as a basic reason for the client's troubles. For example, some clients may complain that they have never had the confidence to think for themselves. They report that their parents always told them what to do without explanation. In their current marriage, they find themselves unable to feel comfortable with any decisions, and they always look to their spouse for the final say. This pattern of dependence may not be as clear to the clients as to psychotherapists, who look specifically for similarities across past and present relationships. Furthermore, clients will probably approach the psychotherapist in a similar fashion. For example, clients might ask for the psychotherapist's advice, stating that they do not know what to do. When the psychotherapist points out the pattern in the clients' behavior, or suggests that it may have developed from the way their parents interacted with them, the psychotherapist is using the technique of interpretation. This technique originated in the psychodynamic models of psychotherapy.

When clients are confronted with having such patterns or focal themes, they may protest that they are not doing this, find it difficult to do anything different, or cannot imagine that there may be a different way of living. These tendencies to protest and to find change to be difficult are called "resistance." Much of the work of psychotherapy involves overcoming this resistance and achieving the understanding of self called "insight."

One of the techniques the psychotherapist uses to deal with resistance is the continued development of the therapeutic relationship in order to demonstrate that the psychotherapist understands and accepts the client's point of view and that these interpretations of patterns of living are done in the interest of the achievement of therapeutic goals by the client. Humanistic psychotherapists have emphasized this aspect of psychotherapeutic technique. The psychotherapist also responds differently to the client from the way others have in the past, so that when the client demonstrates the focal theme in the psychotherapy session, this different outcome to the pattern encourages a new approach to the difficulty. This is called the "corrective emotional experience," a psychotherapeutic technique that originated in psychodynamic psychotherapy and is emphasized in humanistic therapies as well. For example, when the client asks the psychotherapist for advice, the psychotherapist might respond that they could work together on a solution, building on valuable information and ideas that both may have. In this way, the psychotherapist has avoided keeping the client dependent in the relationship with the psychotherapist as the client has been in relationships with parents, a spouse, or others. This is experienced by the client emotionally, in that it may produce an increase in self-confidence or trust rather than resentment, since the psychotherapist did not dominate. With the repetition of these responses by the psychotherapist, the client's ways of relating are corrected. Such a repetition is often called "working through," another term originating in psychodynamic models of therapy.

Psychotherapists have recognized that many clients have difficulty with changing their patterns of living because of anxiety or lack of skill and experience in behaving differently. Behavioral therapy techniques are especially useful in such cases. In cases of anxiety, the client can be taught to relax through "relaxation training" exercises. The client gradually imagines performing new, difficult behaviors while relaxing. Eventually, the client learns to stay relaxed while performing these behaviors with the psychotherapist and other people. This process is called "desensitization," and it was originally developed to treat persons with extreme fears of particular objects or situations, termed phobias. New behavior is sometimes taught through modeling techniques in which examples of the behavior are first demonstrated by others. Behavioral psychotherapists have also shown the importance of rewarding small approximations to the new behavior that is the goal. This shaping technique might be used with the dependent client by praising confident, assertive, or independent behavior reported by the client or shown in the psychotherapy session, no matter how minor it may be initially.

Perspective and Prospects

The goals and techniques of psychotherapy were first discussed by the psychodynamic theorists who originated the modern practice of psychotherapy. Sigmund Freud and Josef Breuer are generally credited with describing the first modern case treated with psychotherapy, and Freud went on to develop the basis for psychodynamic psychotherapy in his writings between 1895 and his death in 1939. Freud sat behind his clients while they lay upon a couch so that they could concentrate on saying anything that came to mind in order to reveal themselves to the psychotherapist. This also prevented the clients from seeing the psychotherapist's reaction, in case they expected the psychotherapist to react to them as their parents had reacted. This transference relationship provided Freud with information about the client's relationship with parents, which Freud considered to be the root of the problems that his clients had. Later psychodynamic psychotherapists sat facing their clients and conversing with them in a more conventional fashion, but they still attended to the transference.

Carl Rogers is usually described as the first humanistic psychotherapist, and he published descriptions of his techniques in 1942 and 1951. Rogers concentrated on establishing a warm, accepting, honest relationship with his clients. Rogers established this relationship by attempting to understand the client from the client's point of view. By communicating this "accurate empathy," clients would feel accepted and therefore would accept themselves and be more confident in living according to their wishes without fear.

Behavioral psychotherapists began to play a major role in this field after Joseph Wolpe developed systematic desensitization in the 1950's. In the 1960's and 1970's, Albert Bandura applied his findings on how children learn to be aggressive through observation to the development of modeling techniques for reducing fears and teaching new behaviors. Bandura focused on how people attend to, remember, and decide to perform behavior they observe in others. These thought processes, or "cognitions," came to be addressed in cognitive psychotherapy by Aaron T. Beck and others in the 1970's and 1980's. Cognitive behavioral therapy became a popular hybrid that included emphasis on how thinking and behavior influence each other.

In surveys of practicing psychotherapists beginning in the late 1970's, Sol Garfield showed that the majority of therapists practice some hybrid therapy or eclectic approach. As it became apparent that no one model produced the desired effects in a variety of clients, psychotherapists utilized techniques from various approaches. An example is Arnold Lazarus's multimodal behavior therapy, introduced in 1971. It appears that such trends will continue and that, in addition to combining existing psychotherapeutic techniques, new eclectic models will produce additional ways of understanding psychotherapy as well as different techniques for practice.

Bibliography

Brems, Christiane. *Psychotherapy: Processes and Techniques*. Boston: Allyn & Bacon, 1999. Synthesizes a wide variety of topics and literature in the field into an excellent resource for quick guidance on a variety of essential therapeutic topics.

Garfield, Sol L. *Psychotherapy: An Eclectic Approach*. New York: John Wiley & Sons, 1980. Focuses on the client, the therapist, and their interaction within an eclectic framework. Written for the beginning student of psychotherapy and relatively free of jargon.

Phares, E. Jerry, and Timothy J. Trull. *Clinical Psychology: Concepts, Methods, and Profession*. 5th ed. Pacific Grove, Calif.: Brooks/Cole, 1997. An overview of clinical psychology that includes excellent chapters summarizing psychodynamic, behavioral, humanistic, and other models of psychotherapy. Written as a college-level text.

Rogers, Carl R. *Client-Centered Therapy*. Boston: Houghton Mifflin, 1951. A classic description of the author's humanistic psychotherapy that is still useful as a strong statement of the value of the therapeutic relationship. Written for a professional audience, though quite readable.

Schaefer, Charles E., ed. *Innovative Psychotherapy Techniques in Child and Adolescent Therapy*. 2d ed. New York: John Wiley & Sons, 1999. A revised edition of *Innovative Interventions in Child and Adolescent Therapy* (1988). Discusses music, dance, journal writing, imagery, adventure-based techniques, biofeedback, hypnosis, touch, and pets and other animals.

Teyber, Edward. *Interpersonal Process in Psychotherapy: A Guide to Clinical Training*. Chicago: Dorsey Press, 1988. An extremely clear and readable guide to modern eclectic therapy. Full of practical examples and written as a training manual for beginning psychotherapy students.

Usher, Sarah Fels. *Introduction to Psychodynamic Psychotherapy Technique*. Madison, Conn.: International Universities Press, 1999. Explains the psychodynamic and psychoanalytical techniques for beginning and intermediate graduate-level clinical students of psychotherapy.

Weissman, Myrna M., John C. Markowitz, and Gerald L. Klerman. *Comprehensive Guide to Interpersonal Psychotherapy*. New York: Basic Books, 2000. This text in basic behavorial science discusses depression and other mental disorders, interpersonal relations, and methods of psychotherapy. A bibliography and an index are provided.

Wolpe, Joseph. *The Practice of Behavior Therapy*. 4th ed. Elmsford, N.Y.: Pergamon Press, 1990. Written by the originator of behavioral psychotherapy. Introduces basic principles, examples of behavioral interventions, and many references to research. Initial chapters are elementary, but later ones tend to be complicated.

Richard G. Tedeschi

See also:

Aversion, Implosion, and Systematic Desensitization Therapies; Behavioral Family Therapy; Cognitive Behavior Therapy; Cognitive Therapy; Group Therapy; Music, Dance, and Theater Therapy; Psychoactive Drug Therapy; Psychoanalysis; Psychotherapy: Children; Psychotherapy: Effectiveness; Psychotherapy: Historical Approaches to Treatment.

PSYCHOTHERAPY
Historical Approaches to Treatment

Type of psychology: Psychotherapy
Fields of study: Classic analytic themes and issues; psychodynamic and neoanalytic models

Psychotherapy as a socially recognized process and profession emerged in Europe during the late nineteenth century. Although discussions of psychological or "mental healing" can be found dating back to antiquity, a cultural role for the secular psychological healer has become established only in modern times.

Principal terms

CATHARSIS: the discharge of emotional tension, yielding relief from symptoms

FUNCTIONAL DISORDERS: signs and symptoms for which no organic or physiological basis can be found

MENTAL HEALING: the healing of a disorder, functional or physical, through suggestion or persuasion

MESMERISM: hypnotic states induced and explained by "animal magnetism"

NONSPECIFIC TREATMENT FACTORS: those factors that can be attributed to the relationship between the patient and therapist and to suggestion and placebo effects

SUGGESTION: the induction of actions or beliefs in a person through subtle means

TRANSFERENCE: the transferring of emotions from childhood onto adult figures in one's life, including a psychotherapist

Overview

The term "psychotherapy" (originally "psycho-therapy") came into use during the late nineteenth century to describe various treatments that were believed to act on the psychic or mental aspects of a patient rather than on physical conditions. It was contrasted with physical therapies such as medications, baths, surgery, diets, rest, or mild electrical currents, which, while producing some mental relief, did so through physical means. The origins of psychotherapy have been variously traced. Some authors call attention to the practices of primitive witch doctors, to the exorcism rites of the Catholic Church, to the rhetorical methods of Greco-Roman speakers, to the naturalistic healing practices of Hippocrates, and to the Christian practice of public (and later, private) confession.

One of the best argued and supported views claims a direct line of development from the practice of casting out demons all the way to psychoanalysis, the most widely recognized form of psychotherapy. The casting out of demons may be seen as leading to exorcism, which in turn led to the eighteenth century mesmeric technique (named for Franz Mesmer) based on the alleged phenomenon of "animal magnetism." This led to the practice of hypnosis as a psychological rather than a physiological phenomenon and finally to the work of Sigmund Freud, a late-nineteenth century Viennese neurologist who, in his treatment of functional disorders, slowly moved from the practice of hypnosis to the development of psychoanalysis.

There are two histories to be sought in the early forms of treatment by psychotherapy: One is an account of the relationship between a patient and a psychological healer; the other is the story of the specific techniques that the healer employs and the reasons that he or she gives to rationalize them. The latter began as religious or spiritual techniques and became naturalized as psychological or physiological methods. The prominence of spiritual revival during the mid- to late nineteenth century in the United States led to the rise of spiritual or mental healing movements, as demonstrated by the Christian Science movement. Religious healing, mental healing, and psychotherapy were often intertwined in the 1890's, especially in Boston, where many of the leading spokespersons for each perspective resided.

The distinction among these viewpoints was the explanation of the cure—naturalistic versus spiritualistic—and to a lesser degree, the role or relationship between the practitioner and the patient. A psychotherapist in the United States or Europe, whether spiritualistic or naturalistic in orientation, was an authority (of whatever special techniques) who could offer the suffering patient relief through a relationship in which the patient shared his or her deepest feelings and most secret

Many people seek out a priest, rabbi, minister, or other spiritual adviser in response to depression, anxiety, and other types of psychological distress. (St. Elizabeths Hospital Museum)

thoughts on a regular basis. The relationship bore a resemblance to that which a priest, rabbi, or minister might have with a member of the congregation. The psychotherapeutic relationship was also a commercial one, however, since private payment for services was usually the case. Freud came to believe that transference, the projection of emotional reactions from childhood onto the therapist, was a critical aspect of the relationship.

Initially, and well into the early part of the twentieth century, psychotherapists treated patients with physical as well as functional (mental) disorders, but by the 1920's, psychotherapy had largely become a procedure addressed to mental or psychological problems. In the United States, its use rested almost exclusively with the medical profession. Psychiatrists would provide therapy, clinical psychologists would provide testing and assessment of the patient, and social workers would provide ancillary services related to the patient's family or societal and governmental programs. Following World War II, all three of these professions began to offer psychotherapy as one of their services.

One could chart the development of psychotherapy in a simplified, time-line approach, beginning with the early use of the term by Daniel H. Tuke in *Illustrations of the Influence of the Mind upon the Body in Health and Disease* in 1872, followed by the first use of the term at an international conference in 1889 and the publication of Sigmund Freud's and Josef Breuer's cathartic method in *Studien über Hysterie* (1895; *Studies in Hysteria*, 1950). Pierre Janet lectured on "The Chief Methods of Psychotherapeutics" in St. Louis in 1904, and psychotherapy was introduced as a heading in the index to medical literature (the *Index Medicus*) in 1906; at about the same time, private schools of psychotherapy began to be established. In 1909, Freud lectured on psychoanalysis at Clark University. That same year, Hugo Münsterberg published *Psychotherapy*. James T. Walsh published his *Psychotherapy* in 1912. During the 1920's, the widespread introduction and medicalization of psychoanalysis in the United States occurred. Client-centered therapy was introduced by Carl Rogers in 1942, and behavior-oriented therapy was developed by Joseph Wolpe and B. F. Skinner in the early 1950's.

Whatever form psychotherapy may take, it nearly always is applied to the least severe forms of maladjustment and abnormal behavior—to those behaviors and feelings that are least disturbing to others. When the patient has suffered a break with reality and experiences hallucinations, delusions, paranoia, or other behaviors that are socially disruptive, physical forms of treatment are often utilized. The earliest examples include "trephining," a Stone Age practice in which a circular hole was cut into the brain cavity, perhaps to allow the escape of evil spirits. The best-known of the Greek theories of abnormal behavior were naturalistic and physicalistic, based on the belief that deviations in levels of bile caused mental derangement. The solution was bleeding, a practice that continued until the early nineteenth century. Rest, special diets, exercise, and other undertakings that would increase or decrease the relevant bile level were also practiced.

Banishment from public places was recommended by Plato. Initially, people were restricted to their own homes. Later, religious sanctuaries took in the mentally ill, and finally private for-profit and public asylums were developed. Institutions that specialized in the housing of the mentally ill began opening during the sixteenth century. Among the best-known institutions were Bethlehem in London, (which came to be known as "Bedlam"), Salpetriere in Paris, and later St. Elizabeth's in Washington, D.C. Beyond confinement, "treatments" at these institutions included "whirling" chairs in which the patient would be strapped; the "tranquilizing" chair for restraining difficult patients; the straitjacket, which constrained only the arms; rest and diet therapies; and hot and cold water treatments.

By the 1930's, electroconvulsive therapy ("shock therapy") was invented; it used an electric charge that induced a grand mal seizure. During the same period, the earliest lobotomy procedures were performed. These surgeries severed the connections between the brain's frontal lobes and lower centers of emotional functioning. What separates all these and other procedures from psychotherapy is the employment of physical and chemical means for changing behavior and emotions, rather than persuasion and social influence processes.

Periodic reforms were undertaken to improve the care of patients. Philippe Pinel, in the late eighteenth century, freed many mental patients in Paris from being chained in their rooms. He provided daily exercise and frequent cleaning of their quarters. In the United States, Dorothea Dix in the mid-1800's led a campaign of reform that resulted in vast improvement in state mental hospitals. In the 1960's and 1970's, some states placed restrictions on the use of electroconvulsive therapy and lobotomies, and the federal government funded many community mental health centers in an attempt to provide treatment that would keep the patient in his or her community. Since the 1950's, many effective medications have been developed for treating depressions, anxieties, compulsions, panic attacks, and a wide variety of other disorders.

Applications

Modern textbooks of psychotherapy may describe dozens of approaches and hundreds of specific psychotherapeutic techniques. What they have in common is the attempt of a person in the role of healer or teacher to assist another person in the role of patient or client with emotionally disturbing feelings, awkward behavior, or troubling thoughts. Many contemporary therapies are derivative of Sigmund Freud's psychoanalysis. When Freud opened his practice for the treatment of functional disorders in Vienna in the spring of 1886, he initially employed the physical therapies common to his day. These included hydrotherapy, electrotherapy, a mild form of electrical stimulation, massage, rest, and a limited set of pharmaceutical agents. He was disappointed with the results, however, and reported feeling helpless.

He turned to the newly emerging procedure of hypnosis that was being developed by French physicians. Soon he was merely urging his patients to recall traumatic episodes from childhood rather than expecting them to recall such memories under hypnosis. In what he called his "pressure technique," Freud would place his hand firmly on a patient's forehead, apply pressure, and say, "you will recall." Shortly, this became the famous method of free association, wherein the patient would recline on a couch with the instruction to say whatever came to mind.

The psychoanalytic situation that Freud invented, with its feature of one person speaking freely to a passive but attentive audience about the most private and intimate aspects of his or her life, was unique in the history of Western civilization.

Psychoanalysis was not the only method of psychotherapy to emerge near the end of the nineteenth century, as an examination of a textbook published shortly after the turn of the century reveals. James J. Walsh, then Dean and Professor of Functional Disorders at Fordham University, published his eight-hundred-page textbook on psychotherapy in 1912. Only two pages were devoted to the new practice of psychoanalysis. For Walsh, psychotherapy was the use of mental influence to treat disease. His formulation, and that of many practitioners of his time, would encompass what today would be termed behavioral medicine. Thus, the chapters in his book are devoted to the different bodily systems, the digestive tract, cardiotherapy, gynecological psychotherapy, and skin diseases, as well as to the functional disorders.

The techniques that Walsh describes are wide ranging. They include physical recommendations for rest and exercise, the value of hobbies as diversion, the need for regimentation, and varied baths, but it is the suggestion and treatment of the patient rather than the disease (that is, the establishment of a relationship with detailed knowledge of the patient's life and situation) that are the principal means for the cure and relief of symptoms. A concluding chapter in Walsh's book compares psychotherapy with religion, with the view that considering religion simply as a curative agent lessens its meaning and worth.

Perspective and Prospects

In the mid-twentieth century, two new psychotherapies appeared that significantly altered the field, although one of them rejected the term, preferring to call itself behavior therapy in order to distinguish its method from the merely verbal or "talk therapies." The first was found in the work of psychologist Carl Rogers. Rogers made three significant contributions to the development of psychotherapy. He originated nondirective or client-centered therapy, he phonographically recorded and transcribed therapy sessions, and he studied the process of therapy based upon the transcripts. The development of an alternative to psychoanalysis was perhaps his most significant contribution. In the United States, psychoanalysis had become a medical specialty, practiced only by psychiatrists with advanced training. Rogers, a psychologist, created a role for psychologists and social workers as therapists. Thus, he expanded the range of professionals who could legitimately undertake the treatment of disorders through psychotherapy. The title of his most important work, *Counseling and Psychotherapy: Newer Concepts in Practice* (1942), suggests how other professions were to be included. In the preface to his book, Rogers indicated that he regarded these terms as synonymous. If psychologists and social workers could not practice therapy, they could counsel.

Behavior therapy describes a set of specific procedures, such as systematic desensitization and contingency management, that began to appear in the early 1950's, based on the work of Joseph Wolpe, a South African psychiatrist, Hans J.

Eysenck, a British psychologist, and the American experimental psychologist and radical behaviorist B. F. Skinner. Wolpe's *Psychotherapy by Reciprocal Inhibition* appeared in 1958 and argued that states of relaxation and self-assertion would inhibit anxiety, since the patient could not be relaxed and anxious at the same time. It was argued that these were specific techniques based upon the principles of learning and behavior; hence, therapeutic benefits did not depend upon the non-specific effects of mere suggestion or placebo. Behavior therapy was regarded by its developers as the first scientific therapy.

In all of its forms, the rise of psychotherapy may be explained in a variety of ways. The cultural role hypothesis argues that psychotherapists are essentially a controlling agency for the state and society. Their function is to help maintain the cultural norms and values by directly influencing persons at the individual level. This view holds that whatever psychotherapists might say, they occupy a position in the culture similar to that of authorities in educational and religious institutions. A related view argues that psychotherapy arose in Western culture to meet a deficiency in the culture itself. Such a view holds that if the culture were truly meeting the needs of its members, no therapeutic procedures would be required.

Psychotherapy has been explained as a scientific discovery, although exactly what was discovered depends on one's viewpoint. For example, behavior therapists might hold that the fundamental principles of behavior and learning were discovered, as was their applicability to emotional and mental problems. Others might hold that nonspecific or placebo effects were discovered, or at least placed in a naturalistic context. Another explanation follows the historical work of Henri Ellenberger and views psychotherapy as a naturalization of early religious practices: exorcism transformed to hypnotism, transformed to psychoanalysis. The religious demons became mental demons and, with the rise of modern psychopharmacology in the 1950's, molecular demons.

More cynical explanations view psychotherapy as a mistaken metaphor. Recalling that the word was originally written with a hyphen, they argue that it is not possible to perform therapy, a physical practice, on a mental or spiritual object. Thus, psychotherapy is a kind of hoax perpetuated by its practitioners because of a mistaken formulation. Others suggest that the correct metaphor is that of healing and hold that psychotherapy is the history of mental healing, or healing through faith, suggestion, persuasion, and other rhetorical means. Whatever one's opinion of psychotherapy, it is both a cultural phenomenon and a specific set of practices that did not exist prior to the nineteenth century and that have had enormous influence on all aspects of American culture.

Bibliography

Ehrenwald, Jan. *The History of Psychotherapy: From Healing Magic to Encounter.* New York: Jason Aronson, 1976. A survey introduction to the history of psychotherapy. Contains excerpts from many original sources.

Ellenberger, Henri F. *The Discovery of the Unconscious: The History and Evolution of Dynamic Psychiatry.* New York: Basic Books, 1970. A comprehensive and scholarly history of nonmedical psychiatry. Traces the development of psychotherapy from exorcism to hypnosis to suggestion to the methods of Sigmund Freud and Carl G. Jung.

Janet, Pierre. *Psychological Healing: A Historical and Clinical Study*. 2 vols. New York: Macmillan, 1925. Reflects the biases of its author but provides detailed descriptions of nonmedical treatments from the middle of the nineteenth century to the early part of the twentieth century. Contains material that can be found nowhere else.

Masson, Jeffrey Moussaieff. *Against Therapy: Emotional Tyranny and the Myth of Psychological Healing*. New York: Atheneum, 1988. Attacks the very idea of psychotherapy by examining selected historical instances from the nineteenth century onward.

Pande, Sashi K. "The Mystique of 'Western' Psychotherapy: An Eastern Interpretation." In *About Human Nature: Journeys in Psychological Thought*, edited by Terry J. Knapp and Charles T. Rasmussen. Dubuque, Iowa: Kendall/Hunt, 1989. Argues that psychotherapy appears only in Western cultures and that it serves as an illustration of what these cultures lack.

Rogers, Carl. *Counseling and Psychotherapy: Newer Concepts in Practice*. Boston: Houghton Mifflin, 1942. Introduces nondirective or client-centered therapy, and provides the first verbatim transcripts of all the therapy sessions for a single patient.

Tallis, Frank. *Changing Minds: The History of Psychotherapy as an Answer to Human Suffering*. New York: Cassell, 1998. An accessible history of psychotherapy that introduces its key figures and explains their most important ideas. Shows how historical and cultural events have influenced ideas about the mind and vice versa.

Valenstein, Elliot S. *Great and Desperate Cures: The Rise and Decline of Psychosurgery and Other Radical Treatments*. New York: Basic Books, 1986. This is a scholarly and readable account of the history of physical therapies for mental disorders. While it focuses on lobotomy, many other forms of treatment are also described.

Terry Knapp

See also:

Abnormality: Behavioral Models; Abnormality: Psychodynamic Models; Analytic Psychotherapy; Cognitive Therapy; Madness: Historical Concepts; Operant Conditioning Therapies; Psychoanalysis; Psychosurgery; Psychotherapy: Children; Psychotherapy: Effectiveness; Psychotherapy: Goals and Techniques.

RATIONAL-EMOTIVE THERAPY

Type of psychology: Psychotherapy
Fields of study: Cognitive therapies

Developed by psychologist Albert Ellis, rational-emotive therapy aims to minimize the client's self-defeating style by helping the client acquire a more rational and logical philosophy of life. It has been successfully applied to marital couples, family members, individual patients, and group clients across a host of psychological difficulties, including alcoholism, depression, anxiety disorders, and sexual dissatisfaction.

Principal terms

A-B-C THEORY OF PERSONALITY: a theory in which activating events (A) are evaluated in light of a person's beliefs (B), which directly influence and shape consequential emotional (behavioral and cognitive) reactions (C)

IRRATIONAL BELIEFS: unreasonable evaluations that sabotage an individual's goals and lead to increased likelihood of experiencing needless pain, suffering, and displeasure

LONG-RANGE HEDONISM: the idea that well-adjusted people seek happiness and avoid pain today, tomorrow, and in the future

RATIONAL-EMOTIVE TREATMENT: a method of personality change that incorporates cognitive, emotional, and behavioral strategies; designed to help resist tendencies to be irrational, suggestible, and conforming

SCIENTIFIC THINKING: the idea that individuals intend to be reasonably objective, rational, and logical; via scientific thinking, attempts are made to construct hypotheses, collect data, and evaluate the validity of these personal hypotheses

Overview

Rational-emotive therapy (RET) was founded in 1955 by Albert Ellis following his disappointment with traditional methods of psychoanalysis. From 1947 to 1953, Ellis had practiced classical analysis and analytically oriented psychotherapy, but he came to the conclusion that psychoanalysis was a superficial and unscientific form of treatment. Specifically, rational-emotive therapy was developed as a combined humanistic, cognitive, and behavioral form of therapy. Although Ellis initially used RET primarily in individual formats, group and workshop formats followed quickly. Ellis would publish approximately fifty books and more than five hundred articles on RET, and he would present more than fifteen hundred public workshops.

According to Ellis in a paper in 1989, the philosophical origins of rational-emotive therapy include the Stoic philosophers Epictetus and Marcus Aurelius. In particular, Epictetus wrote that "people are disturbed not by things, but by the view which they take of them" during the first century C.E.: in *The Encheiridion*. Ellis also gives much credit to the theory of human disturbance highlighted by psycho-therapist Alfred Adler in the development of rational-emotive therapy. Specifically, Ellis was persuaded by Adler's conviction that a person's behavior originates from his or her ideas.

As Ellis began writing about and describing RET in the 1950's and 1960's, clinical behavior therapy was conceptually distinct and distant from Ellis's ideas. The primary similarity was that Ellis employed a host of behavioral techniques in his approach. As time passed, however, behavior therapy engaged in a controver-sial yet productive broadening of what was meant by "behavior" and started to include cognitions as a form of behavior that could be learned, modified, and studied.

Ellis's RET approach shares many similarities with other common cognitive behavioral approaches to treatment. These include Donald Meichenbaum's cogni-tive behavioral modification (focusing on self-instructional processes and adaptive coping statements), Maxie C. Maultsby, Jr.'s rational behavior therapy (which is essentially RET with some adaptations, including written self-analysis techniques and rational-emotive imagery), and Aaron T. Beck's cognitive therapy. Cognitive therapy has many similarities to RET but was developed independently; it uses fewer "hard-headed approaches." For example, Beck advocates the use of collabo-rative empiricism and a focus on automatic thoughts and underlying cognitive schemas. RET strongly emphasizes irrational beliefs, especially "unconditional shoulds" and "absolutistic musts," as the root of emotional and behavioral distur-bances.

There are six principal propositions of rational-emotive therapy as Ellis de-scribed them in 1989. First, people are born with rational and irrational tendencies. That is, individuals may be either self-helping or self-defeating, short-range hedon-ists or long-range hedonists; they may learn by mistakes or repeat the same mistakes, and they may actualize or avoid actualizing their potentials for growth. Second, cultural and family experiences may exacerbate irrational thinking. Third, individuals may seem to think, act, and feel simultaneously. Thinking, however, appears actually to precede actions and feelings. For example, the process of "appraising" a situation usually triggers feelings. Fourth, RET therapists differ from person-centered therapists in that RET practitioners do not believe that a warm interpersonal relationship between therapist and patient is a sufficient or even necessary condition for effective change. RET therapists also do not believe that personal warmth is necessary in order to accept clients fully. In fact, it is important in RET treatment to criticize and point out the deficiencies in a person's behavior and thinking style. Moreover, Ellis argues that RET therapists often need to use "hard-headed methods" to convince clients to employ more self-discipline.

Fifth, rational-emotive therapists use a variety of strategies, including assertive-ness training, desensitization, operant conditioning, support, and role playing. The usual goal of RET is to help rid clients of symptoms and modify underlying thinking styles that create symptoms. Ellis further identifies two basic forms of RET: general RET, which is similar to other forms of cognitive behavior therapy;

and preferential RET, which includes general RET but also emphasizes philosophic restructuring and teaches clients how to dispute irrational thoughts and inappropriate behaviors via rules of logic and the scientific method. Sixth, all emotional problems are caused by people's tendencies to interpret events unrealistically and are maintained by irrational beliefs about them.

Thus, the basic underlying tenet of RET is that emotional disturbances are primarily the result of irrational thinking. Specifically, RET argues that people upset themselves with "evaluative irrational beliefs" (rather than with "nonevaluative" irrational beliefs). For example, in a 1987 essay, Ellis described the following scenario:

> If you devoutly believe that your fairy godmother looks out for you and is always ready to help you, you may live happily and undisturbedly with this highly questionable and unrealistic Belief. But if you evaluate your fairy godmother's help as extremely desirable and go even further to insist that *because* it is desirable, you absolutely *must* at all times have her help, you will almost certainly make yourself anxious (whenever you realize that her magical help that you *must* have may actually be absent) and you will tend to make yourself extremely depressed (when you see that in your hour of need this help does not actually materialize).

Although many forms of irrationality exist, rational-emotive therapy focuses on a client's strong "desires" and "commands." Ellis has developed various lists of irrational beliefs that highlight the most common thinking difficulties of patients. These include such beliefs as "I must do well or very well"; "I am a bad or worthless person when I act weakly or stupidly"; "I need to be loved by someone who matters to me a lot"; "People must treat me fairly and give me what I need"; "People must live up to my expectations or it is terrible"; "My life must have few major hassles"; and "I can't stand it when life is unfair."

Ellis has refined his ideas about irrational thoughts to three primary beliefs. They are "I *must* do well and be approved by *significant* others, and if I don't do as well as I *should* or *must*, there is something really rotten about me. It is terrible that I am this way and I am a pretty worthless, rotten person"; "You (other humans with whom I relate, my original family, my later family that I may have, my friends, relatives, and people with whom I work) *must*, *ought*, and *should* treat me considerately and fairly and even *specially* (considering what a doll I am)!"; and "Conditions under which I live—my environment, social conditions, economic conditions, political conditions—must be arranged so that I easily and immediately, with no real effort, have a free lunch and get what I command." In summary, Ellis defines the three primary irrationalities as "I *must* do well; you *must* treat me beautifully; the world *must* be easy."

Psychological disturbances are based on irrational thinking and behaving. The origin of irrational beliefs and actions stems from childhood. Irrational beliefs are shaped in part by significant others (parents, relatives, and teachers), as well as from misperceptions on the part of children (such as superstitions and overinterpretation). Rational-emotive therapy also maintains that individuals have tendencies, which are both biologically and environmentally determined, for growth and actualization of one's potential. On the other hand, Ellis argues that people also have powerful innate tendencies to condemn themselves, others, and the world when they do not get what they "childishly need." This pattern of self-sabotage is argued by Ellis to be both inborn and acquired during childhood. Moreover, via repetitive self-talk and self-evaluative tendencies, false beliefs are continually re-indoctrinated by the individual. From the RET perspective, self-blame and self-condemnation are the cornerstones of most emotional disturbances. By challenging self-blame and self-condemnation, via an analysis and refutation of irrational beliefs, a client can be helped.

Ellis defines mental health as incorporating self-interest, social interests, self-direction, tolerance, acceptance of ambiguity and uncertainty, scientific thinking, commitment, risk taking, self-acceptance, long-range hedonism, nonperfectionism, and self-responsibility for one's emotional disturbances. Three primary processes seem to be associated with mental functioning and mental disorders: self-talking, self-evaluating, and self-condemning. That is, individuals are constantly engaged in an internal dialogue (self-talk) with themselves, appraising and commenting upon events that occur in their lives. Individuals also are self-evaluating in that humans seek meaning and constantly evaluate events and themselves, frequently placing blame on themselves for events. Self-evaluating is thus often associated with self-condemnation. For example, this condemnation may start in response to evaluating oneself as doing poorly at work or in school, which in turn leads to feeling guilty. This vicious cycle then leads to condemning oneself for condemning oneself, condemning oneself for not being able to stop condemning oneself, and finally condemning oneself for entering psychotherapy and not getting better (Ellis, 1989).

Emotional and behavioral difficulties often occur when simple preferences are chosen above thoughtful decisions. Ellis believes that individuals have inborn growth and actualization tendencies, although they may become sabotaged through self-defeating and self-condemning patterns. Based on the RET model, clients benefit from exposure to three primary insights. Insight number one is that a person's self-defeating behavior is related to antecedent and understandable causes. Specifically, an individual's beliefs are more important in understanding emotional upset than are past or present activating events. Insight two is that individuals actually make themselves emotionally disturbed by re-indoctrinating themselves with irrational and unproductive kinds of beliefs. Insight three is that through hard work and practice, irrational beliefs can be corrected.

Applications

As detailed by Gerald Corey in 1986, practitioners of rational-emotive therapy actively teach, persuade, and direct clients to alter irrational styles of thinking and behaving. RET can be defined as a process of re-education in which clients learn to think differently and solve problems. The first step in treatment often focuses on distinguishing rational (or reasonable) thoughts from irrational (or unreasonable) beliefs. Educational approaches are employed to highlight for the client that he or she has acquired many irrational "shoulds, oughts, and musts." The second step in treatment emphasizes an awareness of how psychological disturbances are maintained through a client's repeated reindoctrination of illogical and unreasonable beliefs. During the third phase of treatment, therapists assist clients in modifying maladaptive thinking styles and abandoning irrational beliefs. Via a variety of cognitive, emotive, and behavioral approaches, self-condemnation and self-blame are replaced with more rational and logical views. Finally, the fourth step in RET involves developing a rational lifestyle and philosophy. Specifically, from internalizing rules of logic and scientific thinking, individuals may prevent future psychological disturbances and live more productive lives.

The A-B-C theory of personality and the A-B-C (D-E) theory of emotional change are also central to RET approaches. "A" refers to an activating event. Activating events can include facts, events, behaviors, or perceived stimuli. "B" refers to beliefs triggered by the event or beliefs about the event. "C" refers to the consequential emotional (behavioral or cognitive) outcomes that proceed directly from beliefs. "D" is the application of methods to dispute or challenge irrational beliefs, and "E" refers to the effect of disputing beliefs on the emotional (behavioral or cognitive) reaction of the client.

Activating events are generally regarded as inherently neutral, and they have no particular emotional meaning in and of themselves. Thus, activating events do not directly cause emotions. Instead, beliefs about events primarily cause emotional reactions. For example, a woman who had been depressed for more than twelve months following the death of her husband from terminal cancer was participating in a hospice therapy group and had demonstrated little or no improvement over the last year. She reasoned that because her husband was dead, she would never feel happy again (nor "should" she feel happy again, since he was dead and she was "not entitled" to experience pleasure without him). She added, "He was the center of my life and I can never expect to feel happiness without him." Her resulting emotional reaction was severe depression, which accompanied her complicated grief and underlying anger.

In an effort to uncover and dispute her unreasonable beliefs, a variety of strategies were employed. First, group members provided feedback about her reasonable and unreasonable ideas following (and during) her husband's death. In particular, group members pointed out that she could expect to experience happiness again in her life since she had experienced pleasure on many occasions before she met her husband, while her husband was away during military service, and while they were married, and she enjoyed activities in which he did not share. Next, her emotional reaction was examined and viewed as being caused not by her husband's death, but instead by the manner in which she interpreted his death (as awful), her own ability to cope and change (as limited), and her future (as hopeless). A variety of behavioral and cognitive strategies were employed to challenge her irrational and self-condemning assumptions. Behavioral homework assignments included increasing activity levels and engaging in pleasurable activities to challenge the notion that she could never experience happiness again. Self-confidence and hope were fostered via strategies which highlighted her ability to cope with stress. This client also found cognitive homework assignments, wherein she listed her irrational beliefs on a daily log and then disputed those beliefs or replaced or modified them with more reasonable statements, to be helpful.

Rational-emotive therapy and its various techniques have been evaluated in at least two hundred studies. Although many of these studies have been associated with various methodological flaws, the effectiveness of RET with a broad range of psychological disturbances is impressive. At the Evolution of Psychotherapy Conference in Phoenix, Arizona, in 1985, Ellis himself identified several limitations of RET (and other therapies). These included several key "irrationalities." Because individuals falsely believe that they are unchangeable, they fail to work to change themselves. Because individuals falsely believe that activating events cause emotional reactions, they blame the activating events and fail to change their beliefs about them. Individuals falsely believe that unpleasant emotional reactions must be good or useful and should be cherished instead of minimized. Individuals are often confused about emotional reactions (for example, concern and caution versus anxiety and panic) and experience difficulty surrendering the inappropriate negative feelings. Because some RET techniques require subtle and discriminative styles of thinking by clients, some clients are not capable of succeeding in therapy. RET is not particularly useful for young children or developmentally delayed individuals (typically RET requires a chronological age of at least eight years and average intelligence).

Perspective and Prospects
Albert Ellis is regarded by many psychologists as the most prominent theorist in the cognitive behavioral school of psychotherapy. His insights and conceptualizations are evident in many of the various cognitive behavioral psychotherapeutic approaches. Specifically, the A-B-C theory of personality is well regarded among cognitive behavioral therapists, and many of Ellis's treatment strategies are frequently used by clinicians across other schools of psychotherapy. On the other hand, Ellis's interpersonal style in treatment has been criticized by many authors. Specifically, a warm, confiding relationship between therapist and client is often de-emphasized in Ellis's writings, and confrontational interactions may be commonly observed in videotapes of rational-emotive therapy. It also appears, however, that more attention is being paid to the quality of the interpersonal relationship between RET practitioner and client. Moreover, the strengths of the RET approach are not based on the style of any particular therapist, but instead are evident in its underlying theory and therapeutic strategies.

Undoubtedly, the influence of rational-emotive therapy in the field of psychotherapy will continue to be prominent. Ellis has written extensively on the application of RET principles to diverse psychological disturbances. The Institute for Rational-Emotive Therapy in New York continues to train hundreds of therapists and serves as a distribution center for most of the books and pamphlets developed by RET therapists.

Bibliography

Corey, Gerald. *Theory and Practice of Counseling and Psychotherapy*. 6th ed. Pacific Grove, Calif.: Brooks/Cole, 2000. Corey reviews many of the primary schools of psychotherapy and specifically highlights the key concepts, therapeutic techniques, and research associated with RET. Also provides a brief critique of RET.

Ellis, Albert. "The Evolution of Rational-Emotive Therapy (RET) and Cognitive Behavior Therapy (CBT)." In *The Evolution of Psychotherapy*, edited by Jeffrey K. Zeig. New York: Brunner/Mazel, 1987. This edited book provides an interesting blend of dialogue, debate, and scholarly review of various schools of psychotherapy. Ellis presents thoughtful answers to questions concerning the future of RET, the primary treatment processes, and training procedures.

_____. "Rational-Emotive Therapy." In *Current Psychotherapies*, edited by Raymond J. Corsini and Danny Wedding. 4th ed. Itasca, Ill.: F. E. Peacock, 1989. Provides a review of the basic concepts, history, theory, and treatment approach of RET. Written by Ellis, this chapter provides much insight into his views of RET and presents a transcript of a treatment session that highlights many of the therapeutic processes involved in RET.

Ellis, Albert, and Shawn Blau, eds. *The Albert Ellis Reader: A Guide to Well-Being Using Rational Emotive Behavior Therapy*. Secaucus, N.J.: Carol Publishing Group, 1998. A collection of thirty of the most popular and controversial articles by Ellis, who updated each piece especially for this volume. Topics include sex, love, marriage, anger, and rational living.

Ellis, Albert, and Windy Dryden. *The Practice of Rational Emotive Behavior Therapy*. 2d ed. New York: Springer, 1997. Includes discussions of individual, couple, family, and group therapies, as well as general theory and practice. Includes bibliographical references and an index.

Ellis, Albert, and Russell Grieger. *Handbook of Rational-Emotive Therapy*. New York: Springer, 1977. Presents an overview of RET with emphasis on the conceptual foundations and fundamental treatment components. Also highlights procedures for conducting RET with children.

Ellis, Albert, and Robert A. Harper. *A New Guide to Rational Living*. Englewood Cliffs, N.J.: Prentice-Hall, 1975. A self-help book emphasizing RET approaches. A classic RET book in that therapists have suggested this book for their clients for many years. Presents a clear, straightforward approach to RET.

Gregory L. Wilson

See also:

Cognitive Behavior Therapy; Cognitive Therapy; Couples Therapy; Depression; Group Therapy; Person-Centered Therapy; Psychotherapy: Effectiveness; Psychotherapy: Goals and Techniques; Strategic Family Therapy.

REALITY THERAPY

Type of psychology: Psychotherapy
Fields of study: Cognitive therapies

Reality therapy is a system of counseling or psychotherapy which attempts to help clients accept responsibility for their behavior. Its aim is to teach clients more appropriate patterns of behavior. Its significance is that it helps clients meet their basic needs more effectively.

Principal terms

FREEDOM: basic to reality therapy; emphasizes that people are free to choose how they act
MORALITY: standards of behaving; the "rightness" or "wrongness" of behavior
RESPONSIBILITY: basic to reality therapy; stresses that people are responsible for their behavior
SUCCESS IDENTITY: what reality therapy strives for; describes people who are able to give and receive love, feel worthwhile, and meet their needs appropriately
VALUE JUDGMENTS: making decisions about one's behavior as to its merit or value

Overview

William Glasser, the founder of reality therapy, believes that people are motivated to fulfill five basic needs: belonging, power, freedom, fun, and survival. When these needs are not met, problems begin. Individuals lose touch with the objective reality of life (what is appropriate behavior and what is not) and often stray into patterns of behavior that are self-defeating or destructive. The reality therapist attempts to help such people by teaching them more appropriate patterns of behavior. This, in turn, will enable individuals to meet their basic needs more effectively.

Reality therapy differs from conventional theories of counseling or psychotherapy in six ways. Reality therapy rejects the concept of mental illness and the use of diagnostic labels; it works in the present, not the past; it rejects the concept of transference (the idea that clients relate to the therapist as an authority figure from their past). Reality therapy does not consider the unconscious to be the basis of present behavior. The morality of behavior is emphasized. Finally, reality therapy teaches individuals better ways to fulfill their needs and more appropriate (and more successful) ways to deal with the world.

In practice, reality therapy involves eight steps. First the therapist makes friends, or gains rapport and asks clients what they want. Then the client is asked to focus on his or her current behavior. The client is helped to make a realistic evaluation of his or her behavior. Therapist and client make a plan for the client to do better, which consists of finding more appropriate (realistic) ways of behaving. The therapist gets a commitment from the client to follow the plan that has been worked out. The therapist accepts no excuses from the client if the plan is not followed. No form of punishment is utilized, however, if the client fails to follow through. Finally, the therapist must never give up on the client.

Paramount to the success of reality therapy is the planning stage, consisting of discovering ways to change the destructive or self-defeating behavior of the client into behavior oriented toward success. Success-oriented behavior leads to a success identity: the feeling that one is able to given and receive love, feel worthwhile, and meet one's needs appropriately. Glasser states that putting the plan into writing, in the form of a contract, is one way to help ensure that the client will follow through. The client, not the therapist, is then held accountable for the success or failure of follow-through. Commitment is, in many ways, the keystone of reality therapy. Resolutions and plans of action become meaningless unless there is a decision (and a commitment) to carry them out.

Like behavior therapists, reality therapists are basically active, directive, instructive, and oriented toward action. Reality therapists use a variety of techniques, including role-play, humor, question-and-answer sessions, and confrontation. They do not employ some commonly accepted therapeutic techniques, such as interpretation, insight, free association, analysis of transference and resistance, and dream analysis. In addition, reality therapists rarely recommend or promote the use of drugs or medications in treatment.

Confrontation is one technique of special consideration to reality therapy. Through confrontation, therapists force clients to evaluate their present behavior and to decide whether they will change it. Reality therapy maintains that the key to finding happiness and success is accepting responsibility. Thus the therapist neither accepts any excuses from the client for his or her self-defeating or destructive behavior nor ignores the reality of the situation (the consequences of the client's present behavior). The client is solely responsible for his or her behavior. Conventional psychotherapy often avoids the issue of responsibility; the client (or "patient") is thought to be "sick" and thus not responsible for his or her behavior.

Throughout reality therapy, the criterion of what is "right" plays an important role in determining the appropriateness of behavior; however, the therapist does not attempt to state the morality of behavior. This is the task and responsibility of the client. Clients are to make these value judgments based on the reality of their situation. Is their current behavior getting them what they want? Does their current behavior lead to success or to failure? The basic philosophy of reality therapy is that people are ultimately self-determining and in charge of their lives. People are, in other words, free to choose how they act and what they will become.

The strengths of reality therapy are that it is relatively short-term therapy (not lasting for years, as classical psychoanalysis does), consists of simple and clear concepts that can be used by all types of helpers, focuses on present behavioral problems, consists of a plan of action, seeks a commitment from the client to follow through, stresses personal responsibility, can be applied to a diverse population of clients (including people in prison, people addicted to drugs and alcohol, and juvenile offenders), and accepts no excuses, blame, or rationalizations.

The weaknesses of reality therapy are that it fails to recognize the significance of the unconscious or of intrapsychic conflict, minimizes the importance of one's past in present behavior, appears overly simplistic (problems are rarely simplistic in nature), may give the therapist an inappropriate feeling of power or control, minimizes the existence of biological or biochemical factors in mental illness, and fails to recognize the significance of psychiatric drugs in the treatment of mental illness.

Applications

Reality therapy can be applied to individuals with many sorts of psychological problems, from mild to severe emotional disorders. It has been used in a variety of counseling situations, including individual and group counseling, marriage and family counseling, rehabilitation counseling, and crisis intervention. The principles of reality therapy have been applied to teaching, social work, business management, and community development. Reality therapy is a popular method of treatment in mental hospitals, correctional institutions, substance abuse centers, and facilities for delinquent youth.

Reality therapists usually see their clients once weekly, for between forty-five minutes and one hour per visit. Therapists come from a variety of disciplines, including psychiatry, psychology, counseling, and social work. Important in applying reality therapy is that the therapist adopt no rigid rules. The therapist has a framework to follow, but within that framework he or she should be as free and creative as possible.

Reality therapy begins with the establishment of a working relationship. Once rapport is established, the process proceeds through an exploration of the client's needs and wants and then to an exploration of the client's present behavior.

Reality therapists stress current behavior. The past is used only as a means of enlightening the present. The focus is on what a client is doing now. Through skillful questioning, clients are encouraged to evaluate current behavior and to consider its present consequences. Is their current behavior getting them what they want or need? If not, why? As this process of questioning and reflecting continues, clients begin to acknowledge the negative and detrimental aspects of their current behavior. Slowly, they begin to accept responsibility for these actions.

Once responsibility is accepted, much of the remaining work consists of helping clients identify specific and appropriate ways to fulfill their needs and wants. This is often considered the teaching stage, since the therapist may model or teach the client more effective behavioral patterns.

Marriage therapy is often practiced by reality therapists; the number of sessions ranges from two to ten. Initially, it is important to clarify the couple's goals for marriage counseling: Are they seeking help in order to preserve the marriage, or have they already made the decision to end the relationship? In marriage counseling, Glasser recommends that the therapist be quite active, asking many questions while trying to understand the overall patterns of the marriage and of the interrelationship.

It is difficult to discuss the application of reality therapy to specific problems, since reality therapists do not look at people as objects to be classified according to diagnostic categories. Reality therapists, like others in the holistic health movement, believe that most ailments—whether physical or psychological—are manifestations of the way people choose to live their lives. William Glasser has stated:

> It makes little difference to a reality therapist what the presenting complaint of the client is; that complaint is a part of the way the client is choosing now to deal with the world. . . . When the client begins to realize that instead of being the victim of some disease or diagnostic category he is a victim of his own ineffective behavior, then therapy begins and diagnosis becomes irrelevant.

The following example shows how the eight steps of reality therapy can be applied to a real-life situation. The client's name is Jim; he is thirty-five years old. For years, Jim has been unable to hold a job. He is twice divorced and is subject to angry outbursts. He has been arrested three times for disorderly conduct. Recently Jim has lost his driver's license because of alcohol intoxication; he has been referred by the court for counseling.

In step one, the therapist makes friends and asks the client what he or she wants. Here the reality therapist, David, will make himself available to Jim as a caring, warm individual but not as someone whom Jim can control or dominate. David will ask, "What is it that you want?" Jim says, "Well, what I want is a job." Once the client states what he or she wants, the therapist can move to step two, asking the client to focus on his or her current behavior. Together David and Jim talk about Jim's behavior—his tendency for angry outbursts, his arrests, and his problems with alcohol.

The third step attempts to get clients to evaluate their present behavior and to see whether what they are now doing is getting them what they want. David asks Jim whether getting in fights is helping him find a job. As this step unfolds, Jim begins to understand that what he is doing is not helping him to become employable. Paramount at this step is that the clients see that their current behavior is within their control: They "choose" to act this way.

Once clients begin to see that what they are doing is not working (not getting them what they want), then the next step (step four) is to help them make a plan to do better. Once Jim realizes that getting in fights and drinking is ineffective and self-defeating, then David will begin to talk with him about a plan to change his behavior and find more appropriate ways of behaving. They plan a course of action. To "cement" this plan, a contract is made. The contract might state that Jim will not get in fights, Jim will control his anger, and Jim will stay out of bars and refrain from alcohol. David may also advise Jim on how to get a job: where to look for work, whom to contact, even what to wear and say during a job interview. Throughout this job search, which may be long and frustrating, David needs to be encouraging and supportive.

Step five involves getting a commitment from the client to follow through. David now asks Jim, "Are you going to live up to the contract? Are you going to change your behavior?" David needs to stress that commitment is the key to making this plan a success. David also must accept only a yes or no answer from Jim. Reality therapy does not accept excuses or reasons why plans are not carried through; this is step six. David's response to excuses should be that he is not interested in why Jim cannot do it; he is interested in when Jim will do it.

Step seven holds that David needs to be "tough" with Jim, but must not punish him if he does not follow through. Instead of finding ways to punish Jim, David may ask instead, "What is it that will get you to follow through?" Reality therapy recognizes that punishment is, in the long run, rarely effective. Step eight is simply never giving up. For most people, change does not come naturally, nor is it easy. A good therapist, like a good friend, does not give up easily. David needs to persevere with Jim. Through perseverance, Jim's life can change.

Perspective and Prospects

The tenets of reality therapy were formed in the 1950's and 1960's as a reaction to the dominant psychotherapeutic approaches of the times, which were closely based on Freudian psychoanalysis. William Glasser, the founder of reality therapy, was trained as a physician and psychoanalyst, but during his psychiatric training in the early 1950's, he became more and more dissatisfied with the psychoanalytic approach. What disturbed him was the insistence of psychoanalysis on viewing the patient as a victim of forces beyond his or her control. In other words, the person was not considered responsible for his or her current behavior.

In 1956, Glasser became a consultant to a school for delinquent female adolescents in Ventura, California, developing a new therapeutic approach that was in sharp opposition to classical psychoanalysis. In 1962, he spoke at a meeting of the National Association of Youth Training Schools and presented his new ideas. The response was phenomenal; evidently many people were frustrated with the current mode of treatment.

Initially Glasser was hesitant to state his dissatisfaction with the conventional approach to treatment, psychoanalysis; however, his faculty supervisor, G. L. Harrington, was supportive. This started a long relationship in which Harrington helped Glasser formulate many of the ideas that became reality therapy.

In 1965, Glasser put his principles of counseling into a book entitled *Reality Therapy: A New Approach to Psychiatry*. Since then, he has written extensively, including *Schools Without Failure* (1968), *The Identity Society* (1972), *Positive Addiction* (1976), *Stations of the Mind: New Directions for Reality Therapy* (1981), *Control Theory: A New Exploration of How We Control Our Lives* (1985), and *The Quality School* (1990). The Institute for Reality Therapy, in Canoga Park, California, offers programs designed to teach the concepts and practice of reality therapy. A journal, the *Journal of Reality Therapy*, publishes articles concerning the research, theory, and application of reality therapy. Reality therapy has seen remarkable success since its conception, and many consider it one of the important approaches to counseling and psychotherapy.

Bibliography

Corey, Gerald. *Theory and Practice of Counseling and Psychotherapy*. 6th ed. Monterey, Calif.: Brooks/Cole, 2000. An excellent source of information on the major theories of counseling and psychotherapy. In one chapter, Corey states the essentials of reality therapy. Also gives a detailed evaluation of the strengths and weaknesses of reality therapy.

Glasser, William. *Control Theory: A New Exploration of How We Control Our Lives*. New York: Harper & Row, 1985. Control theory explains how individuals function. It states that behavior originates from within the individual and is need satisfying. A significant book, easy to read and understand.

_____. "Reality Therapy." In *Current Psychotherapies*, edited by Raymond Corsini. Itasca, Ill.: F. E. Peacock, 1984. In this chapter, Glasser describes in detail the beginnings of reality therapy, his theory of personality, the eight steps of reality therapy, and the processes and mechanisms of psychotherapy. A case example is included to show how the process of reality therapy works.

_____. *Reality Therapy: A New Approach to Psychiatry*. New York: Harper & Row, 1965. Describes Glasser's basic concepts of reality therapy. Glasser also shows how the reality therapist gets involved with the client and how he or she teaches clients more responsible ways to live their lives. This book was a significant contribution to psychotherapy in that it offered an alternative to psychoanalytic therapy.

_____. *Reality Therapy in Action*. Foreword by Peter R. Breggin. New York: HarperCollins, 2000. In a follow-up to his classic *Reality Therapy* (1965), Glasser takes readers into his consulting room and illustrates, through a series of conversations with his patients, exactly how he puts his popular therapeutic theories into practice.

_____. *Schools Without Failure*. New York: Harper & Row, 1968. Glasser applies the concepts of reality therapy to education, showing that many school practices have promoted a sense of failure in students. He proposes a new program to reduce school failure based on positive involvement, group work, no punishment (but discipline), a different grading system, and individual responsibility.

Wubbolding, Robert E. *Reality Therapy for the Twenty-first Century*. Philadelphia: Accelerated Development, 2000. A text on the future of reality therapy. Includes bibliographical references and an index.

Ted Eilders

See also:

Abnormality: Behavioral Models; Abnormality: Cognitive Models; Behavioral Family Therapy; Cognitive Behavior Therapy; Cognitive Therapy; Psychoanalysis; Psychotherapy: Goals and Techniques; Rational-Emotive Therapy.

SCHIZOPHRENIA

Type of psychology: Psychopathology
Fields of study: Organic disorders; schizophrenias

A disease of the brain characterized by withdrawal from the world, delusions, hallucinations, and other disorders in thinking.

Principal terms

CATATONIA: a state in which patients become immobile and fixed in a rigid position for long periods

DELUSION: a false view of what is real

HALLUCINATION: a false or distorted perception of objects or events

HEREDITARY: passed down from generation to generation through the genes

MANIA: a mental disorder marked by extreme hyperactivity, agitation, racing thoughts, and distractibility

Causes and Symptoms

Schizophrenia is a disease of the brain. Eugen Bleuler (1857-1939), a Swiss psychiatrist, first named the disease in a 1908 paper that he wrote entitled "Dementia Praecox: Or, The Group of Schizophrenias." In 1911, he published a book with the same title describing the disease in more detail. Bleuler served as the head of an eight hundred-bed mental hospital in Switzerland and treated the worst and most chronic cases. Beginning in 1896, he embarked on a project to understand the inner world of the mentally ill. He developed work therapy programs for his patients, and he visited them and talked to them almost every day. Bleuler insisted that the hospital staff show the same kind of dedication and support for his clients that he did.

Bleuler's discoveries challenged the traditional view of the causes and treatment of the disease. The traditional view, based on the work of the great German psychiatrist Emil Kraepelin (1856-1926), held that dementia, as it was called, always got worse and that the patient's mind continued to degenerate until death. Kraepelin suggested that the disease, which he called dementia praecox, was hereditary and was the result of a poisonous substance that destroyed brain cells. Bleuler's investigation of living victims led him to reject this view. Instead, he argued, continuing deterioration does not always take place because the disease can stop or go into remission at any time. The disease does not always follow a downhill course. Bleuler's views promised more hope for patients suffering from schizophrenia, which means "to split the mind."

The symptoms of schizophrenia are more well known than the cause. Diagnosis is based on a characteristic set of symptoms that must last for at least several months. The "psychotic symptoms" include a break with reality, hallucinations, delusions, or evidence of thought disorder. These are referred to as positive symptoms. "Negative" symptoms can also be displayed; they include withdrawal

Swiss psychiatrist Eugen Bleuler, who first named the disease "schizophrenia" in a 1908 paper. His discoveries challenged the traditional view of its causes and treatment.

from society, the inability to show emotion or to feel pleasure or pain, total apathy, and the lack of a facial expression. The patient simply sits and stares blankly at the world, no matter what is happening.

Schizophrenia can take many forms. Among the most frequent are those that display acute symptoms under the following labels. Melancholia includes depression and hypochondriacal delusions, with the patient claiming to be extremely physically ill but having no appropriate symptoms. Mania is characterized by withdrawal and a mood of complete disinterest in the affairs of life. Schizophrenia can also be catatonic, in which patients become immobile and seem fixed in one rigid position for long periods of time. Delusional states accompanied by hallucinations frequently involve hearing voices, which often scream and shout abusive and derogatory language at the patient or make outrageous demands. The delusions are often visual and involve frightening monsters or aliens sent to do harm to the afflicted person.

The above symptoms can often be accompanied by disconnected speech patterns, broken sentences, and excessive body movement and purposeless activity. Victims of the disease also suffer through states of extreme anger and hostility. Cursing and outbursts of uncontrolled rage can result from relatively insignificant causes, such as being looked at "in the wrong way." Many times, anniversaries of important life experiences, such as the death of a parent or the birthday of a parent or of the patient, can set off positive and negative symptoms. Hallucinations and mania can also follow traumatic events such as childbirth or combat experiences during war.

The paranoid form of schizophrenia is the only one that usually develops later in life, usually between the ages of thirty and thirty-five. It is a chronic form, meaning that patients suffering from it usually become worse. Paranoid schizophrenia is characterized by a feeling of suspiciousness of everyone and everything, hallucinations, and delusions of persecution or grandiosity. This form becomes so bad that many victims, perhaps one out of three, eventually commit suicide simply to escape their tormentors. Others turn on their alleged tormentors and kill them, or at least someone who seems to be responsible for their terrible condition.

Other chronic forms of the disease include hebephrenic schizophrenia. In this case, patients suffer disorders of thinking and frequent episodes of incoherent uttering of incomprehensible sounds or words. The victims move quickly from periods of great excitement to equally exhausting periods of desperate depression. They frequently have absurd, bizarre delusions such as sex changes, identification with and as godlike creatures, or experiences of being born again and again. Those suffering from "simple" schizophrenia exhibit constant feelings of dissatisfaction with everything in their lives or a complete feeling of indifference to anything that happens. They are usually isolated and estranged from their families or any other human beings. Patients with these symptoms tend to live as recluses with barely any interest in society, in work, or even in eating or in talking to anyone else.

The various types of schizophrenia start at different times in different people. Generally, however, except for the paranoid form, the disease develops during late adolescence. Men show signs of schizophrenia earlier than women, usually by age eighteen or nineteen. It is unusual for signs of the disorder to appear in males after age twenty. In women, symptoms may not appear until the early twenties and sometimes are not evident until age thirty. Sometimes, there are signs in childhood. People who later develop schizophrenia tended to be withdrawn and isolated as children and were often made fun of by others. Not all withdrawn children develop the disease, however, and there is no way to predict who will get it and who will not.

Schizophrenia is a genetic disease. Individuals with the disease are very likely to have relatives—mothers, fathers, brothers, sisters, cousins, grandmothers, or grandfathers—with the disorder. Surveys indicate that 1 percent of all people have the disease. A person with one parent who has the disease is ten times more likely to develop schizophrenia than a member of the general public. Thirty-nine percent of people who have both parents afflicted with the disease also develop schizophrenia.

Other factors are involved in the disease in addition to heredity. E. Fuller Torrey, a leading researcher into the causes of schizophrenia, discovered important information about the origins of the disease in studies that he made of the brains of identical twins. Magnetic resonance imaging (MRI) of their brains showed that individuals diagnosed with the illness had slightly smaller brains than those without the disease. The difference in size was most apparent in the temporal lobe, the area that controls emotions and memory. Apparently, something goes wrong in the development of the temporal lobe of the fetus during the fourth to sixth month of pregnancy. Torrey speculated that this abnormality might result from a viral infection. The antibodies that normally protect the brain seem to get mixed up and attack the brain itself. Why or how this happens is not known. One possibility is that a nutritional deficiency in the mother might cause the temporal lobes to grow in an abnormal manner.

As to why the disease develops later in life rather than at birth, investigators provide the following information. First, the brain develops more slowly than other organs and does not stop developing until late adolescence. Many genetic diseases remain dormant until later in life, such as Huntington's chorea and multiple sclerosis.

Schizophrenia operates by disrupting the way in which brain cells communicate with each other. The neurotransmitters that carry signals from one brain cell to another might be abnormal. Malfunction in one of the transmitters, dopamine, seems to be a source of the problem. This seems likely because the major medicines that are successful in the treatment of schizophrenia limit the production or carrying power of dopamine. Another likely suspect is serotonin, a transmitter whose presence or absence has important influences on behavior.

Treatment and Therapy
Since the 1950's, many medications have been developed that are very effective in treating the symptoms of schizophrenia. Psychotherapy can also be effective and beneficial to many patients. Drugs can be used to treat both positive and negative symptoms. Some such as Haldol, Mellaril, Prolixin, Navane, Stelazine, and Thorazine are used to treat positive symptoms. Clozapine and Risperidone can be used for both positive and negative symptoms. These medications work by blocking the production of excess dopamine, which may cause the positive symptoms, or by stimulating the production of the neurotransmitter, which reduces negative symptoms. Clozapine blocks both dopamine and serotonin, which apparently makes it more effective than any of the other drugs.

The chief problem resulting from the use of such drugs are the terrible side effects that they can produce. The most dreaded side effect, from the point of view of the patient, is tardive dyskinesia (TD). This problem emerges only after many years of use. TD is characterized by involuntary movement of muscles, frequent lip-smacking, facial grimaces, and constant rocking back and forth of the arms and the body. It is completely uncontrollable.

Dystonias are another side effect. Symptoms include the abrupt stiffening of muscles, such as the sudden contraction of muscles in the arms, neck, and face. Most of these effects can be controlled or reversed with antihistamines. Some patients receiving medication are afflicted with effects similar to those movements associated with Parkinson's disease. They suffer from the slowing of movements in their arms and legs, tremors, and muscle spasms. Their faces seem frozen into a sad, masklike expression. These effects can be treated with medication. Another problem is akathisia, a feeling developed by many patients that they cannot sit still. Their jumpiness can be treated with Valium or Xanax. Some of these side effects are so severe or embarrassing that patients cite them as the major reason that they do not take their medicine.

Many patients report great value in family or rehabilitation therapy. These therapies are not intended to cure the disease or to "fix" the family. Instead, they are aimed at helping families learn how to live with mentally ill family members. Family support is important for victims of schizophrenia because they usually are unable to live on their own. Therapy can also help family members understand and deal with their frustration and the constant pain that results from knowing that a family member is very ill and probably will not improve much. Rehabilitation therapy is an attempt to teach patients the social skills that they need to survive in society.

The results of treatment are not always positive, even with medication and therapy. Ten percent of people with schizophrenia commit suicide rather than trying to continue living with the terrible consequences of the disease.

Perspective and Prospects

Hopes for improving the treatment of schizophrenia rest mainly on the continuing development of new drugs. Several studies suggest that psychotherapy directed at improving social skills and reducing stress help many people with the disease improve the quality of their lives. It is known that stress-related emotions lead to increases in delusions, hallucinations, social withdrawal, and apathy. Therapists can help patients find ways of dealing with stress and living in communities. They encourage their patients to deal with feelings of hostility, rage, and distrust of other people. Family therapy can teach all members of a family how to live with a mentally ill family member. Such therapy, along with medication, can produce marvelous results.

One study of ninety-seven victims of schizophrenia who lived with their families, received individual therapy, and took their medications showed far fewer recurrences of acute symptoms than did a group that did not get such help. Among those fifty-four individuals who received therapy who lived alone or with nonfamily members, schizophrenia symptoms reappeared or worsened over the same three-year period of the study. People living alone usually had more severe symptoms to start out with and found it difficult to find housing, food, or clothing, even with therapy. The demands of life and therapy apparently were too much for them. The major problem with this kind of treatment, which seems to work for people in families, is that it is expensive.

Bibliography

Buckley, Peter F., and John L. Waddington, eds. *Schizophrenia and Mood Disorders: The New Drug Therapies in Clinical Practice*. Woburn, Mass.: Butterworth-Heinemann, 2000. A volume on psychopharmacology. Includes bibliographical references and an index.

Chadwick, Peter K. *Schizophrenia: The Positive Perspective*. New York: Routledge, 1997. Presents case studies of schizophrenics. Raises the question of whether schizophrenia should be viewed as a disease to be eradicated or it endows valuable qualities that should be nurtured.

Gorman, Jack M. *The New Psychiatry: The Essential Guide to State-of-the-Art Therapy, Medication, and Emotional Health*. New York: St. Martin's Press, 1996. A well-written, easy-to-understand book by a doctor and researcher that provides the latest information concerning the development of new medications, treatments, and therapies. Valuable information on the new antipsychotic drugs, how they work, and what their possible side effects are.

Gottesman, Irving I. *Schizophrenia Genesis: The Origins of Madness*. New York: W. H. Freeman, 1991. The author, a leading researcher into the genetic causes of schizophrenia, describes recent discoveries on the origins of the disease. He also evaluates different treatments and the many kinds of counseling and therapeutic techniques.

Johnstone, Eve C., et al. *Schizophrenia: Concepts and Clinical Management*. New York: Cambridge University Press, 1999. Covers clinical aspects, including differential and dual diagnosis, and treatment and management problems. Topics include brain imaging, genetics, pharmacology, neuropsychology, health economics, and forensic issues.

Lenzenweger, Mark F., and Robert H. Dworkin, eds. *Origins and Development of Schizophrenia: Advances in Experimental Psychopathology*. Washington, D.C.: American Psychological Association, 1998. Presents a range of empirically based models and viewpoints on the pathogenesis of schizophrenia.

Marsh, Diane T. *Families and Mental Illness: New Directions on Professional Practice*. New York: Praeger, 1992. A good book on the role of families in the care and treatment of the mentally ill. Written for professionals but very useful for anyone who must learn to deal with schizophrenia.

Torrey, E. Fuller. *Surviving Schizophrenia: A Manual for Families, Consumers, and Providers*. 3d ed. New York: Harper & Row, 1995. Perhaps the best single book on the topic, by a leading medical researcher and advocate of more humane care for the mentally ill. Describes the latest research into the origins of the illness and provides useful information and evaluations of the newest drugs and best forms of treatment.

Woolis, Rebecca. *When Someone You Love Has a Mental Illness: A Handbook for Family, Friends, and Caregivers.* New York: Jeremy P. Tarcher/Perigree Books, 1992. A brief, practical guide that gives useful tips on handling the anger, hostility, and bizarre behavior exhibited by people with the disease. Also describes how to help patients to live at home and what to do if suicide is threatened. A very valuable sourcebook.

Leslie V. Tischauser

See also:

Anxiety Disorders; Depression; Hypochondriasis, Conversion, Somatization, and Somatoform Pain; Manic-Depressive Disorder; Paranoia; Psychosis; Schizophrenia: High-Risk Children; Suicide.

SCHIZOPHRENIA
High-Risk Children

Type of psychology: Psychopathology
Fields of study: Organic disorders; schizophrenias

In order to prevent an illness, it is necessary to have information about specific indicators of risk. Researchers have been conducting studies of children whose parents suffer from schizophrenia in order to identify the indicators of risk for this psychiatric illness; preliminary findings indicate that it may someday be possible to prevent the onset of schizophrenia.

Principal terms

ETIOLOGY: the study of the causes of disease
GENETICS: the biochemical basis of inherited characteristics
LONGITUDINAL: dealing with the growth or change in individuals over a period of time
PREMORBID: the period before the onset of a disease
SCHIZOPHRENIA: a serious mental illness that is characterized by psychotic symptoms, such as delusions, hallucinations, and thought disorders

Overview

The term "high-risk" has been applied to biological offspring of schizophrenic parents, because they are known to be at genetic risk for the same disorder shown by their parents. Numerous researchers are studying high-risk children in order to shed light on the origins of schizophrenia. This approach has many advantages over other research methods and has already yielded some important findings.

The importance of research on children at risk for schizophrenia stems from a need to understand the precursors of the illness. Over the years, researchers have studied schizophrenia from many different perspectives and with a variety of methods. Despite many decades of work, however, investigators have not yet been successful in identifying the causes or developing a cure. Some progress has been made in clarifying the nature and course of schizophrenia, and there have been considerable advances in the pharmacological treatment of symptoms; however, the precursors and the origins still remain a mystery.

Because the onset of schizophrenia usually occurs in late adolescence or early adulthood, patients typically do not come to the attention of investigators until they have been experiencing symptoms for some period of time. At that point, researchers have to rely on the patient and other informants for information about the nature of the individual's adjustment prior to the onset of the illness. These retrospective accounts of the patient's functioning are often sketchy and can be biased in various ways. Yet it is well accepted that progress toward the ultimate goal—the prevention of schizophrenia—will not be achieved until researchers are able to identify individuals who are vulnerable to the disorder.

POSSIBLE SIGNS OF SCHIZOPHRENIA IN CHILDREN

❖ trouble discerning dreams from reality
❖ seeing things and hearing voices that are not real
❖ confused thinking
❖ vivid and bizarre thoughts and ideas
❖ extreme moodiness
❖ peculiar behavior
❖ concept that people are "out to get them"
❖ behaving younger than chronological age
❖ severe anxiety and fearfulness
❖ confusing television or movies with reality
❖ severe problems in making and keeping friends

In response to this concern, several investigators, most notably Sarnoff Mednick and Tom McNeil, emphasized the importance of studying the development of individuals known to be at heightened statistical risk for schizophrenia. Specifically, it was proposed that repeated assessments should be conducted so that data on all aspects of the development of at-risk children would be available by the time they enter the adult risk period for schizophrenia. In this way, it might be possible to identify precursors of the illness in subjects who had not yet received any treatment for the disorder. Another major advantage of studying subjects prior to the provision of treatment is that only then is it possible to differentiate true precursors of the illness from the consequences or side effects of treatment for the illness.

By the late 1950's, it was well established that schizophrenia tends to run in families. The general population rate for the disorder is about one in a hundred. In contrast, it has been estimated that children who have one biological parent with schizophrenia have a 10 to 15 percent chance of developing the disorder. When both biological parents are diagnosed with schizophrenia, the risk rate is thought to be around 40 percent. It is apparent, therefore, that offspring of schizophrenic parents are indeed at heightened risk for developing the same disorder. Thus, Mednick encouraged researchers to conduct longitudinal studies of these "high-risk" children.

The first large-scale prospective longitudinal study of high-risk children was initiated in Denmark in the mid-1960's by Mednick and Fini Schulsinger. They followed a group of one hundred children who had at least one schizophrenic parent and two hundred comparison children whose parents had no psychiatric disorder. Since the Danish study was initiated, a number of other research groups have initiated similar high-risk research programs. These projects are now under way in several United States cities (including New York City; Rochester, New York; Minneapolis, Minnesota; and Atlanta, Georgia) as well as in other countries.

Applications

One of the major challenges in conducting high-risk research is locating the sample. Schizophrenia is a relatively rare disorder in that it occurs in about 1 percent of the general population. Moreover, because most schizophrenic patients experience an onset of illness in late adolescence or early adulthood, they are less likely to marry or have children. This is especially true of schizophrenic patients who are men. Consequently, the majority of the subjects of high-risk research are offspring of schizophrenic mothers. Further, of the schizophrenic women who do have children, a substantial portion do not keep their children but instead place them for adoption. This further complicates the task of identifying samples of high-risk children. In order to be assured of identifying a sample of adequate size, researchers in this field establish formal arrangements with local treatment facilities in order to increase their chances of identifying all the high-risk children in their geographic area.

Another important issue confronted by high-risk researchers is the question of when in the child's life span the study should be initiated. Most investigators are interested in identifying the very earliest signs of vulnerability for schizophrenia. Therefore, it is desirable to initiate a high-risk study with subjects who are infants. In this way, investigators will be able to examine the entire premorbid life course of patients. If there are any markers of vulnerability apparent in infancy, they will be able to identify them. The investigator who initiates a study of infant subjects, however, must wait an extended period of time in order to gather any information about their adult psychiatric outcomes. In order to reduce the period between the initiation of the study and the entry of the subjects into the major risk period for schizophrenia, most investigators have initiated high-risk projects on subjects who are in middle or late childhood.

The problem of attrition (loss of subjects) is another one of concern to high-risk researchers. As mentioned, the long-term goal is to compare those high-risk children who succumb to schizophrenia to those who do not. Consequently, the most crucial information will be provided only when the researchers are knowledgeable about the adult psychiatric outcome of the subjects. Because a sample of a hundred high-risk children may eventually yield only ten to fifteen schizophrenic patients, it is of critical importance to investigators that they maintain contact with all subjects so that they can determine their adult psychiatric outcomes.

Finally, the question of how to select an appropriate comparison group is a salient one to high-risk researchers. Again, one of the ultimate goals is to identify specific signs of vulnerability to schizophrenia. An important question is whether the signs identified by researchers are simply manifestations of vulnerability to any adult psychiatric disorder or signs of specific vulnerability to schizophrenia. In order to address this question, many researchers include groups of children whose parents have psychiatric disorders other than schizophrenia.

Reports on the developmental characteristics of high-risk children have been published by eleven high-risk research groups. These studies have revealed some important differences between children of schizophrenic parents and children whose parents have no mental illness. The differences that have been found tend to fall into three general areas: motor functions, cognitive functions, and social adjustment. When compared to children of normal parents, high-risk subjects have been found to show a variety of impairments in motor development and motor abilities. Infant offspring of schizophrenic parents tend to show delays in the development of motor skills, such as crawling and walking. Similarly, studies of high-risk subjects in their middle childhood and early adolescent years reveal deficits in fine and gross motor skills and coordination. It is important to emphasize, however, that these deficiencies are not of such a severe magnitude that the child would be viewed as clinically impaired in motor skills. Yet the deficiencies are apparent when high-risk children, as a group, are compared to children of normal parents.

The occurrence of motor development delays and abnormalities in high-risk children is consistent with the etiologic assumptions made by most researchers in the field. Specifically, such abnormalities would be expected in a disorder that is presumed to be attributable to a central nervous system impairment that is, at least in part, genetically determined.

Numerous studies have found that children at high risk for schizophrenia also show impairments in cognitive functions. Although their scores on standardized tests of intelligence are within the normal range, they tend to be slightly below that of children of normal parents. With regard to specific abilities, investigators have found that high-risk children show deficiencies in their capacity to maintain and focus attention. These deficiencies are apparent as early as the preschool years and involve the processing of both auditory and visual information. Because attentional deficits have been found so consistently in high-risk children, some researchers in the field have suggested that these deficits may be a key marker of risk for schizophrenia.

When compared to children of parents without psychiatric disorder, offspring of schizophrenic parents tend to manifest a higher rate of behavioral problems. These include a higher rate of aggressive behaviors, as well as an increased frequency of social withdrawal. In general, children of schizophrenic parents are perceived as less socially competent than comparison children. It is important to take into consideration, however, that children of parents with other psychiatric disorders are also found to show problems with social adjustment. Consequently, it is unlikely that behavioral adjustment problems are uniquely characteristic of risk for schizophrenia.

Only a subgroup—in fact, a minority—of high-risk children will eventually manifest schizophrenia. The most significant question, therefore, is not what differentiates high-risk children from a comparison group, but rather what differentiates high-risk children who develop schizophrenia from high-risk children who do not. Only a few high-risk research projects have followed their subjects all the way into adulthood. Only limited data are thus available regarding the childhood characteristics that predict adult psychiatric outcome. The findings from these studies confirm the predictions made by the researchers. Specifically, the high-risk children who eventually develop schizophrenia show more evidence of motor abnormalities and attentional dysfunction in childhood than those who do not.

Perspective and Prospects

As is the case with all approaches to research, the high-risk method has some limitations. One limitation concerns whether the findings from these studies can be generalized to a wider population. Although it is true that schizophrenia tends to run in families, it is also true that the majority of schizophrenic patients do *not* have a schizophrenic parent. As a result, the subjects of high-risk research may represent a unique subgroup of schizophrenic patients. The fact that they have a parent with the illness may mean that they have a higher genetic loading for the disorder than do schizophrenic patients whose parents have no mental illness. Moreover, there are undoubtedly some environmental stresses associated with being reared by a schizophrenic parent. In sum, high-risk children who become schizophrenic patients may differ from other schizophrenic patients both in terms of genetic factors and in terms of environment. Some other problems with the method, mentioned above, include subject attrition and the extensive waiting period required before adult psychiatric outcome is determined.

Some investigators have attempted to address the issue of identifying markers of vulnerability with alternative methodologies. For example, it has been shown that children with behavioral problems are more likely to develop schizophrenia in adulthood than are children who manifest no significant behavioral difficulties. Thus, some researchers are conducting longitudinal studies of maladjusted children in order to identify precursors of schizophrenia. Taking a novel approach, one study has utilized childhood home movies of adult-onset schizophrenic patients as a database for identifying infant and early childhood precursors. Up to this point, the findings from these studies are consistent with those from high-risk research.

Based on the research findings, there is good reason to believe that individuals who succumb to schizophrenia in adulthood manifested signs of vulnerability long before the onset of the disorder, perhaps as early as infancy. These findings have some important implications. First, they provide some clues to etiology; they suggest that the neuropathological process underlying schizophrenia is one that begins long before the onset of the clinical symptoms that define the illness. Thus, the search for the biological bases of this illness must encompass the entire premorbid life course. Second, the findings suggest that it may eventually be possible to identify individuals who are at risk for schizophrenia so that preventive interventions can be provided. As time goes on, more of the high-risk children who have been the subjects of these investigations will pass through the adult risk period for schizophrenia. One can therefore anticipate that important new findings from high-risk research will be forthcoming.

Bibliography

Cantor, Sheila. *Childhood Schizophrenia*. New York: Guilford Press, 1998. Presents case histories of fifty-four schizophrenic children. Family histories reveal the increased prevalence in these families of other neuropsychiatric disorders.

Gottesman, Irving I. *Schizophrenia Genesis: The Origins of Madness*. New York. W. H. Freeman, 1991. Provides a comprehensive overview of the genetic determinants of schizophrenia, written by the foremost authority in the field. Very readable; explains the theory and methods of behavioral genetics research and presents a detailed description of the findings.

Lenzenweger, Mark F., and Robert H. Dworkin, eds. *Origins and Development of Schizophrenia: Advances in Experimental Psychopathology*. Washington, D.C.: American Psychological Association, 1998. Presents a range of empirically based models and viewpoints on the pathogenesis of schizophrenia.

Mednick, Sarnoff A., and Thomas F. McNeil. "Current Methodology in Research on the Etiology of Schizophrenia: Serious Difficulties Which Suggest the Use of the High-Risk Group Method." *Psychological Bulletin* 70, no. 6 (1968): 681-693. This classic paper served to introduce the idea of the high-risk method to researchers in the field of psychopathology. It clearly lays out the rationale behind the approach.

Walker, Elaine F., ed. *Schizophrenia: A Life-Course Developmental Perspective.* San Diego: Academic Press, 1991. This book provides an overview of knowledge in the life course of schizophrenia. Chapters are written by experts in the field.

Walker, Elaine F., and Richard J. Lewine. "Prediction of Adult-Onset Schizophrenia from Childhood Home Movies of the Patient." *American Journal of Psychiatry* 147, no. 8 (1990): 1052-1056. Preliminary results from a novel study of the precursors of schizophrenia are presented in this paper. This approach complements the high-risk method in that it holds promise for validating the findings of high-risk research.

Watt, Norman F., et al., eds. *Children at Risk for Schizophrenia.* New York: Cambridge University Press, 1984. This edited volume summarizes the major high-risk projects underway throughout the world at the time it was written. It demonstrates the importance of this work in furthering understanding of the origins of schizophrenia.

Elaine F. Walker

See also:

Abnormality: Biomedical Models; Abnormality: Family Models; Abnormality: Psychodynamic Models; Madness: Historical Concepts; Psychoactive Drug Therapy; Schizophrenia.

SEASONAL AFFECTIVE DISORDER

Type of psychology: Psychopathology
Fields of study: Depression

Seasonal affective disorder is a variant of depression which has received significant research attention since the early 1980's. It may be related to premenstrual syndrome, carbohydrate-craving obesity, and bulimia. Seasonal affective disorder responds to a form of treatment known as phototherapy.

Principal terms

DOUBLE-BLIND STUDY: an experimental design in which neither the experimenter nor the subjects know which subjects are receiving the active treatment
HYPERSOMNIA: sleeping more than ten hours per day
LIBIDO: a person's sex drive
LUX: the amount of light emitted by one candle one meter away; 2,500 lux equals the light from 2,500 candles one meter away
PLACEBO: a treatment that is therapeutically inert

Causes and Symptoms

Seasonal affective disorder (SAD) became the focus of systematic scientific research in the early 1980's. Research originally focused on seasonal changes in mood that coincided with the onset of winter and became known as winter depression. Symptoms consistently identified by Norman Rosenthal and others as indicative of winter depression included hypersomnia, overeating, carbohydrate craving, and weight gain. Michael Garvey and others found the same primary symptoms and the following secondary ones: decreased libido, irritability, fatigue, anxiety, problems concentrating, and premenstrual sadness. Several researchers have found that winter depression is more of a problem at higher latitudes. Thomas Wehr and Norman Rosenthal report on a description of winter depression by Frederick Cook during an expedition to Antarctica in 1898. While winter depression is the form of seasonal affective disorder receiving the most initial attention, there is another variation that changes with the seasons.

Summer depression affects some people in the same way that winter depression affects others. Both are examples of seasonal affective disorder. According to Wehr and Rosenthal, symptoms of summer depression included agitation, loss of appetite, insomnia, and loss of weight. Many people with summer depressions also have histories of chronic anxiety. As can be seen, the person with a summer depression experiences symptoms which are almost the opposite of the primary symptoms of winter depression.

In order to diagnose a seasonal affective disorder, there must be evidence that the symptoms vary according to a seasonal pattern. If seasonality is not present, the diagnosis of SAD cannot be made. The seasonal pattern for winter depression is for it to begin in November and continue unabated through March. Summer depression usually begins in May and continues through September. Siegfried Kasper and others reported that people suffering from winter depression outnumber those suffering from summer depression by 4.5 to 1. Wehr and Rosenthal reported that as people come out of their seasonal depression they experience feelings of euphoria, increased energy, less depression, hypomania, and possibly mania.

Philip Boyce and Gordon Parker investigated seasonal affective disorder in Australia. Their interest was in determining whether seasonal affective disorder occurs in the Southern Hemisphere and, if so, whether it manifests the same symptoms and temporal relationships with seasons as noted in the Northern Hemisphere. Their results confirmed the existence of seasonal affective disorder with an onset coinciding with winter and remission coinciding with summer. Their study also provided evidence that seasonal affective disorder occurs independently of important holidays and celebrations, such as Christmas. There is also a subsyndromal form of seasonal affective disorder. This is usually seen in winter depression and represents a milder form of the disorder. It interferes with the person's life, although to a lesser degree than the full syndrome, and it is responsive to the primary treatment of seasonal affective disorder.

Three hypotheses are being tested to explain seasonal affective disorder. The first is the melatonin hypothesis; the second is the circadian rhythm phase shift hypothesis; and the third is the circadian rhythm amplitude hypothesis.

The melatonin hypothesis is based upon animal studies and focuses on a chemical signal for darkness. Studies show that during darkness, the hormone melatonin is produced in greater quantities; during periods of light, it is produced in lesser quantities. Increases in melatonin level occur at the onset of seasonal affective disorder (winter depression) and are thought to be causally related to the development of the depression.

A second hypothesis is the circadian rhythm phase shift hypothesis. This hypothesis contends that the delay in the arrival of dawn disrupts the person's circadian rhythm by postponing it for a few hours. This disruption of the circadian rhythm is thought to be integral in the development of winter depression. Disruptions in the circadian rhythm are also related to secretion of melatonin.

The third hypothesis receiving much interest is the circadian rhythm amplitude hypothesis. A major tenet of this hypothesis is that the amplitude of the circadian rhythm is directly related to winter depression. Lower amplitudes are associated with depression, and higher ones with normal mood

POSSIBLE SYMPTOMS OF SEASONAL AFFECTIVE DISORDER

❖ regularly occurring symptoms of depression (excessive eating and sleeping, weight gain) during the fall or winter months
❖ full remission from depression occur in the spring and summer months.
❖ symptoms have occurred in the past two years, with no nonseasonal depression episodes
❖ seasonal episodes substantially outnumber nonseasonal depression episodes
❖ a craving for sugary and/or starchy foods

states. The presence or absence of light has been an important determinant in the amplitude of circadian rhythms.

While each of these hypotheses has data to support it, the melatonin hypothesis is falling out of favor. Rosenthal and others administered to volunteers in a double-blind study a drug known to suppress melatonin secretion and a placebo. Despite melatonin suppression, there was no difference in the degree of depression experienced by the two groups (drug and placebo). Both the circadian rhythm phase shift hypothesis and the circadian rhythm amplitude hypothesis continue to have significant research interest and support.

Seasonal affective disorder was officially recognized in 1987 in the American Psychiatric Association's *Diagnostic and Statistical Manual of Mental Disorders*, (rev. 3d ed., DSM-III-R). It was included in the manual as a variant of major depression. In order to diagnose the seasonal variant, the depressed person had to experience the beginning and ending of the depression during sixty-day windows of time at the beginning and ending of the season and had to meet the criteria for the diagnosis of major depression. Additionally, that person had to have experienced more than three episodes of seasonal affective disorder, and two episodes had to have occurred consecutively. Finally, the ratio of 3 to 1 seasonal to nonseasonal episodes had to exist in the absence of any seasonally related psychosocial stressors (such as Christmas). Including the diagnosis in the DSM-III-R not only validated individuals who reported feeling better or worse at different times of year but also encouraged researchers to study the causes, variations, and treatments of this form of depression.

Philip Boyce and Gordon Parker, two Australian scientists, studied seasonal affective disorder in the Southern Hemisphere. Since the Southern Hemisphere has weather patterns reversed from those in the Northern Hemisphere, and since holidays occurring during the winter in the Northern Hemisphere occur during the summer in the Southern Hemisphere, these researchers were able to reproduce Northern Hemisphere studies systematically while eliminating the possible influence of holidays, such as Christmas. Their findings support those of their colleagues in the Northern Hemisphere. There is a dependable pattern of depression beginning during autumn and early winter and ending in the late spring and early summer.

It is important to study the prevalence of seasonal affective disorder in order to understand how many people are affected by it. Siegfried Kasper and others investigated the prevalence of seasonal affective disorder in Montgomery County, Maryland, a suburb of Washington, D.C. The results of their study suggested that between 4.3 percent and 10 percent of the general population is affected to some extent by seasonal affective disorder. Mary Blehar and Norman Rosenthal report data from research in New York City that between 4 percent and 6 percent of a clinical sample met the criteria for seasonal affective disorder. More significantly, between 31 percent and 50 percent of people responding to a survey reported changes to their life which were similar to those reported by seasonal affective disorder patients. There are strong indications that the overall prevalence rate for seasonal affective disorder is between 5 percent and 10 percent of the general population. As much as 50 percent of the population may experience symptoms similar to but less intense than seasonal affective disorder patients.

Prevalence studies have found that the female-male ratio for seasonal affective disorder is approximately 4 to 1. The age of onset is about twenty-two. The primary symptoms of seasonal affective disorder overlap with other diagnoses which have a relatively high female-to-male ratio. For example, people diagnosed with winter depression frequently crave carbohydrate-loaded foods. In addition to carbohydrate-craving obesity, there is another serious disorder, bulimia nervosa, which involves binging on high-carbohydrate foods and has a depressive component. Bulimia nervosa is much more common in females than it is in males.

While most of the research has focused on seasonal affective disorder in adults, it has also been found in children. Children affected with seasonal affective disorder seem to experience a significant decrease in their energy level as their primary symptom rather than the symptoms seen in adults. This is not unusual; in many disorders, children and adults experience different symptoms.

The winter variant of seasonal affective disorder is much more common than the summer variant. It appears that winter depression is precipitated by the reduction in light that accompanies the onset of winter. As a result, it is also quite responsive to phototherapy. Summer depression, the summer variant of seasonal affective disorder, is precipitated by increases in humidity and temperature associated with the summer months. This suggests a different (and currently unknown) mechanism of action for the two variations of seasonal affective disorder.

Treatment and Therapy

The importance of light in the development and treatment of the winter variant of seasonal affective disorder has been demonstrated in a variety of studies world-wide. The general finding is that people living in the higher latitudes are increasingly susceptible to seasonal affective disorder in the winter.

While the mechanism of seasonal affective disorder is still unknown, an important rediscovery has been the use of light to treat it. Phototherapy has been found to be a very important and effective nonpharmacological treatment of the winter form of seasonal affective disorder. Studies have repeatedly shown that bright light, at least 2,500 lux, is more effective than dim light (300 lux). While most studies have compared 2,500-lux light to 300-lux light or other treatments, some researchers have investigated the effect of 10,000-lux light on seasonal affective disorder. Phototherapy treatments using 2,500-lux sources require between two and four hours per day of exposure to reap antidepressant benefits. When 10,000-lux sources of light are employed, the exposure time decreases to approximately thirty minutes a day. Certainly, most people suffering from seasonal affective disorder would prefer to take thirty minutes for their phototherapy treatments than the two to four hours required for 2,500-lux treatments.

Thomas Wehr and others investigated the differences in treatment efficacy when light was applied to the eyes rather than to the skin. They found that the antidepressant benefits were greater when the light was applied to the eyes. This suggests that the eye plays an important role in the effectiveness of phototherapy.

A study by Frederick Jacobsen and others investigated the timing of the phototherapy. This is important because if extending the duration of daylight were necessary for phototherapy to serve as an antidepressant, then the phototherapy must occur in the morning. Also, if phototherapy serves to change the timing of circadian rhythm, it must occur in the morning. The results of this study suggest that the antidepressant effect of phototherapy does not depend upon the timing of the treatment: Both morning and midday treatments were effective in lifting the depression of seasonal affective disorder.

One of the major advantages of phototherapy is that it is a nonpharmacologic approach to treating depression. The fact that no medications are involved allows the patient to avoid the unpleasant and potentially dangerous side effects of medications. Unfortunately, however, phototherapy also has a potentially dangerous side effect. Many researchers are concerned about the possible effect of ultraviolet light on the health of the patient.

Perspective and Prospects

The observation that seasons affect people's moods is not new. Hippocrates, writing in 400 B.C.E., noted in section 3 of his "Aphorisms" that, "Of natures (*temperaments?*), some are well- or ill-adapted for summer, and some for winter." What Hippocrates noticed (and many others since him have noticed) is that there are differences in the way people experience the various seasons. Summer and winter are the most extreme seasons in terms of both light and temperature and, not surprisingly, are the seasons in which most people have problems coping.

As noted above, a physician, Frederick Cook, on an expedition to Antarctica in 1898, noted that the crew experienced symptoms of depression as the days grew shorter. This same report (mentioned by Wehr and Rosenthal) revealed that "bright artificial lights relieve this to some extent." Emil Kraepelin reported in 1921 that approximately 5 percent of his patients with manic-depressive illness also had a seasonal pattern to their depressions. The data from antiquity to the present strongly favor the existence of a form of mood disturbance associated with seasonal variation. Just as the observation of seasonal variations in mood and behavior dates back to antiquity, so does the use of light as a treatment. Wehr and Rosenthal report that light was used as a treatment nearly two thousand years ago. Not only was light used but also it was specified that the light was to be directed to the eyes.

Seasonal affective disorder is a variant of major depressive disorder in the DSM-III-R. It seems to have some degree of relationship to carbohydrate-craving obesity, bulimia nervosa, bipolar disorder (formerly known as manic-depressive illness), and premenstrual syndrome. It affects women more often than men and is more frequently seen covarying with winter than with summer. The winter variant is probably caused by changes in light; it is more severe in the higher latitudes. The summer variant seems to be attributable to intolerance of heat and humidity and would be more prevalent in the lower latitudes. Most of the research both in the United States and internationally has focused on the winter variant and its relationship with light and latitude; there is much less research into the summer variant.

Bibliography

Boyce, Philip, and Gordon Parker. "Seasonal Affective Disorder in the Southern Hemisphere." *American Journal of Psychiatry* 145, no. 1 (1988): 96-99. This study surveyed an Australian sample to determine the extent to which the people experienced symptoms of seasonal affective disorder and to see if the pattern was similar to that of people in the Northern Hemisphere. The results are presented as percentages and are easily understood. Addresses the issue of separating holidays from climatic changes and presents a table of symptoms for seasonal affective disorder.

Garvey, Michael J., Robert Wesner, and Michael Godes. "Comparison of Seasonal and Nonseasonal Affective Disorders." *American Journal of Psychiatry* 145, no. 1 (1988): 100-102. These authors present similarities and differences between affective disorders that covary with seasons and those that do not. Despite the inclusion of statistical analyses, the article is understandable to those without a background in statistics.

Kasper, Siegfried, Thomas A. Wehr, John J. Bartko, Paul A. Gaist, and Norman E. Rosenthal. "Epidemiological Findings of Seasonal Changes in Mood and Behavior." *Archives of General Psychiatry* 46, no. 9 (1989): 823-833. A thorough description of the major prevalence study on seasonal affective disorder. The statistics are fairly advanced, but the authors' use of figures and tables makes the results understandable. An extensive reference list is provided.

Lam, Raymond W., ed. *Seasonal Affective Disorder and Beyond: Light Treatment for SAD and Non-SAD Conditions.* Washington, D.C.: American Psychiatric Press, 1998. Leading clinicians discuss the impact of light and light therapy on conditions such as SAD, premenstrual depression, circadian phase sleep disorders, jet lag, shift-work disorders, insomnia, and behavioral disturbances.

Lam, Raymond W., and Anthony J. Levitt, eds. *Canadian Consensus Guidelines for the Treatment of Seasonal Affective Disorder.* Vancouver, British Columbia: Clinical and Academic Publishing, 1999. A summary of the report of the Canadian Consensus Group on SAD. This is the first comprehensive clinical guide for the diagnosis and treatment of seasonal affective disorder, which affects between 2 percent and 3 percent of the Canadian population.

Rosenthal, Norman E. *Winter Blues: Seasonal Affective Disorder—What It Is and How to Overcome It.* New York: Guilford Press, 1998. A revised and updated edition of *Seasons of the Mind* (1989). An exceptionally clear and well-written presentation of seasonal affective disorder by one of the pioneering investigators in the field. Discusses the risks and benefits of various treatments, including psychotherapy, antidepressant medication, and light therapy. Numerous anecdotes are used to illustrate major points. An excellent book for nonprofessional readers.

Rosenthal, Norman E., and Mary C. Blehar. *Seasonal Affective Disorders and Phototherapy.* New York: Guilford Press, 1997. The authors discuss issues related to the diagnosis and prevalence of the syndrome. In addition, they present mechanisms of action for phototherapy as a treatment and the use of animal models to study seasonal affective disorder. A good summary that avoids being overly technical.

James T. Trent

See also:

Abnormality: Biomedical Models; Depression; Manic-Depressive Disorder.

Sexual Dysfunction

Type of psychology: Psychopathology
Fields of study: Sexual disorders

Sexual dysfunction can occur in the desire, excitement, or orgasm phase of sexual responding: Desire disorders include hypoactive (inhibited) desire, sexual aversion, and excessive desire; problems related to excitement are female sexual arousal disorder and male erectile disorder; problems with orgasm include premature ejaculation and inhibited orgasm; dyspareunia and vaginismus are pain disorders.

Principal terms

DYSPAREUNIA: painful intercourse
ERECTILE DYSFUNCTION: recurrent and persistent inability to attain or maintain a firm erection of the penis despite adequate stimulation
FEMALE SEXUAL AROUSAL DISORDER: failure to obtain or maintain vaginal lubrication despite adequate stimulation
HYPOACTIVE SEXUAL DESIRE: lack of interest in sexual expression with anyone
PREMATURE EJACULATION: unintentional ejaculation before or shortly following insertion of the penis in the vagina
SENSATE FOCUS: a therapeutic exercise involving concentration on sensations produced by touching
SEXUAL AVERSION DISORDER: a dysfunction characterized by extreme fear and avoidance of genital contact with a partner
VAGINISMUS: involuntary spasms of the muscles of the other third of the vagina

Causes and Symptoms

In order to understand sexual dysfunction, it is necessary to examine the process of sexual response. William Masters and Virginia Johnson found that the basic sexual response cycle is the same in both men and women, including the excitement, plateau, orgasmic, and resolution phases. Excitement begins when the individual becomes aroused. Increased levels of sexual tension lead to the plateau phase and to orgasm. During resolution, there is a decrease in sexual tension and a return to an unstimulated state. In both genders, there are two basic physiological responses to sexual stimulation: myotonia (muscle tension) and vasocongestion (filling of blood vessels with blood).

Based on the physiological research of Masters and Johnson, Helen Kaplan proposed a framework that puts more emphasis on the subjective experience of sexual response, dividing it into the phases of desire, excitement, and orgasm. The categories of sexual dysfunction were described in the American Psychiatric Association's *Diagnostic and Statistical Manual of Mental Disorders* (rev. 3d ed., 1987, DSM-III-R) using these frameworks.

Problems with sexual desire include hypoactive sexual desire, sexual aversion,

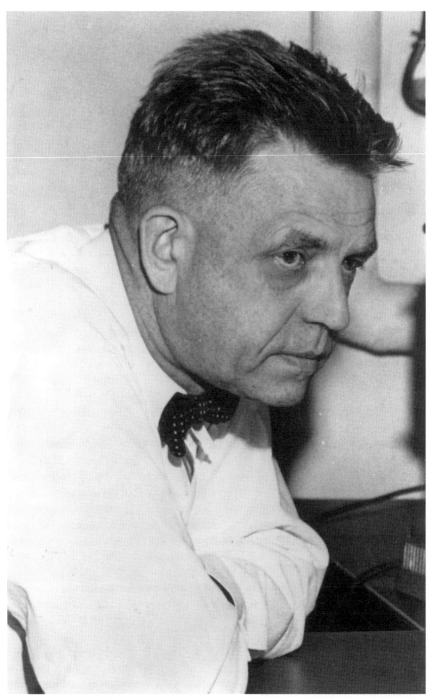

In the 1930's Alfred Kinsey and colleagues began interviewing thousands of volunteers about their sexual behavior. (Library of Congress)

and excessive sexual desire. In cases of hypoactive sexual desire disorder, found in both genders, interest in sex and sexual fantasy are deficient or absent. The problem typically lasts for a given time period, rather than over a lifetime, and sometimes people experience it situationally—such as with a partner but not during mastur-bation. The second type of desire disorder, sexual aversion, occurs when there is a strong fear of sexual relations and a desire to avoid genital contact with a partner. An individual with sexual aversion may still engage in fantasy and masturbation. The sources of sexual desire disorders are not clear, but people who experience sexual aversion sometimes have been the victims of incest or rape. Also, low sexual desire has been associated with depression, fear of loss of control, fear of preg-nancy, marital conflict, and lack of attraction to one's partner. Excessive sexual desire involves a preoccupation with sexuality and the use of sexual activity to reduce tension resulting from pervasive thoughts about sex.

A second category of dysfunction involves the excitement phase. Some people feel sexual desire but are unable to participate in intercourse because of a lack of physiological arousal. It is often situational and in women is characterized by a lack of vaginal lubrication, which can result from biological factors such as low estrogen levels or from psychological factors, including apathy or fear. Equivalent to vaginal lubrication in women is the engorgement and erection of the penis in men. Commonly used terms to describe sexual arousal disorders are "frigidity" in women and "impotence" in men, although researchers now consider them to be derogatory. Instead, the preferred term for women is "female sexual arousal disorder," and the preferred term for men is "erectile dysfunction."

Lifelong erectile dysfunction is characterized by the inability to maintain pene-tration with a partner at any point throughout life, although the person may experience nighttime erections and erections during masturbation. In comparison, nonlifelong erectile inhibition is applied to the man who previously had erections with a partner but is presently unable to experience them. Masters and Johnson think that the label of nonlifelong erectile dysfunction is appropriate when a man is unable to experience an erection in at least one-quarter of his sexual encounters. Erectile problems are frequently caused by a combination of biological and psychological factors. Low levels of testosterone, the use of certain drugs, and disorders that restrict penile blood flow are biological causes. Fatigue, worry, and relationship difficulties are typical psychological problems. Erectile dysfunction is the most common complaint of men who seek sex therapy.

Difficulties of orgasmic response occur in both genders. Women with inhibited orgasm may look forward to sex, experience excitement and lubrication, and enjoy sexual contacts, but they do not reach orgasm. There is an involuntary inhibition of the orgasmic reflex. Difficulty with orgasm is one of the most common sexual complaints among women. Inhibited orgasm is rarely the result of physiological causes. Relatively nonorgasmic women tend to have more negative attitudes toward masturbation, greater guilt feelings about sex, and problems communicat-ing with a partner about the need for stimulation of the clitoris. In comparison, inhibited male orgasm refers to the inability of a man to have an orgasm by ejaculating during intercourse. It is seldom encountered by therapists; it may result from sex guilt, fear of impregnating someone, or dislike for a partner. Another orgasm-related problem for males is premature ejaculation. The preferred definition of premature ejaculation is consistently reaching orgasm so quickly that it greatly reduces a man's own enjoyment of the experience, impairs a partner's satisfaction, or both.

Finally, although men and women both can experience pain involving intercourse, pain is more commonly found in women. Dyspareunia is the technical term. Pain is commonly a result of lack of lubrication because of insufficient arousal or hormone levels. Vaginal infections can also lead to pain; contraceptive substances can also irritate the vagina. Pain at the opening may result from an intact hymen, whereas pain deep in the pelvis during thrusting may be caused by jarring of the ovaries. Another source of deep pain is endometriosis, a condition in which uterine tissue implants on various places in the abdominal cavity. An uncommon type of pain in women is vaginismus, characterized by strong, involuntary contractions of the outer third of the vagina.

Treatment and Therapy

There are several commonly used techniques for treating sexual dysfunction. As necessary, some address the issue of marital conflict and attempt to resolve it. Other techniques focus on individual psychological difficulties in one partner or the other. Sometimes it is necessary to help a couple develop communication skills. Other times, sexual difficulties are rooted in a lack of knowledge, so information and instruction are provided.

One popular technique is systematic desensitization. It involves learning muscle relaxation exercises. A set of scenes that produce anxiety are constructed by the therapist together with the client. The scenes are arranged from least to most anxiety-producing. The goal is to replace the response of anxiety with the response of relaxation. Therapy begins with the client imagining the least anxiety-producing scenes. If anxiety occurs, the client is told to give up the image of the scene and to use the relaxation exercises. The exercise is repeated until the client no longer feels anxiety associated with that scene. Then the next scene is imagined by the client, and so on. The process generally takes from five to fifteen sessions.

Another technique is that of nondemand pleasuring together with sensate focus. To use the exercises of nondemand pleasuring and sensate focus, the couple would be asked to refrain from sexual contacts of any kind until instructed to do so by the therapist. During treatment, the couple would get take-home assignments that gradually increase sexual contact from the point of hugging and kissing to being able eventually to have sexual intercourse. The partners would be assigned to alternate in the roles of giver and receiver. Playing the role of giver would be to explore and touch the receiver's body. The giver would not attempt to arouse the receiver in a sexual manner. To use the sensate focus exercise, the receiver would concentrate on the feelings that come about as a result of the touch of the giver. The receiver would be instructed to prevent or end any kind of stimulation that was uncomfortable or unpleasant by informing the partner to that effect. The next step involves a progression to breast and genital touching while continuing to avoid stimulation that is orgasm-oriented. After the couple attains a satisfactory level of arousal by means of nondemand pleasuring and sensate focus, they engage in nondemand sexual intercourse.

The most effective type of therapy for women who have inhibited orgasm is that of masturbation training. Research indicates that masturbation is the technique that is most likely to produce orgasm in women. If there are negative attitudes toward masturbation, the therapist must first work on those feelings. During the systematic course of masturbation training, the woman is instructed to explore her genitals by touch while in the privacy of her home. Once she becomes comfortable with the exploration, she tries to find the most pleasurable, sensitive area. At another time, she increases the intensity and duration of her self-stimulation and includes fantasy. If the woman has still not had an orgasm, she is often instructed to use a vibrator. Once the woman begins having orgasms, her partner is integrated into her sexual experience.

A common approach for premature ejaculation that was developed by Masters and Johnson is the squeeze technique. During stimulation, when the man signals that he is about to ejaculate, the partner applies a strong pressure directly below the head of the penis, or at the base of the penis, with her hand. The pressure is applied for three to five seconds and ends with a sudden release of the hand. After the sensation of ejaculation goes away, in about twenty to thirty seconds, she begins to stimulate her partner once again. The process is done three or four times per session. Then ejaculation is allowed. Initially, the process is conducted outside the vagina. With increasing practice and greater control, the couple proceeds to have intercourse, but they employ the squeeze technique with the hand as often as needed.

Whatever the source of a person's inability to respond sexually as he or she wishes, the problem can worsen if a fear of failure develops. The fear can lead to self-fulfilling behavior. One element of therapy is the need to identify and eliminate the fear of failure and sexual inadequacy, along with reducing maladaptive thoughts that have a tendency to occur during sexual intimacy. Other useful suggestions for people with problems are to refrain from setting goals of sexual performance and to avoid behaving as a spectator, or monitor, during sex. While involved in monitoring one's own performance, it is difficult to enjoy sexual experiences. It is also useful to understand that failures will occur in any sexual relationship. What is important is the way that an individual or a couple deals with the failures, rather than letting occasional failures ruin a relationship.

Perspective and Prospects

Scientific explanations became the dominant interpretations of human behavior as religious explanations of behavior declined prior to 1990. By the beginning of the twentieth century, scientists were still unable to accept the scientific study of sexual behavior, however; there were many myths concerning sexuality, and the prevalent attitude was that all sexual acts that did not have reproduction as their goal were deviant. For example, the act of masturbation was seen, even by some scientists, as the cause for a variety of human ailments, including insanity, poor eyesight, and digestive problems.

Most of the early knowledge of sexual behavior was based on observations of animals or people in non-Western cultures. The person who was central in the emergence of the modern study of sexuality was Havelock Ellis. He published a number of influential volumes on sexual issues in the early 1900's. Also influential in the study of sexuality was Sigmund Freud, who devised a broad theory of behavior that emphasized sex as the central part of human development. In the mid-1930's, Alfred Kinsey and his colleagues began interviewing thousands of volunteers about their sexual behavior. The findings provided beneficial information and paved the way for other researchers, including Masters and Johnson. Instead of interviewing people about their sexuality, Masters and Johnson directly observed volunteers in the laboratory through one-way glass as the volunteers masturbated and had intercourse. They were the first scientists to study sexual behavior through systematic observation in the laboratory, resulting in a model of the human sexual-response cycle. Before the work of Masters and Johnson, it was believed that men and women were different in their sexual responses. Instead, it was found that men and women have very similar responses.

Once therapists became aware of the sexual functioning of the body, they were able to treat sexual dysfunction by new behavioral means, rather than relying on time-consuming, expensive psychotherapy. Psychotherapy involves a restructuring of the entire personality and is based on the Freudian theory that sexual difficulties are symptoms of emotional conflict originating in childhood. Instead, the therapeutic approaches that grew out of the scientific knowledge about the sexual response cycle were more direct, more effective, and less time-consuming. In conclusion, the scientific study of sex provided information that has helped reduce the amount of ignorance about sexuality. Ignorance is a common underlying cause of sexual dysfunction in general.

Bibliography

Allgeier, Elizabeth Rice, and Albert Richard Allgeier. *Sexual Interactions.* 5th ed. Boston: Houghton Mifflin, 2000. Offers a highly readable description of sexual problems. An excellent and thorough textbook used in colleges and universities across the United States.

American Psychiatric Association. *Diagnostic and Statistical Manual of Mental Disorders, Fourth Edition (DSM-IV).* 4th ed. Washington, D.C.: Author, 1994. In the United States this is the authoritative scheme for classifying psychological disorders. It groups hundreds of psychological disorders and conditions into major categories of mental disorder, including diagnoses for almost every complaint a person could imagine.

Belliveau, Fred, and Lin Richter. *Understanding Human Sexual Inadequacy.* New York: Bantam Books, 1980. A paperback for the layperson that has been officially endorsed by Masters and Johnson. It summarizes the key work of Masters and Johnson on sexual dysfunction and is written in nontechnical language, supplying information that is based on established facts.

Heiman, Julia R., Joseph LoPiccolo, and Leslie LoPiccolo. *Becoming Orgasmic: A Sexual and Personal Growth Program for Women* Rev. ed. New York: Prentice-Hall, 1988. The book gives step-by-step suggestions to try to help women increase their ability to respond sexually in a variety of positive, growth-promoting ways. The suggestions are practical, creative, and interesting. Although the book is specifically written for women, men will also find it useful. The authors are well-respected sex researchers.

Hellstrom, Wayne J., ed. *Male Infertility and Sexual Dysfunction*. New York: Springer, 1997. Discusses the latest advances in research of male infertility, with recent innovations and treatments. Covers all aspects of male infertility and sexual dysfunction, as well as medical, noninvasive, and surgical techniques.

Masters, William H., and Virginia E. Johnson. *Human Sexual Inadequacy*. Boston, Mass.: Little, Brown, 1970. A classic book that is technical and directed toward the professional audience. It is an extremely important book, because Masters and Johnson were the first researchers to use the direct-observation methods that provided a foundation for treating sexual problems.

Newman, Alfred J., M.D. *Beyond Viagra: Plain Talk About Treating Male and Female Sexual Dysfunction*. Montgomery, Ala.: Starrhill Press, 1999. Newman, a urologist, addresses the causes of sexual dysfunction in men and women, how it has historically been treated, how Viagra can help the problem for men, when using this drug is not appropriate, and how Viagra affects women.

Szasz, Thomas Stephen. *Sex by Prescription*. Syracuse, N.Y.: Syracuse University Press, 1990. A short book that criticizes a variety of assumptions that guide the practices of some sex therapists. Also examined are the relationships among cultural beliefs about sexuality during several historical periods. Reactions of the medical community to sexual problems and problems in interpersonal relationships are discussed.

Deborah R. McDonald

See also:

Abnormality: Psychodynamic Models; Couples Therapy; Sexual Variants and Paraphilias.

Sexual Variants and Paraphilias

Type of psychology: Psychopathology
Fields of study: Sexual disorders

Sexual variations, or paraphilias, are unusual sexual activities, in that they deviate from what is considered normal at a particular time in a particular society; paraphilias include behaviors such as exhibitionism, voyeurism, and sadomasochism. It is when they become the prime means of gratification, displacing direct sexual contact with a consenting adult partner, that paraphilias are technically present.

Principal terms

EXHIBITIONISM: a behavior in which a person, who is usually a male, exposes the genitals to an involuntary observer

FETISHISM: a sexual behavior in which a person becomes aroused by focusing on an inanimate object or a part of the human body

FROTTEURISM: pressing or rubbing against a stranger in a public place for sexual gratification

SEXUAL MASOCHISM: the experiencing of sexual arousal by suffering physical or psychological pain

SEXUAL SADISM: the intentional infliction of pain on another person for sexual excitement

TRANSVESTISM: a behavior in which a person obtains sexual excitement from wearing clothing of the opposite gender

VOYEURISM: the derivation of sexual pleasure from looking at the naked bodies or sexual activities of others without their consent

ZOOPHILIA: sexual contact between humans and animals

Causes and Symptoms

Paraphilias are sexual behaviors that are considered a problem for the person who performs them and/or a problem for society because they differ from the society's norms. Psychologist John Money, who has studied sexual attitudes and behaviors extensively, claims to have identified about forty such behaviors.

Exhibitionism is commonly called "indecent exposure." The term refers to behavior in which an individual, usually a male, exposes the genitals to an involuntary observer, who is usually a female. The key point is that exhibitionistic behavior involves observers who are unwilling. After exposing, the exhibitionist often masturbates while fantasizing about the observer's reaction. Exhibitionists tend to be most aroused by shock and typically flee if the observer responds by laughing or attempts to approach the exhibitionist. Most people who exhibit themselves are males in their twenties or thirties. They tend to be shy, unassertive people who feel inadequate and afraid of being rejected by another person. People who make obscene telephone calls have similar characteristics to the people who engage in exhibitionism. Typically, they are sexually aroused when their victims react in a shocked manner. Many masturbate during or immediately after placing an obscene call.

Voyeurism is the derivation of sexual pleasure through the repetitive seeking of situations in which to look, or "peep," at unsuspecting people who are naked, undressing, or engaged in sexual intercourse. Most masturbate during the voyeuristic activity or immediately afterward in response to what they have seen. Further sexual contact with the unsuspecting stranger is rarely sought. Like exhibitionists, voyeurs are usually not physically dangerous. To a degree, voyeurism is socially acceptable, but it becomes atypical when the voyeuristic behavior is preferred to sexual relations with another person or when there is a high degree of risk. Most voyeurs are not attracted to nude beaches or other places where it is acceptable to look because they are most aroused when the risk of being discovered is high. Voyeurs tend to be men in their twenties with strong feelings of inadequacy.

Sadomasochistic behavior encompasses both sadism and masochism; it is often abbreviated "SM." The dynamics of the two behaviors are similar. It is thought that sadists are less common than masochists. Sadomasochistic behaviors have the potential to be physically dangerous, but most people involved in these behaviors participate in mild or symbolic acts with a partner they can trust. Most people who engage in SM activities are motivated by a desire for dominance or submission rather than pain. Interestingly, many nonhuman animals participate in pain-inflicting behavior before coitus. Some researchers think that the activity heightens the biological components of sexual arousal, such as blood pressure and muscle tension. It has been suggested that any resistance between partners enhances sex, and SM is a more extreme version of this behavior. It is also thought that SM offers people the temporary opportunity to take on roles that are the opposite of the controlled, restrictive roles they play in everyday life. The term "sadism" is derived from the Marquis de Sade, a French writer and army officer who was horribly cruel to people for his own erotic purposes. In masochism, sexual excitement is produced in a person by his or her own suffering. Preferred means of achieving gratification include verbal humiliation and being bound or whipped.

Fetishism is a type of sexual behavior in which a person becomes sexually aroused by focusing on an inanimate object or part of the human body. Many people are aroused by looking at undergarments, legs, or breasts, and it is often difficult to distinguish between normal activities and fetishistic ones. It is when a person becomes focused on the objects or body parts ("fetishes") to the exclusion of everything else that the term is most applicable. Fetishists are usually males. Common fetish objects include women's lingerie, high-heeled shoes, boots, stockings, leather, silk, and rubber goods. Common body parts involved in fetishism are hair, buttocks, breasts, and feet.

The term "pedophilia" is from the Greek language and means "love of children." It is characterized by a preference for sexual activity with children and is engaged in primarily by men. The activity varies in intensity and ranges from stroking the child's hair to holding the child while secretly masturbating, manipulating the child's genitals, encouraging the child to manipulate his or her own genitals, or, sometimes, engaging in sexual intercourse. Generally, the pedophile, or sexual abuser of children, is related to, or an acquaintance of, the child, rather than a stranger. Studies of imprisoned pedophiles have found that the men typically had poor relationships with their parents, drink heavily, show poor sexual adjustment, and were themselves sexually abused as children. Pedophiles tend to be older than people convicted of other sex offenses. The average age at first conviction is thirty-five.

Transvestism refers to dressing in clothing of the opposite sex to obtain sexual excitement. In the majority of cases, it is men who are attracted to transvestism. Several studies show that cross-dressing occurs primarily among married heterosexuals. The man usually achieves sexual satisfaction simply by putting on the clothing, but sometimes masturbation and intercourse are engaged in while the clothing is being worn.

Zoophilia involves sexual contact between humans and animals as the repeatedly preferred method of achieving sexual excitement. In this disorder, the animal is preferred despite other available sexual outlets. Necrophilia is a rare dysfunction in which a person obtains sexual gratification by looking at or having intercourse with a corpse. Frotteurism is a fairly common behavior involving a person, usually a male, who obtains sexual pleasure by pressing or rubbing against a fully clothed female in a crowded public place. Often it involves the clothed penis rubbing against the woman's buttocks or legs and appears accidental.

Treatment and Therapy

A problem in the definition and diagnosis of sexual variations is that it is difficult to draw the line between normal and abnormal behavior. Patterns of sexual behavior differ widely across history and within different cultures and communities. It is impossible to lay down the rules of normality; however, attempts are made in order to understand behavior that differs from the majority and in order to help people who find their own atypical behavior to be problematic, or to be problematic in the eyes of the law.

Unlike most therapeutic techniques in use by psychologists, many of the treatments for paraphilias are painful, and the degree of their effectiveness is questionable. Supposedly, the methods are not aimed at punishing the individual, but perhaps society's lack of tolerance toward sexual deviations can be seen in the nature of the available treatments. In general, all attempts to treat the paraphilias have been hindered by the lack of information available about them and their causes.

Traditional counseling and psychotherapy alone have not been very effective in the treatment of modifying the behavior of paraphiliacs, and it is unclear why the clients are resistant to treatment. Some researchers believe that the behavior might be important for the mental stability of paraphiliacs. If they did not have the paraphilia, they would experience mental deterioration. Another idea is that, although people are punished by society for being sexually deviant, they are also rewarded for it. For the paraphilias that put the person at risk for arrest, the danger of arrest often becomes as arousing and rewarding as the sexual activity itself. Difficulties in treating paraphiliacs may also be related to the emotionally impoverished environments that many of them experienced throughout childhood and adolescence. Convicted sex offenders report more physical and sexual abuse as children than do the people convicted of nonsexual crimes. It is difficult to undo the years of learning involved.

Surgical castration for therapeutic purposes involves removal of the testicles. Surgical castration for sexual offenders in North America is very uncommon, but the procedure is sometimes used in northern European countries. The reason castration is used as a treatment for sex offenders is the inaccurate belief that testosterone is necessary for sexual behavior. The hormone testosterone is produced by the testicles. Unfortunately, reducing the amount of testosterone in the blood system does not always change sexual behavior. Furthermore, contrary to the myth that a sex offender has an abnormally high sex drive, many sex offenders have a low sex drive or are sexually dysfunctional.

In the same vein as surgical castration, other treatments use the administration of chemicals to decrease desire in sex offenders without the removal of genitalia. Estrogens have been fairly effective in reducing the sex drive, but they sometimes make the male appear feminine by increasing breast size and stimulating other female characteristics. There are also drugs that block the action of testosterone and other androgens but do not feminize the body; these drugs are called antiandrogens. Used together with counseling, antiandrogens do benefit some sex offenders, especially those who are highly motivated to overcome the problem. More research on the effects of chemicals on sexual behavior is needed; the extent of the possible side effects, for example, needs further study.

Aversion therapy is another technique that has been used to eliminate inappropriate sexual arousal. In aversion therapy, the behavior that is to be decreased or eliminated is paired with an aversive, or unpleasant, experience. Most approaches use pictures of the object or situation that is problematic. Then the pictures are paired with something extremely unpleasant, such as an electric shock or a putrid smell, thereby reducing arousal to the problematic object or situation in the future. Aversion therapy has been found to be fairly effective but is under ethical questioning because of its drastic nature. For example, chemical aversion therapy involves the administration of a nausea- or vomit-inducing drug. Electrical aversion therapy involves the use of electric shock. An example of the use of electric shock would be to show a pedophile pictures of young children whom he finds sexually arousing and to give an electric shock immediately after showing the pictures, in an attempt to reverse the pedophile's tendency to be sexually aroused by children.

Other techniques have been developed to help clients learn more socially approved patterns of sexual interaction skills. In general, there has not been a rigorous testing of any of the techniques mentioned. Furthermore, most therapy is conducted while the offenders are imprisoned, providing a less than ideal setting.

Perspective and Prospects

Beliefs regularly change with respect to what sexual activities are considered normal, so most therapists prefer to avoid terms such as "perversion," instead using "paraphilia." Basically, "paraphilia" means "love of the unusual." Aspects of paraphilias are commonly found within the scope of normal behavior; it is when they become the prime means of gratification, replacing direct sexual contact with a consenting adult partner, that paraphilias are technically said to exist. People who show atypical sexual patterns might also have emotional problems, but it is thought that most people who participate in paraphilias also participate in normal sexual behavior with adult partners, without complete reliance on paraphilic behaviors to produce sexual excitement. Many people who are arrested for paraphilic behaviors do not resort to the paraphilia because they lack a socially acceptable sex partner. Instead, they have an unusual opportunity, a desire to experiment, or perhaps an underlying psychological problem.

According to the approach of Kurt Freund and his colleagues, some paraphilias are better understood as disturbances in the sequence of courtship behaviors. Freund has described courtship as a sequence of four steps: location and appraisal of a potential partner; interaction that does not involve touch; interaction that does involve touch; and genital contact. Most people engage in behavior that is appropriate for each of these steps, but some do not. The ones who do not can be seen as having exaggerations or distortions in one or more of the steps. For example, Freund says that voyeurism is a disorder in the first step of courtship. The voyeur does not use an acceptable means to locate a potential partner. An exhibitionist and an obscene phone caller would have a problem with the second step: They have interaction with people that occurs before the stage of touch, but the talking and showing of exhibitionistic behaviors are not the normal courtship procedures. Frotteurism would be a disruption at the third step, because there is physical touching that is inappropriate. Finally, rape would be a deviation from the appropriate fourth step.

As a result of social and legal restrictions, reliable data on the frequency of paraphilic behaviors are limited. Most information about paraphilias comes from people who have been arrested or are in therapy. Because the majority of people who participate in paraphilias do not fall into these two categories, it is not possible to talk about the majority of paraphiliacs in the real world. It is known, however, that males are much more likely to engage in paraphilias than are females.

Bibliography

Allgeier, Elizabeth Rice, and Albert Richard Allgeier. *Sexual Interactions*. 5th ed. Boston: Houghton Mifflin, 2000. Contains a highly readable description of sexual variations. Photographs, charts, and tables help make the material understandable. Provides a multitude of references. An excellent, thorough textbook.

Evans, David T. *Sexual Citizenship: The Material Construction of Sexualities*. New York: Routledge, 1993. A text on sexual ethics and capitalism. Includes bibliographical references and an index.

Gebhard, P. H., W. B. Pomeroy, B. Wardell, J. H. Gagnon, and C. V. Christenson.

Sex Offenders: An Analysis of Types. New York: Harper & Row, 1965. Also available in paperback from Bantam Books, 1967, this book provides a detailed analysis of many types of atypical sexual behaviors that are against the law, with excellent information about the psychological and social factors that are involved in the development of these behaviors. The authors are well-respected researchers on other aspects of sexuality in addition to paraphilias.

Goldberg, Arnold. *The Problem of Perversion: The View from Self-Psychology.* New Haven, Conn.: Yale University Press, 1995. Explains and interprets perverse behavior by drawing on concepts of psychoanalytic self-psychology. Seeks to make disorders of perversion more understandable and more accessible to treatment.

Laws, D. Richard, and William O'Donohue, eds. *Sexual Deviance: Theory, Assessment, and Treatment.* New York: Guilford Press, 1997. A valuable resource on paraphilias. A comprehensive volume containing information that is both practical and accessible to clinicians and researchers. Includes bibliographical references and an index.

Rosen, Ismond. *Sexual Deviation.* 3d ed. New York: Oxford University Press, 1996. A clinical reference for psychiatrists. Covers biological, genetic, developmental, unconscious, social, psychological, and legal aspects of abnormal sexual behavior. This edition offers chapters on child sexual abuse and gender identity.

Stoller, Robert J. "Sexual Deviations." In *Human Sexuality in Four Perspectives*, edited by Frank A. Beach and Milton Diamond. Baltimore: The Johns Hopkins University Press, 1977. Provides a review of several common atypical sexual behaviors, along with several case studies. Concise and readable. Part of an interesting, well-rounded book on sexuality in general.

Weinberg, Thomas S., and G. W. Levi Kamel, eds. *S and M: Studies in Sadomasochism.* Buffalo, N.Y.: Prometheus Books, 1983. Composed of eighteen articles that provide thought-provoking information on a variety of issues relating to sadism and masochism.

Deborah R. McDonald

See also:
Abnormality; Child Abuse; Cognitive Behavior Therapy.

Sibling Rivalry

Type of psychology: Developmental psychology
Fields of study: Adolescence; attitudes and behavior; infancy and childhood; interpersonal relations

A common form of competition between brothers, sisters, or a brother and sister that is considered normal if it is outgrown and/or does not become destructive to individuals or the family.

Principal terms

DEVELOPMENTAL MILESTONES: the specific achievements accomplished in the normal development of a child (such as motor, cognitive, self-help, social, and communication skills); a child's developmental level affects the expression of sibling rivalry

EXTENDED FAMILY: a type of family that goes beyond the traditional model of parents and children to include other generations or more distant relatives

FAMILY CONSTELLATION VARIABLES: the collection of characteristics that describe the makeup of an individual family, including number of family members, ages, birth order of siblings, gender, and inclusion of any extended family members

INTERPERSONAL SKILLS: the social and communication skills that begin developing in childhood; sibling relationships significantly influence the development of these skills

SIBLING: a general term for brothers and sisters who share the same set of parents; siblings that share only one parent are called half sisters or half brothers

STEPSIBLINGS: siblings who have no relation through biology or adoption except that a parent of one is married to the parent of the other; varied family forms complicate further the traditional rivalry between siblings

Causes and Symptoms

Sibling rivalry is the competition or jealousy that develops between siblings for the love, affection, and attention of either one or both parents. The concept of sibling rivalry has been discussed for centuries, and it is considered a universal phenomenon in families. Although sibling rivalry is generally described in terms of its negative aspects, healthy competition between brothers and sisters can be useful in the individual development of necessary social, communication, and cognitive skills.

While the dynamics of the ways in which brothers and sisters relate to one another cannot be reduced to specifics of age, birth order, gender, and family size, these family constellation variables are important in the development of sibling rivalry. While each element will be discussed separately, it is important to take into account all the relevant factors when looking at causes of sibling rivalry.

The ages of siblings and their birth order are significant factors that have been related to sibling competition. There are many stereotypes associated with being the oldest, youngest, and middle child in the family. For example, typical firstborn children tend to be highly organized and responsible, while youngest children are likely to benefit from more experienced, relaxed parenting and may be more affectionate and spontaneous. Middle children are often more difficult to characterize. They may be at more risk than other children for receiving less attention, and they tend to develop stronger relationships outside the family. Using these stereotypical characteristics as guides for assessing a particular child, it is possible to speculate on the relevance of birth order and age in the development of sibling competition.

The effects of spacing between children has also given rise to a number of theories. It is generally accepted that the closer siblings are in age, the more similar their life experiences are likely to be. As they may have more in common, siblings close in age are also more likely to struggle with each other more frequently. For this reason, siblings who are close in age may engage in more competition with each other than siblings who are separated by more than a few years.

The gender of siblings is also a variable in the development of sibling relationships, including sibling competition. Siblings help each other discover some of the basic characteristics of male and female roles. Growing up with all brothers or all sisters can teach a child much about dealing with one gender. Having a sibling of the opposite sex can offer a child valuable initial information about the opposite sex. The attitudes of parents regarding gender roles also influence the relationships between siblings. Parents who display favoritism toward children based on gender may contribute to sibling jealousy and competition.

For a wide variety of reasons, specific children may be more emotionally vulnerable to feelings of jealousy than their siblings at a given time. For example, in a family with a child who has a disability, other siblings may feel that they do not receive as much attention or the child with special needs may feel different and unwanted.

Emotionally vulnerable children are frequently found in families experiencing high levels of stress. There is evidence that the emotional climate within the family is directly linked to the quality of sibling relationships. It then follows that sibling rivalry may be more problematic in families where there are stressors such as marital conflict, chronically ill family members, or unwanted extended family involvement.

The competition that emerges between siblings can be for material resources such as toys or space within the household. For example, it is not uncommon for an older child to resent having to share a room with a younger brother or sister. Frequently, the competition for material resources stems from a child's uncertainty regarding his or her status in the family. Children may interpret the need to share space as an indication of their lesser importance to parents.

Jealousy can develop when a child perceives favoritism on the part of a parent. This jealousy results from a lack of equality in treatment. Not only is the less-favored child at risk for feeling jealous, but the parental favorite often does not perceive the extra attention as pleasant or comfortable. The challenge in parenting is trying to achieve equality when children are each exceptional beings with their own individual needs. In her book, *Dr. Mom's Parenting Guide* (1991), Marianne Neifert recommends loving children "uniquely," giving each child the message that his or her place in the family is a special one. A parent who consistently favors one child over another through the amount of love and attention shown is encouraging unhealthy rivalry between the children.

Sibling rivalry can manifest itself in a variety of ways. When a new sibling is born, an older child may be either openly or passively hostile to the new baby. This hostility can be displayed in the form of direct verbal or physical attacks on the baby. Sometimes children request that parents return the infant to the hospital or give it away. In other cases, a child may act up or demand attention when the parent is busy with the infant. Serious abuse by siblings is rare, but even mild incidents need attention by parents.

Some children react to a new sibling by displaying regressive behavior such as bed-wetting, asking to be carried, thumb-sucking, excessive crying, or talking baby talk. Other negative behaviors associated with sibling jealousy are lying, aggressiveness, or destructive behaviors. It is also typical for the child to vent frustration or anger on other individuals, pets, or toys when feeling jealous of a sibling. In older children, sibling rivalry may be exhibited by taking the younger child's toys or demanding more parental attention. Another example of rivalry in older children includes a drive to outperform the other sibling in academic or athletic settings.

Unless managed effectively by parents, feelings of jealousy and competition among siblings can undermine a child's development and may continue into adult relationships. Sibling rivalry can be minimized by the active involvement of parents in setting appropriate rules for dealing with conflicts.

Treatment and Therapy

The negative impact of sibling rivalry can be minimized through parental education and attention to the conditions that intensify sibling competition. Attending to the development of a relationship between siblings is an ongoing process which parents can enhance through their involvement in helping children develop good interpersonal skills.

The foundation for dealing effectively with sibling rivalry is an awareness and understanding that sibling competition is a normal, healthy part of family life. Rivalry develops between siblings in nearly every family, and it only becomes problematic when taken to extremes or when ignored and allowed to escalate.

The common behavior problems associated with sibling rivalry occur in the context of many interacting factors: parental expectations; the child's developmental level; the temperament of a particular child; parental discipline; family constellation characteristics such as age, gender, and spacing of children; and the presence of extended family members. There is growing evidence regarding the importance of obtaining assessments and information from family members (including extended family) and other sources such as school or day care personnel when identifying a problem of sibling rivalry.

One of the situations in which parents express the most open concern regarding sibling rivalry is when a new baby is expected or an adoption of a child is imminent.

When a new sibling is expected, the other children can be invited to be actively involved in the preparation. Age-appropriate discussions with each child about pregnancy or adoption are good preventive measures. Parents should be available to answer questions regarding the changes to be expected with the arrival of the additional child. An open, direct discussion with older children can minimize the adjustment difficulties and address initial concerns. Children need regular verbal and demonstrated assurances that they will continue to be loved following the arrival of a new sibling.

Parents can involve an older child in the care of a baby as a means of acknowledging the unique contributions of that child. Expecting an older child to be a regular caretaker, however, may create additional problems and place unnecessary stress on the older brother or sister.

While some older children exhibit negative behaviors associated with the arrival of a baby, others respond positively by becoming more mature and autonomous. Focusing on the individual contributions of an older sibling can minimize the feelings of jealousy when a new child enters the family.

Parents should avoid making either overt or subtle comparisons between siblings and instead focus on the special qualities and achievements of each child. As Neifert suggests, "honor the individual in every child." This is sometimes difficult to accomplish, as many times parents anticipate that subsequent children will be similar to their firstborn. For example, if a first child is successful in sports, a parent may anticipate that the younger sibling will also be athletically inclined. Such unrealistic expectations can foster unhealthy competition and put needless pressure on a younger sibling.

Jealousy between brothers and sisters seldom ends with the adjustment of a new family member and the acknowledgement that an "only" child now has to share parental attention. Balancing the emotional needs of two or more children of differing ages continues to be an important concern of parents as children move through different developmental stages.

The negative behaviors associated with sibling rivalry can stem from other sources as well. Sometimes siblings fight because they are bored or have few appropriate alternatives to taunting a sibling. Sometimes the behavior can be a reaction to stressors outside of the home, such as problems at school or socialization difficulties. A parent's reaction to negative behavior will have a large impact on whether the behavior continues. Parents who can model effective interpersonal skills themselves are likely to influence the development of these same skills in their children.

When jealous behaviors are displayed by siblings, parents need to be sensitive to the source of the feelings. The cause of the competition or rivalry should be the focus of parental interventions, rather than the negative behavior itself. Children should be encouraged to talk about their feelings openly, and parents need to be willing to acknowledge and validate those feelings for each child. After allowing children to express their feelings and showing appreciation for the difficulty of the problem, parents can encourage siblings to work toward a mutual resolution.

One of the common manifestations of sibling rivalry is the expression of anger and, sometimes, the physical or verbal abuse that accompanies the anger. While common, violent displays of anger are not appropriate. Helping children learn to handle anger responsibly is an important task for parents.

In handling fighting between children, parents must assess the level of conflict and intervene appropriately when necessary. Normal bickering between siblings that does not include verbal abuse or threats of physical abuse rarely requires parental involvement. If the situation worsens, however, the following steps can be useful for parents: Acknowledge the angry feelings of each child, then reflect each child's point of view; describe the problem from the position of a respectful bystander, without taking sides on the issue; and express confidence that the children can come up with a reasonable solution.

Parents need to be actively involved in promoting a system of justice within the family which includes age-appropriate rules and consequences for behavior. Examples of ways that parents can manage the behavior are separating siblings when a situation appears dangerous and redirecting children's activities when aggression is likely to occur. Parents can also take responsibility for encouraging and rewarding cooperative play and providing children with appropriate, nonaggressive models for resolving conflict.

Teaching children conflict resolution strategies is an important way for parents to intervene in sibling rivalry problems. Developing the ability to express one's feelings is a valuable step toward conflict resolution. Children should be encouraged to put their feelings into words in appropriate ways. Young children may need help in doing so through the use of statements such as, "You don't like it when I spend so much time caring for your baby sister, do you?" Granting a child permission to fantasize about a given situation may also help in diffusing angry feelings. Encouraging children to verbalize what they wish would happen allows them to address emotions in an honest way. Children should be taught from an early age to develop creative ways to vent their anger. Children can be taught to use physical exercise, write feelings in a journal, or go to their rooms to cool down as appropriate ways to manage anger.

Managing sibling conflict is complex in any family, but even more so in situations where there is a single parent or a blending of families through divorce and remarriage. Because sibling competition stems from a child's anxiety about sharing parental attention, the presence of a single parent can intensify the feelings of insecurity about one's position in the family. Single parents need to be careful not to turn a child into a spouse substitute, instead viewing each child as a unique individual who deserves to be able to mature at his or her own pace. Extended family members, including grandparents, aunts, and uncles, may be useful in helping a single parent meet the individual needs of each child in the family.

When parents remarry, children are required to make adjustments in their relationships and to include new people into their family. Children need to be allowed to express their ambivalent feelings regarding stepsiblings and half siblings, as these feelings are a normal part of this adjustment process. Parents need to accept and tolerate each child's feelings, as long as guidelines of justice and safety are recognized.

Despite the abundant research available on the topic of sibling rivalry, there is still much that is unknown regarding the complex relationships between brothers and sisters. While it is possible to look at generalizations regarding the issues important in sibling rivalry, it is not possible to predict adjustment or maladjustment in a particular child. Information must be gathered from a number of sources and evaluated for each child when planning a course of action to address concerns about sibling rivalry.

Perspective and Prospects

Through the ages, people have assumed that jealousy and rivalry were unavoidable characteristics of sibling relationships. Sibling rivalry has been a common theme in several classic stories. In the Bible, the competition between brothers Cain and Abel and the jealousy which developed between Joseph and his brothers over issues of parental favoritism are but two accounts of sibling rivalry. Such accounts support the assertion that jealousy among siblings is a common phenomenon.

Sigmund Freud's theory of socialization was one of the first to address the concept of sibling rivalry from a scientific perspective. According to Freud, sibling rivalry, with its struggles and controversy, is inherent in all brother-and-sister relationships. Much of what Freud hypothesized regarding sibling competition was grounded in a personal understanding of his own relationships with his siblings. Freud was the oldest child in a family which included five younger sisters and a younger brother.

Competition for parental attention was a dominant theme in Freud's description of the sibling relationship. He emphasized the negative emotions associated with sibling relationships and concluded that, although these feelings diminished as children matured, the rivalry persisted into adulthood. Few of his remarks about sibling relationships addressed gender differences, as Freud described relationships from his own perspective as a male.

Another theorist who addressed the issue of sibling relationships was Walter Toman. In 1961, Toman published the book *Family Constellation: Its Effects on Personality and Social Behavior*. He suggested that birth order, gender, and spacing were significant factors in the development of personality and strongly influenced the nature of personal relationships both within and outside the family of origin. Toman detailed eight sibling positions, such as oldest brother of brothers, youngest sister of brothers, and so on. While the generalizations presented in Toman's work have significance as a basis of comparison, there are too many intervening variables and complexities in family life to use birth order theories as complete explanations for sibling relationships and family roles. Birth order, gender, and spacing are several of the many significant factors that shape the connections between siblings.

Sibling relationships play an important role in each child's development. Since the works of Freud and Toman were published, researchers have expanded their studies of sibling rivalry to include the broader context of the family. There is growing evidence that the emotional climate of the family is directly related to the quality of the relationship of siblings. The parental relationship, factors of vulnerability in specific children, parental expectations, and family constellation variables each contribute to the development and intensity of sibling rivalry between brothers and sisters in a given family.

Bibliography

Akhtar, Salman, and Selma Kramer, eds. *Brothers and Sisters: Developmental, Dynamic, and Technical Aspects of the Sibling Relationship*. Northvale, N.J.: Jason Aronson, 1999. Offers papers on such topics as twin relationships and unconscious womb fantasies, followed by discussions.

Boer, Frits, and Judy Dunn, eds. *Children's Sibling Relationships: Developmental and Clinical Issues*. Hillsdale, N.J.: Lawrence Erlbaum, 1992. This volume is based on presentations from the First International Symposium entitled "Brothers and Sisters: Research on Sibling Relationships, Therapeutic Applications" in 1990. The book highlights developmental principles regarding children and their sibling relationships. In this text, particular attention is paid to children as family members, primarily in relation to siblings.

Faber, Adele, and Elaine Mazlish. *Siblings Without Rivalry: How to Help Your Children Live Together So You Can Live Too*. Expanded ed. New York: Avon Books, 1998. A popular guide for parents on helping children live together successfully. Addresses the complexity of the concept of sibling rivalry in an easy-to-read style. The authors provide messages of reassurance to parents dealing with the competition between children.

Goldenthal, Peter. *Beyond Sibling Rivalry: How to Help Your Children Become Cooperative, Caring, and Compassionate*. New York: Henry Holt, 1999. Argues that conflicts among siblings do not reflect jealousy or a longing for parents' undivided attention but that all family relationships have a bearing on rivalry between brothers and sisters.

Greydanus, Donald E., and Mark L. Wolraich, eds. *Behavioral Pediatrics*. New York: Springer-Verlag, 1992. This outstanding text summarizes contemporary concepts of pediatric mental health science in a very readable form. Although written primarily for health care providers and clinicians, this book provides straightforward information on a wide variety of common behavioral and emotional problems in children. Recommendations are offered for dealing with negative behaviors associated with sibling rivalry.

Kramer, Laurie, and Chad Radey. "Improving Sibling Relationships Among Young Children: A Social Skills Training Model." *Family Relations* 46, no. 3 (July, 1997): 237-246. The authors describe the results of their experiment in which sixty-four families used a method for helping siblings create positive relationships.

Leder, Jane Mersky. *Brothers and Sisters: How They Shape Our Lives*. New York: St. Martin's Press, 1991. This well-written book examines the assumptions that have shaped the way in which sibling relationships have been viewed in the past. The author describes the foundation of the original theories on sibling rivalry and details the characteristics long associated with the development of sibling competitiveness. The characteristics addressed include birth order, gender, age spacing, sibling access, generational messages, ethnic patterns, and environmental and genetic differences.

Mendelson, Morton J. *Becoming a Brother: A Child Learns About Life, Family, and Self.* Cambridge, Mass.: MIT Press, 1990. A case study of the transitions that occurred in one family following the birth of a second child. This personal account of the adaptations that followed the addition of a family member encompasses a family systems perspective regarding family changes and includes a chapter on sibling rivalry.

Neifert, Marianne E. *Dr. Mom's Parenting Guide: Commonsense Guidance for the Life of Your Child.* New York: E. P. Dutton, 1991. This well-written book provides supportive and reassuring answers to important questions commonly asked by parents. Each chapter offers realistic advice for dealing with common parenting issues. One chapter is devoted to a discussion of sibling rivalry, including specific strategies for minimizing or eliminating negative behaviors resulting from competitiveness between siblings.

Carol Moore Pfaffly

See also:

Anxiety Disorders; Bed-Wetting; Behavioral Family Therapy; Child Abuse; Child and Adolescent Psychiatry; Divorce and Separation: Children's Issues; Domestic Violence; Jealousy; Psychotherapy: Children; Stress.

SLEEP APNEA SYNDROMES AND NARCOLEPSY

Type of psychology: Consciousness
Fields of study: Sleep

Sleep apnea syndromes are a class of sleep disorders which result in repeated pauses in breathing during the night and cause repeated interruptions of the sleep cycle. Sleep apnea may be caused by physical obstruction of the upper airway or by neurological difficulties. Narcolepsy, another sleep disorder, is characterized by excessive daytime sleepiness, cataplexy, sleep paralysis, hypnagogic hallucinations, and irregular manifestations of REM sleep. The disorder is lifelong, and its origin is unknown.

Principal terms

APNEA: the cessation of breathing
CATAPLEXY: a brief, sudden episode of muscle weakness or paralysis; in narcoleptic patients, usually triggered by emotion
ELECTROENCEPHALOGRAPHY: a technique used to measure electrical (brain-wave) activity through the scalp
HYPNAGOGIC HALLUCINATIONS: vivid auditory or visual hallucinations which occur at the transition from wakefulness to sleep, or from sleep to wakefulness
INSOMNIA: a complaint of poor, insufficient, or nonrefreshing sleep
RAPID EYE MOVEMENT (REM) SLEEP: a type or stage of sleep characterized by rapid eye movements, vivid dreaming, and lack of skeletal muscle tone

Causes and Symptoms

Sleep apnea syndromes include a variety of conditions, all of which result in the temporary cessation of breathing during sleep. Sleep apnea may affect people of all ages, but it is more common among elderly patients. Individuals with sleep apnea do not necessarily have breathing difficulty while awake, and while many people who do not have apnea experience pauses in breathing during sleep, sleep apnea patients experience much longer pauses (typically fifteen to sixty seconds), and these may occur one hundred to six hundred times per night. Three basic types of apnea exist: obstructive, central, and mixed.

Obstructive sleep apnea (OSA) is caused by an obstruction of the upper airway during sleep and is the most common type of apnea. Breathing effort continues with OSA, but it is ineffective because of the patient's blocked airway. Individuals with OSA will commonly report that they experience excessive daytime sleepiness (EDS). Also, loud snoring occurs at night, which is a result of the vibration of tissues in the upper airway and is caused by the passage of air through a narrow airway. Another feature which is common in OSA patients is excessive body weight. OSA occurs more often in males than in females.

Children are also affected by this disorder; the most common cause is swelling of the tonsils. Therefore, all children are at risk of developing OSA, though some groups of children, such as those with Down syndrome, facial malformation, or muscular disorders, are more at risk than others. Children with OSA are typically underweight, because they usually have difficulty swallowing; they may even enjoy eating less because they are not able to smell or taste food as well as others.

Patients with obstructive sleep apnea frequently report falling asleep while driving, watching television, or reading, but some patients report little or no EDS. OSA patients may also experience intellectual or personality changes, which are probably usually related to EDS, but in severe cases may be attributable to lowered levels of oxygen reaching the brain. Another symptom associated with OSA is erectile impotence.

Central sleep apnea (CSA) is caused by a temporary absence of the effort to breathe while sleeping, and it is considered to be a rare disorder; fewer than 10 percent of all apnea patients experience CSA. CSA differs from OSA in that there is no obstruction of the upper airway, and breathing effort does not continue as it does in OSA. Patients rarely have CSA alone; the majority have both CSA and OSA episodes during the night. CSA is usually diagnosed when more than 55 percent of the episodes are central. Many authors point out that the mechanisms responsible for the two types of apnea may overlap; CSA may be attributable to a failure of the systems which monitor oxygen levels in the blood, resulting in the periodic loss of the breathing effort. CSA patients may experience between one hundred and three hundred episodes per night.

Central sleep apnea patients commonly complain of insomnia, which is poor, insufficient, or nonrefreshing sleep. Other symptoms associated with CSA are depression and decreased sexual drive. Patients with neurological disorders such as encephalitis, brain-stem tumor, and Shy-Drager syndrome may also have CSA. The range of disorders associated with CSA makes it difficult to make absolute statements about the cause of this form of apnea.

The third type of apnea is mixed sleep apnea (MSA). MSA is a pause in breathing which has both obstructive and central components. Most patients with MSA are generally considered to be similar to OSA patients in terms of symptoms, physical causes, and treatment options; however, there are also those MSA patients whose apneic episodes are characterized by long central components, and these individuals are more similar to CSA patients in terms of symptoms, cause, and treatment.

Narcolepsy is a sleep disorder which includes symptoms such as EDS, overwhelming episodes of daytime sleep, disturbed nocturnal sleep, cataplexy (sudden, brief episodes of muscle weakness or paralysis which are emotionally triggered), hypnagogic hallucinations, sleep-onset rapid eye movement (REM) periods (or SOREMPs, the occurrence of REM sleep within fifteen minutes of sleep onset as indicated by electroencephalographic, or EEG, analysis), and sleep paralysis. Four symptoms—EDS, cataplexy, sleep paralysis, and hypnagogic hallucinations—are often referred to as the "narcoleptic tetrad," although all four symptoms are rarely seen in the same patient. Narcoleptics rarely have problems falling asleep at night, but they do awaken more frequently and exhibit more body movements during sleep than normal subjects. Narcoleptics are also frequently disturbed by vivid dreams.

The EDS associated with narcolepsy is most often experienced during boring, sedentary situations, but it may also occur when the person is highly involved with a task. Though narcoleptics may awaken from a "sleep attack" feeling refreshed, narcoleptic sleepiness is persistent and cannot be alleviated by any amount of sleep. For years, many believed that the sleep attacks associated with narcolepsy could be attributable to a sudden "urge" to sleep, but more recent thought suggests that these sleep episodes may result from a sudden failure to resist the ever-present sleepiness that narcoleptics experience.

Not all patients with narcolepsy experience cataplexy. In a study to determine the differences between narcoleptics with cataplexy and those without cataplexy, it was determined that patients who experienced cataplexy had a higher prevalence of hallucinations, sleep paralysis, and nocturnal sleep disturbance. Thus, cataplectics generally seem to be more impaired during sleep and while awake. For this reason, some have suggested that two groups of narcoleptic patients may exist: those with cataplexy and those without cataplexy. During a cataplectic episode, the narcoleptic patient maintains consciousness; however, if the episode is particularly long, the patient may enter REM sleep. Patients with severe cataplexy may experience complete paralysis in all but the respiratory muscles; these episodes can result in injury, although the most common episodes could be characterized by the patient dropping objects, losing posture, or halting motions.

Sleep paralysis in narcolepsy is experienced as the inability to move during the onset of sleep or upon awakening. These episodes may last from a few seconds to ten minutes and can be reversed by external stimuli such as another person touching the patient or calling his or her name. Sleep paralysis can be particularly frightening, although many patients learn that these episodes are usually brief and will end spontaneously. Adding to this fright, however, are the visual, auditory, or tactile hallucinations which may accompany sleep paralysis. Sleep paralysis and hypnagogic hallucinations occur in about 60 percent of narcoleptic patients. Much like patients with sleep apnea, narcoleptics may exhibit psychopathology, but it is most likely related to effects of their disturbed sleep rather than to the sleep disorder itself.

Individuals with apnea may repeatedly experience dangerously low levels of oxygen in their blood while sleeping. Oxygen is essential to the body's proper functioning, and if one does not receive the amount of oxygen the body needs, health may be affected in some way; heart disease and stroke are strongly associated with the occurrence of apnea. While it is not known if apnea actually causes these complications, the association is important nevertheless. Exposure to such low levels of oxygen in the blood over a prolonged period may result in increased blood pressure and poor circulation, as well as disturbance of heart rhythms.

Since both narcolepsy and apnea patients often experience nocturnal sleep difficulties, their quality and quantity of sleep is lowered. As a result, many patients with both disorders experience excessive daytime sleepiness. This may present itself as a problem during such activities as work or driving. Studies indicate that narcolepsy and apnea patients are more likely to have automobile accidents, poor job performance, and less job satisfaction than those without a sleep disorder, in part because of the fact that these patients often fall asleep during such activities. Diagnosis of sleep apnea and narcolepsy in a sleep disorders clinic involves a number of measurements. The Multiple Sleep Latency Test measures the tendency of a patient to fall asleep during the day. This test, in addition to polysomnographic recording and the patient's medical history, aids in determining the proper treatment for these disorders.

Treatment and Therapy

Treatment of sleep apnea depends on a number of factors, which include frequency and type of apnea, quality of nighttime sleep, amount of oxygen in the blood during sleep, frequency and type of heart rhythm disturbance, and the tendency to sleep during waking hours. CSA patients may be treated using oxygen administration during sleep, which reduces the number of central apnea events, drug therapy, or mechanical ventilation, but all treatments for CSA have the potential to increase the occurrence of OSA in these patients. Various treatments available to patients with obstructive or mixed apnea include weight loss, drug therapy, surgery, and medical management.

Weight loss can be an important part of treatment for patients with OSA. In many cases, weight loss alone results in a reduction of the frequency and severity of apnea. Since adequate weight loss may take months, however, this option alone is not likely to be feasible for serious cases of apnea. Drug therapy has met with limited success in treating apnea patients, but there are many drugs which are being studied, and these may prove effective in treating the disorder. Surgical treatment for severe cases of apnea was, in the past, limited to tracheostomy. More recently, however, removal of unnecessary tissue in the area of obstruction has been found to reduce apnea events significantly in certain patients. Facial reconstruction is also an option in more severe cases.

Treatments for apnea which involve medical management are constantly being developed. These include the insertion of a tube which bypasses the point of obstruction, allowing normal breathing to occur, and continuous positive airway pressure (CPAP). CPAP is a technique that uses air pressure to eliminate the closure of the airway in the nasal passages. In effect, CPAP provides a "splint" for the area that causes the obstruction; it also increases lung volume. This treatment is comfortable and easy to use for most patients, and is thus very promising.

Treatments for narcolepsy all center on managing its symptoms, as there is no cure for narcolepsy itself. Fortunately, cataplexy, sleep paralysis, and hypnagogic hallucinations improve or disappear over time in approximately one-third of all narcoleptic patients. Medication may be prescribed to decrease the severity of daytime sleepiness, nocturnal sleep disturbance, and cataplexy. Regularly scheduled naps throughout the day may be used as an effective supplement to medication. Such naps may also reduce the need for medications by relieving the effects of insufficient sleep. Many doctors employ this method of treatment, because it is important for patients to adjust their lifestyle in order to deal with the effects of narcolepsy.

Perspective and Prospects

The scientific study of sleep began in the nineteenth century, although there was certainly interest in sleep prior to that time. Technological advances during the 1930's and 1940's allowed scientists to investigate the processes of sleep with more precision than before. In 1929, Hans Berger first recorded the EEG activity of humans. This development led to the discovery of patterns of brain-wave activity during sleep and the later description of REM sleep. This period of technological growth began the modern era of sleep studies; since that time, much has been learned about sleep and how it relates to other physiological processes.

Recognition of sleep apnea as a distinct sleep disorder began in 1966, and it is estimated today that as many as one in every thirty to fifty adults has sleep apnea to the extent that their quality of life is affected in some manner. Since its description, sleep apnea has received intensive investigation by a variety of medical specialists; in sleep apnea studies, it is not uncommon to see a heart surgeon working with a psychologist and a child specialist. This is attributable to the fact that sleep apnea can be the result of a number of physical or neurological problems, and it affects patients in a number of different ways.

Between one in a thousand and one in ten thousand women and men experience narcolepsy, and the usual age of onset is between fifteen and thirty-five. In half the cases, the onset of narcoleptic symptoms is preceded by severe psychological stress, an abrupt change in the sleep-wake schedule, or some other special circumstance. Scientists suspect a genetic factor in the occurrence of narcolepsy that may involve the immune system, but data also suggest that a strong environmental factor may play a role in the development of the disorder.

In an essay in *Principles and Practice of Sleep Medicine* (1989), Christian Guillemenault writes that the word "narcolepsy" was first used in 1880 to describe a pathological condition characterized by recurring, irresistible episodes of sleep which were of short duration. Interest in the disorder grew, and in 1960 it was discovered that a narcoleptic patient exhibited sleep-onset REM periods. This phenomenon became one of the cornerstone symptoms in the diagnosis of narcolepsy, and narcolepsy has since been described as primarily a disorder of REM sleep.

Investigation of sleep is showing how important sleep is to human physical and psychological health. Many theories exist which attempt to account for why people sleep; studies indicate that tissue restoration is enhanced during sleep, the ability to concentrate suffers if one is deprived of sleep for a significant period of time, and one may experience distinct mood changes without proper sleep. As stated earlier, cardiovascular complications are frequently associated with sleep apnea, as are work-related accidents and changes in intellectual ability. Sudden infant death syndrome (SIDS) is thought by some to be associated with sleep apnea. For these reasons, the study of sleep apnea, narcolepsy, and sleep in general is crucial to the health of many people. As psychologists and physicians further understand the processes involved in human and animal sleep, they will come closer to providing more effective treatment for patients with sleep apnea and narcolepsy.

Bibliography

Anch, A. Michael, C. P. Browman, M. M. Mitler, and James K. Walsh. *Sleep: A Scientific Perspective*. Englewood Cliffs, N.J.: Prentice-Hall, 1988. The authors cover the entire spectrum of sleep study in this work, integrating the history of sleep studies with more recent knowledge of the field. The book addresses physiological as well as psychological issues and gives sufficient definitions, information, and references for those who wish to study sleep in a more in-depth manner.

Dement, William C. *Some Must Watch While Some Must Sleep*. San Francisco: W. H. Freeman, 1974. A book by a scientist who many consider to be the leading authority in the field of sleep studies. Easily read by high school or college students. Very informative; provides an excellent starting point for further study.

Dement, William C., and Christopher Vaughan. *The Promise of Sleep: A Pioneer in Sleep Medicine Explores the Vital Connection Between Health, Happiness, and a Good Night's Sleep*. New York: Random House, 1999. Explains what happens during sleep, taking readers on a tour of the body and mind.

Issa, Faiq G., Paul M. Surrat, and John E. Remmers, eds. *Sleep and Respiration*. New York: John Wiley & Sons, 1990. A compilation of articles and discussions by many of the leading scientists of the field. Especially helpful are the sections after each chapter in which the topic is discussed among specialists. Somewhat advanced, but a basic knowledge of sleep disorders is sufficient for understanding most of the material in this book.

Kryger, Meir H., Thomas Roth, and William C. Dement, eds. *Principles and Practice of Sleep Medicine*. 3d ed. Philadelphia: W. B. Saunders, 2000. A very comprehensive work on the subject of sleep disorders. The entire spectrum of sleep and its disorders is covered, with extensive material on treatment practices. A large glossary and numerous references make this book an ideal tool.

Mendelson, Wallace B. *Human Sleep: Research and Clinical Care*. New York: Plenum Medical Book Company, 1987. Provides an overview of research and treatment practices for a number of sleep disorders.

Swanson, Jenifer, ed. *Sleep Disorders SourceBook: Basic Consumer Health Information About Sleep and Its Disorders, Including Insomnia, Sleepwalking, Sleep Apnea, Restless Leg Syndrome, and Narcolepsy*. Detroit: Omnigraphics, 1999. Helps readers identify symptoms of the major sleep disorders. Describes sleep requirements, sleep changes through the life span, sleep medications, and the cost of sleep deprivation to society.

Alan K. Gibson
Shirley A. Albertson Ownes

See also:

Brain Disorders; Child and Adolescent Psychiatry; Geriatric Psychiatry; Insomnia.

STRATEGIC FAMILY THERAPY

Type of psychology: Psychotherapy
Fields of study: Group and family therapies

Strategic theory and interventions have been highly influential in the founding of modern family therapy. Strategic family therapy focuses on influencing family members by carefully planned interventions and the issuance of directives for resolving problems. At times, these directives may appear to be in direct opposition to the goals of treatment (an approach referred to as paradox). Strategic therapy is one of the most widely studied, taught, and emulated approaches to treating family (and individual) dysfunction.

Principal terms

AGORAPHOBIA: an intense fear of being in places or situations in which help may not be available or escape could be difficult

DOUBLE BIND: receiving contradictory messages; a form of communication which often occurs when a family member sends two messages, requests, or commands that are logically inconsistent, contradictory, or impossible

PARADOXICAL INTERVENTION: a therapy technique in which a therapist gives a patient or family a task that appears to contradict the goals of treatment

REFRAMING: redefining an event or situation in order to alter its meaning

RESTRAINING STRATEGIES: a form of paradoxical intervention wherein the therapist discourages, restrains, or denies the possibility of change

SYMPTOM PRESCRIPTION: a form of paradoxical intervention wherein the therapist encourages or instructs patients to engage in behaviors that are to be eliminated or altered

Overview

Families engage in complex interactional sequences that involve both verbal and nonverbal (for example, gestures, posture, intonation, volume) patterns of communication. Family members continually send and receive complicated messages. Strategic family approaches are designed to alter psychological difficulties which emerge from problematic interactions between individuals. Specifically, strategic therapists view individual problems (for example, depression, anxiety) as manifestations of disturbances in the family. Psychological symptoms are seen as the consequences of misguided attempts at changing an existing disturbance. For example, concerned family members may attempt to "protect" an agoraphobic patient from anxiety by rearranging activities and outings so that the patient is never left alone; unfortunately, these efforts only serve to foster greater dependency, teach avoidant behaviors, and maintain agoraphobic symptoms. From a strategic viewpoint, symptoms are regarded as communicative in nature. That is, symptoms have distinct meanings within families and usually appear when a family member feels trapped and cannot break out of the situation via nonsymptomatic ways.

The strategic model views all behavior as an attempt to communicate. In fact, it is impossible not to communicate, just as it is impossible not to act. For example, an adolescent who runs away from home sends a message to his or her parents; similarly, the parents communicate different messages in terms of how they react. Frequently, the intended message behind these nonverbal forms of communication is difficult for family members to discern. Moreover, when contradictions appear between verbal and nonverbal messages, communication can become incongruent and clouded by mixed messages.

Gregory Bateson, who was trained as an anthropologist and developed much of the early theory behind strategic approaches, worked with other theorists to develop the double-bind theory of schizophrenia. A double-bind message is a particularly problematic form of mixed communication that occurs when a family member sends two messages, requests, or commands that are logically inconsistent, contradictory, or impossible. For example, problems arise when messages at the content level ("I love you" or "Stay close to me") conflict with nonverbal messages at another level ("I despise you" or "Keep your distance"). Eventually, it is argued, a child who is continually exposed to this mixed style of communication, that is, a "no-win" dilemma, may feel angered, helpless, and fearful, and responds by withdrawing.

Since Bateson's early work in communication theory and therapy, the strategic approach has undergone considerable revision. At least three divisions of strategic family therapy are frequently cited: the original Mental Research Institute (MRI) interactional view, the strategic approach advocated by therapists Jay Haley and Cloe Madanes, and the Milan systemic family therapy model. There is considerable overlap among these approaches, and the therapy tactics are generally similar.

The MRI interactional family therapy approach shares a common theoretical foundation with the other strategic approaches. In addition to Bateson, some of the prominent therapists who have been associated with the institute at one time or another are Don Jackson, Jay Haley, Virginia Satir, and Paul Watzlawick. As modified by Watzlawick's writings, including *The Invented Reality* (1984), the MRI model emphasizes that patients' attempts to solve problems often maintain or exacerbate difficulties. Problems may arise when the family either overreacts or underreacts to events. For example, ordinary life difficulties or transitions (for example, a child beginning school, an adult dealing with new work assignments) may be associated with family overreactions. Similarly, significant problems may be treated as no particular problem. The failure to handle such events in a constructive manner within the family system eventually leads to the problem taking on proportions and characteristics which may seem to have little similarity to the original difficulty. During family therapy, the MRI approach employs a step-by-step progression of suggested strategies toward the elimination of a symptom. Paradoxical procedures, which are described later, represent a mainstay of the MRI approach.

Haley and Madanes's approach to strategic family therapy argues that change occurs through the process of the family carrying out assignments (to be completed outside therapy) issued by the therapist. As described in Madanes's *Strategic Family Therapy* (1981), strategic therapists attempt to design a therapeutic strategy for each specific problem. Instead of "suggesting" strategies, as in the MRI approach, therapists issue directives which are designed deliberately to shift the organization of the family in order to resolve the presenting problem. Problems are viewed as serving a function in the family and always involve at least two or three individuals. As detailed in Haley's *Leaving Home: The Therapy of Disturbed Young People* (1980) and *Ordeal Therapy: Unusual Ways to Change Behavior* (1984), treatment includes intense involvement, carefully planned interventions designed to reach clear goals, frequent use of therapist-generated directives or assignments, and paradoxical procedures.

The Milan systemic family therapy model is easily distinguished from other strategic approaches because of its unique spacing of therapeutic sessions and innovative team approach to treatment. The original work of therapists Mara Selvini-Palazzoli, Luigi Boscolo, Gianfranco Cecchin, and Guiliana Prata has been described as "long brief" family therapy and was used to treat a wide variety of severe problems such as anorexia and schizophrenia. The first detailed description of the Milan group's approach was written by the four founding therapists and called *Paradox and Counterparadox: A New Model in the Therapy of the Family in Schizophrenic Transition* (1978). The original Milan approach incorporated monthly sessions for approximately one year. The unusual spacing of sessions was originally scheduled because many of the families seen in treatment traveled hundreds of miles by train to receive therapy. Later, however, the Milan group decided that many of their interventions, including paradox, required considerable time to work. Thus, they continued the long brief model. Another distinguishing factor of the Milan group was its use of therapist-observer teams who watched treatment sessions from behind a two-way mirror. From time to time, the therapist observers would request that the family therapist interrupt the session to confer about the treatment process. Following this discussion, the family therapist would rejoin the session and initiate interventions, including paradox, as discussed by the team of therapist observers who remained behind the mirror. In 1980, the four originators of the Milan group divided into two smaller groups (Boscolo and Cecchin; Selvini-Palazzoli and Prata). Shortly thereafter, Selvini-Palazzoli and Prata continued pursuing family research separately. The more recent work of Boscolo and Cecchin is described in *Milan Systemic Family Therapy* (1987), while Selvini-Palazzoli's new work is presented in *Family Games* (1989), which she wrote with several new colleagues.

Applications

Jay Haley argued that conventional mental health approaches were not providing effective treatment. Based on his work with schizophrenics, he observed that patients typically would improve during their hospitalizations, return home, and then quickly suffer relapses. He also suggested that if the patient did improve while away from the hospital, then a family crisis would often ensue, resulting in the patient's eventual rehospitalization. Thus, effective treatment from a strategic framework often required family members to weather crises and alter family patterns of communication so that constructive change could occur.

Related to Haley's work with hospitalized patients was his treatment of "disturbed" young adults who exhibited bizarre behavior and/or continually took illegal drugs. In *Leaving Home: The Therapy of Disturbed Young People*, Haley suggests that it is best to assume that the problem is not an individual problem, but a problem of the family and young person separating from each other. That is, young adults typically leave home as they succeed in work, school, or career and form other intimate relationships. Some families, however, become unstable, dysfunctional, or distressed as the son or daughter attempts to leave. In order to regain family stability, the young adult may fail in attempts to leave home (often via abnormal behavior). Furthermore, if the family organization does not shift, then the young adult may be destined to fail over and over again.

Haley's approach to treating such cases includes several stages of strategic therapy. First, the entire family attends the initial interview, and the parents are put in charge of solving their child's problems. During treatment, the parents are told that they are the best therapists for their child's problems. Because the family is assumed to be in conflict (as shown by the patient's problems), requiring the family to take charge and become active in the treatment of the identified patient allows for greater opportunities to intervene around the conflict. In particular, it is assumed that the hierarchy of the family is in confusion and that the parents must take an active role in shifting the family's organization. Also, all family members are encouraged to adopt a position in which they expect the identified patient's problems to become normal.

As the identified patient improves, the family will often experience a crisis and become unstable again. A relapse of the identified patient would follow the usual sequence for the family and return stability (and familiarity) to the system. Unfortunately, a relapse would only serve to perpetuate the dysfunction. Therefore, the therapist may further assist the family by dealing with concerns such as parental conflicts and fears, or attempt to assist the young adult by providing opportunities away from therapy sessions which foster continued growth. Eventually, termination is planned, based on the belief that treatment does not require the resolution of all family problems, but instead those centered on the young adult.

Strategic therapists share a common belief in the utility of paradoxical procedures. In fact, the history of modern paradoxical psychotherapy is frequently credited as beginning with the MRI group, although paradoxical techniques have been discussed by various theorists from other orientations. Paradox refers to a contradiction or an apparent inconsistency that defies logical deduction. That is, strategic paradox is employed as a means of altering behavior through the use of strategies in apparent opposition to treatment goals. The need for paradoxical procedures is based on the assumption that families are very resistant to change and frequently attempt to disrupt the therapist's effort to help them. Thus, if the therapist suggests common therapeutic tactics (for example, communication homework, parenting suggestions), then the family may resist (for example, may "forget" to do the homework, sabotaging the exercise) and fail to improve. On the other hand, if the therapist tells the family to do what they are already doing, then the family may resist by getting better.

A variety of explanations have been offered to explain the manner in which paradox works. In *Change: Principles of Problem Formation and Problem Resolution* (1974), written by Watzlawick and his colleagues, paradox is described as producing a special type of change among family members. That is, there are two levels of change: first-order and second-order change. First-order change is change within a family system (for example, a parent increasing punishment as the child's behavior becomes more disruptive). First-order change is typically conducted in a step-by-step fashion and involves the uses of problem-solving strategies. On the other hand, second-order change refers to changing the family system itself, and it typically occurs in a sudden and radical manner. The therapist attempts to change the system by unexpected, illogical, or abrupt methods. Paradoxical procedures are designed to effect second-order change. A paradoxical approach might be to encourage the child to act out every time he or she believes that the parents are about to have a fight. In such a case, the family system may be transformed by family members receiving important feedback about the manner in which they operate, by increased understanding of one another's impact on the system, and by efforts to discard "old family rules" by initiating new procedures for effective family living.

Several different classes of paradoxical interventions are highlighted in Gerald Weeks and Luciano L'Abate's book *Paradoxical Psychotherapy: Theory and Practice with Individuals, Couples, and Families* (1982). These include reframing, prescribing the symptom, and restraining.

Reframing refers to providing an alternative meaning or viewpoint to explain an event. A common example of reframing is Tom Sawyer, who described the boredom of whitewashing a fence as pleasurable and collected cash from his peers for the opportunity to assist him. Reframing provides a new framework from which to evaluate interactions (for example, "Mom is smothering" versus "Mom is caring and concerned").

Prescribing the symptom refers to encouraging or instructing patients to engage in the behavior that is to be eliminated or altered. Symptom prescription is the most common form of paradox in the family therapy literature. Following the presentation of an appropriate rationale to the family (for example, to gain more assessment information), the therapist offers a paradoxical instruction to the family, typically as part of the week's homework. For example, a child who frequently throws temper tantrums may be specifically instructed to engage in tantrums, but only in certain locations at scheduled times. Another common use of paradox involves symptom prescription for insomniacs. A patient with onset insomnia (difficulty falling asleep) may be encouraged to remain awake in order to become more aware of his or her thoughts and feelings before falling asleep. As might be guessed, anxiety is often associated with onset insomnia, and such an intervention serves to decrease anxiety about failing to fall asleep by introducing the idea that the patient is supposed to stay awake. Frequently, patients describe difficulty completing the homework because they "keep falling asleep too quickly."

Restraining strategies include attempts to discourage, restrain, or even deny the possibility of change; the therapist might say, "Go slow," or, "The situation appears hopeless," or, "Don't change." The basis for restraining strategies is the belief that many patients may not wish to change. Why would patients seek treatment and spend money toward that end if they do not wish to improve? All change involves risk, and with risk comes danger and/or uncertainty. Moreover, the future may be less predictable following change. In fact, it is possible to conceive of most recurring patterns of family dysfunction or individual difficulties as a heavy overcoat. At times, the heavy overcoat serves a useful purpose by protecting one from harsh weather. As time passes, however, the overcoat becomes uncomfortable as the weather becomes warmer. Still, many people dread taking off the overcoat because they are used to it, it has become familiar, and the future seems uncertain without it. From the patient's viewpoint, discomfort may be more acceptable than change (and the uncertainty it brings).

Perhaps the most common restraining strategy is predicting a relapse. In predicting a relapse, the patient is told that a previous problem or symptom will reappear. By so doing, the therapist is in a no-lose situation. If the problem reappears, then it was predicted successfully by the therapist, is understood by the therapist, and can be dealt with by the therapist and patient. If the problem does not reappear, then the problem is being effectively controlled by the patient.

Perspective and Prospects

Strategic approaches, based on communication theories, developed from research conducted at the Mental Research Institute (MRI) in Palo Alto, California, in the 1950's. In contrast to psychodynamic approaches, which emphasize the importance of past history, trauma, and inner conflicts, strategic therapies highlight the importance of the "here and now," and view psychological difficulties as emerging from problematic interactions between individuals (family members or married partners). Moreover, strategic therapists tend to follow a brief model of treatment, in contrast to many individual and family therapy approaches.

The effectiveness of family therapy approaches, including strategic approaches, is difficult to measure. Although there has been a clear increase in research evaluating the efficacy of family interventions since about 1980, the results are less than clear because of difficulties with research methodologies and diverse research populations. For example, psychodynamic therapists prefer to use case studies rather than experimental designs to determine effectiveness. Strategic therapists have conducted only a handful of research studies, but these results are encouraging. A structural-strategic approach developed by psychologist M. Duncan Stanton has demonstrated effectiveness in the treatment of drug abuse. Also, the Milan approach has been found to be effective for a variety of problems identified by families who participated in a three-year research program. Further research is warranted, however, before definitive conclusions about the empirical effectiveness of strategic approaches can be reached.

In conclusion, strategic family therapy has shaped the field of family therapy. Innovative approaches such as paradox have been associated with strategic therapy for years, and advances continue to be seen from the respective groups of strategic therapists. Although strategic approaches such as paradoxical directives are frequently regarded as controversial and perhaps risky, the importance of some strategic contributions to the field of family therapy—in particular, the recognition of multiple levels of communication, and of subtle nuances of power struggles in relationships—is widely accepted.

Bibliography

Eron, Joseph B., and Thomas W. Lund. *Narrative Solutions in Brief Therapy*. New York: Guilford Press, 1998. Presents an approach that combines the elements of strategic and narrative traditions in family therapy.

Goldenberg, Irene, and Herbert Goldenberg. *Family Therapy: An Overview*. 5th ed. Belmont, Calif.: Wadsworth, 2000. An updated review of the major family therapy approaches, including strategic family therapy. Also provides a background on family development, and highlights issues in family therapy research and training.

Haley, Jay. *Leaving Home: The Therapy of Disturbed Young People*. New York: McGraw-Hill, 1980. Presents a treatment program for disturbed young people and their families. Describes the use of intense involvement and rapid disengagement with such families. Haley is one of the foremost theorists and therapists in strategic approaches.

Madanes, Cloe. *Strategic Family Therapy*. Reprint. San Francisco: Jossey-Bass, 1991. Provides an overview of strategic family therapy from one of the primary therapists in the field. Describes the philosophy and common approaches employed by strategic therapists in the treatment of a variety of presenting problems.

Stanton, M. Duncan. "Strategic Approaches to Family Therapy." In *Handbook of Family Therapy*, edited by Alan S. Gurman and David P. Kniskern. New York: Brunner/Mazel, 1981. Summarizes the strategic family therapy approach and highlights the central components of the MRI group, Milan school, and other notable strategic therapists. Also highlights the dimensions of healthy and dysfunctional families from a strategic model. Finally, briefly outlines some research on the effectiveness of the model in treating a variety of disorders.

Weeks, Gerald R., and Luciano L'Abate. *Paradoxical Psychotherapy: Theory and Practice with Individuals, Couples, and Families*. New York: Brunner/Mazel, 1982. Provides an overview of paradoxical approaches and details a variety of considerations in using paradox in treatment. Presents a compilation of paradoxical methods and describes some of the theories underlying these methods.

Gregory L. Wilson

See also:

Abnormality: Family Models; Behavioral Family Therapy; Couples Therapy; Divorce and Separation: Adult Issues; Divorce and Separation: Children's Issues; Modeling Therapies; Play Therapy; Psychotherapy: Children; Psychotherapy: Effectiveness; Psychotherapy: Goals and Techniques.

STRESS

Type of psychology: Stress
Fields of study: Coping; critical issues in stress; stress and illness

The stress response consists of physiological arousal, subjective feelings of discomfort, and the behavioral changes people experience when they confront situations that they appraise as dangerous or threatening. Because exposure to extreme situational or chronic stress causes emotional distress and may impair physical functioning, it is important to learn effective stress coping strategies.

Principal terms

COGNITIVE APPRAISAL: an assessment of the meaningfulness of an event to an individual; events that are appraised as harmful or potentially harmful elicit stress

EMOTION-FOCUSED COPING: minimizing negative emotions elicited by a stressor by using techniques such as relaxation and denial and paying little attention to the stressor itself

LEARNED HELPLESSNESS: motivational, cognitive, and emotional deficits resulting from exposure to a stressor that is perceived to be uncontrollable

PROBLEM-FOCUSED COPING: minimizing negative emotions elicited by a stressor by changing or avoiding the stressor

STRESSOR: an event that is appraised as dangerous or threatening and that elicits a stress response

Overview

In the past, the term "stress" designated both a stimulus (a force or pressure) and a response (adversity, affliction). More recently, it has usually been used to denote a set of changes that people undergo in situations that they appraise as threatening to their well-being. These changes involve physiological arousal, subjective feelings of discomfort, and overt behaviors. The terms "anxiety" and "fear" are also used to indicate what people experience when they appraise circumstances as straining their ability to cope with them.

The external circumstances that induce stress responses are called stressors. Stressors have a number of important temporal components. Exposure to them may be relatively brief with a clear starting and stopping point (acute stressors) or may persist for extended periods without clear demarcation (chronic stressors). Stressors impinge on people at different points in their life cycles, sometimes occurring "off time" (at times that are incompatible with personal and societal expectations of their occurrence) or at a "bad time" (along with other stressors). Finally, stress may be induced by the anticipation of harmful circumstances that one thinks one is likely to confront, by an ongoing stressor, or by the harmful effects of stressors already encountered. All these factors affect people's interpretations of stressful events, how they deal with them, and how effective they are at coping with them.

Although there are some situations to which almost everyone responds with high levels of stress, there are individual differences in how people respond to situations. Thus, though most people cringe at the thought of having to parachute from an airplane, a substantial minority find this an exciting, challenging adventure. Most people avoid contact with snakes, yet others keep them as pets. For most people, automobiles, birds, and people with deep voices are largely neutral objects, yet for others they provoke a stress reaction that may verge on panic.

The key concept is cognitive appraisal. Situations become stressors for an individual only if they are construed as threatening or dangerous by that individual. As demonstrated in a study of parachuters, by psychologists Walter D. Fenz and Seymour Epstein, stress appraisals can change markedly over the course of exposure to a stressor, and patterns of stress arousal differ as a function of experience with the stressor. Fenz and Epstein found that fear levels of veteran jumpers (as evaluated by a self-report measure) were highest the morning before the jump, declined continuously up to the moment of the jump, and then increased slightly until after landing. Fear levels for novice jumpers, in contrast, increased up to a point shortly before the jump and then decreased continuously. For both groups, the peak of stress occurred during the anticipatory period rather than at the point of the greatest objective danger (the act of jumping).

Stress reactions are measured in three broad ways: by means of self-report, through behavioral observations, and on the basis of physiological arousal. The self-report technique is the technique most commonly used by behavioral scientists to evaluate subjective stress levels. The State Anxiety Scale of the State-Trait Anxiety Inventory, developed by psychologist Charles Spielberger, is one of the most widely used self-report measures of stress. Examples of items on this scale are "I am tense," "I am worried," and "I feel pleasant." Subjects are instructed to respond to the items in terms of how they currently feel.

Self-report state anxiety scales may be administered and scored easily and quickly. Further, they may be administered repeatedly and still provide valid measures of momentary changes in stress levels. They have been criticized by some, however, because they are face valid (that is, their intent is clear); therefore, people who are motivated to disguise their stress levels can readily do so.

Overt behavioral measures of stress include direct and indirect observational measures. Direct measures focus on behaviors associated with stress-related physiological arousal such as heavy breathing, tremors, and perspiration; self-manipulations such as nail biting, blinking, and postural orientation; and body movement such as pacing.

Speech disturbances, both verbal (for example, repetitions, omissions, incomplete sentences, and slips of the tongue) and nonverbal (for example, pauses and hand movements), have been analyzed intensively, but no single measure or pattern has emerged as a reliable indicant of stress. Another way in which people commonly express fear reactions is by means of facial expressions. This area has been studied by psychologists Paul Ekman and Wallace V. Friesen, who concluded that the facial features that take on the most distinctive appearance during fear are the eyebrows (raised and drawn together), the eyes (open, lower lid tensed), and the lips (stretched back).

Indirect observational measures involve evaluating the degree to which people avoid feared objects. For example, in one test used by clinical psychologists to assess fear level, an individual is instructed to approach a feared stimulus (such as a snake) and engage in increasingly intimate interactions with it (for example, looking at a caged snake from a distance, approaching it, touching it, holding it). The rationale is that the higher the level of fear elicited, the earlier in the sequence the person will try to avoid the feared stimulus. Other examples include asking claustrophobics (people who are fearful of being closed in) to remain in a closed chamber as long as they can and asking acrophobics (people who fear heights) to climb a ladder and assessing their progress.

Physiological arousal is an integral component of the stress response. The most frequently monitored response systems are cardiovascular responses, electrodermal responses, and muscular tension. These measures are important in their own right as independent indicants of stress level, and in particular as possible indices of stress-related diseases.

Applications

The concept of stress has been used to help explain the etiology of certain diseases. Diseases that are thought to be caused in part by exposure to stress or poor ability to cope with stress are called psychophysiological or psychosomatic disorders. Among the diseases that seem to have strong psychological components are ulcers and coronary heart disease. The role of stress in ulcers was highlighted in a study by Joseph V. Brady known as the "executive monkey" study. In this study, pairs of monkeys were yoked together in a restraining apparatus. The monkeys received identical treatment except that one member of each pair could anticipate whether both of them would be shocked (he was given a warning signal) and could control whether the shock was actually administered (if he pressed a lever, the shock was avoided). Thus, one monkey in each pair (the "executive monkey") had to make decisions constantly and was responsible for the welfare of both himself and his partner. Twelve pairs of monkeys were tested, and in every case the executive monkey died of peptic ulcers within weeks, while the passive member of each pair remained healthy. This experiment was criticized because of flaws in its experimental design, but it nevertheless brought much attention to the important role that chronic stress can play in the activation of physiological processes (in this case, the secretion of hydrochloric acid in the stomach in the absence of food) that can be damaging or even life-threatening.

Although being in the position of a business executive who has to make decisions constantly can be very stressful, research indicates that it may be even more damaging to be exposed to stress over long periods and not have the opportunity to change or control the source of stress. People and animals who are in aversive situations over which they have little or no control for prolonged periods are said to experience "learned helplessness." This concept was introduced by psychologist Martin E. P. Seligman and his colleagues. In controlled research with rats and dogs, he and his colleagues demonstrated that exposure to prolonged stress that cannot be controlled produces emotional, motivational, and cognitive deficits. The animals show signs of depression and withdrawal, they show little ability or desire to master their environment, and their problem-solving ability suffers.

Learned helplessness has also been observed in humans. Seligman refers to Bruno Bettelheim's descriptions of some of the inmates of the Nazi concentration camps during World War II, who, when faced with the incredible brutality and hopelessness of their situation, gave up and died without any apparent physical cause. Many institutionalized patients (for example, nursing home residents and the chronically ill) also live in environments that are stressful because they have little control over them. Seligman suggests that the stress levels of such patients can be lowered and their health improved if they are given maximum control over their everyday activities (such as choosing what they want for breakfast, the color of their curtains, and whether to sleep late or wake up early).

Research findings have supported Seligman's suggestions. For example, psychologists Ellen Langer and Judith Rodin told a group of elderly nursing home residents that they could decide what they wanted their rooms to look like, when they wanted to go see motion pictures, and with whom they wanted to interact. A second comparable group of elderly residents, who were randomly assigned to live on another floor, were told that the staff would care for them and try to keep them happy. It was found that the residents in the first group became more active and reported feeling happier than those in the second group. They also became more alert and involved in different kinds of activities, such as attending movies and socializing. Further, during the eighteen-month period following the intervention, 15 percent of the subjects in the first group died, whereas 30 percent of the subjects in the second group died.

Altering people's perception of control and predictability can also help them adjust to transitory stressful situations. Studies by psychologists Stephen Auerbach, Suzanne Miller, and others have shown that for people who prefer to deal with stress in active ways (rather than by avoiding the source of stress), adjustment to stressful surgical procedures and diagnostic examinations can be improved if they are provided with detailed information about the impending procedure. It is likely that the information enhances their sense of predictability and control in an otherwise minimally controllable situation. Others, who prefer to control their stress by "blunting" the stressor, show better adjustment when they are not given detailed information.

Perspective and Prospects

Physiologist Walter B. Cannon was among the first scientists to describe how people respond to stressful circumstances. When faced with a threat, one's body mobilizes for "fight or flight." One's heart rate increases, one begins to perspire, one's muscles tense, and one undergoes other physiological changes to prepare for action—either to confront the stressor or to flee the situation.

Physician Hans Selye examined the fight-or-flight response in more detail by studying physiological changes in rats exposed to stress. He identified three stages of reaction to stress, which he collectively termed the general adaptation syndrome

(GAS). This includes an initial alarm reaction, followed by a stage of resistance, and finally by a stage of exhaustion, which results from long-term unabated exposure to stress and produces irreversible physiological damage. Selye also brought attention to the idea that not only clearly aversive events (for example, the death of a spouse or a jail sentence) but also events that appear positive (for example, a promotion at work or meeting new friends) may be stressful because they involve changes to which people must adapt. Thus, these ostensibly positive events (which he called eustress) will produce the nonspecific physiological stress response just as obviously negative events (which he called distress) will.

How an individual cognitively appraises an event is the most important determinant of whether that event will be perceived as stressful by that person. Psychologist Richard S. Lazarus has delineated three important cognitive mechanisms (primary appraisals, secondary appraisals, and coping strategies) that determine perceptions of stressfulness and how people alter appraisals. Primary appraisal refers to an assessment of whether a situation is neutral, challenging, or potentially harmful. When a situation is judged to be harmful or threatening, a secondary appraisal is made of the coping options or maneuvers that the individual has at his or her disposal. Actual coping strategies that may be used are problem focused (those that involve altering the circumstances that are eliciting the stress response) or emotion focused (those that involve directly lowering physiological arousal or the cognitive determinants of the stress response). Psychologists have used concepts such as these to develop stress management procedures that help people control stress in their everyday lives.

Bibliography

Brady, Joseph Vincent. "Ulcers in Executive Monkeys." *Scientific American* 199 (October, 1958): 95-98. This article describes a classic series of studies in which monkeys subjected to psychological stress in a laboratory apparatus developed gastrointestinal lesions.

Cox, Tom, et al., eds. *Encyclopedia of Stress.* 3 vols. San Diego: Academic Press, 2000. The first comprehensive reference source on stressors, the biological mechanisms involved in the stress response, the effects of activating the stress response mechanisms, and the disorders that may arise as a consequence of acute or chronic stress.

Hobfoll, Stevan E. *Stress, Culture, and Community: The Psychology and Philosophy of Stress.* New York: Plenum Press, 1998. Focuses on how stress evolves and is resolved in the interplay between individuals and their social connections with family and culture.

Kaplan, Howard B., ed. *Psychosocial Stress: Perspectives on Structure, Theory, Life-Course, and Methods.* New York: Harcourt Brace, 1999. Brings researchers, clinicians, and academics up to date on the many facets of research on stress. Includes bibliographical references and indexes.

Lazarus, Richard S., and Susan Folkman. *Stress, Appraisal, and Coping.* New York: Springer, 1984. Lazarus and Folkman review the history and development of the concepts of stress and coping. The book, which is organized around their cognitive appraisal theory of emotion, includes sections on coping and health and adaptation, and on approaches to stress management.

Rodin, Judith. "Managing the Stress of Aging." In *Coping and Health*, edited by Seymour Levine and Holger Ursin. New York: Plenum Press, 1980. In this chapter, Rodin emphasizes that stress produced by the perception of loss of personal control is particularly prevalent among the elderly. She describes interventions and coping-skills training techniques that have been useful in enhancing the sense of control and reducing the stress levels of institutionalized older people.

Seligman, Martin E. P. *Helplessness: On Depression, Development, and Death.* San Francisco: W. H. Freeman, 1975. Seligman describes how being placed in a situation in which one is powerless to influence important outcomes produces "learned helplessness" and associated stress and depression. Many examples from studies with animals and humans are given. Ways of combating learned helplessness by giving people progressively greater control are also described.

Toates, Fredrick, and Milton Keynes. *Stress: Conceptual and Biological Aspects.* New York: John Wiley & Sons, 1996. Describes the relationship between behavioral phenomena and the biological foundations of stress.

Stephen M. Auerbach

See also:

Anxiety Disorders; Biofeedback and Relaxation; Depression; Phobias; Posttraumatic Stress; Stress: Behavioral and Psychological Responses; Stress: Coping Strategies; Stress: Physiological Responses; Stress: Prediction and Control.

STRESS
Behavioral and Psychological Responses

Type of psychology: Stress
Fields of study: Coping; critical issues in stress; stress and illness

Stress is an adaptive reaction to circumstances that are perceived as threatening. It motivates people and can enhance performance. Learning to cope with adversity is an important aspect of normal psychological development, but exposure to chronic stress can have severe negative consequences if effective coping mechanisms are not learned.

Principal terms

COPING STRATEGIES: techniques used to lower one's stress level
DAILY HASSLES: seemingly minor everyday events that are a constant source of stress
PHOBIAS: stresses induced by unrealistic fear of specific situations
STATE ANXIETY: often used interchangeably with *fear* and *stress;* denotes a momentary, transitory reaction to a situation that is perceived as threatening or dangerous
TRAIT ANXIETY: relatively stable individual differences in proneness to experience state anxiety; people high in trait anxiety are especially threatened by situations involving fear of failure or social/interpersonal threats

Overview

The term "stress" is used to designate how human beings respond when they confront circumstances that they appraise as dangerous or threatening and that tax their coping capability. Stressful events (stressors) elicit a wide range of responses in humans. They not only bring about immediate physiological changes but also affect one's emotional state, the use of one's intellectual abilities and one's efficiency at solving problems, and one's social behavior. When experiencing stress, people take steps to do something about the stressors eliciting the stress and to manage the emotional upset they are producing. These maneuvers are called coping responses. Coping is a key concept in the study of the stress process. Stress-management intervention techniques are designed to teach people the appropriate ways to cope with the stressors that they encounter in their everyday lives.

The emotional state most directly affected by stress is anxiety. In fact, the term "state anxiety" is often used interchangeably with the terms "fear" and "stress" to denote a transitory emotional reaction to a dangerous situation. Stress, fear, and state anxiety are distinguished from trait anxiety, which is conceptualized as a relatively stable personality disposition or trait. According to psychologist Charles

Spielberger, people high in trait or "chronic" anxiety interpret more situations as dangerous or threatening than do people who are low in trait anxiety, and they respond to them with more intense stress (state anxiety) reactions. Instruments that measure trait anxiety ask people to characterize how they usually feel, and thus they measure how people characteristically respond to situations. Measures of trait anxiety (such as the trait anxiety scale of the State-Trait Anxiety Inventory) are especially useful in predicting whether people will experience high levels of stress in situations involving threats to self-esteem or threat of failure at evaluative tasks.

Common phobias or fears of specific situations, however, especially when the perceived threat has a strong physical component, are not related to individual differences in general trait anxiety level. Measures of general trait anxiety are therefore not good predictors of people's stress levels when they are confronted by snakes, an impending surgical operation, or the threat of electric shock. Such fears can be reliably predicted only by scales designed to evaluate proneness to experience fear in these particular situations.

Seemingly minor events that are a constant source of irritation can be very stressful, as can more focalized events that require major and sometimes sudden readjustments. Psychologists Richard Lazarus and Susan Folkman have dubbed these minor events "daily hassles." The media focus attention on disasters such as plane crashes, earthquakes, and epidemics that suddenly disrupt the lives of many people, or on particularly gruesome crimes or other occurrences that are likely to attract attention. For most people, however, much of the stress of daily life results from having to deal with ongoing problems pertaining to jobs, personal relationships, and everyday living circumstances. According to Lazarus and Folkman, exposure to such daily hassles is actually more predictive of negative health outcomes than is frequency of exposure to major life events.

People often have no actual experience of harm or unpleasantness regarding things that they come to fear. For example, most people are at least somewhat uneasy about flying on airplanes or about the prospect of having a nuclear power plant located near them, though few people have personally experienced harm caused by these things. Although people tend to pride themselves on how logical they are, they are often not very rational in appraising how dangerous or risky different events actually are. For example, there is great public concern about the safety of nuclear reactors, though they in fact have caused very few deaths. The same general public that smokes billions of cigarettes (a proved carcinogen) per year also supported banning an artificial sweetener because of a minuscule chance that it might cause cancer.

People tend to think of stress as being uniformly negative—something to be avoided or at least minimized as much as possible. Psychologists Carolyn Aldwin and Daniel Stokols point out, however, that studies using both animals and humans have indicated that exposure to stress also has beneficial effects. Rats handled as infants are less fearful, are more exploratory, are faster learners, and have more robust immune systems later in life. In humans, physical stature as adults is greater in cultures that expose children to stress (for example, circumcision, scarification, sleeping apart from parents) than in those that are careful to prevent stress exposure—even when nutrition, climate, and other relevant variables are taken into account. Although failure experiences in dealing with stressful circumstances can inhibit future ability to function under stress, success experiences enable learning of important coping and problem-solving skills that are then used to deal effectively with future stressful encounters. Such success experiences also promote a positive self-concept and induce a generalized sense of self-efficacy that in turn enhances persistence in coping with future stressors.

Stress is a normal, adaptive reaction to threat. It signals danger and prepares people to take defensive action. Over time, individuals learn which coping strategies are successful for them in particular situations. This is part of the normal process of personal growth and maturation. Stress can, however, cause psychological problems if the demands posed by stressors overwhelm a person's coping capabilities. If a sense of being overwhelmed and unable to control events persists over a period of time, one's stress signaling system ceases to work in an adaptive way. One misreads and overinterprets the actual degree of threat posed by situations, makes poor decisions as to what coping strategies to use, and realizes that one is coping inefficiently; a cycle of increasing distress and ineffective coping may result. Some people who have experienced high-level stress for extended periods or who are attempting to deal with the aftereffects of traumatic stressors may become extremely socially withdrawn and show other signs of severe emotional dysfunction.

Applications

The fact that stress has both positive and negative effects can be exemplified in many ways. Interpersonally, stress brings out the worst and the best in people. A greater incidence of negative social behaviors, including less altruism and cooperation and more aggression, has generally been observed in stressful circumstances. Psychologist Kent Bailey points out that, in addition to any learning influences, this may result from the fact that stress signals real or imagined threats to survival and is therefore a potent elicitor of regressive, self-serving survival behaviors. The highly publicized 1964 murder of Kitty Genovese in Queens, New York, which was witnessed by thirty-eight people (from the safety of their apartments) who ignored her pleas for help, exemplifies this tendency, as does the behavior during World War II of many Europeans who either did not stand up for the Jews and other minorities who were oppressed by the Nazis or conveniently turned their heads. Everyone has heard, however, of selfless acts of individual heroism being performed by seemingly ordinary people who in emergency situations rose to the occasion and risked their own lives to save others. Even in a Europe dominated by Adolf Hitler, there were people who risked great harm to themselves and their families to save others. In addition, in stressful circumstances in which cooperation and altruism have survival value for all concerned, as in the wake of a natural disaster, helping-oriented activities and resource sharing are among the most common short-term reactions.

Stress may enhance as well as hinder performance. For example, the classic view of the relationship between stress and performance is represented in the

Yerkes-Dodson inverted-U model, which posits that both low and high levels of arousal decrease performance, whereas intermediate levels enhance performance. Although this model has not been unequivocally validated, it seems to be at least partially correct, and its correctness may depend upon the circumstances. On the one hand, psychologists Gary Evans and Sheldon Cohen concluded that, in learning and performance tasks, high levels of stress result in reduced levels of working-memory capacity and clearly interfere with performance of tasks that require rapid detection, sustained attention, or attention to multiple sources of input. On the other hand, psychologist Charles Spielberger found that in less complex tasks, as learning progresses, high stress levels may facilitate performance.

Psychologist Irving Janis examined the relationship between preoperative stress in surgical patients and how well they coped with the rigors of the postoperative convalescent period. He found that patients with moderate preoperative fear levels adjusted better after surgery than those with low or high preoperative fear. He reasoned that patients with moderate fear levels realistically appraised the situation, determined how they would deal with the stressful aspects of the recovery period, and thus were better able to tolerate those stressors. Patients low in preoperative fear engaged in unrealistic denial and thus were unprepared for the demands of the postoperative period, whereas those high in preoperative fear became overanxious and carried their inappropriately high stress levels over into the recovery period, in which that stress continued to inhibit them from realistically dealing with the demands of the situation. The negative effect of unrealistically low fear levels is also exemplified in the description by psychologists Walter Fenz and Seymour Epstein of two first-time sky divers who surprised everyone with their apparent total lack of concern during training and on the morning of their first jump. Their reactions changed dramatically, however, once they entered the aircraft. "One began vomiting, and the other developed a coarse tremor. Both pleaded for the aircraft to be turned back. Upon leaving, they stated that they were giving up jumping."

Janis's investigation was particularly influential because it drew attention to the question of how psychologists can work with people to help them cope with impending stressful events, especially those (such as surgery) that they are committed to confronting and over which they have little control. Findings by psychologists Thomas Strentz and Stephen Auerbach indicate that in such situations it may be more useful to teach people emotion-focused coping strategies (those designed to minimize stress and physiological arousal directly) than problem-focused strategies (those designed to change the stressful situation itself). In a study with volunteers who were abducted and held hostage for four days in a stressful simulation, they found that hostages who were taught to use emotion-focused coping techniques (such as deep breathing, muscular relaxation, and directed fantasy) adjusted better and experienced lower stress levels than those who were taught problem-focused techniques (such as nonverbal communication, how to interact with captors, and how to gather intelligence).

Perspective and Prospects

Stress has many important adaptive functions. The experience of stress and learning how to cope with adversity is an essential aspect of normal growth and development. Coping strategies learned in particular situations must be generalized appropriately to new situations. Exposure to chronic stress that cannot be coped with effectively can have severe negative consequences. Work by pioneering stress researchers such as Hans Selye brought attention to the physiological changes produced by exposure to chronic stress, which contribute to diseases such as peptic ulcers, high blood pressure, and cardiovascular disorders. Subsequent research by psychiatrists Thomas Holmes and Richard Rahe and their colleagues indicated that exposure to a relatively large number of stressful life events is associated with the onset of other diseases such as cancer and psychiatric disorders, which are less directly a function of arousal in specific physiological systems.

Studies by these researchers have led psychologists to try to understand how best to teach people to manage and cope with stress. Learning to cope with stress is a complex matter because, as Richard Lazarus has emphasized, the stressfulness of given events is determined by how they are cognitively appraised, and this can vary considerably among individuals. Further, the source of stress may be in the past, the present, or the future. The prospect of an impending threatening encounter (such as a school exam) may evoke high-level stress, but people also experience stress when reflecting on past unpleasant or humiliating experiences or when dealing with an immediate, ongoing danger. Sometimes, people deal with past, present, and future stressors simultaneously.

It is important to distinguish among present, past, and future stressors, because psychological and behavioral responses to them differ, and different kinds of coping strategies are effective in dealing with them. For example, for stressors that may never occur but are so aversive that people want to avoid them if at all possible (for example, cancer or injury in an automobile accident), people engage in preventive coping behavior (they stop smoking, or they wear seat belts) even though they are not currently experiencing a high level of anxiety. In this kind of situation, an individual's anxiety level sometimes needs to be heightened in order to motivate coping behavior.

When known stressors are looming (for example, a surgical operation the next morning), it is important to moderate one's anxiety level so that one can function effectively when actually confronting the stressor. The situation is much different when one is trying to deal with a significant stressor (such as sexual assault, death of a loved one, or a war experience) that has already occurred but continues to cause emotional distress. Some persons who cannot adjust adequately are diagnosed as having "post-traumatic stress disorder." Important aspects of coping with such stressors include conceptualizing one's response to the situation as normal and rational rather than "crazy" or inadequate, and reinstatement of the belief that one is in control of one's life and environment rather than subject to the whims of circumstance.

Bibliography

Auerbach, Stephen M. "Assumptions of Crisis Theory and Temporal Model of Crisis Intervention." In *Crisis Intervention with Children and Families*, edited by Stephen M. Auerbach and Arnold L. Stolberg. Washington, D.C.: Hemisphere, 1986. This chapter examines some basic issues pertaining to psychological responses to extremely stressful events, including the role of the passage of time, individual differences, and previous success in dealing with stressful events. Crisis intervention and other stress-management programs are also reviewed.

_____. "Temporal Factors in Stress and Coping: Intervention Implications." In *Personal Coping: Theory, Research, and Application*, edited by B. N. Carpenter. Westport, Conn.: Praeger, 1991. Focuses on how behavioral and psychological stress responses differ depending on whether the stressor is anticipated, currently ongoing, or has already occurred. The types of coping strategies that are likely to be most effective for each kind of stressor are described, and many examples are given.

Briere, John. *Psychological Assessment of Adult Posttraumatic States*. Washington, D.C.: American Psychological Association, 1997. Provides an analysis of posttraumatic disturbance and its measurement. Discussions include the etiology of posttraumatic states, the symptomatology and phenomenology of stress, and structured assessments.

Driskell, James E., and Eduardo Salas, eds. *Stress and Human Performance*. Mahwah, N.J.: Lawrence Erlbaum Associates, 1999. Focuses specifically on how stress impacts performance and on interventions to overcome these effects.

Greenberg, Jerrold S. *Comprehensive Stress Management*. Dubuque, Iowa: Wm. C. Brown, 1990. An easy-to-read text giving an overview of psychological and physiological stress responses and stress-management techniques. Separate sections on applications to occupational stress, the college student, the family, and the elderly.

Janis, Irving Lester. *Psychological Stress*. New York: John Wiley & Sons, 1958. Describes some of Janis's early investigations evaluating relationships between stress and behavior. The focus is on his pioneering study evaluating the relationship between preoperative stress levels in surgical patients and their ability to adapt to the rigors of the postoperative convalescent period.

Møller, Anders Pare, Manfred Milinski, and Peter J. B. Slater, eds. *Stress and Behavior*. San Diego: Academic Press, 1998. Includes discussions of the nature of immunocompetence; developmental instability as a general measure; welfare, stress, and feelings; and skepticism.

Monat, Alan, and Richard S. Lazarus, eds. *Stress and Coping*. 3d ed. New York: Columbia University Press, 1991. This anthology consists of twenty-six brief readings under the headings of effects of stress, stress and the environment, coping with the stresses of living, coping with death and dying, and stress management. The selections are readable as well as informative, and the editors give a useful overview prior to each section in which they summarize the relevance and importance of each reading.

Stephen M. Auerbach

See also:

Anxiety Disorders; Biofeedback and Relaxation; Depression; Phobias; Post-traumatic Stress; Stress; Stress: Coping Strategies; Stress: Physiological Responses; Stress: Prediction and Control.

STRESS
Coping Strategies

Type of psychology: Stress
Fields of study: Coping

When people are exposed to a stressful demand, they respond by coping; coping attempts either to reduce the demand, to reduce its effect, or to help one change the way one thinks about the demand. Coping can either help one in stressful situations or increase the kind and number of problems created by the demand.

Principal terms

COGNITIVE: any activity that involves thought, such as remembering, thinking, or problem solving

COPING: responses which are directed to dealing with demands upon an organism; these responses may either improve or reduce long-term functioning

PROGRESSIVE RELAXATION: a stress-management technique which involves intentionally testing and relaxing each of the major muscles in the body until complete relaxation is achieved

STRESS RESPONSE: the body's response to a demand

STRESSOR: anything that produces a demand on an organism

Overview

Coping includes all the possible responses to stressors in one's environment. As a stressor makes demands on an organism and initiates a stress response, the organism initiates behaviors and thoughts which attempt to remove the stressor or to reinterpret its effects. Coping often reduces the negative effects of the stressor, but sometimes coping creates new and different problems.

Coping strategies may emphasize the physical, social, or psychological components of stress and the stress response. Coping strategies may attempt to eliminate or moderate the initial source of the stress reaction (stimulus-directed coping), reduce the magnitude of the stress response (response-directed coping), or change the way the stressor is perceived (cognitive coping).

The coping strategies directed toward the stressor itself in stimulus-directed coping may eliminate the cause of the problem. The physical changes which occur in response to stress are very much like pain in that they warn that something in the environment is unusual and is a potential threat. Taking action to eliminate the threat not only removes the present demand but also reduces the possibility of continued stress.

Several stress-management techniques are directed toward reducing the influence of the stressor itself. Improving problem-solving skills and knowledge about the problem increases understanding and improves access to solutions. Time-management techniques can also reduce stress by eliminating its source. Solving the most important problems first and improving the quality of time spent on tasks reduces stress by eliminating the problem sooner. Changes in the work environment can also reduce stress. Eliminating sources of stress in the workplace, improving communication between workers and management, allowing workers to have control over their jobs, using workers who are capable of doing the job, and rewarding workers for good job performance can all reduce job-related stress. Sometimes stress reduction involves changing jobs or eliminating the stress-producing activity or relationship. Even with good stimulus-directed coping skills, it is not always possible to eliminate the stressor itself.

Many of the techniques of stress management are directed toward reducing the stress response. The pattern of physiological arousal in a stress response feels uncomfortable to most people; moreover, the related physiological changes can increase one's chances of illness or injury. The stress response is often treated as a physical illness. Prescribed medication, such as tranquilizing drugs, may be provided to reduce the unpleasant symptoms of the stress response such as anxiety, muscle tension, and pain. Sometimes people medicate themselves, choosing alcohol or other nonprescription drugs to reduce the symptoms of the stress response. All these medications do reduce the effects of stress over the short term, but they also tend to create problems of their own. Medications can be habit forming and may continue to be used after the stressful situation is gone. They may promote an artificial contentment and limit the possibility of finding a permanent solution to the problem creating the stress. Tranquilizing medications also tend to produce sleepiness, slowed reaction time, poor coordination, and inhibitions in judgment. These effects may hinder work productivity and safety.

One physical approach to coping with stress involves increasing the level of exercise. Regular strenuous exercise has a wide range of benefits. It reduces tension in muscles, improves cardiac fitness, and improves the functioning of the central nervous system. Muscles, particularly those in the neck and back, tend to react to stress by becoming tight and rigid. This tightness then results in symptoms such as tension headaches and backaches. Exercise promotes cardiac fitness, which improves the strength of the heart and circulatory system and improves the resistance of the circulatory system to the demands of stressful events. Exercise also improves the ability to think clearly, as it improves circulation to the brain. Many traditional athletic activities can help reduce stress (although highly competitive events may add stressors of their own). Athletic activities can also have a psychological impact, as they provide social support and distraction from stressful situations.

The importance of social factors in coping with stress was first proposed by John Cassel in 1974. Friends and family can make it possible to cope more effectively with stressful situations. The freedom to express feelings and to gain insight from hearing the problem described from another perspective can improve understanding of the stressor. The opportunity to gain useful information about problem solving and access to economic or material support makes coping with stressful events and circumstances possible. The impact of social support is reflected in research which suggests that a woman with even one relationship with someone in whom she could confide is 90 percent less likely to suffer from depression than a woman with no close relationships. Family gatherings, recreation, and community activities help to form a social support network which is then available to provide listeners when one needs to talk, advice when one needs to listen, and the tools needed to accomplish the task of coping with stress.

Psychological coping strategies include techniques that change the way one thinks about the stressor or the stress response. Much of the stress response results from one's emotional reaction to events. Cognitive reappraisal and restructuring can help one to think of a stressful event as a positive challenge and can eliminate much of the arousal associated with stress. Imaging techniques are used to help the stressed individual see herself or himself as healthy and as successfully coping with the sources of stress.

Coping can also involve denying that the stressor exists or that it is a problem. Becoming emotionally detached can reduce the harmful effects of stress as physical arousal levels are prevented from increasing in the stressful situation, but this denial can also be harmful if it lasts for a long period of time or if it replaces an attempt to deal with the stressor. Denial of stressful events is seen by many theorists as a major contributor to mental and physical illness.

When considering the many possible approaches to coping with stress, it is important to remember that different individuals and different stressors can make one strategy more effective than another. Each individual will need to explore the options to find the most effective coping strategy.

Applications

Just as the stress response involves a general reaction of the body to a demand, many of the techniques used to cope with stress have an element in common. This common thread can be described as control. If one feels that one is in control of a situation, one is less likely to interpret it as threatening, and therefore stressful. If one learns to control one's thoughts about a stressor or to control one's physical reactions to the stressor, one is more likely to be successful at coping with stress.

Research on the effects of control has included animals and humans and has focused on many different types of control. For example, from what is known about stress, job stress should be related to physical illness, but this is not always found in the research literature. What has been found is that people with both high job demand and a lack of control over their work are more likely to have coronary heart disease.

Some of the earliest research on stress placed monkeys in a problem-solving situation. One monkey could prevent electric shocks from occurring by learning to solve a problem. A second monkey received a shock every time the first monkey did, but could do nothing to prevent the shocks from occurring. At autopsy, the second monkey, with less control over the situation, had more indications of stress-related physiological arousal.

One approach to stress that can give people a feeling of control is to teach them relaxation techniques; these range from meditation to progressive relaxation to biofeedback techniques. One benefit of such techniques is that they reduce or eliminate the temptation to use medication to reduce stress responses. Progressive relaxation, one form of this training, involves tensing specific muscle groups for a brief period and then allowing that group of muscles to relax before continuing to the next. The tension both focuses attention on the muscle to be relaxed and fatigues the tensed muscle, making relaxation easier.

Biofeedback has been used successfully to reduce the physical tensions and resulting pain often associated with the stress response. Biofeedback uses electronic instruments to make physical changes more observable. Instrumentation which measures physical changes in skin temperature, sweating, muscle tension, and blood pressure has been used to make people more aware of their bodies' functions. With training, the individual can learn to reduce the muscle tension which has been producing headaches or to regulate problems causing gastrointestinal activity.

Perspective and Prospects

Stress has been recognized as contributing to mental and physical health and illness, job satisfaction and dissatisfaction, and the ability to perform well in any setting. From Hans Selye's contributions concerning understanding the general nature of the physiological response to stressors to the research connecting the stress response to illness, stress has become a factor to be considered in a wide variety of life situations.

There have been two major approaches to the problem of coping with stress. One has involved the attempt to describe and define stress responses in the hope of determining the causes and controlling factors. The second approach focuses on the control the symptoms presented to doctors and therapists. Defining stress and the stress response includes not only Selye's physiological definition of the stress response but also cognitive factors such as locus of control. Julian Rotter proposed that behavior in and understanding of situations are determined by the perceived source of events. A person with an internal locus of control will feel that he or she is the determining factor in success or failure in life. The person with an external locus of control is more likely to place the responsibility on fate or luck and to feel that his or her action will not make much difference. These two interpretations of events have a number of implications for coping, as the coping strategy chosen may lead to a more effective or less effective solution to the stressful situation.

An external locus of control may lead to less active participation in coping and to more negative outcomes. An internal locus of control has been related to successful therapy and lower levels of depression, suggesting the use of effective coping strategies. Albert Bandura proposed a similar concept: self-efficacy. Individuals who are high in self-efficacy believe that they can change things by taking action. They are more likely to choose coping strategies which attempt to remove or reduce the influence of the stressor rather than withdrawing or denying that the stressor exists and thereby failing to remove its influence.

Bibliography

Charlesworth, Edward A., and Ronald G. Nathan. *Stress Management: A Comprehensive Guide to Wellness.* New York: Atheneum, 1985. This book is easy to understand and provides a description of the stress response; it outlines many of the methods used to cope more successfully. Includes questionnaires to help one to assess one's current functioning as well as excellent and easy-to-follow instructions on relaxation. Cognitive techniques for stress reduction are also described. Sources for tapes and related materials are listed.

Goldberg, Philip. *Executive Health: How to Recognize Health Danger Signals and Manage Stress Successfully.* New York: Business Week, McGraw-Hill, 1978. This book puts stress management into a business context, both for the employee and for management. It provides a good general outline of the problem and suggests possible routes leading to solutions.

Goliszek, Andrew G. *Breaking the Stress Habit: A Modern Guide to One-Minute Stress Management.* Winston-Salem, N.C.: Carolina Press, 1987. This small but impressive book includes a detailed description of the stress response. Questionnaires are included which allow one to examine one's own problems; a wide variety of suggestions for the reduction of stress-related problems is included. Topics include job burnout, stress and aging, and time management, as well as tension-reduction techniques.

Gottlieb, Benjamin H., ed. *Coping with Chronic Stress.* New York: Plenum Press, 1997. Explores the circumstances and experiences that give rise to chronic stress and the ways in which individuals adapt to them.

Kahn, Ada P. *Stress A to Z: A Sourcebook for Facing Everyday Challenges.* New York: Facts on File, 1998. Focuses on practical ways to recognize stress and offers positive advice on how to cope with it.

Powell, Trevor J., and Simon J. Enright. *Anxiety and Stress Management.* New York: Routledge, 1990. This book was written for therapists who must help people deal with anxiety and stress. It is clearly written and can be understood by the layperson. Includes an excellent description of anxiety as a response to stressors and gives the reader an idea of what a therapist might do to help someone suffering from severe problems with stress. Self-help techniques are also explained.

Shaffer, Martin. *Life After Stress.* New York: Plenum Press, 1982. This book is less detailed in its discussion of the stress response and self-assessment of stress levels. It provides relaxation instructions (including photographs) and suggestions for time management, managing work stress, nutrition, exercise, and improving communication and reducing stress in family relationships.

Susan J. Shapiro

See also:

Biofeedback and Relaxation; Post-traumatic Stress; Stress; Stress: Behavioral and Psychological Responses; Stress: Physiological Responses; Stress: Prediction and Control.

STRESS
Physiological Responses

Type of psychology: Stress
Fields of study: Biology of stress; critical issues in stress; stress and illness

The human body contains a number of regulatory mechanisms that allow it to adapt to changing conditions. Stressful events produce characteristic physiological changes that are meant to enhance the likelihood of survival. Because these changes sometimes present a threat to health rather than serving a protective function, researchers seek to determine relations between stressors, their physiological effects, and subsequent health.

Principal terms

FIGHT-OR-FLIGHT RESPONSE: a sequence of physiological changes, described by Walter B. Cannon, that occur in response to threat and prepare the organism to flee from or fight the threat

GENERAL ADAPTATION SYNDROME: a physiological process by which the organism responds to stressors and attempts to reestablish homeostasis; consists of three stages: alarm, resistance, and exhaustion

HOMEOSTASIS: the tendency of the human body to strive toward an optimal or balanced level of physiological functioning

PARASYMPATHETIC NERVOUS SYSTEM: a branch of the nervous system responsible for maintaining or reestablishing homeostasis

STRESS RESPONSE: the physiological, emotional, cognitive, and/or behavioral changes that result from a stressful event, including increased heart rate, anxiety, confused thinking, and/or avoidance behaviors

STRESSOR: any psychological or physical event that produces the physiological, emotional, cognitive, and/or behavioral changes characteristic of a stress response

SYMPATHETIC NERVOUS SYSTEM: a branch of the nervous system that is responsible for activating the fight-or-flight response

Overview

Although the term "stress" is commonly used (if not overused) by the general population to refer to various responses to events that individuals find taxing, the concept involves much more. For centuries, scientific thinkers and philosophers have been interested in learning more about the interactions between the environment (stressful events), emotions, and the body. Much is now known about this interaction, although there is still much left to discover. In the late twentieth century, particularly, much has been learned about how stressful events affect the activity of the body (or physiology); for example, it has been established that these physiological responses to stressors sometimes increase the risk of development or exacerbate a number of diseases. In order best to understand the body's response to stressful events (or stressors), the general sequence of events and the specific responses of various organ systems must be considered.

Almost all bodily responses are mediated at least partially by the central nervous system: the brain and spinal cord. The brain takes in and analyzes information from the external environment as well as from the internal environment (the rest of the body), and it acts to regulate the activities of the body to optimize adaptation or survival. When the brain detects a threat, a sequence of events occurs to prepare the body to fight or to flee the threat. Walter B. Cannon, in the early twentieth century, was the first to describe this "fight-or-flight" response of the body. It is characterized by generalized physiological activation. Heart rate, blood pressure, and respiration increase to enhance the amount of oxygen available to the tissues. The distribution of blood flow changes to optimize efficiency of the tissues most needed to fight or flee: Blood flow to the muscles, brain, and skin increases, while it decreases in the stomach and other organs less important for immediate survival. Increased sweating and muscle tension help regulate the body's temperature and enhance movement if action is needed. Levels of blood glucose and insulin also increase to provide added energy sources, and immune function is depressed. Brain activity increases, resulting in enhanced sensitivity to incoming information and faster reactions to this information.

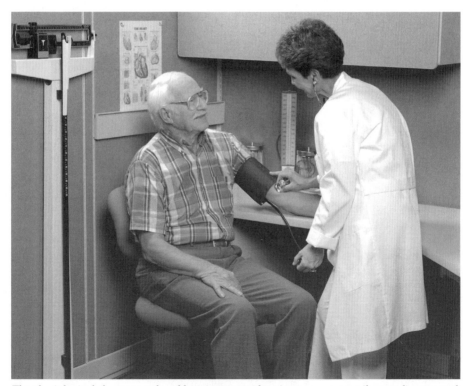

The physiological changes produced by exposure to chronic stress can contribute to diseases such as high blood pressure, peptic ulcers, and cardiovascular disorders. (Digital Stock)

Taken together, these physiological changes serve to protect the organism and to prepare it to take action to survive threat. They occur quite rapidly and are controlled by the brain through a series of neurological and hormonal events. When the brain detects a threat (or stressor), it sends its activating message to the rest of the body through two primary channels, the sympathetic nervous system (SNS) and the pituitary-adrenal axis. The SNS is a branch of the nervous system that has multiple, diffuse, neural connections to the rest of the body. It relays activating messages to the heart, liver, muscles, and other organs that produce the physiological changes already described. The sympathetic nervous system also stimulates the adrenal gland to secrete two hormones, epinephrine and norepinephrine (formerly called adrenaline and noradrenaline), into the bloodstream. Epinephrine and norepinephrine further activate the heart, blood vessels, lungs, sweat glands, and other tissues.

Also, the brain sends an activating message through its hypothalamus to the pituitary gland, at the base of the brain. This message causes the pituitary to release hormones into the bloodstream that circulate to the peripheral tissues and activate them. The primary "stress" hormone released by the pituitary gland is adrenocorticotropic hormone (ACTH), which in turn acts upon the adrenal gland to cause the release of the hormone cortisol. The actions of cortisol on other organs cause increases in blood glucose and insulin, among many other reactions.

In addition to isolating these primary stress mechanisms, research has demonstrated that the body secretes naturally occurring opiates—endorphins and enkephalins—in response to stress. Receptors for these opiates are found throughout the body and brain. Although their function is not entirely clear, some research suggests that they serve to buffer the effects of stressful events by counteracting the effects of the SNS and stress hormones.

One can see that the human body contains a very sophisticated series of mechanisms that have evolved to enhance survival. When stressors and the subsequent physiological changes that are adaptive in the short run are chronic, however, they may produce long-term health risks. This idea was first discussed in detail in the mid-twentieth century by physiologist Hans Selye, who coined the term "general adaptation syndrome" to describe the body's physiological responses to stressors and the mechanisms by which these responses might result in disease. Selye's general adaptation syndrome involves three stages of physiological response: alarm, resistance, and exhaustion. During the alarm stage, the organism detects a stressor and responds with SNS and hormonal activation. The second stage, resistance, is characterized by the body's efforts to neutralize the effects of the stressor. Such attempts are meant to return the body to a state of homeostasis, or balance. (The concept of homeostasis, or the tendency of the body to seek to achieve an optimal, adaptive level of activity, was developed earlier by Walter Cannon.) Finally, if the resistance stage is prolonged, exhaustion occurs, which can result in illness. Selye referred to such illnesses as diseases of adaptation. In this category of diseases, he included hypertension, cardiovascular disease, kidney disease, peptic ulcer, hyperthyroidism, and asthma.

Selye's general adaptation syndrome has received considerable attention as a useful framework within which to study the effects of stressors on health, but there are several problems with his theory. First, it assumes that all stressors produce characteristic, widespread physiological changes that differ only in intensity and duration. There is compelling evidence, however, that different types of stressors can produce very different patterns of neural and hormonal responses. For example, some stressors produce increases in heart rate, while others can actually cause heart rate deceleration. Thus, Selye's assumption of a nonspecific stress response must be questioned. Also, Selye's theory does not take into account individual differences in the pattern of response to threat. Research during the later twentieth century has demonstrated that there is considerable variability across individuals in their physiological responses to identical stressors. Such differences may result from genetic or environmental influences. For example, some studies have demonstrated that normotensive offspring of hypertensive parents are more cardiovascularly responsive to brief stressors than individuals with normotensive parents. Although one might conclude that the genes responsible for hypertension have been passed on from the hypertensive parents, these children might also have different socialization or learning histories that contribute to their exaggerated cardiovascular reactivity to stressors. Whatever the mechanism, this research highlights the point that individuals vary in the degree to which they respond to stress and in the degree to which any one organ system responds.

Applications

Coinciding with the scientific community's growing acknowledgment that stressful events have direct physiological effects, much interest has developed in understanding the relations between these events and the development and/or maintenance of specific diseases. Probably the greatest amount of research has focused on the link between stress and heart disease, the primary cause of death in the United States. Much empirical work also has focused on gastrointestinal disorders, diabetes, and pain (for example, headache and arthritis). Researchers are beginning to develop an understanding of the links between stress and immune function. Such work has implications for the study of infectious disease (such as flu and mononucleosis), cancer, and acquired immunodeficiency syndrome (AIDS).

A number of types of research paradigms have been employed to study the effects of stressors on health and illness. Longitudinal studies have identified a number of environmental stressors that contribute to the development or exacerbation of disease. For example, one study of more than four thousand residents of Alameda County, California, spanning two decades, showed that a number of environmental stressors such as social isolation were significant predictors of mortality from all causes. Other longitudinal investigations have linked stressful contexts such as loud noise, crowding, and low socioeconomic status with the onset or exacerbation of disease.

A major drawback of such longitudinal research is that no clear conclusions can be made about the exact mechanism or mechanisms by which the stressor had its impact on health. Although it is possible, in the Alameda County study, that the relationship between social isolation and disease was mediated by the SNS/hormonal mechanisms already discussed, individuals who are isolated also may be less likely to engage in health care behaviors such as eating healthy diets, exercising, and maintaining preventive health care. Thus, other research paradigms have been used to try to clarify the causal mechanisms by which stressors may influence particular diseases. For example, laboratory stress procedures are used by many scientists to investigate the influence of brief, standardized stressors on physiology. This type of research has the advantage of being more easily controlled. That is, the researcher can manipulate one or a small number of variables (for example, noise) in the laboratory and measure the physiological effects. These effects are then thought to mimic the physiological effects of such a variable in the natural environment.

This research primarily is conducted to ask basic questions about the relations between stressors, physiology, and subsequent health. The findings also have implications, however, for prevention and intervention. If a particular stressor is identified that increases risk of a particular disease, prevention efforts could be developed to target the populations exposed to this stressor. Prevention strategies might involve either modifying the stressor, teaching people ways to manage more effectively their responses to it, or both.

During the last two or three decades, applied researchers have attempted to develop intervention strategies aimed at controlling the body's physiological re-sponses to stress. This work has suggested that a number of stress management strategies can actually attenuate physiological responsivity. Most strategies teach the individual some form of relaxation (such as deep muscle relaxation, biofeed-back, hypnosis, or meditation), and most of this work has focused on populations already diagnosed with a stress-related disease, such as hypertension, diabetes, or ulcer. The techniques are thought to produce their effects by two possible mecha-nisms: lowering basal physiological activation (or changing the level at which homeostasis is achieved) and/or providing a strategy for more effectively respond-ing to acute stressors to attenuate their physiological effects. Research has not proceeded far enough to make any statements about the relative importance of these mechanisms. Indeed, it is not clear whether either mechanism is active in many of the successful intervention studies. While research does indicate that relaxation strategies often improve symptoms of stress-related illnesses, the causal mechanisms of such techniques remain to be clarified.

Perspective and Prospects

The notion that the mind and body are connected has been considered since the writings of ancient Greece. Hippocrates described four bodily humors (fluids) that he associated with differing behavioral and psychological characteristics. Thus, the road was paved for scientific thinkers to consider the interrelations between environment, psychological state, and physiological state (that is, health and illness). Such considerations developed most rapidly in the twentieth century, when advancements in scientific methodology permitted a more rigorous exami-nation of the relationships among these variables.

In the early twentieth century, Walter B. Cannon was the first to document and discuss the "fight-or-flight response" to threatening events. He also reasoned that the response was adaptive, unless prolonged or repeated. In the 1940's, two physicians published observations consistent with Cannon's of an ulcer patient who had a gastric fistula, enabling the doctors to observe directly the contents of the stomach. They reported that stomach acids and bleeding increased when the patient was anxious or angry, thus documenting the relations between stress, emotion, and physiology. Shortly after this work was published, Hans Selye began reporting his experiments on the effects of cold and fatigue on the physiology of rats. These physical stressors produced enlarged adrenal glands, small thymus and lymph glands (involved in immune system functioning), and increased ulcer formation.

Psychiatrists took this information, along with the writings of Sigmund Freud, to mean that certain disease states might be associated with particular personality types. Efforts to demonstrate the relationship between specific personality types and physical disease endpoints culminated in the development of a field known as psychosomatic medicine. Research, however, does not support the basic tenet of this field, that a given disease is linked with specific personality traits; thus, psychosomatic medicine has not received much support from the scientific community. The work of clinicians and researchers in psychosomatic medicine paved the way for late twentieth century conceptualizations of the relations between stress and physiology. Most important, biopsychosocial models that view the individual's health status in the context of the interaction between his or her biological vulnerability, psychological characteristics, and socio-occupational environment have been developed for a number of physical diseases.

Future research into individual differences in stress responses will further clarify the mechanisms by which stress exerts its effects on physiology. Once these mechanisms are identified, intervention strategies for use with patients or for prevention programs for at-risk individuals can be identified and implemented. Clarification of the role of the endogenous opiates in the stress response, for example, represents an important dimension in developing new strategies to enhance individual coping with stressors. Further investigation of the influence of stressors on immune function should open new doors for prevention and intervention, as well.

Much remains to be learned about why individuals differ in their responses to stress. Research in this area will seek to determine the influence of genes, environment, and behavior on the individual, elucidating the important differences between stress-tolerant and stress-intolerant individuals. Such work will provide a better understanding of the basic mechanisms by which stressors have their effects, and should lead to exciting new prevention and intervention strategies that will enhance health and improve the quality of life.

Bibliography

Briere, John. *Psychological Assessment of Adult Posttraumatic States*. Washington, D.C.: American Psychological Association, 1997. Provides an analysis of post-traumatic disturbance and its measurement. Discussions include the etiology of post-traumatic states, the symptomatology and phenomenology of stress, and structured assessments.

Fuller, M. G., and V. L. Goetsch. "Stress and Stress Management." In *Behavior and Medicine*, edited by Danny Wedding. New York: Mosby-Year Book, 1990. Provides an overview of the field, focusing particularly on the physiological response to stress.

Hubbard, John R., and Edward A. Workman, eds. *Handbook of Stress Medicine: An Organ System Approach*. Boca Raton, Fla.: CRC Press, 1997. Focuses on the relationship between stress and the physiology and pathology of the major organ systems of the body.

Jacobson, Edmund. *You Must Relax*. New York: McGraw-Hill, 1934. A rare classic which may be available in the special collections section of the library. Jacobson is considered the founder of modern relaxation training. This book is worth seeking for the pictures of Jacobson's patients after undergoing his relaxation procedure as well as for Jacobson's thoughtful insights.

Lovallo, William R. *Stress and Health: Biological and Psychological Interactions*. Thousand Oaks, Calif.: Sage Publications, 1997. Introduces the concept of psychological stress, its physiological mechanisms, and its effects on health and disease. Includes bibliographical references and indexes.

Rabin, Bruce S. *Stress, Immune Function, and Health: The Connection*. New York: Wiley-Liss, 1999. Provides introductory coverage of stress and the complex relationship among the immune, endocrine, and nervous systems.

Selye, Hans. *The Stress of Life*. New York: McGraw-Hill, 1956. A thoroughly readable account of Selye's work and thinking about stress and health. Available at most bookstores, a must for those interested in learning more about stress.

Toates, Fredrick, and Milton Keynes. *Stress: Conceptual and Biological Aspects*. New York: John Wiley & Sons, 1996. Describes the relationship between behavioral phenomena and the biological foundations of stress.

Virginia L. Goetsch
Kevin T. Larkin

See also:

Abnormality: Biomedical Models; Biofeedback and Relaxation; Psychosomatic Disorders; Stress; Stress: Behavioral and Psychological Responses; Stress: Coping Strategies; Stress: Prediction and Control.

STRESS
Prediction and Control

Type of psychology: Stress
Fields of study: Coping

Foreknowledge of stress and various forms of control over potential or pending stressors affects the negative psychological and physiological effects of those stressors. The ability to predict and exercise some form of control over stressors is a useful and necessary addition to effective coping repertoires.

Principal terms

AVERSIVE: unpleasant, threatening, and/or painful

COGNITIVE: of or relating to thoughts or ideas

CONDITIONED: learned through the process of conditioning by association or through trial and error

HYPOTHESIS: a theoretical assumption or guess that is subject to proof or disproof

NONCONTINGENCY: nondependency or absence of any relationship between two variables

PSYCHOPHARMACOLOGICAL: pertaining to chemicals or drugs that have effects on mental states

STIMULUS: any action or situation that elicits a response; can be internal (thoughts, feelings) or external (people, events, sounds)

STRESSOR: a stimulus that produces a state of psychological or physiological tension

Overview

Stress is a ubiquitous phenomenon in human life. Though it may in some cases be beneficial, attention is ordinarily drawn to its negative effects. In that regard, stress is both a psychological and physiological response to aversive life events, situations, and stimuli, as well as to an accumulation of or overexposure to mundane stimuli or common hassles. Because of the primary or secondary role of stress in most medical and psychological pathology, stress management and coping exact considerable attention from both professionals and laypeople.

With rare exceptions, everyone faces—at some time or another in their lives—the necessity of experiencing a stressor that is unavoidable, such as the need to leave home for the first time, taking a crucial test for which one is unprepared, or undergoing a painful or life-threatening medical procedure. Most people would agree that being able to predict the onset and intensity of such stressors seems to make them somehow more tolerable. Prediction allows people to make defensive preparations, to develop new coping methods, and to brace themselves for the ordeal to come. As a matter of fact, prediction is apparently so important that humans would prefer to suffer a painful stressor immediately rather than tolerate an uncertain postponement.

In two 1966 studies, Pietro Badia and his colleagues found that humans given a choice of being shocked immediately or with a variable amount of delay showed a distinct preference for getting it over with immediately. If humans or animals must tolerate a delay in experiencing something stressful and unpleasant, it would appear that both prefer some sort of signal preceding and announcing that stressor. Badia and his colleagues demonstrated, for example, that rats not only preferred signaled shocks but also were willing to tolerate longer and more intense shocks, providing they were announced.

According to Russell G. Geen, two hypotheses have been proposed to account for the signal preferences. The first is the preparatory-response hypothesis, which suggests that the signal sets off automatic or conditioned anticipatory defense reactions, making the stressor more tolerable. The second is the safety-signal hypothesis, which proposes that the signal makes the intervening time until stressor onset more tolerable. Both hypotheses emphasize the notion that stressor predictability provides people with a sense of control that serves to moderate stress effects.

Humans are able to tolerate life better when they have, or believe they have, a fair amount of control over their day-to-day lives. Knowing what is happening is preferable to being in the dark, having a strategy or defense ready is preferable to being unprepared, and being able to avoid or terminate a stressor is better than sitting there and suffering. In 1973, James R. Averill described behavioral, cognitive, and decisional methods of stress control. He first delineated two kinds of behavioral control: self-regulation and stressor modification. With self-regulation, people can choose to self-administer the inescapable stressor, or they can choose when and/or where to suffer the stressor. Research has shown that humans prefer to self-administer painful stimuli such as electric shocks, a finding that mirrors the relatively common tendency for people to want, for example, to remove their own splinter.

Stressor modification, on the other hand, involves being able to escape, avoid, or reduce the aversiveness of the stressor. A number of studies have demonstrated, for example, that subjects who know that they have the means to terminate a stressor suffer less physical stress than subjects who believe that they have no control. Note that it is the individual's belief in his or her ability to control and not the actual exercise of control that appears to reduce the stress.

Frequently, however, people are powerless to self-regulate or modify a stressor. In those cases, information about the stressor can provide people with a sense of control through the use of cognitive processes. Cognitive processes can moderate or minimize the effects of stressors in several possible ways. For example, detailed prescience of a stressor allows the individual to focus on less harmful or threatening aspects of the stressor or to think about the stressor differently (to see it as a challenge rather than a threat). In addition, one can tolerate a stressor better by knowing the nature of the discomfort the stressor will cause and how the stressor will materialize. Research is generally supportive of the idea that having information about an otherwise uncontrollable stressor allows people to rid themselves of uncertainty about the stressor and to eliminate any stress resulting from that uncertainty.

Decision control has to do with the individual's perception that he or she is free to choose between alternative stressors. Despite how distasteful any two or three alternative aversive events may be, the freedom to choose between them tends to reduce the overall level of stress. Having choices—even unpleasant choices— gives one a sense of control and acts to moderate stress. On the other hand, the effects of a perceived loss or absence of control can result in reactance (a struggle to gain control) or, at the other extreme, a form of learned helplessness (a surrender to the stressor and all of its effects).

Applications

Stress prediction and control lends itself to a wide variety of mundane applications as well as to broader social and individual issues, such as crowding, learned helplessness, and individual differences in stress proneness.

In the physician's or dentist's office, many things take place that are stressful to the uninformed or timid soul. For example, an individual who is about to undergo his or her first root canal procedure may find the pending event threatening and consequently stressful. Stress in this case results from uncertainty about the qualitative effects of the procedure, expectations of pain and discomfort, and feelings of lack of control. Technology and training provide the contemporary dentist with the means to minimize pain and discomfort and to describe accurately the sensations associated with various aspects of the procedure. Such information provides the basis for cognitive control and a reduction in the overall level of stress. When behavioral control is impossible, information can become the instrumentality of control.

In general, humans seem to have a need for control, even in the absence of clearly identifiable stressors. A perceived lack of control in the face of ambient nonnoxious stimuli can also be stressful. How the individual responds to perceived lack of control forms the basis for the discussion of such phenomena as crowding, learned helplessness, and the Type A coronary stress-prone pattern.

As the earth's population increases, the effect of crowding on human behavior becomes a matter of increasing concern. There is a prevalent—but not universally held—view that crowding is stressful. There is, however, no consensus about the reasons for the stressfulness of crowding.

Those who study crowding generally agree that density is a necessary, but not sufficient, factor in crowding. Crowding is therefore regarded as a subjective aversive feeling that may or may not be related to objective density. Two hypotheses tie density to crowding. The first hypothesis suggests that feelings of crowding happen when density is perceived to constrain behavior, such as when heavy freeway traffic blocks freedom of movement. This loss of freedom is a threat to behavioral and decisional control that results in negative affect or stress.

The second hypothesis is that the individual feels crowded when the near presence of others is unpleasantly arousing or overstimulating. When overaroused, the individual suffers impaired coping and decision-making capabilities. Again, the perception of crowding is subjective and is often mitigated by situational or cultural norms. For example, the density one comfortably sustains at the well-attended football game would likely be intolerable in one's own living room. Thus situational density norms moderate the feeling of loss of control, which, as suggested earlier, tends to be inherently stressful.

Elevators provide natural settings for studying the effects of crowding. There are many behavioral indicators of the increasing discomfort people suffer as the elevator fills to capacity. People stand facing the door with eyes cast downward, fixed straight ahead, or focused on the elevator floor indicator as if exercising some form of psychokinesis. Occupants generally attempt to maintain some semblance of interpersonal spacing, however crowded the elevator becomes. Only the individuals standing by—and commanding—the control panels manifest something different in the way of behavior as they press the buttons. Indeed, in 1978, Judith Rodin and her colleagues found that elevator occupants who stand away from elevator controls report feeling more crowded, more aroused, and less in control.

Generally speaking, when individuals perceive a loss of control in the face of an imminent stressor, there is an attempt to adjust or cope with the stressor (for example, to reestablish control by running away from it). There are times, however, when the means of regaining control is not manifest—when there is no apparent way to cope. In the absence of any control, the individual may develop a sense of helplessness that causes him or her to suffer the stressor and its effects. Sometimes after repeated instances of an inability to control outcomes, the individual may develop the belief that he or she is incapable of coping, even in cases where the means of control exist. This generalization of one's inability to control and to suffer whatever the stressor has to hand out is called "learned helplessness."

That learned helplessness exists is probably not arguable. Depressed patients often manifest an unreasonable resignation to whatever might go wrong. Some people attribute the passivity of some Jews in Nazi extermination camps to the phenomenon of learned helplessness. Some evidence, however, tends to suggest that learned helplessness in the face of stressors of any kind is not so much the result of noncontingency between behavior and outcomes as it is a function of personality and attributional style.

Some humans carry on a mighty struggle for control of themselves and their surroundings, while others manifest no such need. People who manifest the competitive, hostile, impatient, and aggressive characteristics that typify the Type A coronary stress-prone pattern seem, according to David Glass, to react to threats to their control and freedom with vigorous actions to regain their sense of command. If the Type A person's struggle to regain control is unsuccessful, frustration, exhaustion, and a drastic decrease in attempts to control will follow. Repeated failure at attempts to control robs Type A people of their motivation and renders them helpless.

Perspective and Prospects

According to Charles Spielberger, the term "stress" is a Latin derivative that was "first used during the 17th century to describe distress, oppression, hardship, and adversity." In the eighteenth and nineteenth centuries, the meaning of stress changed to that of some pressure or force acting on a physical object or person resulting in some form of strain, possibly the basis for the colloquial phrase "stress and strain." During the nineteenth century, speculation about the connection between stress and illness began, but it was not until the early twentieth century that professionals, such as the distinguished Canadian physician Sir William Osler, began to make the connection between stress, worry, and heart disease.

The massive contemporary interest in stress, its ill effects, and its management, including prediction and control, found its impetus in the work of physician and researcher, Hans Selye. In 1936, Selye described a systematic and progressive physiological reaction to unremitting stressors that he called the general adaptation syndrome (GAS) or the biologic stress syndrome. Selye's work highlights the human body's innate defensive response to perceived threats, whether physical or psychological, internal or external.

Much has been learned about the details of the physiological stress reaction since 1936, especially about the role of the sympathetic nervous system and hormones. This acquired knowledge has led to the discovery of psychopharmacological agents (for example, tranquilizers) that control, relieve, or combat the physical and mental effects of stress. Such remedies, however, require medical prescription and supervision, do not eliminate or affect stress at its origins, and provide only symptomatic relief.

Increasing attention has therefore been given to nonchemical means of controlling or eliminating stress and its effects. Such means include relaxation techniques, lifestyle changes, biofeedback techniques, and the development of behavioral, cognitive, and decisional controls over stressors. Researchers have also investigated other possible influential factors, such as individual differences in stress vulnerability or proneness as well as individual differences in stress perception.

Stress prediction and control as a means of softening or eliminating stress will be a continuing subject of research and individual stress management development for the foreseeable future. The effects of relaxation techniques and stress prediction and control on stress effects accentuate the human potential for self-prevention, control, and healing of stress effects. Maximizing and mastering this human potential has highly beneficial portents for health, happiness, and the lowering of health care costs.

Bibliography

Averill, James R. "Personal Control over Aversive Stimuli and Its Relationship to Stress." *Psychological Bulletin* 80, no. 4 (1973): 286-303. Original presentation of author's descriptive hypothetical scheme for behavioral, cognitive, and decisional control of stressors.

Geen, Russell G. "The Psychology of Stress." In *Personality: The Skein of Behavior*. St. Louis: C. V. Mosby, 1976. Survey of research relating to helplessness, uncertainty, stress, and control.

Geen, Russell G., William W. Beatty, and Robert M. Arkin. "Stress and Motivation." In *Human Motivation: Physiological, Behavioral, and Social Approaches*. Boston: Allyn & Bacon, 1984. Addresses stress prediction and control, including principal applications to such phenomena as crowding and learned helplessness.

Goldberger, Leo, and Shlomo Breznitz, eds. *Handbook of Stress: Theoretical and Clinical Aspects.* New York: Free Press, 1982. Comprehensive compendium of articles by noted researchers of stress processes, stressors, treatment, management, and support.

Gottlieb, Benjamin H., ed. *Coping with Chronic Stress.* New York: Plenum Press, 1997. Explores the circumstances and experiences that give rise to chronic stress and the ways in which individuals adapt to them.

Kahn, Ada P. *Stress A to Z: A Sourcebook for Facing Everyday Challenges.* New York: Facts on File, 1998. Focuses on practical ways to recognize stress and offers positive advice on how to cope with it.

Spielberger, Charles Donald. *Understanding Stress and Anxiety.* New York: Harper & Row, 1979. Stress manual by a stress researcher and specialist. Discusses what stress is, what its sources are, and how to adjust to and live with others.

Ronald G. Ribble

See also:

Anxiety Disorders; Biofeedback and Relaxation; Stress; Stress: Behavioral and Psychological Responses; Stress: Physiological Responses; Stress: Prediction and Control.

SUBSTANCE ABUSE

Type of psychology: Psychopathology
Fields of study: Biological treatments; nervous system; substance abuse

Substance abuse is the use of any substance in amounts or frequencies that violate social, personal, or medical norms for physical or behavioral health; these substances are often addictive.

Principal terms

DEPENDENCE: the presence of withdrawal signs when use of a substance is discontinued

HALLUCINOGENS: drugs that can alter perception, including LSD, PCP, peyote, psilocybin, and possibly marijuana

INHALANTS: volatile drugs, including glue, gasoline, propellants, and some anesthetics

OPIATES: substances derived from the opium poppy, including morphine, heroin, codeine, and Demerol

SEDATIVES/HYPNOTICS: nonopiate substances that cause a slowing of behavioral arousal, including alcohol, tranquilizers, and barbiturates

SELF-MEDICATION: a theory that substance abuse is a form of self-treatment in order to alleviate measured or perceived pain/dysphoria

STIMULANTS: drugs that cause behavioral and/or physiological stimulation, including amphetamine, cocaine, and their respective derivatives; caffeine; nicotine; and some antidepressants

TOLERANCE: the need for greater amounts of a substance over time in order to achieve a previous effect

Causes and Symptoms

Substance abuse is studied in psychology from personality, social, and biological perspectives. Social and personality studies of the substance abuser have produced theories with four principal themes: The abuser displays inability to tolerate stress, immaturity in the form of inability to delay gratification, poor socialization, and/or environmental problems. Biological theories of substance abuse maintain that at least two major factors can result in abusive disorders: the need to relieve some form of pain and the seeking of pleasure or euphoria. Pain is broadly defined as any feeling of dysphoria. Because both pain and euphoria can be produced by psychosomatic or somatopsychic events, these two biological categories can subsume most of the stated nonbiological correlates of substance abuse.

There are several forms of substance abuse, including chronic abuse, intermittent abuse (sprees), active abuse that involves drug seeking, and passive abuse that involves unintentional repeated exposure to drugs. In each case, abuse is determined by a physical or psychological reaction or status that violates accepted professional or personal health norms.

Substance abuse may or may not involve the development of tolerance or physical dependence and may or may not result in easily detectable symptomatology. Tolerance, the need for greater amounts or more frequent administration of a substance, can develop over time or can be acute. In addition, the amount of a substance needed to produce tolerance varies widely among drugs and among individuals. Similarly, the withdrawal signs that indicate dependence need not be the same among individuals and are not always obvious, even to the abuser. Thus, an individual can be an "invisible" abuser.

There are several types of abused substances, and some of these are not typically viewed as problematic. Major categories include sedatives/hypnotics, such as alcohol; opiates, such as heroin; stimulants, including cocaine and caffeine; inhalants, such as nitrous oxide ("laughing gas"); and hallucinogens, including phencyclidine (PCP or "angel dust"). Food is an example of a substance not usually considered a substance of abuse, but it has definite abuse potential.

The experience of pain or the seeking of euphoria as causes of substance abuse can be measured physically or can be perceived by the individual without obvious physical indicators. The relative importance of pain and euphoria in determining the development and maintenance of substance abuse requires consideration of the contributions of at least five potential sources of behavioral and physical status: genetic predisposition, dysregulation during development, dysregulation from trauma at any time during the life span, the environment, and learning. Any of these can result in or interact to produce the pain or feelings of euphoria that can lead to substance abuse.

The key commonality in pain-induced substance abuse is that the organism experiences pain that it does not tolerate. Genetic predisposers of pain include inherited diseases and conditions that interfere with normal pain tolerance. Developmental dysregulations include physical and behavioral arrests and related differences from developmental norms. Trauma from physical injury or from environmental conditions can also result in the experience of pain, as can the learning of a pain-producing response.

Several theories of pain-induced substance abuse can be summarized as self-medication theories. In essence, these state that individuals abuse substances in order to correct an underlying disorder that presumably produces some form of dysphoria. Self-medication theories are useful because they take into account the homeostatic (tendency toward balance) nature of the organism and because they include the potential for significant individual differences in problems with pain.

Relief from pain by itself does not account entirely for drug use that goes beyond improvement in health or reachievement of normal status and certainly cannot account entirely for drug use that becomes physically self-destructive (an exception occurs when pain becomes more motivating than the need to preserve life). Thus, the desire for euphoria is also studied. This type of substance abuse can be distinguished from the possible pleasure produced by pain relief because it does not stop when such relief is achieved.

Euphoria-induced substance use, or pleasure seeking, is characteristic of virtually all species tested. The transition from pleasurable use to actual abuse is also widespread, but often limited in other species when life-threatening conditions are produced. Some theorists have proposed that pleasure seeking is an innate drive not easily kept in check even by socially acceptable substitutes. Thus, euphoria-induced substance abuse is conceived of as pleasure seeking gone awry. Other theorists believe that euphoria-induced substance abuse is related to biological causes such as evolutionary pressure. For example, some drug-abuse researchers believe that organisms that could eat rotten, fermented fruit (partly alcohol) may have survived to reproduce when others did not.

Laboratory studies of the biological bases of substance abuse involve clinical (human) and preclinical (animal) approaches. Such research has demonstrated that there are areas of the brain that can provide powerful feelings of euphoria when stimulated, indicating that the brain is primed for the experience of pleasure. Direct electrical stimulation of some areas of the brain, including an area first referred to as the medial forebrain bundle, produced such strong addictive behaviors in animals that they ignored many basic drives including those for food, water, mating, and care of offspring.

Later research showed that the brain also contains highly addictive analgesic and euphoriant chemicals that exist as a normal part of the neural milieu. Thus, the brain is also predisposed to aid in providing relief from pain and has coupled such relief in some cases with feelings of euphoria. It is not surprising, therefore, that substance abuse and addictive behaviors can develop so readily in so many organisms.

Treatment and Therapy

The effects of typical representatives of the major categories of abused substances can be predicted. Alcohol, a sedative/hypnotic, can disrupt several behavioral functions. It can slow reaction time, movement, and thought processes and can interfere with needed rapid eye movement (REM) sleep. It can also produce unpredictable emotionality, including violence. Abusers of alcohol develop tolerance and dependence, and withdrawal can be life-threatening. Heroin, an opiate, has analgesic (pain-killing) and euphoriant effects. It is also highly addictive, but withdrawal seldom results in death. Marijuana, sometimes classified as a sedative, sometimes as a hallucinogen, has many of the same behavioral effects as alcohol. Stimulants vary widely in their behavioral effects. Common to all is some form of physiological and behavioral stimulation. Some, such as cocaine and the amphetamines (including crystal methamphetamine, or "ice"), are extremely addictive and seriously life-threatening and can produce violence. Others, such as caffeine, are relatively mild in their euphoriant effects. Withdrawal from stimulants, especially the powerful forms, can result in profound depression. Hallucinogens are also a diverse group of substances that can produce visual, auditory, tactile, olfactory, or gustatory hallucinations, but most do so in only a small percentage of the population. Some, such as PCP, can produce violent behavior, while others, such as lysergic acid diethylamide (LSD), are not known for producing negative emotional outbursts. Inhalants usually produce feelings of euphoria, but they are seldom used by individuals beyond the adolescent years.

It is noteworthy that some of the pharmacological effects of very different drugs are quite similar. Marijuana and alcohol affect at least three of the same brain biochemical systems. Alcohol can become a form of opiate in the brain following some specific chemical transformations. These similarities raise an old question in substance abuse: Is there a fundamental addictive mechanism common to everyone that differs only in the level and nature of expression? Older theories of drug-abuse behavior approached this question by postulating the "addictive personality," a type of person who would become indiscriminately addicted as a result of his or her personal and social history. With advances in neuroscience have come theories concerning the possibility of an "addictive brain," which refers to a neurological status that requires continued adjustment provided by drugs. This is a modification of self-medication theories.

An example of the workings of the addictive brain might be a low-opiate brain that does not produce normal levels of analgesia or normal levels of organismic and behavioral euphoria (joy). The chemical adjustment sought by the brain might be satisfied by use or abuse of any drug that results in stimulation of the opiate function of the brain. As discussed above, several seemingly unrelated drugs can produce a similar chemical effect. Thus, the choice of a particular substance might depend both on brain status and on personal or social experience with the effects and availability of the drug used.

The example of the opiate-seeking brain raises at least two possibilities for prevention and treatment, both of which have been discussed in substance-abuse literature: reregulation of the brain and substitution. So far, socially acceptable substitutes or substitute addictions offer some promise, but reregulation of the dysregulated brain is still primarily a hope of the future. An example of a socially acceptable substitute might be opiate production by excessive running, an activity that can produce some increase in opiate function. The success of such a substitution procedure, however, depends upon many variables that may be quite difficult to predict or control. The substitution might not produce the required amount of reregulation, the adjustment might not be permanent, and tolerance to the adjustment might develop. There are a host of other possible problems.

Perspective and Prospects

Use and probable abuse of psychoactive substances date from the earliest recorded history and likely predate it. Historical records indicate that many substances with the potential for abuse were used in medicinal and ceremonial or religious contexts, as tokens in barter, for their euphoriant properties during recreation, as indicators of guilt or innocence, as penalties, and in other practices.

Substance abuse is widespread in virtually all countries and cultures, and it can be extremely costly, both personally and socially. There is no doubt that most societies would like to eliminate substance abuse, but current practices have been relatively unsuccessful in doing so. It is obvious that economic as well as social factors contribute both to abusive disorders and to the laws regulating substance use, and possibly create some roadblocks in eliminating abuse.

In psychology, the systematic and popular study of substance abuse became most extensive during the period when such abuse was most popular, the 1960's and 1970's. Research into psychological, social, environmental, therapeutic, and some biological aspects of abuse proliferated during these years, and the reasons proposed to explain abuse disorders were almost as numerous as the authors proposing them. During the early 1980's, drug-abuse research experienced a somewhat fallow period, but with discoveries of the brain mechanisms involved in many disorders, a resurgence has occurred. Many disorders previously thought to be the result of nonbiological factors are now known to have strong neural determinants. Both psychosomatic and somatopsychic events affect the nervous system, and the resurgence of brain-oriented research reflects this understanding.

Future research on substance abuse is likely to focus on more of the biological determinants and constraints on the organism and to try to place substance-abuse disorders more in the contexts of biological self-medication and biological euphoria. Many people erroneously consider biological explanations of problematic behaviors to be an excuse for such behaviors, not an explanation. In fact, discoveries regarding the neural contributions to such behaviors are the basis on which rational therapies for such behaviors can be developed. Recognizing that a disorder has a basis in the brain can enable therapists to address the disorder with a better armamentarium of useful therapeutic tools. In this way, simple management of such disorders can be replaced by real solutions to the problems created by substance abuse.

Bibliography

Bukstein, Oscar Gary. *Adolescent Substance Abuse: Assessment, Prevention, and Treatment.* New York: John Wiley & Sons, 1995. Offers in-depth review of the causes, treatment, and prevention of substance abuse in adolescents. Critically evaluates most theoretical models of drug abuse and abusers and explores a wide range of issues concerning contributing biological factors.

Gomberg, Edith S. Lisanky, and Ted D. Nirenberg, eds. *Women and Substance Abuse.* Norwood, N.J.: Ablex, 1993. Discusses the use of tobacco, alcohol, and other drugs among women in the United States. Includes bibliographical references and indexes.

Hardman, Joel G., and Lee E. Limbird, eds. *Goodman and Gilman's The Pharmacological Basis of Therapeutics.* 9th ed. New York: McGraw-Hill, 1996. A standard reference for students interested in an overview of the pharmacological aspects of selected addictive drugs. Contains a chapter called "Drug Addiction and Drug Abuse." Of greater interest to those interested in pursuing the study of substance abuse from a neurological and physiological perspective.

Julien, Robert M. *A Primer of Drug Action.* 8th ed. New York: W. H. Freeman, 1998. An introductory treatment of types and actions of many abused and therapeutic substances. A useful, quick reference guide for psychoactive effects of drugs used in traditional pharmacological therapy for disorders and of abused substances. Contains good reference lists and appendices that explain some of the anatomy and chemistry required to understand biological mechanisms of substance abuse.

Leavitt, Fred. *Drugs and Behavior.* 3d ed. Thousand Oaks, Calif.: Sage Publications, 1995. Inclusive coverage from a psychological perspective of the effects of drugs on many types of behaviors. Includes sections on licit and illicit drugs, theories of drug use and abuse, prevention and treatment, and development of drugs. Important because it considers the effects of drug use on a large range of behaviors and physical states and because it presents a relatively integrated view of biopsychological information on drugs.

Ray, Oakley Stern, and Charles Ksir. *Drugs, Society, and Human Behavior.* 8th ed. St. Louis: Times Mirror/Mosby, 1999. A good text for the newer student of substance abuse who not only wishes to understand the substances and their biological significance but also is interested in current methods of prevention and treatment. Of special interest are the interspersed history and comments regarding the social aspects of abused substances.

U.S. Department of Health and Human Services. *Drug Abuse and Drug Abuse Research: The First in a Series of Triennial Reports to Congress.* Rockville, Md.: National Institute on Drug Abuse, 1984. An excellent summary of research on selected substances of abuse. The rest of the series should also be of great interest to the reader interested in substance-abuse research. The strength of this series is the understandable language and style used to convey recent research. Treatment, prevention, and specific drug research are summarized, and a well-selected reference list is provided for each chapter.

_____. *Theories on Drug Abuse: Selected Contemporary Perspectives.* Edited by Dan J. Lettieri, Mollie Sayers, and Helen Wallenstein Pearson. Rockville, Md.: National Institute on Drug Abuse, 1980. An older but good compendium of theoretical positions related to the question of substance abuse. Theories covered include the gamut of empirical and nonempirical thought concerning the predisposition to, development of, maintenance of, and possible termination of abuse disorders. Perspectives are biological, personal, and social. Of interest are a quick guide to theory components and an extensive list of references.

Rebecca M. Chesire

See also:

Addictive Personality and Behaviors; Alcoholism; Codependent Personality; Depression; Psychoactive Drug Therapy; Suicide.

SUICIDE

Type of psychology: Psychopathology; stress
Fields of study: Anxiety disorders; critical issues in stress; depression; substance abuse

Suicide is the deliberate taking of one's own life, usually the result of a mental disorder, although sometimes deliberated in the face of life-threatening physical illness.

Principal terms

"NO SUICIDE" CONTRACT: an agreement, verbally or in writing, that a suicidal person will not act on these urges

PSYCHOSOMATIC: referring to physical symptoms caused by psychological problems

RATIONAL SUICIDE: suicide to avoid suffering when there is no underlying cognitive or psychiatric disorder

RITUAL SUICIDE: a formal, ceremonial, and proscribed form of suicide performed for social reasons in Japanese history

SEROTONIN: an abundant chemical nerve signal in the brain which is involved in modulating aggression

SUICIDE CLUSTER: the occurrence of several suicides immediately following a much-publicized suicide

SUICIDE GESTURE: a superficial suicidal action in which the intention is not to die but to solicit help

Causes and Symptoms

Suicide is the deliberate taking of one's own life. Most often, suicidal individuals are trying to avoid emotional or physical pain that they believe they cannot bear. Suicide is seen as a solution to an otherwise insoluble problem. Each year, there are about 30,000 suicides in the United States, with 200,000 family survivors. Women attempt suicide more often than men, but men complete suicide more often than women because men tend to use more lethal means, such as a gun. Adolescents and the elderly are two high-risk groups.

When an individual contemplates suicide to avoid the physical pain of a terminal illness and does not have a mental disorder, that form of suicidal thought is called "rational" suicide. This does not imply that this form of suicide is appropriate, moral, or legal but merely that the suicidal thoughts do not arise from a mental disorder (nonrational). Social views on rational suicide vary by culture. For example, many Dutch people consider rational suicide to be acceptable, whereas most Americans do not.

Most suicidal people encountered by physicians, psychologists, social workers, and other mental health professionals experience suicidal thoughts as a result of a mental disorder. The suicidal thoughts and impulses are seen as symptoms of the

POSSIBLE WARNING SIGNS FOR SUICIDE

- ❖ verbal threats such as "You'd be better off without me" or "Maybe I won't be around anymore"
- ❖ expressions of hopelessness and/or helplessness
- ❖ previous suicide attempts
- ❖ daring and risk-taking behavior
- ❖ personality changes (such as withdrawal, aggression, moodiness)
- ❖ depression
- ❖ giving away prized possessions
- ❖ lack of interest in the future

underlying disorder and require treatment just as any other symptom. The treatment may involve protecting the person against his or her suicidal actions, even to the point of involuntary commitment to a mental hospital.

The rationale behind society's willingness temporarily to deny suicidal individuals' usual civil rights by involuntary commitment is that they are considered to be not "acting in their right mind" by virtue of their mental illness. Thus, they deserve the protection of society until their illness is treated. In fact, suicidal thoughts usually do abate when suicidal patients are treated. The vast majority of these individuals are appreciative afterward; they are glad that they were prevented from killing themselves, as they no longer wish to do so.

The most common mental illness that causes suicidal thoughts is depression. In fact, suicidal thoughts are considered to be a symptom of clinical depression. Other mental disorders associated with suicidal ideation include panic disorders, schizophrenia, alcoholism and other substance abuse disorders, and certain personality disorders.

Although suicide may occur at any time of the year, there is a seasonal variation in its peak incidence. Suicides are most common in both men and women in May; women have a second peak around October and November. This seasonal variation may be attributable to seasonal differences in the incidence of depression.

Why people commit suicide appears to have a multifactorial etiology. There are biological, psychological, and social factors that interact in a complex way to contribute to the causes of suicide in a given individual.

These biological factors include genetic contributions to the development of mental disorders such as clinical depression. In addition, studies have shown that suicidal people have an abnormality in a biochemical nerve communication system within the brain. This system involves a common neurotransmitter, serotonin, which is released at the end of one nerve, travels across a gap to the adjacent nerve, and attaches to that nerve. When the serotonin attaches to the adjacent nerve at a specialized receptor site, it initiates changes within the nerve. In this manner, one nerve communicates with its neighbors. In suicidal patients, the metabolites of serotonin that are found in spinal fluid are present in unusually low quantities. Therefore, it is assumed that inadequate amounts of serotonin exist in the brain at those times. Serotonin is thought to be involved in those areas of the brain that control aggression. Low serotonin levels may increase aggressive urges. In a depressed patient, the aggression is turned inward and the person has thoughts of taking his or her own life.

There is also evidence, although not as strong, that low levels of another neurotransmitter, dopamine, may predispose an individual to suicide. The simple

Studies show that women who attempt suicide are more likely to choose nonviolent and less lethal methods, such as pills, rather than violent and lethal methods, such as guns. (PhotoDisc)

loss of brain cell mass also increases the risk of suicide. This loss occurs with many forms of dementia and to a minor degree from normal aging. It is known that the elderly have an increased risk of completed suicide.

Alcohol and addictive drugs may also cause suicidal ideation. Such thoughts may occur while the individual is intoxicated or during withdrawal. Paradoxically, suicidal thoughts may also arise while the patient is taking antidepressant medications. Fortunately, this side effect is uncommon, arising in approximately 1.5 to 6.5

percent of patients. It does not appear that any one antidepressant is more likely to cause this reaction than another.

Psychological factors contributing to suicide include a depressed and/or anxious mood, hopelessness, and a loss of normal pleasure in life activities. Chronically depressed people often have diminished problem-solving skills during periods of depression and can see no way out of their difficulties; suicide is seen as the only solution. There are also personality characteristics that contribute to suicide. In women, borderline personality disorder is often associated with suicide attempts. This disorder is characterized by widely fluctuating moods, rages, feelings of emptiness or boredom, and unstable relationships.

The social factors involved in suicide include cultural acceptance or rejection of suicide. Japanese people have accepted ritual suicide within their culture and sanction suicide as a response to a severe loss of face or social esteem. The Dutch government has legalized rational suicide, while American society generally has a more negative view of the suicide act. Other social factors that increase the likelihood of suicide include social instability, divorce, unemployment, immigration, and exposure to violence as a child. In the United States, European Americans commit suicide more often than African Americans. Native Americans have a high incidence of suicide. In general, good social support reduces the risk of suicide.

Some patients engage in suicidal gestures; that is, they say they want to kill themselves and take actions such as swallowing some pills or superficially cutting their wrists, but there is no real intention to die. They act this way as a cry for help. For some, this may be the only way to receive attention for what troubles them. Unfortunately, the suicide gesture may go awry and unintended death may occur. Anyone who speaks of suicide or engages in what may appear to be a gesture should be taken seriously.

Most people who are suicidal have ambivalent feelings: Part of them wants to die, part does not. This is one of the reasons that the majority of suicidal people tell others of their intention in advance of their attempts. Most have visited their personal physician in the months prior to the suicide. Adolescents sometimes hint at their wish to die by giving away their prized possessions just prior to an attempt.

Anyone experiencing suicidal thoughts should be thoroughly evaluated by a professional trained in the assessment of suicidal patients. If the risk of suicide is considered to be high enough, the patient will have to be protected. This may require hospitalization, either voluntary or involuntary. It may mean removing suicidal means from that person's environment, such as removing guns from the home. Having someone stay with the patient at all times may be required. These steps should be individualized, taking into account the patient's situation.

Treatment and Therapy
Treatment of the underlying cause of the suicidal ideation is very important. Depression and anxiety can be treated with medications and/or psychotherapy. There are treatment programs for alcoholism and drug abuse. Usually, successful treatment of the underlying mental disorder results in the suicidal thoughts going away.

While they await the resolution of the suicidal ideation, patients need to be offered support and hope. Sometimes, a "no suicide" contract is helpful. This is simply a commitment on the part of the patient not to act on any suicidal thoughts and to contact the health professional if the urges become worse. While this contract may be written down, it is usually verbal.

Suicide prevention includes the early detection and management of the mental disorders associated with suicide. Because social isolation increases the risk of suicide, patients should be encouraged to develop and actively maintain strong social supports such as family, friends, and other social groups (such as church, clubs, and sports teams).

It may also be helpful to provide counseling to teenagers after an acquaintance has committed suicide, as this may prevent social contagion and suicide clusters. A suicide cluster is when several teenagers commit suicide after learning of the suicide of an acquaintance or a person who is attractive to them, such as a music or film star. Suicide clusters have increased among the young.

Family members of a suicide victim often go through a grieving process which is more severe than that which occurs after death from other causes. The stigma of suicide and mental illness is strong, and surviving family members often have greater feelings of both guilt and abandonment. Family survivors also have increased psychosomatic complaints, behavioral and emotional problems, and an increased risk of suicide themselves. Referral to a suicide survivor group may be helpful.

An understanding of the causes, detection, and treatment of suicide has led to the development of a number of suicide hotlines and suicide prevention centers. There is evidence that, after these support groups are introduced into a community, the suicide rate for young women decreases. It is not yet known if they have any effect on other groups, such as young men or the elderly.

Most people who contemplate suicide do not seek professional treatment even if they tell people around them of their suicidal ideas. Thus, it is important for physicians, clergy, teachers, parents, and mental health workers to remain alert to the possibility of suicidal thoughts in those in their care. If someone is depressed or very anxious, they should be asked if they have suicidal thoughts. Such a question will not plant the idea in their heads, and they may be relieved that they are being asked. Once someone with suicidal ideation is identified, evaluation and treatment should proceed quickly. The following sample composite cases illustrate the application of the concepts described in the overview.

Mary is a seventeen-year-old senior in high school. She is from a broken home and was severely abused by her father prior to her parents' divorce ten years ago. Her teachers think that she is a bright underachiever who has a rather dramatic personality. Her friends see her as moody and easily angered. Her relationships with boyfriends are intense and always end with deep feelings of hurt and abandonment. Her mother is best described as cold, aloof, and preoccupied with herself.

Mary is brought to the school counselor by one of her friends when Mary threatens to kill herself and superficially scratches her wrists with a safety pin. The counselor learns that Mary has just broken up with her boyfriend, a young man at a local junior college. She is devastated. When she tried to tell her mother about it, her mother seemed uninterested and said that Mary always makes too much of such little things. It was the next morning that she scratched herself in front of her friend.

While more information is needed, this case illustrates a suicide gesture. In this case, Mary does not want to die but instead wants someone to realize how distressed she is. She feels rejected by her boyfriend and then by her mother. One can suspect a gesture rather than a serious suicide attempt by the superficial, nonlethal means (scratching with a safety pin) and by the likelihood of discovery (done in front of a friend).

Tom is a forty-eight-year-old accountant. He is separated from his wife and three children and lives alone in an apartment. He has no real friends, only drinking buddies. Like his father and two uncles, Tom is an alcoholic. Each day after work, he stops at his favorite bar and drinks between eight and twelve beers.

He is brought to the emergency room of the local hospital by the police, who found him sitting on the steps of a church sobbing. He threatened to kill himself if his wife did not take him back. The emergency room doctor noted the strong odor of alcohol on his breath and ordered a blood alcohol test, which showed that he was legally intoxicated. Tom insisted that he would kill himself by running in front of a moving bus if he could not be with his family. The emergency room doctor had Tom's belt, pocketknife, and potentially dangerous items taken from him and arranged for a staff member to sit with him until he was sober. Six hours later, his blood alcohol had returned to near zero. Tom no longer felt despondent and had no more suicidal thoughts. He was embarrassed by his statements a few hours before. An alcoholism counselor was called, and outpatient treatment for his alcoholism was arranged.

This case illustrates suicidal ideation caused by alcohol intoxication. As often happens, the suicidal ideation resolves when the patient becomes sober. The primary treatment is for the underlying addictive disorder.

Sally is a fifty-three-year-old married mother of two. She is a part-time hairdresser and normally a very active, happy person. For the past three weeks, however, she has gradually lost all interest in her job, her children, her home, and her hobbies. She feels irritable and sad most of the time. Although she is tired, she does not sleep well at night, waking up very early each morning, unable to return to sleep. She is worried by the fact that she is having intrusive thoughts of killing herself. Sally imagines she could end all this dreariness by overdosing on sleeping pills and never waking up. She is a strict Catholic and knows it is against her religion to commit suicide. She calls her parish priest.

After a brief conversation, her priest meets her at the office of a psychiatrist who acts as a consultant for the diocese. The psychiatrist diagnoses major depression as the cause of Sally's suicidal ideation. She has a good social support network, so the psychiatrist decides to treat her as an outpatient and has her agree to a "no suicide" contract. Sally is also started on antidepressant medication, which gradually lifts her depression over a period of two to three weeks. Simultaneously, her suicidal thoughts leave her.

This case illustrates suicidal thoughts caused by depression. If Sally had been more depressed or her suicidal urges stronger, she would probably have needed hospitalization. If she had required hospitalization and had refused to go voluntarily, the psychiatrist could have had her committed according to the laws of the state where he practiced. Most states require a signed statement by two physicians or one physician and a licensed clinical psychologist. They must attest that the patient is a danger to himself or herself and that no less restrictive form of treatment would suffice.

Harry is a sixty-seven-year-old resident of a hospital, where he has been for the past two years. He has a serious neurological disorder called amyotrophic lateral sclerosis (also called Lou Gehrig's disease). It has caused progressive weakness such that he cannot even breathe on his own. Harry is permanently connected to a respirator attached to a tracheotomy tube in his throat. He has few visitors and mostly stares off and thinks.

Harry tells his nurse that he is "sick of it all" and wants his doctors to disconnect him from the respirator and let him die. His neurologist requests a psychiatric evaluation. The psychiatrist confirms the patient's wish to die. There is no evidence of dementia or other cognitive disorder, nor is the patient showing any evidence of a mental illness. Subsequently, a meeting is called of the hospital ethics committee to make recommendations. Membership on the committee includes physicians, nurses, an ethicist, a local minister, and the hospital attorney.

This case illustrates a difficult example of rational suicide. The patient has a desire to die and is not suffering from any mental disorder. In this case, he is requesting not to take his own life actively but to be allowed to die passively by removal of the respirator. Some people do not consider this to be suicide at all. They make a distinction between passively allowing a natural process of dying to occur and actively taking one's own life. If this patient requested a lethal overdose of potassium to be injected into his intravenous tubes, such action would be considered suicide and ethically different. In either event, these matters are more ethical, social, and legal than psychiatric.

Perspective and Prospects

Throughout history, there have been numerous examples of suicide. In Western culture, early views on the subject were mainly from a moral perspective and suicide was viewed as a sin. Mental illness in general was poorly understood and often thought of as weakness of character, possession by evil spirits, or willful bad behavior. Thus, mental illness was stigmatized. Even though society now has a better medical understanding of mental illness, there is still a stigma attached to mental illness and to suicide. This stigma contributes to underdiagnosis and undertreatment of suicidal individuals, as many sufferers are reluctant to come forth with their symptoms.

Yet, suicide remains an important public health problem, as it is the ninth most common cause of death in the United States (although it is third for adolescents and second for young adults). There are about thirty thousand known suicides in the United States annually. The actual incidence may be higher because an unknown number of accidental deaths or untreated illnesses may actually be undiagnosed suicides. Suicide is more common among young adults and the elderly, with a relative sparing of the middle aged. The rate of suicide is rising among teenagers. The lifetime prevalence of suicide attempts among American adults is about 2.9 percent.

As most cases of suicidal ideation never come to the attention of health professionals, a high index of suspicion should be maintained. Those people who express suicidal thoughts should be taken seriously and thoroughly evaluated. Increased levels of awareness of suicide may help to improve detection and treatment of this potentially preventable cause of death.

Bibliography

Aldridge, David. *Suicide: The Tragedy of Hopelessness*. Philadelphia: Jessica Kingsley, 1998. Advocates a holistic approach to treatment that takes into account the social context of the patient and involves family in the intervention process.

Burns, David D. *Feeling Good: The New Mood Therapy*. New York: William Morrow, 1980. This popular book describes a cognitive approach to depression and addresses suicidal thoughts. Intended for the layperson.

DePaulo, J. Raymond, Jr., and Keith R. Ablow. *How to Cope with Depression*. New York: McGraw-Hill, 1989. This book was written by two physicians; DePaulo is a national authority on depression. Contains a full chapter on suicide and depression.

Hafen, Brent Q., and Kathryn J. Frandsen. *Youth Suicide: Depression and Loneliness*. 2d ed. Evergreen, Colo.: Cordillera Press, 1986. An excellent review of all aspects of teenage suicide, with practical suggestions for helping the suicidal young person.

Lester, David. *Making Sense of Suicide: An In-Depth Look at Why People Kill Themselves*. Philadelphia: The Charles Press, 1997. This book may be helpful for beginning counselors and family members or friends interested in learning more about suicidal behavior.

Peck, M. Scott. *Denial of the Soul: Spiritual and Medical Perspectives on Euthanasia and Mortality*. New York: Harmony Books, 1997. This book discusses controversial issues related to euthanasia and suicide.

Stearns, Ann K. *Living Through Personal Crisis*. Chicago: Thomas More Press, 1984. The author is a clinical psychologist who discusses how to deal with losses, including the death of a loved one. There is a short but effective section on recognizing the signs of suicidality and when to seek professional help.

Steinberg, Maurice D., and Stuart J. Youngner, eds. *End-of-Life Decisions: A Psychosocial Perspective*. Washington, D.C.: American Psychiatric Press, 1998. Addresses the role of psychiatry in dealing with issues ranging from terminal illness in children to making difficult treatment decisions for AIDS patients to physician-assisted suicide.

Peter M. Hartmann

See also:

Addictive Personality and Behaviors; Alcoholism; Anxiety Disorders; Child and Adolescent Psychiatry; Dementia; Depression; Geriatric Psychiatry; Grief and Guilt; Neurosis; Schizophrenia; Stress; Teenage Suicide.

TEENAGE SUICIDE

Type of psychology: Psychopathology; stress
Fields of study: Adolescence; critical issues in stress; depression

Teenage suicide is a profoundly tragic and unsettling event. The rise in adolescent suicide has been so dramatic since the 1960's that it cannot be ignored as a passing problem; attention has been directed toward gaining insight into the myths, causes, warning signs, treatments, and preventive measures of adolescent suicide.

Principal terms

BEHAVIORAL PSYCHOLOGY: a school of psychology that studies only observable and measurable behavior

COGNITIVE LIMITATIONS: a lack of development in mental activities such as perception, memory, concept formation, reasoning, and problem solving

COGNITIVE PSYCHOLOGY: a school of psychology devoted to the study of mental processes; behavior is explained by emphasizing the role of thoughts and individual choice regarding life goals

DEPRESSION: a psychological disorder characterized by lowered self-esteem, feelings of inferiority, and sadness

PSYCHODYNAMIC ORIENTATION: psychotherapeutic thinking that is based loosely on the theories of Freud and his theory of psychoanalysis

SUICIDE: self-destruction in which the victim clearly intended to kill himself or herself; the act must be successful to be categorized as suicide

SUICIDE ATTEMPT: a situation in which the individual commits a life-threatening act that does not result in death; the act must have the intent or give the appearance of actually jeopardizing the person's life

Causes and Symptoms

The statistics on teenage suicide are shocking. Suicide is the fifth leading cause of death for those under age fifteen, and it is the second leading cause of death for those ages fifteen to twenty-four. Perhaps even more disturbing are the statistics regarding the classification of attempted suicides. Although it is difficult to determine accurately, it is estimated that for every teenager who commits suicide there are approximately fifty teenagers who attempt to take their own lives. According to John Santrock, as many as two in every three college students has thought about suicide on at least one occasion.

According to Linda Nielson, the dramatic increase in youth suicide is primarily a result of the change in the male suicide rate. From 1970 to 1980, male suicides increased by 50 percent, with only a 2 percent increase among females. Females attempt suicide at higher rates than males but are less likely to suceed. Males are much more likely to use violent and lethal methods, such as shooting or hanging. Females are more likely to use passive means to commit suicide; the use of drugs and poisons, for example, is more prevalent among females than males.

As alarming as these figures may be, it should be noted that suicide is still very rare among the young. The National Center for Disease Control has estimated that suicide claims the lives of only 0.0002 percent of all adolescents. Nevertheless, preventing suicide would save thousands of adolescent lives each year. The problem of suicide is complex, and studying it has been especially difficult because suicidal death is often denied by both the medical professional and the victim's family. The whole subject of suicide is carefully avoided by many people. As a result, the actual suicide rate among adolescents may be significantly higher than the official statistics indicate.

There are no simple answers to explain why adolescents attempt suicide, just as there are no simple solutions that will prevent its occurrence; however, researchers have discovered several factors that are clearly related to this drastic measure. These include family relations, depression, social interaction, and the adolescent's concept of death.

Family factors have been found to be highly correlated with adolescent suicide. A majority of adolescent suicide attempters come from families in which home harmony is lacking. Often there is a significant amount of conflict between the adolescent and his or her parents and a complete breakdown in communications. Many suicidal youths feel unloved, unwanted, and alienated from the family. Almost every study of suicidal adolescents has found a lack of family cohesion.

Most adolescents who attempt suicide have experienced serious emotional difficulty prior to their attempt. For the majority, this history involves a significant problem with depression. The type of chronic depression that leads some adolescents to commit suicide is vastly different from the occasional "blues" most people experience from time to time. When depression is life-threatening, adolescents typically feel extremely hopeless and helpless, and believe there is no way to improve their situation. These feelings of deep despair frequently lead to a negative self-appraisal in which the young person questions his or her ability to cope with life.

Further complicating the picture is the fact that clinically depressed adolescents have severe problems with relating to other people. As a result, they often feel isolated, which is a significant factor in the decision to end one's life. They may become withdrawn from their peer group and develop the idea that there is something wrong with society. At the same time, they lack the ability to recognize how their inappropriate behavior adversely affects other people.

Another factor that may contribute to suicidal thoughts is the adolescent's conception of death. Because of developmental factors, a young person's cognitive limitations may lead to a distorted, incomplete, or unrealistic understanding of death. Death may not be seen as a permanent end to life and to all contact with the living; suicide may be viewed as a way to punish one's enemies while maintaining the ability to observe their anguish from a different dimension of life. The harsh and unpleasant reality of death may not be realized. Fantasy, drama, and "magical thinking" may give a picture of death that is appealing and positive. Adolescents' limited ability to comprehend death in a realistic manner may be further affected by the depiction of death in the songs they hear, the literature they read, and the films they watch. Frequently death is romanticized. Often it is presented in euphemistic terms, such as "gone to sleep" or "passed away." At other times it is trivialized to such an extent that it is the stimulus for laughter and fun. Death and violence are treated in a remarkably antiseptic fashion.

Treatment and Therapy

Suicide is a tragic event for both the victim and the victim's family. It is also one of the most difficult problems confronting persons in the helping professions. In response, experts have focused their attention on trying to understand better how to prevent suicide and how to treat those who have made unsuccessful attempts to take their own lives.

It is believed that many suicides can be prevented if significant adults in the life of the adolescent are aware of various warning signals that often precede a suicide attempt. Most adolescents contemplating suicide will emit some clues or hints about their serious troubles or will call for help in some way. Some of the clues are easy to recognize, but some are very difficult to identify.

The adolescent may display a radical shift in characteristic behaviors related to academics, social habits, and relationships. There may be a change in sleeping habits; adolescents who kill themselves often exhibit difficulty in falling asleep or maintaining sleep. They are likely to be exhausted, irritable, and anxious. Others may sleep excessively. Any deviation from a usual sleep pattern should be noted. The individual may experience a loss of appetite with accompanying weight loss. A change in eating habits is often very obvious.

A pervasive feeling of hopelessness or helplessness may be observed. These feelings are strong indicators of suicide potential. Hopelessness is demonstrated by the adolescent's belief that his or her situation will never get better. It is believed that current feelings will never change. Helplessness is the belief that one is powerless to change anything. The more intense these feelings are, the more likely it is that suicide will be attempted. The adolescent may express suicidal thoughts and impulses. The suicidal adolescent may joke about suicide and even outline plans for death. He or she may talk about another person's suicidal thoughts or inquire about death and the hereafter. Frequently, prized possessions will be given away. Numerous studies have demonstrated that drug abuse is often associated with suicide attempts. A history of drug or alcohol abuse should be considered in the overall assessment of suicide potential for adolescents.

A variable that is often mentioned in suicide assessment is that of recent loss. If the adolescent has experienced the loss of a parent through death, divorce, or separation, he or she may be at higher

---

POSSIBLE WARNING SIGNS FOR TEEN SUICIDE

- ❖ suicide threats, direct and indirect
- ❖ obsession with death
- ❖ poems, essays, and drawings that refer to death
- ❖ dramatic change in personality or appearance
- ❖ irrational, bizarre behavior
- ❖ overwhelming sense of guilt, shame, or refection
- ❖ changed eating or sleeping patterns
- ❖ severe drop in school performance
- ❖ giving away belongings

risk. This is especially true if the family is significantly destabilized or the loss was particularly traumatic. A radical change in emotions is another warning sign. The suicidal adolescent will often exhibit emotions that are uncharacteristic for the individual. These may include anger, aggression, loneliness, guilt, grief, and disappointment. Typically, the emotion will be evident to an excessive degree.

Any one of the above factors may be present in the adolescent's life and not indicate any serious suicidal tendency; however, the combination of several of these signs should serve as a critical warning and result in some preventive action.

The treatment of suicidal behavior in young people demands that attention be given to both the immediate crisis situation and the underlying problems. Psychologists have sought to discover how this can best be done. Any effort to understand the dynamics of the suicidal person must begin with the assumption that most adolescents who are suicidal do not want to die. They want to improve their lives in some manner, they want to overcome the perceived meaninglessness of their existence, and they want to remove the psychological pain they are experiencing.

The first step in direct intervention is to encourage talking. Open and honest communication is essential. Direct questions regarding suicidal thoughts and/or plans should be asked. It simply is not true that talking about suicide will encourage a young person to attempt it. It is extremely important that the talking process include effective listening. Although it is difficult to listen to an individual who is suicidal, it is very important to do so in a manner that is accepting and calm. Listening is a powerful demonstration of caring and concern.

As the adolescent perceives that someone is trying to understand, it becomes easier to move from a state of hopelessness to hope and from isolation to involvement. Those in deep despair must come to believe that they can expect to improve. They must acknowledge that they are not helpless. Reassurance from another person is very important in this process. The young person considering suicide is so overwhelmed by his or her situation that there may seem to be no other way of escape. Confronting this attitude and pointing out how irrational it is does not help. A better response is to show empathy for the person's pain, then take a positive position which will encourage discussion about hopes and plans for the future.

Adolescents need the assurance that something is being done. They need to feel that things will improve. They must also be advised, however, that the suicidal urges they are experiencing may not disappear immediately, and that movement toward a better future is a step-by-step process. The suicidal young person must feel confident that help is available and can be called upon as needed. The adolescent contemplating suicide should never be left alone.

If the risk of suicide appears immediate, professional help is indicated. Most desirable would be a mental health expert with a special interest in adolescent problems or in suicide. Phone-in suicide prevention centers are located in virtually every large city and many smaller towns, and they are excellent resources for a suicidal person or for someone who is concerned about that person. In order to address long-term problems, therapy for the adolescent who attempts suicide should ideally include the parents. Family relationships must be changed in order to assist the young person in feeling less alienated and worthless.

Perspective and Prospects

Suicide has apparently been practiced to some degree since the beginning of recorded history; however, it was not until the nineteenth century that suicide came to be considered a psychological problems. Since that time, several theories which examine the suicidal personality have been developed.

Émile Durkheim was one of the first to offer a major explanation for suicidal behavior. In the late nineteenth century he conducted a now-classic study of suicide and published his book *Le Suicide: Étude de sociologie* (1897; *Suicide: A Study in Sociology*, 1951). He concluded that suicide is often a severe consequence of the lack of group involvement. He divided suicide into three groupings: egoistic, altruistic, and anomic suicides.

The egoistic suicide is representative of those who are poorly integrated into society. These individuals feel set apart from their social unit and experience a severe sense of isolation. He theorized that people with strong links to their communities are less likely to take their lives. Altruistic suicide occurs when individuals become so immersed in their identity group that group goals and ideals become more important than their own lives. A good example of this type of suicide would be the Japanese kamikaze pilots in World War II: They were willing to give up their lives in order to help their country. The third type, anomic suicide, occurs when an individual's sense of integration in the group has dissolved. When caught in sudden societal or personal change that creates significant alienation or confusion, suicide may be viewed as the only option available.

Psychologists with a psychodynamic orientation explain suicide in terms of intrapsychic conflict. Emphasis is placed on understanding the individual's internal emotional makeup. Suicide is viewed as a result of turning anger and hostility inward. Sigmund Freud discussed the life instinct versus the drive toward death or destruction. Alfred Adler believed that feelings of inferiority and aggression can interact in such a way as to bring a wish for death in order to punish loved ones. Harry Stack Sullivan viewed suicide as the struggle between the good me, bad me, and not me.

Other areas of psychology offer different explanations for suicidal behavior. Cognitive psychologists believe that suicide results from the individual's failure to utilize appropriate problem-solving skills. Faulty assessment of the present or future is also critical and may result in a perspective marked by hopelessness. Behavioral psychologists propose that past experiences with suicide make the behavior an option which may be considered; other people who have taken their lives may serve as models. Biological psychologists are interested in discovering any physiological factors that are related to suicide. It is suggested that chemicals in the brain may be linked to disorders which predispose an individual to commit suicide.

Research in the area of suicide is very difficult to conduct. Identification of those individuals who are of high or low suicidal risk is complex, and ethical considerations deem many research possibilities questionable or unacceptable. Theory construction and testing will continue, however; the crisis of adolescent suicide demands that research address the causes of suicide, its prevention, and treatment for those who have been unsuccessful in suicide attempts.

Bibliography

Hyde, Margaret O., and Elizabeth Held Forsyth. *Suicide: The Hidden Epidemic.* New York: Franklin Watts, 1978. A book written for grades nine through twelve. Discusses the misconceptions of suicide, self-destructive patterns, and motivation theories. Includes a chapter that specifically addresses teenage suicide. Contains a list of suicide prevention centers located across the nation.

Klagsbrun, Francine. *Too Young to Die.* 3d ed. New York: Pocket Books, 1984. An excellent book that combines scientific research with practical examples in a manner that is easy to comprehend. Discusses myths, causes, and prevention of suicide; offers concrete suggestions for talking to a suicidal person. Includes a list of hotlines and suicide prevention centers.

Mitchell, Hayley R. *Teen Suicide.* San Diego: Lucent Books, 2000. Examines some of the causes of suicidal behavior in teenagers, including mental health issues and outside pressures. Discusses prevention efforts and help for survivors.

Murphy, James M., M.D. *Coping with Teen Suicide.* New York: Rosen Publishing Group, 1999. A self-help book for teenagers designed to help them or their troubled friends cope with stress, frustration, and depression instead of killing themselves.

Peck, Michael L., Norman L. Farberow, and Robert E. Litman, eds. *Youth Suicide.* New York: Springer, 1985. Provides a comprehensive overview of adolescent suicide. Written especially for the individual who is interested in working with suicidal youth, but an excellent resource for all who want to increase their understanding of this topic. Contains information on the psychodynamics of suicide, the impact of social change, the role of the family, and intervention strategies.

Petti, T. A., and C. N. Larson. "Depression and Suicide." In *Handbook of Adolescent Psychology*, edited by Vincent B. Van Hassett and Michel Herson. New York: Pergamon Press, 1987. A well-written chapter that makes the complicated factors involved in depression and suicide accessible to the general audience. The authors discuss the causes of both depression and suicide, as well as how the two are related. Addresses how to help the suicidal adolescent. Very readable and informative.

Robbins, Paul R. *Adolescent Suicide.* Jefferson, N.C.: McFarland, 1998. Covers prevalence, racial and gender differences, methods used, associated behavioral problems, psychological profiles, precipitating events, teenage suicide clusters, effects on family and friends, treatment, and strategies for intervention and prevention.

Dolye R. Goff

See also:

Child and Adolescent Psychiatry; Community Psychology; Depression; Identity Crises; Stress; Suicide.

TRANSACTIONAL ANALYSIS

Type of psychology: Psychotherapy
Fields of study: Cognitive therapies; humanistic therapies; interpersonal relations

Transactional analysis (TA) is a school of psychotherapy and personality theory. Many of TA's key concepts, such as therapeutic contracts, games, and life scripts, have been accepted in the general psychotherapy community.

Principal terms

ADULT: the part of the personality that is objective, solves problems, and processes data

CHILD: the feeling, spontaneous, and impulsive part of the personality; the child ego state is subdivided into three subphases: free, adapted, and intuitive

DECISION: an early childhood choice in which the individual defines his or her life stance

DISCOUNTING: a response to the self or to another person that undermines self-esteem

EGO STATE: the building block of TA; the mental attitude of an individual at a given moment, such as parent, adult, or child

GAMES: a series of transactions in which one or both players end up feeling hurt or "not OK"

LIFE SCRIPT: a "script" that resembles a drama or mythological role that an individual reenacts as a result of family conditioning

PARENT: the part of personality that is incorporated from one's real parents; the parent ego state is either nurturing or critical

RACKET: an unhappy feeling that results from a game; chronic feelings that are maintained in order to justify an "I am not OK" life position

STROKE: a form of personal recognition that may include a touch, a kind word, or public praise; strokes may be positive or negative

Overview

Transactional analysis (TA) is a theory of personality and social interaction originated by Eric Berne in the mid-1950's. TA's popularity has been primarily as a form of psychotherapy and a method for improving social interactions between people in almost any setting—from the group therapy room to business and industry. Berne rejected psychoanalytic therapy, which he considered a type of game called "archaeology," in favor of his own short-term, action-oriented, commonsense approach to psychotherapy. Before entering a group psychotherapy session, Berne would ask himself, "How can I cure everyone in this room today?" In 1964, Berne's book *Games People Play* created a popular interest in a theory of personality and psychotherapy unequaled in the history of psychology; the book sold more than a million copies.

The basic concepts of transactional analysis describe an individual personality and the individual's repetitive patterns of interacting with others. Three distinct ego states compose the individual personality: "parent," "adult," and "child." Berne observed these as distinct phases in his patients' self-presentations. The child ego state within each individual is defined by the feeling, creative, and intuitive part within the person. The child ego state may be approval-seeking or defiant. The funloving or "free" side of the child state is curious, spontaneous, and impulsive. Parental discipline, when too harsh or inconsistent, often damages this spontaneous and free child; the adapted child is what then results. The adapted child can have a broken or rebellious spirit and may develop depression or addictions. In either case, the individual, authentic self becomes distorted because of an excessively compliant or defiant adaptation.

The adult ego state is objective and, in a sense, resembles a computer. The adult retrieves, stores, and processes data about physical and social reality. Problem solving and task-oriented behavior are the domain of the adult. If one were trying to build a bridge or do homework, the adult ego state would serve best; however, many problems require the assistance of the intuitive and creative child to be solved most effectively.

The parent ego state is an internalization of one's biological parents or other substitute authority figures in early childhood. The parent state judges, criticizes, and blames. This harsh side of the parent state is the critical parent. In contrast, Berne also recognized the nurturing parent that soothes, encourages, and gently supports the individual. The nurturing parent calls forth the free child, while the critical parent conditions the adapted child. The parent ego state is like a tape recording of the "dos and don'ts" of one's family of origin and culture; it may contain obsolete information. When in the parent state, one may point or shame with an extended index finger or disapproving scowl.

Transactions are basic units of analysis for the TA therapist. A transaction occurs when one individual responds to the behavior of another. Transactions are called complementary when both persons interact from compatible ego states. For example, a feverish child asks her parent for a glass of water, and the parent complies. A crossed transaction occurs when individuals in incompatible ego states interact. For example, a whining and hungry child asks a parent for an ice cream cone, and the parent (speaking from her adult ego state) reminds the child that it would not be nutritious. The child cannot incorporate the adult data. Another important type of transaction is the ulterior one. An ulterior transaction occurs when the spoken message is undercut by a hidden agenda. To exemplify this, Berne cited a cowboy who asks a woman to leave the dance and go look at the barn with him. The face value of his adult-to-adult question is subtly undercut by a child-to-child sexual innuendo.

Ulterior transactions, when not clearly understood by both parties, lead to "games." A game by definition is a social transaction in which either both or one member of the duo ends up feeling "bad." This bad feeling is experienced as a payoff by the game perpetrator; the game pays off by confirming the player's existential life position. For example, the game that Berne called "blemish" involves an existential life position of "I am not OK, you are not OK." In this game, the player exhaustively searches his or her partner for some defect, such as a personality quirk or physical imperfection. Once this defect or blemish is found, the player can hold it up as proof that others are not OK. One thus avoids examining one's own blemish while providing that "others are no good." An example of this can be seen in the chronic bachelor who cannot find a woman who measures up to his perfectionistic standards for marriage.

"Rackets" are the negative feelings that one experiences after a game. Racket feelings are chronic and originate in the early stroking patterns within one's family of origin. In the game of "blemish," the player will ultimately feel lonely and sad, while the victim may feel hurt and rejected. Berne compared rackets to stamp collecting: When one collects ten books of brown stamps from playing blemish, they can be cashed in for a divorce or suicide.

Life scripts emerge through repetitive interactions with one's early environment. Messages about what to expect from others, the world, and self become ingrained. A script resembles an actor's role in a drama. An important outcome of one's early scripting is the basic decision one makes about one's existential position. Specifically, the basic identity becomes constellated around feelings of being either OK (free child) or not OK (adapted child). Coping strategies are learned that reinforce the basic decision. Life scripts can often be discovered by asking individuals about their favorite games, heroes, or stories from their childhood. Once individuals become aware of their life scripts, they can be presented with the option of changing them. If a script does not support a person's capacity to be an authentic winner in life, the TA therapist will confront it. TA holds that people are all born to win.

Applications

Transactional analysis has been applied to the areas of individual and group psychotherapy, couples and family relationship problems, and communication problems within business organizations. This widespread application of TA should not be surprising, since TA's domain is wherever two human beings meet. Berne believed that the playing of games occurs everywhere, from the sandbox to the international negotiation table. Consequently, wherever destructive patterns of behavior occur, TA can be employed to reduce dysfunctional transactions.

TA's most common application is in psychotherapy. The TA therapist begins by establishing a contract for change with his client. This denotes mutual responsibilities for both therapist and client and avoids allowing the client to assume a passive spectator role. The therapist also avoids playing the "rescuer" role. For example, Ms. Murgatroyd (Berne's favorite hypothetical patient name), an attractive thirty-two-year-old female, enters therapy because her boyfriend refuses to make the commitment to marry her. Her contract with the therapist and group might be that she will either receive a marriage commitment from her boyfriend or will end the relationship. As her specific games and life script are analyzed, this contract might undergo a revision in which greater autonomy or capacity for intimacy becomes her goal.

During the first session, the therapist observes the client's style of interacting.

The therapist will be especially watchful of voice tone, gestures, and mannerisms and will listen to her talk about her current difficulties. Since games are chronic and stereotypical ways of responding, they will appear in the initial interview. For example, her dominant ego state might be that of a helpless, whining child looking for a strong parent to protect her. Ms. Murgatroyd may describe her boyfriend in such bitter and negative terms that it is entirely unclear why a healthy adult would want to marry such a man. Discrepancies of this sort will suggest that a tragic script may be operating.

During the first few interviews, the transactional analysis includes game and script analysis. This might require some information about Ms. Murgatroyd's early childhood fantasies and relationships with parents, but would eventually return to her present behavior and relationship. This early history would be used primarily to help the therapist and client gain insight into how these childhood patterns of interacting are currently manifesting. Once the games and script have been clearly identified, the client is in a much better position to change.

After several interviews, in which Ms. Murgatroyd's past and recent history of relationships is reviewed, a pattern of her being rejected is evident. She acknowledges that her existential position is "I am not OK, you are not OK." Her repeated selection of men who are emotionally unavailable maintains her racket feelings of loneliness and frustration. She begins to see how she puts herself in the role of victim. Armed with this new awareness, she is now in a position to change her script. Through the support of the therapist and group, Ms. Murgatroyd can learn to catch herself and stop playing the victim.

Berne believed that the original script could best be changed in an atmosphere of openness and trust between the client and therapist. Hence the TA therapist will at all times display respect and concern for his or her client. At the appropriate time in therapy, the therapist delivers a powerful message to the client which serves to counteract the early childhood messages that originally instated the script. Ms. Murgatroyd's therapist, at the proper time, would decisively and powerfully counterscript her by telling her, "You have the right to intimacy!" or "You have the right to take care of yourself, even if it means leaving a relationship." Since the existential life position is supported by lifelong games and scripts, which resist change, TA therapists often employ emotionally charged ways of assisting a client's script redecision.

To catalyze script redecision, a client is guided back in time to the original scene where the destructive message that started the losing life script was received. Simply being told differently by a therapist is not always strong enough to create an emotionally corrective experience that will reverse a life script. Once in the early childhood scene, the client will spontaneously enter the child ego state, which is where the real power to change lies. This time, during the therapeutic regression, the choice will be different and will be for the authentic self.

Ms. Murgatroyd, who is struggling to change an early message, "Don't be intimate," needs to reexperience the feeling she had at the time she first received this message and accepted it from her adapted child ego state. In the presence of the therapist and group, she would role-play this early scene and would tell herself and the significant parent that she *does* have the right to be intimate. These words would probably be spoken amid tears and considerable emotional expression. The parent(s) would be symbolically addressed by her speaking to an empty chair in which she imagines her significant parent sitting: "Whether you like it or not, I'll be intimate!" She would tell herself that it is OK to be intimate. This time she will make a new decision about her script based on her authentic wants and needs, rather than on faulty messages from early childhood. Ms. Murgatroyd's further TA work might involve new contracts with the therapist and group as she integrates her new script into her daily life.

Perspective and Prospects
Transactional analysis evolved as a form of short-term psychotherapy beginning in the mid-1950's. Eric Berne's early work in groups as a major in the Army during World War II helped him identify the need for both group and short-term therapy. The human growth and potential movement of the 1960's added further momentum to the transactional analysis approach. TA's recognition of the innate goodness of the free child prior to the damage of early parental injunctions and self-defeating scripts was consistent with the then-emerging humanistic schools of psychology. Berne began using TA as an adjunct to psychoanalysis, but he eventually rejected the psychoanalytic idea of the dynamic unconscious. Berne's move away from the unconscious and Freudian system paralleled developments in other schools of psychology. Both behavioral psychologists and the cognitive school wished to move away from what they saw as "depth psychology" fictions.

The general thesis of TA that current behavior is premised on responses to emotional trauma of early childhood is generally agreed upon by most psychologists. Early life experience teaches people to script a behavioral pattern, which they then repetitively act out in adulthood. Behavioral and humanistic schools alike recognize the formative role that early experiences play in adult behavior patterns; these ideas are not original to TA. TA's contribution is to have created a vocabulary that demystifies many of these ideas and provides a readily learned method of psychotherapy.

Most of the TA jargon and concepts can be readily seen to correspond to equivalent ones used by other psychologists. Sigmund Freud's constructs of the superego, ego, and id bear a noteworthy similarity to Berne's parent, adult, and child. The superego as the internalized voice of parental and societal values to regulate behavior nearly coincides with Berne's parent ego state. Freud's ego and the adult ego state similarly share the responsibility of solving the individual's problems with a minimum of emotional bias. Freud's id as the instinctual, spontaneous part of the personality shares many characteristics with Berne's child ego state.

Berne's concept of a game's "payoff" is clearly what the behaviorist call a reinforcer. The idea of scripts corresponds to the notion of family role or personality types in other personality theories. For example, an individual with a dominant child ego state would be labeled an orally fixated dependent type in Freudian circles.

The psychological role of dysfunctional families has become a topic of conversation for many nonspecialists. The explosion of twelve-step self-help groups has evidenced growing concern about America's mental health; the prominent role of shame and abandonment experiences in early childhood is receiving widespread interest. This surge of interest in making mental health services available to all society is a continuation of what TA practitioners pioneered several decades earlier. It is likely that future developments in the mental health field will draw upon the rich legacy of TA.

Finally, pure transactional analysis as practiced by Berne in the 1960's right before his death has been modified by TA therapists who combine it with emotive and experiential techniques. Many TA therapists found that life scripts failed to change when their clients merely executed new adult decisions. Powerful therapeutic experiences in which the individual regresses and relives painful experiences were necessary. These enable the client to make script redecisions from the child ego state, which proved to be an effective source of change. Future TA therapists are likely to continue enhancing their methods of rescripting by eclectically drawing upon new methods of behavior change that go beyond traditional TA techniques. The intuitive child ego state, upon which TA therapists freely draw, promises creative developments in this school of psychotherapy.

Bibliography

Berne, Eric. *Games People Play*. New York: Grove Press, 1964. A national best-seller that provides a highly readable introduction to the basic ideas of TA and games. Provides an interesting catalog of the most common games played in groups of many kinds. The reader will find that he or she can immediately apply the ideas contained here.

_____. *What Do You Say After You Say Hello?* New York: Grove Press, 1972. This is another excellent primary source for the reader who wants to apply TA to everyday life. Focuses on games and on Berne's final development of his script theory shortly before his death.

Corey, Gerald. *Theory and Practice of Counseling and Psychotherapy*. 6th ed. Pacific Grove, Calif.: Brooks/Cole, 2000. TA is covered in a brief twenty-five pages but is treated with excellent scholarship. Ideal for the reader who would like a sound overview of TA before moving on to the particular works of Berne. A two-page bibliography is included. TA is critically appraised and compared to other approaches.

Dusay, J., and K. Dusay. "Transactional Analysis." In *Current Psychotherapies*, edited by Raymond J. Corsini and Danny Wedding. 4th ed. Itasca, Ill.: Peacock, 1989. This forty-two-page article contains five pages of bibliography and is cowritten by a leading TA therapist and writer. Thorough and scholarly. The Dusays go into considerable depth in explaining Berne's ideas. A detailed discussion of egograms, the drama triangle, and many more key TA concepts are excellently covered. Recommended for the reader who wants a serious introduction to TA.

Goulding, Mary McClure, and Robert L. Goulding. *Redecision Therapy*. New

York: Brunner/Mazel, 1979. This three hundred-page book is written by the two therapists who pioneered the integration of TA with Gestalt therapy. Both Gouldings studied directly with Berne and Fritz Perls. An overview of TA, contracts, and stroking is covered. The clinical use of TA with depression, grieving, and establishing "no suicide contracts" is handled with many case examples and some transcripts of actual sessions. Recommended for the advanced student of TA.

James, Muriel, and Dorothy Jongeward. *Born to Win*. Reading, Mass.: Addison-Wesley, 1971. Another TA work that became a best-seller. An optimistic and humanistic version of TA mixed with Gestalt experiments gives the reader a rich firsthand experience of TA. Contains many experiential and written exercises that enable readers to diagnose their own scripts and rackets. A practical program in how to apply the ideas of TA immediately to improve one's life is provided.

Lennox, Carolyn E., ed. *Redecision Therapy: A Brief Action-Oriented Approach*. Northvale, N.J.: Jason Aronson, 1997. Characterizes the redecision therapist as a director in an improvisational theater.

Stewart, Ian. *Developing Transactional Analysis Counselling*. Thousand Oaks, Calif.: Sage Publications, 1996. Divided into the sections "Principles of TA" and "Thirty Ways to Develop your TA Counselling." Includes bibliographical references and an index.

Paul August Rentz

See also:

Abnormality: Cognitive Models; Abnormality: Humanistic-Existential Models; Cognitive Therapy; Group Therapy; Psychotherapy: Goals and Techniques; Psychotherapy: Historical Approaches to Treatment; Rational-Emotive Therapy.

Type A Behavior Pattern

Type of psychology: Personality; stress
Fields of study: Personality theory; stress and illness

The Type A behavior pattern has been related to coronary artery disease; individuals who have the Type A behavior pattern have been shown to be at a greater risk of coronary artery disease in some studies.

Principal terms

CATECHOLAMINES: hormones released from the adrenal glands in response to stressful situations

HARD-DRIVING BEHAVIOR: a Type A trait that comes from a perception of being more responsible, conscientious, competitive, and serious than other people

HURRY SICKNESS: the perception that more needs to be done or should be done in a given period of time

JOB INVOLVEMENT: a Type A trait that comes from the perception of having a challenging, high-pressure job

SPEED AND IMPATIENCE: two traits of the Type A behavior pattern caused by a perception of time urgency

Causes and Symptoms

The Type A behavior pattern, often simply called the Type A personality, identifies behaviors which have been associated with coronary artery disease. Although these behaviors appear to be stress related, they are not necessarily involved with stressful situations or with the traditional stress response. Instead, the behaviors are based on an individual's thoughts, values, and approaches to interpersonal relationships. In general, Type A individuals are characterized as ambitious, impatient, aggressive, and competitive. Individuals who are not Type A are considered Type B. Type B individuals are characterized as relaxed, easygoing, satisfied, and noncompetitive.

Cardiologists Meyer Friedman and Ray H. Rosenman began work on the Type A behavior pattern in the mid-1950's. It was not until the completion of some retrospective studies in the 1970's, however, that the concept gained credibility. During the 1950's, it was noticed that younger and middle-aged people with coronary artery disease had several characteristics in common. These included a hard-driving attitude toward poorly defined goals; a continuous need for recognition and advancement; aggressive and at times hostile feelings; a desire for competition; an ongoing tendency to try to accomplish more in less time; a tendency to think and act faster and faster; and a high level of physical and mental alertness. These people were classified as "Pattern A" or "Type A."

Following their work on identifying the characteristics of the Type A personality or behavior pattern, Friedman and Rosenman began conducting studies to determine if it might actually cause coronary artery disease. First they conducted several correlational studies to determine if there was a relationship between the Type A behavior pattern and metabolic function in humans. They found that healthy persons with the Type A behavior pattern had elevated levels of fat in the blood (serum cholesterol and triglycerides), decreased blood-clotting time, increased catecholamine secretion (which increases heart contractility) during normal work hours, and decreased blood flow to some tissues. These studies indicated that the Type A behavior pattern may precede coronary artery disease.

Following these studies, Friedman, Rosenman, and their research team initiated the Western Collaborative Group Study in 1960. This large study, which went on for more than eight years, attempted to determine if the presence of the Type A behavior pattern increased the risk of coronary artery disease. The results of Rosenman and Friedman's study in 1974 indicated that the subjects with the Type A pattern had more than twice the incidence of the disease than subjects with the Type B pattern. More specifically, Type A individuals (when compared to Type B individuals) were twice as likely to have a fatal heart attack, five times more likely to have a second heart attack, and likely to have more severe coronary artery disease (of those who died). These results were found when other known risk factors, such as high blood pressure, smoking, and diet, were held constant. This study was followed by numerous other studies which linked coronary artery disease to the Type A behavior pattern. In 1978, the National Heart, Lung and Blood Institute sponsored a conference on the Type A behavior pattern. As a result of the Review Panel on Coronary-Prone Behavior and Coronary Heart Disease, a document was released in 1981 which stated that the Type A behavior pattern is related to increased risk of coronary artery disease.

Another product of the Western Collaborative Group Study was a method for assessing the Type A behavior pattern, developed by Rosenman in 1978. This method was based on a structured interview. A predetermined set of questions were asked of all participants. The scoring was based on the content of the participants' verbal responses as well as their nonverbal mannerisms, speech style, and behaviors during the interview process. The interview can be administered in fifteen minutes. Since the interview was not a traditional type of assessment, however, many interviewers had a difficult time using it.

In an effort to simplify the process for determining Type A behavior, many self-report questionnaires were developed. The first developed and probably the most-used questionnaire is the Jenkins Activity Survey, which was developed by C. David Jenkins, Stephen Zyzanski, and Rosenman in 1979. This survey is based on the structured interview. It gives a Type A score and three related subscores. The subscores include speed and impatience, hard driving, and job involvement. The Jenkins Activity Survey is a preferred method, because the questionnaire responses can be tallied to provide a quantitative score. Although this instrument is easy to use and provides consistent results, it is not considered as good as the structured interview because many believe the Type A characteristics can best be identified by observation.

The Type A behavior pattern continues to be studied, but research appears to have reached a peak in the late 1970's and early 1980's. Researchers are challenging the whole concept of coronary-prone behavior, because many clinical studies have not shown high correlations between the Type A behavior pattern and the progression of coronary artery disease. Other risk factors for coronary artery disease, such as smoking, high blood pressure, and high blood cholesterol, have received increasing attention.

The Type A behavior pattern, or personality, has been used to explain in part the risk of coronary artery disease; however, many risk factors for the disease have been identified. Since the various risk factors interact with one another, it is difficult to understand any one risk factor clearly.

Efforts have been made to explain the mechanism by which the Type A behavior pattern affects coronary artery disease. It has been theorized that specific biochemical and physiological events take place as a result of the emotions associated with Type A behavior. The neocortex and limbic system of the brain deliver emotional information to the hypothalamus. In a situation that arouses the Type A characteristics, the hypothalamus will cause the pituitary gland to stimulate the release of the catecholamines epinephrine and norepinephrine (also known as adrenaline and noradrenaline) from the adrenal glands, as well as other hormones from the pituitary itself. These chemicals will enter the blood and travel throughout the body, causing blood cholesterol and fat to increase, the ability to get rid of cholesterol to decrease, the ability to regulate blood sugar levels to decrease (as with diabetics), and the time for the blood to clot to increase. This response by the body to emotions is normal. The problem with Type A individuals arises because they tend to maintain this heightened emotional level almost continually, and the constant release of pituitary hormones results in these negative effects on the body being continuous as well.

The connection between Type A behavior and coronary artery disease actually results from the continuous release of hormones controlled by the pituitary gland. Through complex mechanisms, the constant exposure to these hormones causes several problems. First, cholesterol is deposited on the coronary artery walls as a result of the increase in blood cholesterol and the reduced ability to rid the blood of the cholesterol. Second, the increased ability of the blood to clot results in more clotting elements being deposited on the arterial walls. Third, clotting elements can decrease blood flow through the small capillaries which feed the coronary arteries, resulting in further complications with the cholesterol deposits. Fourth, increased insulin in the blood further destroys the coronary arteries. Therefore, the reaction of the pituitary gland to the Type A behavior pattern is believed to be responsible for the connection with coronary artery disease.

Treatment and Therapy

Fortunately, it is believed that people with the Type A behavior pattern can modify their behavior to reduce risk of coronary artery disease. As with many health problems, however, denial is prevalent. Therefore, it is important that Type A individuals become aware of their problem. In general, Type A individuals need to focus on several areas. These include hurry sickness, speed and impatience, and hostility.

Type A individuals try to accomplish more and more in less and less time (hurry sickness). Unfortunately, more is too often at the expense of quality, efficiency, and, most important, health. Type A individuals need to make fewer appointments related to work, and they need to schedule more relaxation time. This includes not starting the day in a rush by getting out of bed barely in time to get hurriedly to work. Finally, Type A individuals need to avoid telephone and other interruptions when they are working, because this aggravates hurry sickness. Therefore, it is recommended that individuals who suffer from hurry sickness avoid scheduling too much work; take more breaks from work (relaxation), including a lunch hour during which work is not done; and have calls screened in order to get blocks of working time.

Type A individuals typically do things rapidly and are impatient. For example, they tend to talk rapidly, repetitiously, and narrowly. They also have a hard time with individuals who talk slowly, and Type A individuals often hurry these people along by finishing their sentences. Additionally, Type A individuals try to dominate conversations, frequently focusing the discussion on themselves or their interests. In an effort to moderate speed and impatience, Type A individuals need to slow down, focus their speech in discussions to the specific problem, and cut short visits with individuals who waste their time. They should spend more time with individuals who enhance their opportunities.

The other area is hostility, or harboring destructive emotions. This is highly related to aggressiveness. Aggressive Type A individuals must learn to use their sense of humor and not look at situations only as challenges set up to bother or upset them. One way to accomplish this is for them consciously to attempt to socialize with Type B individuals. Obviously, this is not always possible, since the Type A individuals have certain other individuals with whom they must associate, such as colleagues at work and certain family members. Nevertheless, Type A individuals must understand their hostilities and learn to regulate them. In general, Type A individuals must learn to control their feelings and relationships. They must focus more attention on being well-rounded individuals rather than spending most of their time on work-related successes. Type A individuals can learn the Type B behavior pattern, resulting in a lower risk for coronary artery disease.

Perspective and Prospects

The Type A behavior pattern was defined by two cardiologists, Meyer Friedman and Ray H. Rosenman, in the 1950's at the Harold Brunn Institute for Cardiovascular Research, Mt. Zion Hospital and Medical Center, in San Francisco. Since that time, many researchers have studied the Type A behavior pattern. Initially, most of the researchers were cardiologists. Gradually, more and more psychologists have become involved with Type A research.

Since the concept of relating coronary heart disease with human behavior was developed by cardiologists instead of psychologists, it was initially called the Type A behavior pattern rather than the Type A personality. "Personality" relates to an individual's inner traits, attitudes, or habits and is very complex and generally studied by psychologists. As Type A was defined, however, it only related specific behaviors with disease and was observed openly. Therefore, it seemed appropriate to label Type A a behavior pattern. Over the years, Type A has been assumed to be a personality; technically, this is not accurate, although many people now refer to it as the Type A personality.

Another reason Type A is most accurately considered a behavior pattern rather than a personality relates to the way it is assessed. Whether the structured interview or the written questionnaire is utilized, a predetermined set of questions and sequence are used. While this approach can assess a behavior pattern adequately, different skills which allow the interviewer to respond appropriately to an individual's answers and probe specific responses further are needed to assess personality.

The Type A behavior pattern evolved as a risk factor for coronary artery disease. The original need for this idea was not psychologically based. Instead, it was based on a need to understand further the factors that are involved with the development of coronary artery disease, a major cause of death. Therefore, the role of the Type A behavior pattern in psychology has been limited. Nevertheless, Type A studies have benefited humankind's understanding of an important disease and, to a certain extent, the understanding of psychology.

The future study of the Type A behavior pattern is in question. Research continually shows conflicting results about its role in coronary artery disease. As more research is conducted by both medical clinicians and psychologists, the true value of the Type A behavior pattern will become evident. Until then, health care professionals will continually have to evaluate the appropriateness of using the Type A behavior pattern as an identifier of the risk of artery or heart disease.

Bibliography

Chesney, Margaret A., and Ray H. Rosenman, eds. *Anger and Hostility in Cardiovascular and Behavior Disorders*. Washington, D.C.: Hemisphere, 1985. Integrating psychology and the Type A behavior pattern, this book provides in-depth information on the technical aspects of behavior. Although some portions of the book are technical, the introductions to each chapter provide historical and nontechnical information related to the broader topic of behavior.

Friedman, Meyer. *Type A Behavior: Its Diagnosis and Treatment*. New York: Plenum Press, 1996. Describes the most effective means of correctly diagnosing the disorder and presents a method for treating this life-threatening disorder.

Friedman, Meyer, and Ray H. Rosenman. *Type A Behavior and Your Heart*. New York: Alfred A. Knopf, 1974. Summarizes the history of Type A behavior and presents information as it relates to individuals. Very basic, it is meant to provide an understanding of Type A behavior for the general public. The basics of changing Type A behavior are also presented.

Friedman, Meyer, and D. Ulmer. *Treating Type A Behavior—and Your Heart*. New York: Alfred A. Knopf, 1984. Friedman's second book written for the general public focuses on what an individual can do to change Type A behavior. It is nontechnical and provides basic information in an easy-to-read form.

Houston, B. Kent, and C. R. Snyder, eds. *Type A Behavior Pattern: Research, Theory, and Intervention*. New York: John Wiley & Sons, 1988. Contains thirteen chapters by various authors. The first three chapters nicely introduce the topic in relatively simple terms. Subsequent chapters tend to be more technical and require a better background for understanding. A wealth of references are listed throughout.

Jenkins, C. D., S. J. Zyzanski, and R. H. Rosenman. *The Jenkins Activity Survey.* New York: Psychological Corporation, 1979. Contains the survey used for assessing Type A behavior. Includes the scoring procedure, which is easy to understand and administer.

Johnson, Ernest H., W. Doyle Gentry, and Stevo Julius, eds. *Personality, Elevated Blood Pressure, and Essential Hypertension.* New York: Hemisphere, 1992. Contains a chapter entitled "Type A Behavior Pattern and Cardiovascular Reactivity: Is There a Relationship with Hypertension?" Includes bibliographical references and an index.

Price, Virginia Ann. *Type A Behavior Pattern.* New York: Academic Press, 1982. A good technical resource for Type A behavior. Very comprehensive. The introductory chapters provide the nontechnical reader with valuable, understandable information. More than three hundred references are listed at the end of the book.

Bradley R. A. Wilson

See also:

Abnormality: Biomedical Models; Anxiety Disorders; Biofeedback and Relaxation; Stress; Stress: Coping Strategies; Stress: Physiological Responses.

Psychology
and
Mental Health

CATEGORY LIST

Abnormality
Abnormality
Abnormality: Behavioral Models
Abnormality: Biomedical Models
Abnormality: Cognitive Models
Abnormality: Family Models
Abnormality: Humanistic-Existential
  Models
Abnormality: Legal Models
Abnormality: Psychodynamic Models
Abnormality: Sociocultural Models
Diagnosis and Classification
Madness: Historical Concepts

Anxiety Disorders
Agoraphobia and Panic Disorders
Amnesia, Fugue, and Multiple Personality
Anxiety Disorders
Aversion, Implosion, and Systematic
  Desensitization Therapies
Eating Disorders
Hypochondriasis, Conversion,
  Somatization, and Somatoform Pain
Insomnia
Lobotomy
Neurosis
Obsessive-Compulsive Disorder
Paranoia
Phobias
Psychoactive Drug Therapy
Psychosurgery

Childhood and Adolescent Disorders
Anorexia Nervosa and Bulimia Nervosa
Attention-Deficit Disorder
Autism
Bed-Wetting
Child Abuse
Child and Adolescent Psychiatry
Divorce and Separation: Children's Issues
Down Syndrome
Eating Disorders
Identity Crises
Juvenile Delinquency
Phobias
Play Therapy

Psychotherapy: Children
Schizophrenia: High-Risk Children
Sibling Rivalry
Teenage Suicide

Depression
Depression
Electroconvulsive Therapy
Grief and Guilt
Manic-Depressive Disorder
Psychoactive Drug Therapy
Seasonal Affective Disorder
Suicide
Teenage Suicide

Developmental Issues
Behavioral Family Therapy
Child Abuse
Child and Adolescent Psychiatry
Couples Therapy
Divorce and Separation: Adult Issues
Divorce and Separation: Children's Issues
Domestic Violence
Geriatric Psychiatry
Identity Crises
Juvenile Delinquency
Midlife Crises
Sexual Variants and Paraphilias
Sibling Rivalry
Strategic Family Therapy

Diagnosis
Behavioral Assessment and Personality
  Rating Scales
Diagnosis and Classification
Personality: Psychophysiological Measures

Emotional Disorders
Agoraphobia and Panic Disorders
Aggression: Definitions and Theoretical
  Explanations
Aggression: Reduction and Control
Amnesia, Fugue, and Multiple Personality
Anxiety Disorders
Child Abuse
Child and Adolescent Psychiatry

Treatments

Analytical Psychotherapy
Aversion, Implosion, and Systematic
    Desensitization Therapies
Behavioral Family Therapy
Biofeedback and Relaxation
Cognitive Behavior Therapy
Cognitive Therapy
Community Psychology
Couples Therapy
Electroconvulsive Therapy
Gestalt Therapy
Group Therapy
Lobotomy
Mental Health Practitioners
Modeling Therapies
Music, Dance, and Theater Therapy

Operant Conditioning Therapies
Person-Centered Therapy
Play Therapy
Psychiatry
Psychoactive Drug Therapy
Psychoanalysis: Classical Versus Modern
Psychosurgery
Psychotherapy: Children
Psychotherapy: Effectiveness
Psychotherapy: Goals and Techniques
Psychotherapy: Historical Approaches to
    Treatment
Rational-Emotive Therapy
Reality Therapy
Strategic Family Therapy
Transactional Analysis

INDEX